BRACKNELL'S

GREAT WAR FALLEN

III - CROWTHORNE AND SANDHURST

BY

ANDREW RADGICK

Grosvenor House
Publishing Limited

This book is published by
Grosvenor House Publishing Ltd
28-30 High Street, Guildford, Surrey, GU1 3EL.
www.grosvenorhousepublishing.co.uk

A CIP record for this book
is available from the British Library

ISBN 978-1-78148-686-3

CONTENTS

INTRODUCTION

In 2009, a new mass grave of bodies from World War One was found near Fromelles; 250 Australian and British soldiers are now buried in a new cemetery. This item on the national news prompted me to visit the Bracknell War Memorial, located beside the Royal British Legion in the town centre, to look at the names from the town recorded on it. There are none.

I then started on a journey of discovery, tracking down lists of names, initially in the town, but then right across the borough of Bracknell Forest. I visited churches and graveyards, I looked in Books of Remembrance, I gained entrance to schools, both current and closed, and found Rolls of Honour from clubs. Some names appear on more than one list; others discovered during my researches do not feature on any.

Who were these men and where did they come from? My research has discovered they come from all classes and ages, from farm labourers to young men educated at Eton College. Stanley Wade from Chavey Down was just sixteen; John Quick from Bracknell was more than thirty years older. A few are buried in the local cemeteries; many are listed on the huge memorials in France and Belgium, their bodies never recovered. Others are even further afield in the Balkans, the Near East, and India. It is estimated that 880,000 men from the United Kingdom lost their lives in the war to end all wars, plus a further 200,000 more from other countries in the British Empire and Commonwealth. Britain lost ten per cent of its male population between the ages of eighteen and forty (Germany lost 15% of its active males). While many died from injuries on the battlefield, others died from illness or in Prisoner of War camps. Practically every city, town and village across the country lost men. Some survived, only to die from their injuries soon after; others perished in the wave of Spanish Flu that swept across Europe in the aftermath of the conflict.

The advent of the internet has been invaluable in this project with so much information now readily available online. Birth registration, census returns, military records, cemetery information, newspapers, War Diaries and fellow researchers can all be accessed without leaving the house, while a Google search uncovers many other sources. Sometimes it is all too easy to get overwhelmed with facts, or get distracted and go off at a tangent to the main direction of research. So where does one start on a project like this?

From the initial idea of looking on Bracknell's War Memorial, I then found there were two lists in the town's churches, one inside Holy Trinity, partly hidden behind furniture and flags, and another in St Michael and Magdalene, Easthampstead. The latter has a cross inscribed with the names around its base in the churchyard, plus a marble tablet inside the church, detailing the units with which the men served, a vital clue in some instances, and a hindrance in others. But what about the churches that existed before the redevelopment of Bracknell? Only the Roll of Honour from the Congregational Chapel in Bracknell High Street, demolished in 1968, has survived; it is now located in St. Paul's United Reformed Church in Harmanswater. Binfield has two churches; the list on the triptych inside All Saints has a few additional names to the memorial in the grounds of St Mark's. Warfield and Winkfield Churches are obviously proud of their men, with the names prominently displayed and immaculately maintained. The latter again includes military details, and further names that have come to light since the original commemoration, have been added by a grateful parishioner. The interior of Cranbourne Church was gutted by a fire in 2006, but a replacement Roll of Honour, again with military details, has been erected to supplement the memorial and cross outside. The Roll of Honour at Crowthorne is uniquely situated inside the lych gate, on four panels. This is the longest list of names from any community within the borough, containing the names of more than one hundred men from the village who did not return. Some have only an initial with their surname, making it a challenge to find them, while others are more fully named and more easily identified. Sandhurst offers the most clues, listing rank as well as military unit against every name. But this is a reconstituted list, the original having been lost when the building housing it burnt down. A few errors have come to light during my research. I also looked at the lists in All Saint's, Ascot and St. Sebastians, Wokingham (on Nine Mile Ride), as although the churches are outside the borough, part of their parishes fall within our area.

As well as churches, some schools recorded those who had passed through their doors. Fifteen former pupils from Ranelagh School in Bracknell are listed; forty-six from Crowthorne Church of England School on Duke's Ride. Another Church School existed on Forest Road, just to the west of its junction with Binfield Road. Today, it is a private house with a tribute to the thirteen former pupils mounted in a recess in the side of the garage wall. This poignant list was probably erected just after hostilities ceased by those living in the immediate neighbourhood, before the authorities decided on the official memorials erected around the country. It is a rare survivor of many that were erected by streets, or small pockets of grateful people, up and down the country. Although located just over the border in Wokingham Borough, many of the names are those of Binfield men and has been included in this book. The private schools of Wellington College in Crowthorne, with several hundred former pupils, masters, staff and servants, Eagle House School between Sandhurst and Crowthorne, and Lambrook School in Winkfield Row, all poignantly display Rolls of Honour prominently. These latter three are not included in this publication.

Three other lists came to light from personal contacts during my research. I am indebted to Vera Bain, Chairman of Bracknell Bowling and Social Club, for allowing me to photograph the list there. It mentions all thirty-three former members who fought in the conflict, three of whom did not return. I would also like to thank local historian Ruth Timbrell who gave me a copy of her photograph from the now demolished Bracknell Working Men's Club, located in Stanley Road, just off Bracknell High Street. It contains the names of almost one hundred men who came back, as well as the twenty who did not. A casual conversation with a former member of staff at Binfield Club led me to the Roll of Honour in that building, listing practically all the men of the village who took part in the fighting.

When we talk of those who died in the First World War, we immediately think of the vast War Cemeteries and Memorials in Western Europe. For example, there are over fifty-four thousand names listed on the Menin Gate at Ypres, all men with no known grave. There are other huge memorials, among them Arras, Loos, Pozieres, Thiepval and Tyne Cot. There are nearly three thousand War Cemeteries in France alone. But battles were fought in the Balkans, and men from the borough are buried in Salonika, Skopje, Haidar Pasha (now a suburb of Istanbul), and on the island of Limnos in the Aegean. In the near east, the remains of our men are in Basra,

Beersheba, Jerusalem, Gaza, Tehran, and Kantara, on the east side of the Suez Canal. In India, we are represented in Madras and the Delhi War Cemetery, and listed on the Memorial there. Closer to home are the three massive Naval Memorials at Chatham, Portsmouth and Plymouth. Local men died in the Haslar Naval Hospital at Gosport and Netley Military Hospital at Southampton, and buried in the cemeteries alongside. Brookwood Military Cemetery near Woking contains also three of our natives.

While most never came home again, a few are buried in the local churchyards. There are three victims of the Great War in Larges Lane Cemetery, seven are remembered at Easthampstead, two in Binfield Cemetery. Warfield has two burials (although both were veterans and never served overseas in this conflict), five are in Cranbourne Churchyard (another is listed on a family grave), nine at Crowthorne, and a further two at Sandhurst. A few other names are listed on plaques erected inside the churches. The extension to the churchyard of Ascot (All Saint's) also lies within the borough, just off Priory Road in Chavey Down, and contains seven graves from World War I, while the churchyard at Wokingham St Sebastian's, on Nine Mile Ride, has the grave of a man listed at Easthampstead.

Probably the most useful website used in this research was www.ancestry.co.uk. It contains census returns, birth, marriage and death registrations, and military records.

Censuses were taken every ten years, starting in 1841. They generally only become available to the public after one hundred years, but the 1911 census was released early, and has been available for about five years at the time of writing. You hope to find every person listed in every census, but it does not always work out like that. Women married, people used nicknames, occasionally the enumerator only recorded initials rather than full names. A young lad, working away from home, may not be listed by either his parents or his employer, each assuming the other has done it. Ages or place of birth are either not known or falsified. Members of the forces on active service are not included, nor are many married women in the 1911 census who supported the suffragette movement. People moved in the three years between the 1911 census and the start of the war, so sometimes it can be difficult to find a name locally from just the census information, or find a link to a man living in a different part of the country.

Births are registered locally and then sent to central offices for recording and indexing; a few might get lost or not sent. An illegitimate child may be listed under the mother's maiden name or the father's (this may not be who the mother later marries). If a name has not been chosen, the child is just listed as male or female. In later life, another name may be used. For example, Jack Provins from Sandhurst was registered and appears in the first two censuses after his birth as Raymond. Christian names get reversed so Henry William becomes William Henry. Marriages failed but divorce was expensive and a social disgrace; the 'accepted' norm was for the couple to separate and be free to remarry after seven years - John Quick of Bracknell appears to have done this. An unmarried couple living together was also socially less acceptable; either the woman is listed as a 'housekeeper' in the census, or occasionally they are listed as married when no marriage has taken place. Although the population was becoming more mobile, the majority still lived and died in the same district. But with wounded soldiers being brought back for treatment, this may not be the case as deaths would frequently occur in hospitals far away from home. If a boy has added a year or more to get into the army, subtracting his age from the year of death will not necessarily give his year of birth.

The key to unlocking a man's military record is his service number. This may change if the men in units are renumbered, or if he is moved between regiments (or even between services – many young men dreamed of getting into the Royal Flying Corps, which became the Royal Air

Force in 1918). The first record to check is Soldiers Died in the Great War (SDGW). In 1921, His Majesty's Stationery Office published, on behalf of and by authority of the War Office, two lists of those who died during the Great War. One volume listed nearly 42,000 Officers, and another eighty volumes recorded the 'other ranks'. The latter record more information, often including place of birth and residence, as well as where the soldier attested. The man's service number, rank, regiment and battalion are included, date of death, location and type of casualty. Only men who are still in the army and who have served abroad are listed, so any who died during training, or had been discharged before their death, will not appear in these lists.

If a solider has served abroad, he will have a Medal Rolls Index Card (MIC). Regiment and service number changes will be listed, but not the dates when these occurred. All men who served overseas were eligible for the British War and Victory medals. Those who came under fire between the start of the conflict and 22nd November 1914 were eligible for the 1914 Star; those after this date but before end of 1915, were eligible for the 1914/5 Star. For these latter two awards, the date of eligibility (the date the man landed on foreign soil) is usually recorded, plus the theatre of war (France, Balkans, etc). Other medals, awarded for bravery, should also be listed. Often, but not always, the date of death is recorded, and for Officers, but rarely for other ranks, address of next of kin to whom medals are to be sent.

Originally there would have been a Service Record for every soldier who served, but around two thirds of soldiers' service records from the First World War were lost in a fire during the Second. But for those that do exist, it can open an intimate picture of the man and his life. The first page should be his attestation and records his stated age, trade, marital status, and date of signing up. A physical description follows on the next page, which duplicates some of the information from a medical inspection he would have had, as well as current address, and details of any marriage and children. There should also be a military summary of important dates, such as mobilisation, arrival overseas, spells in hospital, disciplinary matters, medals and decorations, etc. There may be letters and official documents between the Military Authorities and next of kin, even a list of a casualty's effects to be returned. Many other files, invaluable for WWI research, were lost in the fire, including information on Officers, the Royal Artillery, the Machine Gun Corps, the Royal Army Medical Corps, the Labour Corps, the Royal Air Force, honours and awards, casualty returns, prisoners of war, court martial proceedings, and daily orders covering postings, promotion, punishments and casualties.

More biographical information may turn up in the De Ruvigny Roll of Honour, also viewable online. Published in five volumes at the end of the conflict, this originally set out to list the details of every man killed, but as the war dragged on and losses grew, this became an unrealistic target. But there are still over 26,000 casualties listed, with varying amounts of information, the more detailed usually being for Officers, where the families had provided it.

The other genealogy site I have used in research is www.findmypast.co.uk. Again, censuses and birth, marriage and death registrations are available. The search mechanism differs from that of ancestry; sometimes an entry will show up on one site but not the other. But it also has entries for naval casualties which include date and place of birth, rank and last ship, cause of death, and name and address of relative notified. Even more information is available on men who served in the Royal Marine Light Infantry, which also includes the service history, plus a section of miscellaneous notes which may turn up some nuggets. Similar amounts of information are also listed in the Royal Marine Medal Rolls.

Scottish and Irish censuses (the latter for 1901 and 1911 only, earlier ones having being destroyed in the struggle for independence) are available at www.scotlandspeople.gov.uk and www.census.nationalarchives.ie respectively.

Full service records for naval personnel and officers in the Royal Air Force are available at The National Archives at Kew and downloadable from their website www.nationalarchives.gov.uk. The majority of Army Officer Service Records are also held. Also available are War Diaries for the vast majority of army regiments, although not all have been digitised yet. Some are also available online elsewhere, including the Royal Berkshire Regiment, in which many local men served, at www.thewardrobe.org.uk. More information on men from the flying services may also be found on www.flightglobal.com.

Over one million men and women of the Commonwealth forces, who died in the First World War, are listed on the Commonwealth War Graves Commission website at www.cwgc.org. Military details, stated age at death, next of kin and place of burial, or memorial where the casualty is listed, can be found, along with details on location and history of resting places. More men are being added to this list on a regular basis as new casualties come to light or omissions identified.

In the early part of the twentieth century, there were opportunities overseas in the Colonies for adventurous young men. Canada in particular was eager for new settlers, and some men from Bracknell and its surrounds crossed the Atlantic to forge a new life. When war broke out, new battalions were formed to fight for the mother country, and they joined up to fight with the Canadian Expeditionary Force. The attestation forms for most men from Canada, plus the circumstances of the death of many of them, are now online at www.collectionscanada.gc.ca. A few had gone even further afield, and fought under the Australian flag. Attestation and service records for men from Australia are available at www.naa.gov.au.

The Victoria Cross (V.C.) was the highest military honour to be awarded. Officers were also eligible for the Distinguished Service Order (D.S.O.) and the Military Cross (M.C.); for other ranks the equivalent awards were the Distinguished Conduct Medal (D.C.M) and Military Medal (M.M.). The London Gazette records citations for military decorations (except for the Military Medal), and also many promotions of Officers. These can be viewed at www.london-gazette.co.uk, but the search facility is a bit hit-and-miss. Some battalions also awarded a 'Green Ticket' to men who had been nominated for awards but failed to receive them. The War Diary of the 8th Battalion, Royal Berkshire Regiment makes several references to them being given.

Most of the photos of men in this book have come from the Reading Standard newspaper. Starting in February 1916, a monthly edition was published containing pictures of casualties, heroes, and brothers serving in the conflict. These are now available on a set of CDs. The picture of Allan Wiggett from Binfield, while being held as a Prisoner of War, was discovered in his Service Record at The National Archives. The remainder have mainly been discovered on the internet.

The Great War Forum at www.1914-1918.invisionzone.com is a great source of information, with many members willing to share their extensive information and experience on anything about the conflict, right down to the smallest detail. It is not unknown for a solider to be identified from an anonymous photo.

It must be remembered that all the information recorded at the time was either written by hand or occasionally produced on typewriters. Errors creep in, either accidentally or by men falsifying information. Some men served under an alias for a variety of reasons, and young lads added one or more years to their age to join up. Later transcription errors or 'typos' can also muddy the waters, leading the researcher down false trails or obscuring the truth. Sometimes you discover conflicting information and have to look elsewhere to verify the truth. Some records are lost or destroyed. As has been mentioned above, well over half of soldier's service records were lost in a fire. More information exists about officers than the ordinary rank and file. But what is the truth? Official War Diaries, written on a daily basis at the front, only record one side of the story, and were written to put our leaders in a good light. Of those charged with writing them, some are more efficient than others. One was obviously written by a frustrated author, containing huge amounts of detail on the conditions, the landscape, and the supposed feelings of the men, waiting to go 'over the top.' Some record the weather or others things of local interest. "We were successfully relieved by The Queen's at night, the relief taking 1 hour 55 minutes, again a record." "Leave rules came out, 1 Officer and 3 other ranks every fourteen days, which means at the end of eighteen months, every Officer will get home, and at the end of twelve years, every man." Others are less forthcoming with details. During the German Spring Offensive in 1918, when a desperate rearguard action was being fought, the War Diary entries can be particularly terse, just when we would wish for more information. For some, the details of their horses or even, in the case of the artillery, the guns, take precedence over the men. While the names of towns, villages and prominent landmarks appear in the diaries, some features of the landscape are referred to by the names used by troops on the ground or Amy staff (for example, Lone Pine, Brown Line, or Piccadilly Circus). Military maps used reference co-ordinates, meaningless to anyone without the map in front of them, and these have not been used in this publication.

Similarly, many regimental histories were written in the years immediately after the conflict when Britain was still patting itself on the back after victory. But it is also easy to misread things with the benefit of hindsight. Communications were poor; telephone lines were frequently disrupted, runners became casualties, signals were obscured by fog, smoke or gas. New technology was unreliable – the first tanks broke down or got stuck in the mud. Marching was often the way of moving from one part of the battlefield to another; flight was a still relatively recent innovation. We must take what we have and try to interpret it.

In the course of this project, the names of men have been discovered who died in the War and had a connection with the area, yet they are not commemorated on any local War Memorial. The passage of time means that it can never be known why a man was not included on one of the local memorials, but there are several possible reasons. Whilst a man may have been born in the area, surviving family members may have died, or moved away, by the time the memorials were being erected. Quite simply, there was no-one left to remember him. A single man, whose connection being perhaps having only briefly worked in the area. The family may not have come to live in the area until some time after the War, and the man may be commemorated on a memorial nearer his actual home. It may be that the family never saw the invitation to submit names, or thought that the man didn't qualify (for whatever reason), under whatever the criteria set by the organising committee for the particular memorial. Other families may have held out hope of their missing man returning, and the placing of his name on a list of those who perished would finally extinguish that hope. Advertisements appear in the Reading Mercury from 1919 onwards, aimed at returning Prisoners of War, asking for any information on men, still listed as missing. Or maybe the family simply didn't want him remembered in this way. Several of the memorials are inside a church. If the family felt the memorial was too closely connected with the Anglican Church, they may have chosen not to put his name forward. When reading the minutes of the Memorial Committee at Crowthorne, it becomes obvious the final position of the memorial, in the lych gate of St John's Church, was highly controversial, and many people did not want it placed there. On the other side of the same coin, the man's name might be excluded because the family was insufficiently connected with the church. In Crowthorne, a dialogue took place as to whether names would be included in the village or at St Sebastians on Nine Mile Ride, but more than one man finished up being listed at both! Occasionally, a name may appear on a memorial of a man who was not killed. One of the names at Wokingham had to be corrected; two men with similar names fought, with the wrong one being listed as killed. A name on the memorial at Pontardawe in South Wales was removed when the soldier returned from France four years after it was unveiled, having suffered from amnesia for the intervening period. William Hart, an Australian, was reported missing in August 1918 and presumed to have been killed. But he resurfaced two years later, using a different name, in the U.S. Army in Honolulu! No-one ever established how he came to be an American soldier.

Conversely, a name appears on a memorial, and no local man can be identified. Who was Herbert Cartwright who appears on a panel in Crowthorne lych gate? No-one with the surname appears in the 1911 census in the area. Only by investigating the eight men of that name who died in the conflict, can a reasonable guess be made. Or A. Cox? Arthur? Alfred? Bert Wood (Easthampstead) and Jack Franks (Bracknell Holy Trinity) would have been readily identifiable a century ago, but not now. Crowthorne has the added difficulty of Broadmoor Hospital. When conscription was introduced, a list of reserved occupations was also compiled, of work deemed vital for the war economy. "Attendants on lunatics", as the nurses at Broadmoor were then described, was one of these occupations, and men, attempting to avoid being called up, worked at the institution. This exemption lasted until June 1918; for this reason, there is no Roll of Honour in the chapel at Broadmoor.

Since 1908 the British Army had offered three forms of recruitment. A man could join the army as a professional soldier of the regular army, as a part-time member of the Territorial Force, or as a soldier of the Special Reserve. There was a long-running battle, with politicians and military men taking both sides, about whether Britain should have a system of national conscripted service. By 1914 this had not come about, and Britain's army was entirely voluntary.

A man wishing to join the army could do so providing he passed certain physical tests and was willing to enlist for a number of years. The recruit had to be taller than 5 feet 3 inches, and aged between 18 and 38 (although he could not be sent overseas until he was aged 19). He would join at the Regimental Depot or at one of the normal recruiting offices. The man had a choice over the regiment he was assigned to. He would typically join the army for a period of seven years full-time service with the colours, to be followed by another five on the National Reserve. When war was declared, there were 350,000 former soldiers on the National Reserve, ready to be called back to fill the establishment of their regiments.

The Territorial Force came into existence in 1908 as a result of the reorganisation of the former militia and other volunteer units. It provided an opportunity for men to join the army on a part-time basis. These units were recruited locally, and became more recognised and supported by the local community than the regulars. Men trained at weekends or in the evenings, and went away to a summer camp. Territorials were not obliged to serve overseas, but were enlisted on the basis that in the event of war, they could be called upon for full-time service. The physical criteria for joining the Territorials were the same as for the Regular army, but the lower age limit was 17. Not long after war was declared, all men in the Territorials were asked if they wished to serve overseas, but in some cases, it was assumed they did, and they had to 'opt out' rather than 'opt in'. If all your pals were going off to fight, would you want to stay behind, even if officially you were too young to go?

The Special Reserve was another form of part-time military service. Special Reservists enlisted for six years, had to accept the possibility of being called up in the event of a general mobilisation, and to undergo all the same conditions as men of the Army Reserve. This meant that it differed from the TF in that the men could be sent overseas.

On his appointment as Secretary of State for War shortly after the declaration of the war, Field-Marshal Lord Kitchener issued a call for volunteers to increase the size of the army. He did not believe that the Territorial Force was an appropriate structure for doing this. The poster of the moustachioed Lord Kitchener, pointing his finger at the reader, with the slogan "Your Country Needs You", is probably the most famous in history, although recent research has claimed the poster was an urban myth, and was never used. The men would only have to enlist 'for the duration of the war,' but legally, they were joining the regular army. There was no recruiting office in Bracknell, the nearest being in Wokingham and Ascot. Most local men attested at the former, although many went to Reading, many from Sandhurst went to Camberley, and a handful from the north of the borough signed up in Windsor or Maidenhead. Others, for whatever the reason, went further afield, to London, Sussex, and even, in the case of Harry Willis from Binfield, to Yorkshire. The wartime volunteers had a choice over the regiment and unit they joined. They had to meet the same physical criteria as the regulars, but men who had previously served in the army would now be accepted up to the age of 45. There are many recorded instances of underage, and indeed overage, men being accepted into the service. It was not necessary to produce evidence of age, or even of one's name, in order to enlist, and Recruitment Officers were paid for each man they enlisted. If a youngster, keen to join, was known by the local recruiting officer, he could go elsewhere and join with no questions asked. If a boy was too short or insufficiently developed, surely a few months of army training and food would bring him up to the mark.

Although death was part of everyday life, war was not. Most children, especially in large families, had lost a sibling at a young age, and old relatives were 'laid out' in the front room of the home before the funeral took place. Battles, on the other hand, took place far away overseas, and before the advent of photographs, were depicted by paintings or idealised drawings in newspapers, showing heroic men in scarlet uniforms performing heroic deeds. For the youth of the time, soldiers were heroes. The British Army had been practically invincible (the Boer War was a sharp reality check), and boys were brought up on a list of stories and books, extolling the fighting man, his bravery and courage. In school, pictures of great military heroes adorned the walls, and famous days in the military calendar, such as the Battle of Waterloo, were commemorated. Between five and ten per cent of children born in 1900 were given names associated, in one way or another, with the Boer War. The British Empire covered a quarter of the globe, and a posting in the armed forces gave youths a chance to travel that was simply not available to the ordinary youngster. India, South Africa, Hong Kong, and the West Indies were all far-away exotic places, out of reach of all but the top end of society. The media gave one-sided, glamorous reports of conflicts, where the British were always superior, always victorious, and always had right on their side. The chance of going to France, of putting the evil Bosche in his rightful place, and of being home again by Christmas, proved too much of an opportunity to be missed by many teenagers of the time. But while soldiers were heroes to the youth, the adult population had a different view of the Army. The fighting force was full of dodgy characters, men on the edge of society, those escaping a life of drudgery or the arm of the law, and where it was possible to desert one night, by climbing over the depot wall, and re-enlist in the next county the following morning with a different name in a different regiment.

The public response to Kitchener's appeal was rapid, and at times overwhelming, but soon died down to average only 100,000 men per month. While many were inspired to enlist by the news, drum-beating and pressure to conform, some joined up for all manner of reasons, including a natural desire to quit a humdrum or arduous job, take a chance of seeing another country, or to escape family or troubles. Many travelled considerable distances to attend a depot or recruiting office for a particular unit. They would be attracted to a Regiment or Corps by its reputation, the fact that it was the local one, or where they had relatives or pals. Members of the Territorial Force were used for home duties in the early stages, and Boy Scouts were used to safeguard railways, telegraphs and reservoirs, or act as despatch riders.

War was declared on 4th August 1914, and the first contact between Germany and British troops occurred on the 23rd of the same month. The British were totally outnumbered; the Germans had two and a half times as many men, and twice as many guns. The numbers volunteering did not remain constant. Even the initial perceived rush to join did not happen. The queues at recruiting offices in the early days mainly consisted of recalled Reservists. It was only the news of major setbacks to the British Army, or of enemy atrocities, that caused a surge in numbers. The retreat from Mons in August 1914, January 1915 (after Christmas), German attacks on Ypres and their use of poison gas, the sinking of the passenger ship 'Lusitania', and the Zeppelin bombing raids led to another increase in the spring of 1915, while the execution of the nurse Edith Cavell and other bad news increased the number of volunteers in the autumn. While some 300,000 enlisted in the first month of the war, the number rose by 50% in September.

But by spring 1915, it had become clear that voluntary recruitment was not going to provide the numbers of men required. The Government passed the National Registration Act on 15th July 1915 as a step towards stimulating recruitment, and to discover how many men between the ages of 15 and 65 were engaged in each trade. The results of this census became available to the authorities by mid-September 1915.

On 11th October 1915, Lord Derby, who had played a major part in raising volunteers, was appointed Director-General of Recruiting. He brought forward a scheme five days later, always called the Derby Scheme, for raising the numbers. It was half-way to conscription. Disappointed at the results of the Derby Scheme, the Government introduced the Military Service Act on 27th January 1916. All voluntary enlistment was stopped. All British males were now deemed to have enlisted, that is, they were conscripted, if they were aged between 18 and 41, resided in Great Britain (excluding Ireland), and were unmarried or a widower on 2nd November 1915. Conscripted men were no longer given a choice of which service, regiment or unit they joined. This act was extended to married men on 25th May 1916. Some occupations were considered necessary to the running of the country or the War effort, and men in these jobs were exempt for being called up (these were known as Starred Occupations). This list was regularly updated, with some 'necessary' occupations being dropped; attendants at Broadmoor were exempt until June 1918, although several of them ignored the protection, and joined up anyway. There was also an appeals mechanism for men who objected to serving, whether for health, family or moral grounds, but with many appealing, the system became overburdened and slow, postponing the conscription of many who were only trying to avoid being called up. The tribunal in Bracknell in November 1917 found a coal branch inspector, a grocer's manager, and a pharmacist exempt, but only until another re-evaluation the following year.

From September 1916, men called up were first assigned to a unit of the Training Reserve. It had been found that the traditional regimental means of training was not keeping up with the flood of men coming through, and the TR was established as a means of doing so. A further extension of the Act on 10th April 1918, followed a serious political crisis concerning the provision of manpower, which along with a large extension of the British section of the Western Front, was cited as a prime cause of the defeat of the Fifth Army in March 1918. This act reduced the minimum age of recruitment to 18. The introduction of conscription made it very much more difficult for a recruit to falsify his age and name. Conscription ceased on 11th November 1918 and all conscripts were discharged, if they had not already been so, on 31st March 1920.

As casualties mounted, parents of under-age boys, serving at the front, became alarmed, and clamoured for their return. Training could be as short as fourteen weeks before men were sent to the fighting, ill-prepared for what awaited them. It has been estimated that as many as 15% of the volunteers were under-age, although not all of them reached the front; a few lasted barely four days' training before being discharged, and one fifth less than a month. But at a conservative estimate, over 250,000 enlisted. For those who reached the front, many were ill-equipped physically, mentally and emotionally to cope with what they encountered, and the extreme cold of the winter weather. Stanley Spencer from Chavey Down died aged just sixteen; Harold McEune from Crowthorne enlisted at the same age. In Parliament, the parents of these youngsters had a champion, Sir Arthur Markham, a Liberal MP from Nottinghamshire. A wealthy industrialist from Mansfield, employing 25,000 men in mining and the iron and steel industry, he concentrated his efforts on his constituents' welfare and interests. Many of his workers heeded the call to enlist, and after talking to some of them, he was quick to ask why they were called upon before the Government were in a position to equip them. The question of under-age soldiers soon came to his attention, and a perceived indifference of the issue from the War Office drove him on. The introduction of the Derby Scheme and registration cards all but eliminated the problem at home, although some boys managed to still beat the system (including a 14-year old who reached the front line by assuming the place of an older brother who had deserted while home on leave). But that still left the thousands of under-age boys serving in the front line overseas. Instructions were issued to commanders, but with 'get-out' clauses, and reluctance on the part of some, many boys that should have been sent back were not. If the young man was a well-trained, efficient soldier who was fighting well, and who wanted to continue to serve his country, why should he be released? Newspapers were also sending mixed messages, one minute decrying the use of boys for fighting; highlighting the heroics of a young teenager the next. Holding camps were set up at the French Channel ports for young soldiers removed from the line, who could be rapidly recalled if necessary due to excessive 'wastage' on the front line. The authorities were slow to realise what to do with these young men; the Army was geared up to ship men to the front, or the injured to England; they had no plans for young men there on a more permanent basis. It was left to a few volunteers to arrange distractions for those who were typically young tearaways, and for whom the Army had imposed the first meaning and discipline on their lives. Education, sports, and entertainment were organised, with mixed results; an old Officer who spent over an hour talking about the correct way to salute was not as well received as an undersized young lad, talking about his experiences in the trenches in limited, but colourful, language. Other problems were faced by those sent back to England. Men who had been invalided out of the Army were awarded a Silver War Badge which could be worn in public places, indicating their unfitness for service. But for under-age boys, especially those of large stature, there was no such 'mark', and many were seen as shirkers, who should have been fighting, but had somehow evaded the call. Army life and improved food had made them taller and heavier than the average. Women in particular, would give a white feather to those they thought should have been away, fighting for the country.

In the second half of March 1918, the Germans launched a massive offensive in a last-ditch attempt to win the war. The United Sates had proclaimed a strict policy of neutrality at the beginning of the conflict, although she was an important supplier to Britain and the Allies. Even the loss of 128 American passengers on the 'Lusitania', sunk by a German submarine in May 1915, was not enough to drag America into the fighting, although their call for attacks on passenger vessels to cease was heeded. But in January 1917, the Germans resumed unrestricted submarine warfare. They also invited Mexico to join the fighting, in return offering them money and help to regain territories lost to the United States seventy years earlier. Britain intercepted the telegram, and reluctantly, America entered the war, bringing another four million troops to the side of the Allies.

From 1914, Germany and her allies had been fighting on two fronts; facing the French and British in the west, and Russia in the east. The Russian Revolution of October 1917, and Russia's subsequent peace treaty with Germany, allowed the Central European powers to move all their resources to the Western Front. These factors, combined with economic troubles at home, brought about by Britain's naval blockade of the North Sea, preventing food and materials reaching Germany, and mismanagement at home, gave Germany the momentum for a big push to win the war. Britain's troops were also in need of a rest and training after offensives at Ypres and Cambrai in 1917, as well as the diversion of some troops to Italy. The British line now stretched over 120 miles, much longer than it had been the previous year; Britain's resources were being stretched thinly. The German push gained 25 miles in places, against a line that had been almost stable for two or three years. Over 90,000 British and Empire troops were taken Prisoner of War in six weeks.

Following the 'war to end all wars', a flu pandemic spread across the world, taken back by soldiers returning to their homes. Men, who had survived the conflict, died in their own beds from an unseen enemy. The official cut-off date for war casualties was 31st August 1921, so those who died from the disease are officially registered as having died as a result of the war. Those who died on 1st September 1921 are not. How many later deaths were due to physical and mental injuries, sustained during the fighting, will probably never be known.

The Bracknell area is not unique in its list of casualties, but every man who gave his life defending the country is unique. The fallen are not just names on a list; they are real people, sons, husbands, fathers. Each one has a story; this book tells their stories.

CROWTHORNE

ST JOHN'S CHURCH

The Crowthorne War Memorial, consisting of four panels in the lych gate containing more than one hundred names, was unveiled on 20th February 1921.

HAROLD G. ANNETTS

The late Pte. H. G. ANNETTS, 10th Batt., 7, Broadmoor, Crowthorne.— Killed in action, Aged 22.

Harry George Annetts was born at Crowthorne in 1893, and baptised on 21st May. He was the only boy in a family of four surviving children, a younger sister having died in infancy. His father worked as an attendant at Broadmoor, while an elder sister became a teacher at Crowthorne School. Harry worked as a plumber's apprentice after leaving school. He volunteered for service, attesting at Basingstoke, and joined the 10th Battalion, Hampshire Regiment. Formed at the outbreak of war, the battalion had been in Ireland until May 1915 before moving to Basingstoke, and two months later left for the Balkans. Harold was still doing his training when they went, but followed in September, and was in Gallipoli for a few days before they left and moved to Salonika early the following month. In December, they were at Kosturino in Serbia. The Regimental History describes the action: "The key to the position was Rocky Peak, a detached hill southwest of Ormanli, which was attacked in force on the 6th, when the enemy entered our trenches, but was driven out by a counter-attack. Early on the following day, the attack was resumed and in greater force. The shelling was very heavy, and fog helped them considerably, and they made good use of the dead ground in which they were collecting and which prevented the British guns from giving the infantry really effective support. The Bulgarian guns proved very effective, gradually demolishing the ill-sited trenches of the Hampshires and making their position untenable, while the loss of Rocky Peak allowed mountain guns and machine guns to enfilade the position from the right. The pressure steadily increased, the Bulgarians were in great force and their heavy losses did not deter their efforts to advance. Eventually about 2pm, the Hampshire's left company had to be withdrawn from their virtually demolished front trenches to get some shelter behind the crest. This move was unfortunately mistaken by the next company of the Hampshires for the beginning of an ordered retirement, to which it conformed. All ranks were very tired, having had no food for two days, while most men had lost packs and great-coats. After two bitterly cold but quiet days, practically untroubled by the enemy, a fresh retirement was ordered on the 10th, the Hampshires being directed to Doiran Station. One officer and twenty men from each battalion remained behind to conceal the move from the enemy. The losses could now be ascertained, killed and missing, mainly the latter, came to over 180." The march to Doiran started just after midnight on the 11th, and took eleven hours. Early next morning, they were ordered to take up a position behind the boundary line to the west of Doiran Station in thick fog, a movement that was completed by dawn. It was another 24 hours before the fog cleared, and even then, the enemy made no attempt to move. The War Diary stated, "*the* spirit of *the* men *is* excellent, though they are having a bad time due to lack of clothing and bad damp and fogs." After another quiet day, the battalion marched to Kilindia on the 15th, and entrained for Salonika. Harry's official date of death is 14th December, but it is likely he was killed a few days earlier, and the paperwork had only just caught up. His body and grave could not be located after the war, and his name is listed in the Doiran Memorial.

ROGER D. BAKER

Roger Dyke Baker was born at Thruxton, near Andover, Hampshire, on 24th July 1879. He was one of five children, and also had three half-brothers from his father's first marriage. His father, the local vicar, died in 1896, and his mother was forced to leave the rectory, and moved to Streatley, Berkshire. The family had a private income, and employed up to five servants. Roger was educated privately at a preparatory school in Hastings, before going to Rugby School. He attended the Royal Military Academy at Sandhurst, and obtained a commission with the 2nd Battalion, East Lancashire Regiment, in 1898. He served in the Waziristan Campaign (1901-2) on the northwest frontier of India, and also in East Africa in operations in Somaliland (1904). In 1908, he married Florence Ann Lockyer in London, but they were to have no children. He passed through the Staff College in 1913, and on the outbreak of war was appointed Assistant Embarkation Officer at Southampton. On 24th September the same year, he was appointed Brigade Major to the 38th Brigade, 13th Division, with which he went to Gallipoli, leaving from Avonmouth in June 1915, and landing on the peninsula on 7th July. On 1st August, the Brigade was withdrawn to Mudros, and two days later, Roger, along with Brigadier-General Anthony Baldwin, in charge of the 38th Infantry Brigade, left for Anzac Cove for reconnaissance purposes. The battalion followed next day, arriving at 9pm, and spent the night in bivouacs in Victoria Gully. They remained there on the 5th, but were shelled all day and "lost *a* fair number of men through shelling." On the 9th, Brigadier-General Baldwin led an attack on Chunuk Bair. The Brigade War Diary for the following day reads, "At 3am …. we were heavily attacked by the enemy and subjected to severe rifle fire. This attack, however, was beaten back. At 5am, the enemy delivered another attack, and succeeded in driving our troops back on our right flank for a short distance. However, the position they took rendered it impossible for us to hold the hill above 'The Farm', and we were forced to retire. Just before retiring, Brigadier-General Baldwin was killed," and a book on Officer casualties adds, "all his staff fell with him." The War Diary for the 6th Battalion, East Lancashire Regiment, records a re-organisation on 11th August, including the appointment of a new Brigade Major. Roger died of wounds on the 13th and was buried in East Mudros Military Cemetery, having been taken back to the island for treatment to his injuries. General Shaw, Commanding the 13th Division, wrote: "During the time he was with me …. he was all that a young Staff Officer ought to be – knowledgeable, brave, energetic and tactful. He died doing his duty strenuously, as he always did. His loss was a great one, both to the 38th Brigade and the Services generally." General Finch Pearse: "He always made the Service his profession. His abilities and determination of character were of the highest order, and had he been spared, there must have been a brilliant career before him. His straightforwardness, earnestness, keenness and loyalty, combined with his unusual sense of humour, endeared him to all who knew him. He was a staunch friend, an exhilarating companion and deservedly popular." Although Roger appears to have no connections with Crowthorne, his mother's family lived in the village, and a relative must have put his name forward for the list on the village War memorial.

SIDNEY L. BARRATT

Sidney Lloyd Barratt was born in Wokingham in 1880. He was one of five children, two others dying in infancy. Sidney's father worked as a carpenter, and the family soon moved to Sandhurst, and then Napier Road, Crowthorne. Sidney also worked as a carpenter and joiner after leaving school, but is missing from the 1911 census. However, the records state he was working as a carpenter at Broadmoor immediately prior to joining the Army. He married Ethel Haddrell on 5th August 1912 in Wokingham; she had been working at a laundry attached to Wellington College, close to Crowthorne station. He volunteered for service, attesting at Camberley on 9th November 1915, and joined the Royal Engineers. He was 5'6" tall, with brown eyes, black hair, and a pale complexion, and had a mole on his left shoulder. He went to France at the end of July the following year, but returned to the depot at Newark, Nottinghamshire, six months later, where he was diagnosed as suffering from tuberculosis, brought on from cold and wet conditions at Simoncourt, Arras. The Medical Board, which considered his case in June, heard his illness began with a chill, general aches and pains, and a cough. Pains in his back were especially marked. On admission to Marcham Road Sanitorium, Abingdon on 2nd February, there were "definite signs of tubercle at both lung apices. He appeared very ill, sallow and emaciated, had persistent vomitings, was sleepless and had diarrhoea (enteric) with offensive stools." His current appearance was "bad", and his weight had not increased in response to treatment. The cough continued to be troublesome, especially in the early morning. There were definite signs of tuberculosis in both lungs. It was also noted he was "of good character." He was discharged from the army as medically unfit and requiring sanatorium treatment on 26th June, and awarded a Silver War Badge. Sidney died on 12th January 1918, and is buried in the graveyard on the north side of Crowthorne Church. The Reading Mercury of 26th January 1918 carried a report of the burial: "The funeral of Mr Sidney Barratt took place in Crowthorne Churchyard on Thursday last week. The deceased, who was 37 years of age, was the popular secretary of the Crowthorne Football Club. The first part of the service was *held* at the Wesleyan Church."

The late Sergt. WM. BARTLETT, late captain Crowthorne F.C.—Killed in action.

WILLIAM BARTLETT

William Bartlett was born in 1892 at Sandhurst. He was one of six children, one of whom died in infancy. Although the family lived at Owlsmoor, his father worked at the Royal Military Academy at Sandhurst. William worked as a building labourer after leaving school, and later as a house painter, possibly working alongside an uncle who lived with the family. William volunteered for service, attesting at Camberley, and joined the 7th Battalion, Royal West Surrey Regiment. His initial training was carried out in and around Colchester, before the battalion moved to Salisbury Plain in May, with an inspection by the King the next month. Embarkation for France began on 24th July, with William's draft arriving three days later. There was no major action for the battalion until the Battle of the Somme the following year. They were based near Montauban, a village in German hands, which it was their objective to capture. The days preceding the attack, in which the enemy positions were relentlessly bombarded, had mixed effects. In front of the West Surreys, it was pretty effective; the enemy trenches were badly damaged and lightly held, and the Royal Flying Corps reported large explosions at the enemy dumps. Just before 7:30am on 1st July, two mines laid by one of the Royal Engineer Tunnelling Companies were blown, which were the signal for the lead units to advance from the British front trenches. Units in the centre were held up by fire from a crater field in No Man's Land, the results of mine warfare in the area in May. The enemy had occupied the craters, and had built some strong points which survived the bombardment. Undamaged machine guns fired from these when the battalion began to advance. Gradually, as the day wore on, the enemy were driven back and the pressure on the battalion eased, but it was not until 5.15pm that Montauban Alley was taken. The enemy artillery, having been badly damaged in this area, did not greatly interfere with the work of evacuation of the wounded, bringing up of supplies, and consolidation of the ground won, which now began in earnest. However, enemy shell fire falling on the area intensified and stayed heavy, causing many casualties, and making relief and re-supply very problematic. They were finally relieved the following day. On the 11th, the battalion were in the front line again, northwest of Maricourt. Two days later, they were ordered to attack the northern portion of Trones Wood, an area with which they were not familiar. The leading Company moved forward from Dublin Trench at 5:30pm. The battalion were greatly impeded by a relief moving up into Longueval Alley at the same time. At 8pm, they assaulted Trones Wood from the northern extremity over a front of 750 yards. Men from another battalion, who were to assist in the assault, became disorganised owing to casualties due to shell fire when moving up to the attack, and only about one and a half platoons arrived in time to partake in the assault. The advance was met by very heavy rifle, machine gun and shell fire, and checked. At 8:50pm, a message was received that the northern portion of Trones Wood would be re-bombarded, and that the attack was not to be pressed if success seemed unlikely. At 9pm, the remaining men reorganised for the defence of Longueval Alley, and some three hours later, instructions were received that the battalion might withdraw to the German old front line position if Longueval Alley was sufficiently held, which they did a couple of hours later. The attack had cost over two hundred casualties. Corporal William Bartlett was one of those found to be missing; his body was never recovered, and his name is listed on the Thiepval Memorial.

JAMES S. BEDFORD

James Sydney Bedford, known as Sydney, was born at Wokingham in 1888. He was the youngest of eleven children, six of whom failed to live more than a few years. The family lived on London Road, opposite All Saints Church, and Sydney's father worked as a bricklayer until his death in 1902. The family then moved to New Wokingham Road, Crowthorne, where his mother took in laundry, assisted by two of her daughters, while Sydney worked as a hair dresser. He joined the 1st Battalion, Royal West Surrey Regiment, possibly under the Derby Scheme, attesting at Wokingham. The War Diary records a draft of 154 men arriving on 31st May, which probably included James, but comments, "First batch of Derby recruits among them; rather a poor lot physically." However, it has been impossible to find a medal card for James, which would include information on when he went to France. The battalion took part in the Arras Offensive and Third Battle of Ypres in 1917, and the Battle of Hazebrouck in 1918. On the night of 11th/12th April, they were billeted in huts near Meteren, which was shelled heavily all night. The camp was hit by a shell the following day, just as orders were being given to the Company

Commanders, wounding eight men. Although the high ground they were to occupy was held by Germans with machine guns, they captured it with very few casualties. They held the positions all day, no troops succeeded in joining up on either flank, and they came under machine gun and rifle fire, as well as shelling, but held firm. An attack was beaten off early the following morning, but three outposts of 'B' Company were later overwhelmed, forcing that company to withdraw. A general withdrawal was ordered for 1pm which was accomplished, although under heavy machine gun fire from the right and shrapnel from field guns. There was continued heavy fighting all day, and a slow withdrawal of the battalion as the Germans succeeded in getting better positions and firing on them. Sydney was wounded at some time during these two days of action, and died of his wounds on 13th April; he is buried in Lijssenthoek Military Cemetery. James's name also appears on the Rolls of Honour at both Sandhurst and Wokingham St Sebastians.

Pte. W. BELL, 2.4th Batt., Bell View, Owlsmoor. — Wounded and missing.

WILLIAM W. BELL

William Walter Bell was born at Owlsmoor on 8th January 1893, and baptised at St Michael's, Sandhurst, on 5th March, the eldest of four children. His father worked as a mess waiter at the Royal Military Academy at Sandhurst. After leaving school, William worked as a printer's apprentice. He had joined the 1/4th Battalion, Hampshire Regiment, a Territorial Battalion, before the war, attesting at Salisbury Plain. The battalion sailed for India in 1914, before returning to Basra in March the following year. The Regimental History describes the situation: "Earlier in the year, the British had made some tactical moves to seize important or threatening points beyond Basra. After an early string of cheap successes, eyes increasingly fell on the Mesopotamian capital, Baghdad. The 6th (Poona) Division advanced, leaving a very thinly stretched supply line of hundreds of miles behind it, only to receive a bloody repulse at Ctesiphon. A ragged and dispiriting retreat back to Kut-al-Amara began. The Turks pursued the retreating Division to Kut, and soon surrounded and cut it off. British forces in Mesopotamia were now growing, and these formations were ordered to advance north along the Tigris to relieve Kut. They ran into strong and stoutly defended lines and suffered some hard knocks; although they got close to Kut, the garrison there was surrendered on 29th April 1916. It was an enormous blow to British prestige and a morale-booster for the Turkish Army. An attack on El Hanna, on 21st January was part of this advance. 'Zero' was fixed for 6:30am, but a mirage prevented the gunners from seeing their targets, so the attack had to be postponed till 7:45am, by which time the Turks had fully realised what was coming. The Hampshires had been under fairly heavy long-range rifle fire even before 'Zero', and had had a few men hit. The fire was heavy, and the battalion had a long stretch to cover, even to gain our old front trench. With no support coming up and heavy casualties, the advance was held up short of the Turkish line. On the extreme left, some men managed to join Black Watch in the Turkish trenches and lend a hand in a struggle which they maintained for over an hour against heavy odds, though no more support reached them. Eventually, they were overwhelmed, only a few survivors regaining our lines. Meanwhile, the rest of the battalion could merely hang on behind such cover as they could scrape together with their entrenching tools and wait till darkness allowed them to move and to try to assist the wounded. A pelting rain and bitter cold added to the trials to be endured, and stamina and endurance were severely taxed." Well over half the attacking infantry were casualties, including William's battalion, who lost almost 250 men. William was killed in the fighting; his body was never recovered, and his name is listed on the Basra Memorial.

CYRIL E. F. BEVIR

Cyril Edward Felix Bevir, who had an older sister, was born on 30th May 1891 at Wellington College, where his father was a teacher and House Master. He was baptised in Crowthorne Church on 29th July. He was privately educated at Temple Grove School, Mortlake, and Rugby School, before going up to Pembroke College, Cambridge, where he ran for his College at cross country. He gained a commission with the Royal Field Artillery, and went to France in September 1914 with the 6th Division. After serving as an Artillery Observation Officer with the Royal Flying Corps, Cyril was posted to 'X' Battery, Royal Horse Artillery, lent to the 28th Division, and again borrowed by the R.F.C. On rejoining his battery, he was wounded at Zonnebeke in April 1915, and invalided home. After recovering, he returned to the front in August, as Adjutant to the 76th Brigade, Royal Field Artillery, Guards Divisional Artillery, having been promoted to Lieutenant the previous month. Towards the end of October, the batteries were at Annequin, firing on the Hohenzollern Redoubt and enemy trenches. The Brigade was ordered to retire on the 28th, and some of the officers took over to keep the guns firing until the relief arrived. Cyril was killed by a gunshot wound to the head, while looking for another officer who was missing. He was buried in a small local cemetery named Quality Street. The Colonel wrote: "The Signaller who was with him told me they got into bad shell fire, and laid down for a bit, and your boy told him, 'Well, we've got to get through with it', and they both got up to go on, when a shrapnel burst in front of them, killing your son. He was a very good Adjutant, and was imperturbable when there were any fires or worry, and always kept his head. The Service has lost a good Officer," and a brother Officer: "I am sure he has told you what a happy family we used to be at Cahir, and I cannot express in a letter, the affection we all had for him. The men, too, loved him, and there are no better judges. He was just the same in France as at home in peace time; never so happy at home as when charging a big fence on a bad horse, and never so cheery on service as when things were going really badly. He was the best type of gunner officer." In October 1915, Cyril's father wrote to the War Office, asking why his son's name has not been included in the official casualty lists in The Times, but the response has not been found. His father was writing again, this time a letter dated 30th June 1919, to Buckingham Palace: "The parents of 2/Lt. C. N. F. Bevir desire humbly to express to his Most Gracious Majesty the King, their grateful thanks for a most kindly thought in sending to them, the beautiful scroll which they will ever greatly value." Almost a year later, a copy of a further letter from Cyril's service file, sent to Cyril's father is filed: "I am writing with reference already sent to you regarding the place of burial of 2/Lt. C. N. F. Bevir, RFA. I am to inform you that in accordance with the agreement with the French and Belgian governments to remove all scattered graves and all cemeteries of less than 40 graves, also certain other cemeteries which were situated in places unsuitable for permanent retention, it has been found necessary to exhume the bodies buried in certain areas. The body of 2/Lt. C. N. F. Bevir has therefore been removed from a point near Philosophe, and reburied in Veille Chapelle New Military Cemetery, Lacoutre, NNW of Bethune. I am to add that the necessity for the removal is much regretted, but was unavoidable for the reasons given above. You may rest assured that the work of reburial has been carried out carefully and reverently, special arrangements having been made for the appropriate religious service to be held."

Pte. ARTHUR BOYDE, 7th Batt. Royal Sussex Regt.

A. BOYDE

Arthur Boyde was born at Sandhurst in 1893. He was one of seven children, another two dying in infancy. His father, a local man from Finchampstead, worked as a night watchman at Wellington College for well over twenty years, and the family lived on Wokingham Road, and later on Addiscombe Road. Arthur went into domestic service after leaving school, and in the 1911 census, held a position of footman at an address in West London. However, he may well have been working in Sussex at the outbreak of war, as he immediately volunteered, attesting at Bexhill-on-Sea Town Hall on 19th August 1914, and joined the 7th Battalion, Royal Sussex Regiment. He was only 5'4" tall, but weighed just over ten stone, with grey eyes, light brown hair, and a fresh complexion. His initial training was done in the Folkestone area, before the battalion moved to Aldershot in March the following year, and crossed the Channel to Boulogne at the end of May. They were involved in the Battle of Loos in September, and although in a 'quiet area' from mid December to mid January, still suffered heavy casualties. A month later, they were moved to the area round Hohenzollern Redoubt, where underground mine warfare was very active. Four mines were exploded under the Redoubt on 2nd March 1916, allowing the infantry to capture the craters, giving them important observation over enemy lines. Severe fighting continued in this area for several weeks, and although Arthur was wounded on 21st March, he remained on duty. He was granted a few days' leave in England the following month, but soon returned and was involved in the Battle of the Somme. On 7th July, the battalion were in trenches near Ovillers, and attacked after an intense bombardment. At 8:28am, the front line crawled out of trenches to get in line on top of the ground. For the previous few minutes, a heavy German barrage had been put on to the new assembly trench and over the old front line trenches. At 8:30am, the whole Brigade advanced in line. Arthur's battalion got a good share of machine gun fire, and were heavily shrapnelled by whizz bang (high velocity shell) guns and Jack Johnsons (German shells which burst with black smoke). On reaching the line, they got enfilade machine gun fire, and found the Germans either decamping, or in their deep dug-outs. The clearing-up process then started, under machine gun fire from the southeast. Germans were in groups, some fighting, some surrendering, and there was a good deal of individual sniping, and some bomb-throwing. Although each man had to carry over twenty bombs in sandbags, many of them were dropped and the supply had to be saved, even after collecting German bombs, of which there were a number in the dug-outs, but no dump could be found. Up to this time, no communication could be obtained; several messengers volunteered, but none of them ever reached Brigade Headquarters. Rain began to fall and continued throughout day, making the trenches into a kind of porridge mud. After 6pm, men from the Essex Regiment came up, and supplemented the line. There are no casualty figures in the War Diary for this period, but one can assume the losses were heavy. Arthur was one of those killed, and he is buried in Ovillers Military Cemetery. He is also recorded on the list of war dead at Sandhurst.

G. BOYDE

Cpl. GEORGE BOYDE,
Oxford and Bucks L.I.

George Boyde was born in Sandhurst in 1888, and was an elder brother of Arthur's. He too worked in domestic service, and is listed as first footman at a house in Shrewsbury in the 1911 census. He also volunteered for service, attesting at Woking, and joined the 7th Battalion, Oxford and Bucks Light Infantry. The battalion went to France in September 1915, with George marrying Kathrine Widdows in Oxfordshire, a few months before he sailed. The battalion were only in France for a couple of months before moving to Salonika. Just after Christmas, units began moving from Lembet to Happy Valley Camp, and were all in place by early February 1916. In August, the Division took part in the capture of Horseshoe Hill, and fought in both the Battles of Dorian the following year, the second occurring on 8th to 9th May. George's battalion were involved during the night, and the War Diary contains a report on the action: "The assaulting Companies, 'A' and 'B', left our lines, reaching the north side of Jumeaux Ravine with very few casualties. As they were forming up in wave formation, they were apparently seen, as trench mortar fire was opened, Major Homan, two Company Commanders, and one Company Sergeant Major all being badly wounded by it. Except for one gun firing high explosives into the left of our left assaulting company, and causing about ten casualties, our barrage was very accurate, so that our first wave was able to creep within about twenty yards of the enemy's trench before assaulting. The wire was no obstacle at all. Our first wave met with practically no resistance, there being about ten dead Bulgars and a few live ones, who were easily disposed of. Parties of bombers were sent along the trench, while the first wave of the left company manned the enemy's parados, preparatory to forming for the advance. The crossing of the Jumeaux had been made so easily that our first three companies suffered quite considerable casualties while waiting 45 minutes in the preparatory position for the assault. An effort was made to alter the time of assault, but this proved impossible. The following fifteen minutes' wait in the first line trench, till the barrage was to make its second lift, cost us heavy casualties, especially in the left company. 2/Lieut. Kelly, 'B' Company, had been badly wounded in the leg just before the assault, and 2/Lieut. Hutchins, the only officer left of the company, was wounded in the leg by shrapnel. The supporting company, 'C' Company, now seems to have been engaged, although no intimation to that effect reached the Battalion H.Q. 2/Lieut. Garland, 'C' Company, hearing that 'B' Company had lost all its officers, took charge of 'B' Company, bringing up one platoon on the left, as 'B' Company had been held up by trench mortar fire. The third and fourth waves failed to carry the attack on. Lieut. Steels, although already wounded, now took a platoon of his supporting company to fill in the gap between 'A' and 'B' Companies. I cannot say what ultimately happened to the rest of 'C' Company, as all its officers, and most of its N.C.O.s, are missing. 'D' Company, who were in reserve, reached Green Pan with very few casualties about 0300 hours. Trench mortar and artillery fire continued very heavy all over the captured position. While 'B' Company was held up, 'A' Company, on the right, easily attained their objectives, and began consolidation. About a quarter of an hour after their arrival, about two hundred enemy counter-attacked from Deep Ravine. They were easily repulsed by our artillery and Lewis gun fire, suffering very heavy casualties. Matters were critical, as our left could make no further advance. In addition to their bad mauling by the enemy's fire, it appeared certain that one of our heavy guns was still firing on to our left. 2/Lieut. Hutchins actually saw four of his men killed by the shells from this gun." By the time the battalion came back after the fighting to bivouacs in Vladaja Ravine, fifteen officers and nearly 450 men were casualties; only 45 remaining on duty. Corporal George Boyde was missing; his body was never found, and his name is listed on the Doiran Memorial. He is also recorded on the list of war dead at Sandhurst.

W. BOYDE

Pte. WALTER BOYDE. 7th Batt. Oxford and Bucks L.I.

Walter Boyde was a brother of Arthur and George, born at Sandhurst in 1892. Unlike his two older siblings, he was still living at home in 1911, and was working as an assistant at the East Berkshire Golf Club, founded some eight years earlier by masters of Wellington College. He too volunteered for service, attesting at Woking, and joined the 7th Battalion, Oxford and Bucks Light Infantry at the same time as George; they have consecutive service numbers. It is not known whether they fought side by side, but one can only imagine his feelings when his brother was killed. At the beginning of 1918, the Allied troops in Salonika were prepared for a major offensive, intended to end the war in the Balkans. The Greek Army had been reorganised and joined the Allied force. The offensive began in July, but the British contingent did not play a significant part until early September, when they attacked a series of fortified hills. The final assault began along the whole front on 15th September, the British being engaged in the Lake Doiran area. This battle was a disaster for the British Divisions, who had to frontally assault Pip Ridge, a two thousand foot high, heavily defended mountain ridge, with fortresses built on some of the higher mountains, notably Grand Couronne. This was what the Bulgarians had been working on in the first months of 1916 and early 1917. They sustained very heavy casualties, and a report from a Staff Officer of the 28th Division called it "a futile massacre." By the end of the month, they were pursuing the enemy, crossing the Serbian-Bulgarian boundary on the 25th; hostilities with Bulgaria ceasing two days later. The Division advanced towards Adrianople, the war with Turkey still being underway, but this too was to stop soon. The 26th Division had suffered just over eight thousand men casualties during the war, but a much larger number had been sick with malaria, dysentery and other diseases rife in the Salonika theatre. Walter succumbed to disease on 14th January 1919, one of almost forty men in the battalion to suffer that month, and is listed on the addenda panel of the Haidar Pasha Memorial. This panel was added to the memorial at a later date, to commemorate some 170 men, buried in cemeteries whose graves can no longer be maintained by the Commonwealth War Graves Commission. Walter is buried in Batoum British Cemetery in Georgia. He is also recorded on the list of war dead at Sandhurst.

ALAN BROWN

The late Pte. C. A. BROWN, 2nd Batt., 19, St. Edward's Road, Reading.—Killed in action. Aged 26.

Charles Alan Brown was born at Crowthorne in 1890, and baptised 28th September. He was one of seven children, two of whom died in infancy. His father worked at Broadmoor, where Alan also got a job as assistant attendant after leaving school. He married Elsie Staniford in 1913, and volunteered for service, attesting at Reading early in 1915, joining the 2nd Battalion, Coldstream Guards. He arrived in France four days before Christmas that year. The battalion were not involved in any major battles in the first half of 1916. In June, the 2nd Guards Brigade were ordered up to relieve some of the Canadians for a few days, and arrived north of Vlamertinghe on the 14th in motor buses and lorries. Getting into new trenches was always a lengthy process, especially when most of them were blown in and ruined; this was done in the night of the 15th, which fortunately proved to be fairly quiet. The following two nights were very disturbed, with a gas alarm on the 17th, although no gas was detected later. A General recorded in his diary: "Started to go round the line about 10pm. We got safely and with no trouble to the Coldstream Head-Quarters at a place called Les Tuilleries. As I was discussing the situation with Hopwood (Second-in-Command, 1st Battalion), an intense bombardment started on our front trenches, shortly followed by the S.O.S. signal. Then came the gas alarm, and we had to don our gas helmets and wait. The bombardment was very intense for forty minutes, and our guns were retaliating for all they were worth. About midnight, it seemed quieter, and so I went on to the Scots Guards Head-Quarters. In a few minutes, the Germans started a second intense bombardment; the noise was terrific, and the whole place was lit up with the flashes of the bursting shells, but we could smell no gas; a good many wounded were brought in. The bombardment ceased about 3am and then we went back, carrying a wounded man on a stretcher, and arriving at 5am." He continued on the 20th: "Ypres heavily shelled again this morning with 5.9 inch. Shells seem to be falling all around, judging by the crashing noise, and the fall of bricks and branches of the trees into our quarters." The battalion were relieved by the Canadians on the 22nd. Alan was killed on the 20th, and is buried in Essex Farm Cemetery. The General recorded in his dairy, "Casualties during these five days amounted to eighty - all ranks – a small percentage considering the heavy fire to which the men had been exposed."

BASIL A. CARR

Basil Alderson Carr was born on 31st July 1879 at Broadstairs, Kent. He was one of six children, a seventh dying in infancy. His father was a Church of England rector, firstly at Broadstairs, Kent, for about twenty years, and then at Adisham, near Canterbury. The family also employed three or four servants. Basil was educated at a preparatory school in Ramsgate and Marlborough College, before graduating at Cambridge University in 1901, and gaining an M.A. in 1910. He was assistant schoolmaster at Sunningdale School from 1905 to 1911, before becoming joint headmaster at The Towers, a preparatory school near Crowthorne Station, for boys who anticipated going on to Wellington College. Basil joined the Royal Berkshire Regiment, Special Reserve, attesting on 8th December 1915 at Reading. He was about 6'1" tall, weighed twelve stone, had blue eyes, brown hair, a sallow complexion, had a scar on his right kneecap and a warty mole under his left armpit, and needed glasses to read. With mobilisation looming in February 1917, he applied for a commission, and was accepted at No. 2 R.G.A. Cadet School at Maresfield Park, near Uckfield, Sussex. He obtained his commission with the Special Reserve, Royal Garrison Artillery in May, and went to France with the 61st Siege Battery on 1st July. The unit was at Wancourt, a couple of miles southeast of Arras, until the 14th, before moving to Oost Dunkirk, arriving two days later. On the 25th, he was one of several men in an observation post. Around 6pm, the post was fired upon, with three men being wounded, and a telephonist killed. An hour and a half later, Basil, and a young Second Lieutenant, who had been in France for just over two months, were killed by a shell when returning from the post. They are buried, side by side, in Coxyde Military Cemetery. The list of personal effects returned to his sister included Basil's wrist watch with guard and strap, signet ring, two cheque books, pocket book, leather purse, and cards. He had made a will before going overseas, and left just over £4000, with his brother as joint executor. Basil is also listed on the Roll of Honour at Wellington College, and the War Memorial in Adisham, near Dover, Kent, where his parents were living at the time of his death. The parish church there also contains his original wooden grave marker, in the form of a cross. His uncle, Arthur Carr, was rector at St Sebastian's Church, from 1882 to 1895, and later Basil's brother held the same position.

HERBERT CARTWRIGHT

Herbert Cartwright was born at Birkenhead, Cheshire, in 1871. He was the youngest of three surviving children, a fourth dying in infancy. His father worked as a general labourer, but Herbert served an apprenticeship as a joiner after leaving school. He married Betsy Piercy in 1894, and they moved to Southampton where he worked as a carpenter, possibly at the nearby Royal South Hants Hospital. By 1911, they had moved again to South Farnborough, where Herbert had a position as Clerk of Building Works for Hampshire County Council. He was conscripted into the 641st Company, Army Service Corps, Mechanical Transport Company. The Mechanical Transport Companies of the Army Service Corps, called Ammunition Parks, operated dumps, or stores, for the heavy guns and howitzers of the Royal Garrison Artillery, with their attendant equipment and ammunition, and the motorised transport to haul them. Herbert's unit was working with 57 Siege Battery, who operated four 8-inch howitzers, before being attached to III Corps Heavy Artillery. This meant he would have been involved in the Battle of the Somme in 1916, and probably phases of the Arras Offensive and third Battle of Ypres the following year. In the final year of the war, III Corps were involved in both the First and Second Battles of the Somme, the Battle of Amiens, the Battles of the Hindenburg Line, and the Final Advance in Artois. The Heavy Artillery had received a letter of congratulation from their Brigadier General after the first day's action at Amiens: "I wish to offer my personal thanks and congratulations to all ranks and all units of the III Corps Heavy Artillery on the hard work done during the past week, and the good shooting done today. The enemy was taken completely by surprise this morning, and the day has been a very successful one to which all ranks have helped to contribute." By the start of November 1918, the unit was at Bouvines, southeast of Lille, where there work was described as "small and uneventful." On the 10th, they moved to Tournai, where, just before midnight, they heard the news that the Germans had accepted the armistice. On the 22nd, some of the Officers visited Brussels to be present when the Belgian king returned, but Major Owen "shamed himself …. *and* stayed in bed" on the 24th, and a week later was "still indisposed and away from *the* office." The British king passed Tournai on 7th December, some three hundred men going out to see him. On the 22nd, demobilisation started, with miners and postal workers being the first to be sent home, but there was a "great dissatisfaction among all ranks as a result of orders received that all other branches of *the* service are being given preferential treatment in demobilisation." Just after Christmas, the War Diary reported a problem with motorcycles being stolen (four in less than a week), and by the second week of January, this had extended to "war material and soldiers' personal effects *being stolen* by civilians." At the end of the month, all petrol was put into a dump, surrounded by wire, and guarded 24 hours a day, to prevent further thefts by the local populace. By now, the main work consisted in salving German war material, and repairing the local roads. Although there is no mention of it in the War Diary, influenza was affecting the men; Herbert succumbed on 25th February 1919, and is buried in Ath Communal Cemetery, Belgium, one of three men from the unit to die in the same week. On the preceding day, the War Diary had reported, "Large numbers of men who proceeded to UK on leave during last month and early part of this, have failed to return, and are being discharged in England," and ninety more from the unit were demobilised in France at the beginning of March.

CHARLES A. CHAMBERLAIN

Charles Alfred Chamberlain was born in 1886 at Buscot, near Faringdon, then part of Berkshire, and was one of six children. At the time, his father worked as a farm labourer, but just before 1900, he moved the family to Forest Road, Wokingham, near to Ashridge Farm, where he worked as a yard man. Later, he would switch to being a nursery gardener in Wokingham. Charles worked with his father, firstly as a dairy boy, and then as a garden labourer at Wixenford, now Ludgrove School. He volunteered for service, attesting at Reading, and joined the 8th Battalion, Royal Berkshire Regiment. Training was done at Reading before a move to Sutton Verey, near Warminster, Wiltshire, in May 1915, and the battalion went to France three months later. New boots had been issued on leaving Warminster, and the three days of marching that followed caused a lot of footsores to some of the men. On August 17th, they were in trenches for the first time. Most of the next month was spent in billets, with short periods in the front line trenches, before they were involved in their first major action, an attack on the German position east of Hulluch on 25th September, part of the Battle of Loos. Charles was in England early in 1916, and married local girl Elsie Greenman. Later the same year, the battalion took part in the Battles of Albert and Pozieres, as well as the Second Battle of Passchendaele in 1917. On 20th March 1918, while holding the front line near Cerizy, north-west of Moy, a warning was received of an impending enemy attack. The offensive started at 4:30am the following morning, with a powerful barrage and gas shells launched on the British front line, whilst the back areas were also heavily shelled. It was very foggy and communications had been broken by the bombardment, so Battalion Headquarters knew nothing of the attack until 10am, when a report was received that the front line had been broken. The Germans began working round the flanks, opening machine gun fire on the trenches from the rear which, along with snipers on all sides, inflicted heavy casualties. By the time the mist lifted, the battalion were virtually surrounded and a withdrawal was ordered; only 182 men made it back. Fighting continued for another week, by which time over 450 men had become casualties. Charles was one of those missing at the end of the day's fighting on the 21st; his body was never found, and his name is listed on the Pozieres Memorial. By the time the Crowthorne War Memorial was being erected, his parents were living in the village, but he is also listed on the Roll of Honour at Wokingham St Sebastians. His widow remarried in 1924; she had already lost a brother (William Greenman) and a husband to the conflict, and had worked in domestic service for the Hinde family, who also lost two sons. It is difficult now to realise just how compact and close-knit communities were a hundred years ago.

The late Corpl. E. J. CHAPMAN, 1st Coldstream Guards, Broadmoor, Crowthorne. Killed in action.

E. CHAPMAN

Ewart Frederick Chapman was born in 1889 at Weston-super-Mare, Somerset, and had a younger brother. His parents seemed to have lived apart (from the census entries), and his father had various jobs including tailor, stone sawyer and market gardener, and claimed to be a widower in 1911, some forty years before his wife died! In 1904, Ewart joined the Army, attesting at Devizes, Wiltshire, and joined the Coldstream Guards, but by 1911, had completed his service, and was living in Hartley Wintney as a boarder, and working as a bootmaker. By the outbreak of war, he was living at an address in Broadmoor, and was recalled to the 1st Battalion, Coldstream Guards, then at Aldershot, and served as a Lance Corporal. The battalion sailed for France on 21st August, and were soon taking part in the Battle of Mons, the Battle of the Marne and Battle of the Aisne. On 21st October, they marched from Poeringhe to Pilkem, and were ordered to attack in the direction of Langemarck. By nightfall, the village had been secured, but the Germans attacked strongly over the course of the next two days. On the 24th, the battalion were located in positions at Bixschoote, north of Ypres. In the evening, the entire 1st (Guards) Brigade was in the process of being relieved by a French Territorial Regiment, when the enemy "opened a severe bombardment which delayed the relief and it was almost dawn before the 1st Battalion Coldstream were replaced by the French Territorials who took over the trenches." Ewart is listed as missing on this date, so it is likely he was caught directly by shell fire and as his body was never found, he is listed on the Ypres (Menin Gate) Memorial.

E. EDWARD CLACEY

Ernest Edward Clacey, known as Edward, was born in Little Sandhurst in 1897, the youngest of eight children. His father worked as a bricklayer, and the family moved frequently, Edward's siblings being born in Croydon, Caversham and Yateley. Edward spent some of his childhood at Winnersh, but by the time of the 1911 census, he had left school, and was working as an errand boy at a laundry business in Sandhurst. His mother had died in 1906, and his father remarried a few months before the census was taken. Edward was conscripted into the army, attesting at Camberley, mobilised in March 1916, and joined the Oxfordshire and Buckinghamshire Light Infantry, although the records do not state which battalion. At some stage, he was transferred to the 1/6th Battalion, West Yorkshire Regiment, possibly towards the end of April 1918, when the 5th Battalion, Oxfordshire and Buckinghamshire Light Infantry was reduced to basic staff. In the same month, Ernest's new battalion were involved in fighting in the River Lys valley and surrounding hills, and halting the German advance and attacks, and later in the year would be part of the final advance in Picardy. Just before this, on 7th October, they moved to Cagnicourt, making part of the journey by bus, arriving just before dawn on the 8th. Next day, the morning was spent in tactical training, but in the afternoon, they were suddenly called on to march to Haynecourt, west of Cambrai, and spent the night in bivouacs. They continued to move up to the front, and were in position under a railway embankment by 5:00am on the 11th. Four hours later, the attack began, and soon German prisoners were "flocking back." Just over an hour later, the West Yorkshires were well beyond some high ground, but not long after, the units on their flanks began to withdraw under a German counter-attack, supported by tanks. However, the counter-attack failed to develop, and they were able to hold their position, although a barrage of high explosives and shells put down on their posts made holding them difficult. Edward, now a Corporal, was killed in the attack; his body was never found, and he is listed on the Vis-en-Artois Memorial.

JOHN A. CLACEY

John Alexander Clacey was born at Wokingham Without in 1878, the parish of St Sebastian's church on Nine Mile Ride, one of nine children. He does not appear to be closely related to Edward, although Clacey is a common surname in the area. His father was a farm labourer, and

John also worked as a labourer after leaving school. On 14th April 1900, in search of adventure and excitement, he joined the Royal Berkshire Regiment, attesting at Reading, and set sail for South Africa with the 2nd Battalion a month later. He was nearly six feet tall, weighed nine stone, with grey eyes, brown hair, and a fresh complexion. John spent just over a year in South Africa, fighting in the Boer War, although the battalion were not involved in any major actions. He returned to England, and was discharged in June 1901, his term of engagement having been completed. On leaving the army, he returned to live in Crowthorne, and back to labouring as a job. He married Alice Forder later the same year, and they had two children. In 1908, he joined the 4th Battalion, Royal Berkshire Regiment, a Territorial Battalion, was mobilised on the outbreak of war, and went to France at the end of March 1915. By June the following year, his Territorial Service expired, and he attested again at Reading as a regular soldier, giving his occupation as servant, and transferred to the 3rd Battalion (a reserve battalion), and then the 5th Battalion. By the time of his death, he had been promoted to Lance Corporal (although his medal card states he was a sergeant). The battalion took part in the Arras Offensive in the spring of 1917. On 19th July, they relieved the 9th Battalion, Essex Regiment, east of Monchy le Preux. At 3pm, a small attack was made by 'D' Company, with the intention of joining up certain trenches in front. The men had to cross just over one hundred yards to trenches which were thought to be lightly held, but were met with a hail of bombs and obstinate resistance. Some of them got into the trench, but were vastly outnumbered and, having run out of bombs, were forced to retire after only fifteen minutes. This apparently simple mission cost over forty casualties; John was one of fourteen men missing at the end of the day. His body was never recovered, and his name is listed on the Arras Memorial.

GORDON W. COLEBROOK

Photo by] [Walton Adams.
Tpr. G. W. COLEBROOK, Reading.—Missing.

Gordon Wilfred Colebrook, known as Fred, was born in 1895 at Reading, the youngest of five children. His father ran a small, successful business in Reading, selling meat and fish, which allowed the family to employ a couple of servants, and to send the two sons to private schools. For Fred, this was at Hilton Hall, at Prestwich, just north of Manchester. Fred had joined the Berkshire Yeomanry, a mounted arm of the Territorial Force, before the war, and spent two weeks in the summer most years, training at Churn Camp, five miles south of Didcot. The Berkshire Yeomanry went there again at the end of August 1914 to prepare. On arrival of the Brigade Headquarters, it was found that no provision had been made for encampment of troops, and men had to bivouac in the open for the first few days; luckily, the weather was fine. No water was available, but within a few days, cast iron pipes had been laid to bring water to the camp from Blewbury, a short distance to the northeast. In the second half of September, the training began. They remained in Reading until April 1915, when they sailed for Egypt, and were based at Abbassia, Cairo. On 2nd August, Fred wrote to his parents: "We are at present thinking that we may move but we do not know anything definite, but we may know more in a day or two." Eleven days later, he was writing again: "We are moving from here this evening and going somewhere overseas, but of course I do not know where. It will most probably be Lemnos or some base like that, so there is no need to worry at all. We entrain about midnight and are going as infantry. We have got proper infantry packs and though they weigh about 60 lbs, they are fairly comfortable when properly adjusted. George Murley is not going (*George Murley*

BRACKNELLS GREAT WAR FALLEN III

survived the war, only to die in the flu epidemic at the end of 1918), as they are not taking any motor cyclists. Lewis also is getting a commission so he will not come with us *(Thomas Lewis also survived the war, dying at the age of ninety in 1979)*. I am in the same squadron as Hubert, but not in his troop *(Hugh Blyde from College Road, Reading, was a Second Lieutenant at this time. He married Fred's sister Lily in 1916, was wounded in 1917, but survived the war, and died in 1962)*. I hope we shall get some letters pretty soon, as we miss a mail here that comes in tonight. I must close now as I have some packing to do, but not to worry about me a bit, you may be sure I shall take every care of myself. Everyone has had their hair clipped close all over and looks very funny." Another letter arrived at the Colebrook household at the same time: "My Dear Mr Colebrook, We have received orders to go to the Dardanelles dismounted and are leaving at Midnight tonight. We do not like the idea of being dismounted, but cavalry are not required, and we must do our bit and do it well. Fred is coming with 'A' Squadron so I shall see him and do everything in my power for him .... If anything should happen to me, everything I have is for Lil .... Hugh." The Berkshires arrived in Alexandria early in the morning of the 14th, having travelled overnight by train. "I had a very good journey to Alex, and slept well under the seat," wrote Fred. There, they boarded the S.S. 'Lake Michigan' for "an (exact) destination known only to those of a high rank, packed like sardines in a troopship, so overloaded that many of the men had to spend the whole of the .... voyage on deck." The ship arrived at Mudros on the 17th, having sailed a circuitous route to avoid enemy submarines, but did not land; the men were transferred to another ship and continued to Gallipoli. On arrival, they were met by a steam launch towing six boats, each capable of holding fifty men, and went ashore at Suvla Bay in these. Frank Millard, another Reading man, wrote to his parents of the landing: "[We] reached Gallipoli quite safely on August 18th, and although we have been here but 36 hours, we have had quite an exciting time. We did not actually land under fire, but had just disembarked and were carrying our maxims and ammunition off the landing place, when I heard a long whistling, followed by a report. I didn't know what it was at the time, but was soon informed by a Naval officer, who simply said 'Grease - they're on you,' when 'yours truly' picked up two boxes of ammunition, and 'greased' and that quickly." After getting settled, the men were taken off to build a road, before returning to have a swim, which was interrupted by some enemy shells falling in the sea. The next day Frank told his family, "We are not fed badly, and even in this short time we are becoming quite good cooks. Our little dugout consists of a hole scraped in the ground about a foot deep, with a few stones stacked on the earth outside, and some bushes stacked round it. Its outward appearance is very pretty, but inside it might easily be more comfortable. However, things will improve as we go on, so why worry? I don't think we shall be out here long, so you may see me home sooner than you expect." He omitted to mention that two men had already been wounded. On the 20th, there was speculation of a move, and at 8pm, they moved along the coast towards Lala Baba. The rate of march only averaged about one mile per hour, due to frequent halts to allow supply carts to pass both ways along the very narrow road. The 2nd Mounted Division, of which the Berkshire Yeomanry were a part, were the reserve for an attack on Scimitar Hill on the 21st. The Berkshires led the Troop Column towards Chocolate Hill and came under heavy shrapnel fire while crossing a plain, which they later discovered was aptly named 'Shrapnel Valley'. But despite several men going down injured, "there was not the slightest disorder .... the formation of the regiment was perfect." One man described it was "just like being in a hail-storm." They reached the shelter of Chocolate Hill at 4:45pm, with orders to attack the Turkish trenches just 45 minutes later, while it was still daylight. The earlier attack had failed to reach its objective, and the Yeomanry were required to move forward, uphill over unknown territory, in mist and smoke from burning shrubbery which hid their objective, with snipers shooting from trees on both sides. "We got within 800 yards of them, and then down came the shrapnel and shells." By now, they had fixed bayonets, and after pausing some one hundred yards from the Turkish line, a charge was called for. There are several accounts of what happened from then on. "How did the charge begin? Well, an officer shouted, as far as I can recollect, 'Come on, lads! We'll give 'em beans!' That is not exactly according to drill-books and regulations as I know them; but it was enough. It let the boys loose, and they simply leapt forward and went for the Turkish trenches." "The final charge is impossible to describe. As soon as we got over the gully, there was a fusillade of shells and rifles, and machine guns seemed all around us. It seemed impossible to live through, and that was where we had most casualties. We, or what was left of us, took two lines of trenches." "Although there had been many casualties, the Regiment then swept over the ridge into the enemy's trenches, Major Gooch being the first man in. Part of the ground captured was held by the Regiment, with other Yeomanry, until early the next morning, when, under orders, a retirement was conducted in good order, as the position was considered untenable in the daytime." "…. owing to enfilade fire down the left, the trench could not be held, and after about ten minutes had to be evacuated." "Our Brigade, with the Berks doing the leading, got right on top of the hill we were set to capture, by means of two bayonet charges after continual rushes, but the order came that all Yeomanry were to retire to a certain spot. It did seem a pity after what we had done and given." "Personally I got it coming back, but came across several wounded and did what little I could to relieve them, arriving at our trenches about 10 a.m. on Sunday morning. I was just in time for the roll call, and when hearing the figures it was as much as I could do to keep my pecker up." An unknown trooper would later write home: "Sorry to say, the Berks Yeomanry got rather badly cut up: cannot seem to find any of my pals." Hugh Blyde wrote again on 28th August: "Dear Mr Colebrook, I am dreadfully grieved to write to you again without any news of Fred. Major Wigan has just gone back wounded, but not badly, and he has promised me to do everything he can to get news. I have also written to Major Hughes and Lewis who are in Cairo. This has been an awful affair, and we have lost half the Regiment. I hope and pray that before long we shall have news. It is just possible that he may be a prisoner, as we took the line of trenches, but had to retire owing to very heavy shrapnel and machine gun fire. Fred was in the next troop to me from the start, and as we advanced across the open for about a thousand yards, we were quite close to each other, and we shouted across as we advanced up a Hill; it was rather thickly wooded and we could not see each other. Afterwards, when the order was given to charge, Fred was seen rushing into the Turkish trench. After a time we retired back a few yards, and held the position all night. I enquired for him, but could not find out where he was. We then searched round and still no trace. A lot of men from each troop are missing. Fred was perfectly splendid and very brave. All his friends that are left are very sad, and if anything could be done, it would be a great joy." Hugh's brother, Wilfred, was also with the Berkshire Yeomanry, and wrote to Fred's parents: "Dear Mr & Mrs Colebrook, I am writing this somewhere in Gallipoli, I must not say where, to tell you that we have been in action. We were fighting for twelve hours straight on end. We had a very hot time and the casualties have been heavy, for I am sorry to tell you Fred is missing, and although we have tried our best to trace him, we have so far not been successful. Try not to worry as Hubert and I are making all possible enquiries. I will of course let you know as soon as we hear any news of him, unfortunately I was not near him during the fight as I have been transferred to another troop. It has been a most terrible experience, and how

Hubert and I have got through so far without being hit I do not know - we have all had the most narrow escapes. We have had several casualties among the officers, and Hubert is acting Adjutant and I am promoted Corporal. We are now in reserve and are living in dug outs, we are shelled nearly all day but if we keep in our dug outs are quite safe. The food is very good considering, and thank goodness the weather so far has been quite fine. I expect we shall take our place in the trenches with the other regiments soon .... There is not a great quantity of water here, and the only chance of a bathe is a dip in the sea when we have the opportunity. A man in this regiment named Potts has been recommended for, and will probably get, the Victoria Cross for rescuing a comrade under fire. *(Fred Potts, himself wounded, dragged a badly injured comrade back to the British lines, using a shovel as an improvised sledge; the journey of six hundred yards took 48 hours. He received the Victoria Cross from King George V at Buckingham Palace in December 1915).* So far the life out here is fairly rough, we have to do our own cooking and sleep in all our own clothes day in and day out, but thanks to our fine transport, we always have plenty of food and water to drink which is a great thing. You must excuse this rough scribble as writing facilities here are not great. Please keep up hope and try not to worry about Fred, as Hubert and I are doing our best to find out about him, and of course will let you know all we can, and hope to trust he will come out safe and sound in the end. I expect by the time you receive this you will have seen the account in the papers." Another friend had received a letter from one of Fred's sisters and replied on October 10th: "I received your letter yesterday asking me if I could give you any information about your brother. As you probably noticed from the date of my letter, it was written a day or two after the big battle when they were collecting the names, etc of our casualties, and I was then told that your brother had been killed. Since then I have news he was posted as missing. My informant at the time was L/Cpl Sturgess, who I am sorry to say has since died of wounds, and so I can get no more information from that source. Sturgess told me he was killed at the first Turkish trench. I have made all the enquiries possible amongst the very few of his friends that are left, but can get nothing definite. The last time I saw your brother personally was just before we advanced up Hill 70, about an hour before the final charge was pushed home, and *he* was then alright, as we spoke together for a minute or so, and he left me with a joke about something or other. Since the battle, us of the Machine Gun Section have been posted nearly all the way along the line of trenches which border round the scene of that day's fight, and during that time have been attached to several different regiments who were engaged in burying the dead, and I made enquiries off of them as to whether they had come across any of our fellows but they said not, and all the news I could get was that a lot of our people were captured by the Turks during the night and early morning, and no doubt a lot of the missing were taken prisoner, in which case if your brother is amongst these, he will be treated fairly well as I believe the Turks are setting the Germans a fine example in this way! I am sure you will not think me presumptuous in offering you and your family my deepest sympathy in your great trial, as during the time we were in Egypt, your brother and I were great friends and I feel his loss very much, and I can only say that if the worse has happened, you can rest assured that he died as gallant a death as any Englishman can wish. While we are out here I will keep him in mind, and if I can get hold of any more information I will at once let you know." Fred was later confirmed as killed; his body was never found, and his name is listed on the Helles Memorial. By the time of his death, the family had moved to Crowthorne, so his name is on the village War Memorial. A memorial was also discovered in 2008 in a reclamation yard, with Fred being one of twenty names listed on it. After much investigation, it was found to come from Trinity Congregational Church, Reading, which was demolished in 1980. At the time of writing, discussions are in place to re-erect it in an appropriate location.

GEORGE H. CONDICK

George Henry Condick was born in 1886 at Farnborough, Hampshire, one of ten children. His father worked as a domestic gardener. After leaving school, George worked in a local shop, firstly as a fruit boy, but then moved to Crowthorne to work as an assistant at a grocer's in the village. He married Gertrude Bulpit, a servant at Wokingham St Sebastian's Vicarage, in 1911, and they had three children. George volunteered for service, attesting at Wokingham, and joined the 8th Battalion, Royal Berkshire Regiment. The battalion left for France on 7th August 1915, and were in the trenches ten days later. Their first major action came on 25th September in an attack on the German position east of Hulloch, part of the Battle of Loos. The 1st Brigade, of which the Berkshires were a part, got forward into the outskirts of the village, capturing some gun positions on the way, and forced the surrender of a German detachment that held up the advance elsewhere. In the following year, they were involved in several phases of the Battle of the Somme, entering the front trenches on 10th July. George was later transferred to the 6th Battalion. Although there is no date for this transfer in the records, the War Diary records the arrival of a draft, accompanied by a Sergeant (George's rank by now), on 7th October 1916. This battalion took part in Operations on the Ancre, a phase of the Arras Offensive, and the Third Battle of Ypres, which started at the end of July 1917, and would last until November. On 11th October, when a relief was taking place at 4:30am at a strong point in the southwest corner of Glencorse Wood, the position was rushed by the Germans in a counter-attack, and the Berkshires were ordered to support an attack to recapture it. The strong point was recovered, though not without considerable loss. An attack ordered for 10:15am was subsequently cancelled. On the night of 12th/13th, they were withdrawn from the front line, a process that took all day as the Germans were shelling the area, and it was deemed too dangerous to move in large numbers. George was reported missing on the 12th; his body was never recovered, and his name is listed on the Tyne Cot Memorial.

E. J. COOK

James Edward Cook (known as Edward) was born in 1880 at Kemble, near Cirencester, Gloucestershire, and was one of ten children. His father, who died in 1897, worked on local farms in the area. After leaving school, Edward moved to Oxford, and worked on the railways, cleaning railway engines. He married Mary Hughes in Reading in 1903, and moved there to set up home, working in the flour department at Huntley and Palmer's biscuit factory on King's Road. Founded in 1841 with eight employees, the business became the town's largest employer with over five thousand working there by the turn of the century. Pay was typically £1 per week, plus a pound of broken biscuits! This bonus was probably much appreciated by his four sons. Edward joined the Army under the Derby Scheme, attesting at Reading, was mobilised in May 1916, and joined the 6th Battalion, Royal Berkshire Regiment. It is not known precisely when Edward arrived in France, but the War Diary records several drafts arriving during the first half of September. The battalion were involved in phases of the Battle of the Somme until November that year, so he would have been involved in some of the later fighting. In 1917, they were involved in operations on the Ancre, a part of the Arras Offensive, and phases of the Third Battle of Ypres. Edward's death is a bit of a mystery as the date recorded is 6th November 1917. According to the War Diary, this was a "quiet day," and nothing much is being recorded around this date, although whoever was charge with writing the diary at this time was somewhat lax in his job, as ten men were killed on the 6th, and nearly thirty during the month. They had gone into the front line on the 4th, and were relieved on the 7th, so it is possible a shell hit the trench and Edward was just in the wrong place at the wrong time. Alternatively, the death of an officer is recorded, so a patrol, including Edward, may have gone out and been killed. Whatever happened, his body was never found, and his name is listed on the Tyne Cot Memorial. As his family appear to have lived in Reading, it is not known why his name appears on the memorial at Crowthorne.

A. COX

Alexander Cox was born at Oxford in 1880, one of four children. His father worked as a saddler in the city for over twenty years. Alexander is missing from the 1901 census (which may indicate he was out of the country with the Army), but was living at Stadhampton, Oxfordshire, and listed his occupation as domestic butler in 1911. By now he was married, having wed Rhoda Hollister in 1909. By 1916, Alexander had moved to Crowthorne, and was working at a house called Heatherley, on the Wellington College estate. Although not part of the College, the school held two leases on it, and the lessee had the option of sending his boys to Wellington. Alexander joined the Army under the Derby Scheme, attesting at Wokingham, was mobilised in May 1916, and joined the 7th Battalion, Royal Berkshire Regiment. The battalion had been in Salonika since the previous November, but there is no mention in the War Diary of a draft arriving until January the following year. The battalion spent the end of 1916 digging defences or making roads when not in the trenches. Apart from occasional raids on the enemy line, or patrols being sent out to spy on their positions, there was little action beyond avoiding the bombardments. After the stabilisation of the line in August 1916, action had been confined to "minor operations undertaken with a view to continually harassing the enemy, entrenched in mountainous and rocky country, and to inflicting as much loss as possible, both in material and personnel." Offensive operations were resumed in the latter half of April 1917. On the 24th, a serious attack was made, south and southwest of Dorian, preceded by three days of bombardment. The Berkshire men set off at 9:45pm, and had difficult terrain to cross. 'C' and 'D' Companies reached their objectives despite coming under heavy fire, but 'A' was held up by a steep-sided ditch. 'C' and 'D' began consolidating their positions, but were violently counter-attacked and, having run out of bombs and with three of their Lewis guns destroyed, were forced to retire. At 4:30am the following morning, orders were received to abandon the attack and to retire to the starting positions. Over 250 casualties were suffered in the attack. Alexander was wounded and died six days later; he is buried in Mikra British Cemetery, Kalamaria.

The late Corpl. H. COX, 4th Batt. Crowthorne.—Killed in action.

G. H. COX

George Harry Cox was born in Binfield in 1895. He was illegitimate, but his birth was registered with the surname Squires, presumably the name of the father. George was brought up by his grandparents, and one of their daughters was in domestic service in Poole, Dorset in the 1891 census; a young man by the name of Ernest Squires, also living in Poole at the time, may have been the father. In the 1901 census, George and his family were living at The Square, Bracknell, an area at the bottom of the High Street. His grandfather, an agricultural labourer, died in 1908, and George, his grandmother, and an aunt moved to Crowthorne; by this time he had left school and was working as a general labourer. He volunteered for service at the beginning of 1915, attesting at Guildford, and joined the 4th Battalion, Grenadier Guards. He went to France in early November, but not before marrying Emily Cosh just before setting off. The battalion were not involved in the major fighting on the Somme in July 1916, but took part in two actions in September that year, as well as the First Battle of Passchendaele in 1917. On 30th November, the Germans were reported to have broken through the British Line near Gonnelieu, and the battalion were ordered to Metz, encountering men and equipment coming in the opposite direction as they did so. The Commanding Officer received several different orders and instructions over the next few hours, making planning and organisation very difficult. An earlier attack on Gonnelieu by the 16th Brigade had failed, and at 6:30am the next day, the Grenadiers were involved in a new assault, having just three hours to get ready. The accompanying shelling by the artillery was described as "feeble," and it was not long before they were met by very heavy and accurate machine gun and rifle fire. George was with No. 1 Company who appear to have had the easiest time and fewer casualties, but he was missing at the end of the day's action. His body was never recovered, and his name is listed on the Cambrai Memorial, Louverval. George had been due to go leave a few days earlier, but had postponed it so as to coincide with that of his brother-in-law.

FREDERICK T. DAVIS

Frederick John Davis was born at Bagshot in 1897, the youngest of three children. He spent part of his childhood at Windlesham before the family moved to Crowthorne. His father was a farm carter, possibly working at Broadmoor Farm as they lived close to the hospital. Frederick joined the 2/4th Battalion, Royal Berkshire Regiment, a Territorial Regiment, having attested in Reading. The battalion trained on Salisbury Plain before going to France, landing at Le Havre in late May 1916, and took part in the attack at Fromelles later the same year, and operations on the Ancre in 1917. There are two different dates recorded in the records for Frederick's death, the 2nd August 1917 and the 22nd. As the battalion were training for several days at the beginning of the month, and no other men from the battalion were killed on that day, it is assumed the latter date is the correct one. On 21st August, the battalion moved into assembly trenches at Wieltje, northeast of Ypres, for an attack the following day. Their role was to follow close behind the leading platoons, assaulting each enemy strong point as it was reached, either taking or blockading it, allowing the leading battalions to continue their advance. Zero was at 4:45am. The first strong point was Pond Farm which resisted two attacks, but finally fell in the afternoon. Hindu Cottage, the second strong point, was surrounded, as marshy ground prevented a frontal attack. A private from 'A' Company, who had lost his own platoon, managed to get into the strong point, and held nineteen Germans prisoner for forty-eight hours until relieved by an Officer from the 2/6th Gloucestershires; he was awarded a Military Medal. A third strong point, Schuler, was also taken with the capture of 76 Germans, and although in an isolated position, was also held for forty-eight hours until relieved. Three further strong points could not be reached due to heavy machine gun fire from the right, but the position reached was consolidated and the battalion finally relieved on the night of the 23rd/24th. 32 men were killed in the attack, over one hundred wounded and around eighty missing. Frederick was one of the latter, and his name is listed on the Tyne Cot Memorial.

[Photo by Donna Roms.
Pte. A. R. DEAN, 1th Batt. Royal Berks Regt., Broadmoor, Crowthorne. Wounded.

ALBERT R. DEAN

Albert Reginald Dean was born at Crowthorne in 1894, and baptised 4th August. He was one of six children, but an elder brother died a few months after Albert was born. His father had worked as an attendant at the asylum at Littlemore, just south of Oxford before moving to Crowthorne, and would become the principal attendant at the local facility. While his elder surviving brother moved to Yorkshire to work in the coal mines, Albert remained in the area, working as a servant at Wellington College. He volunteered for service, attesting at Wokingham, and joined the 3rd Battalion, Royal Berkshire Regiment for his training, before transferring to the 1st Battalion, and going to France in August 1915. The battalion took part in the Battle of Loos a month later, and the Battle of Delville Wood and the Battle of the Ancre, the last large British attack of the following year. On 13th November 1916, they were at Serre, and started moving forward in readiness for an attack the following day. They came under heavy artillery and machine gun fire all morning as well as from mine-throwers, and snipers were active in the afternoon; nine men were killed during the course of the day and more than twenty wounded. At 5am the following morning, they advanced across No Man's Land, suffering casualties from machine gun fire, as well as from British artillery "shorts." These were especially heavy on the right, and there were insufficient men left when they reached the German trenches. Despite this, they managed to capture several prisoners, and captured part of Serre Trench, the objective. Initially reported wounded, Albert was later confirmed killed (almost half the battalion were casualties on the day), and is buried in New Munich Trench British Cemetery, Beaumont-Hamel. His brother was also wounded during the war, but survived the conflict.

R. DEAN

Henry Russell Deane, known as Russell, was born in 1898 at Peckham, South London. He was the eldest of three surviving children, a fourth dying in infancy. His grandfather had been farm bailiff on the Broadmoor estate, and his father, who was born in Crowthorne, worked briefly as an attendant at the hospital before marrying and moving to London, where he took up various positions as a clerk. Russell volunteered for service within a few days of war being declared, despite only being sixteen years old, attesting in London, and joined the 2nd Battalion, Royal Fusiliers, a Territorial Battalion. A month later, the battalion sailed from Southampton to Malta, a voyage that took ten days, where they remained until 2nd January the following year, arriving in Marseilles four days later, and progressing northwards to join the fighting. Later that year, they were involved in fighting at Hooge. In January 1916, the War Office authorised the re-formation of the London Division which concentrated in the Hallencourt area, and took part in a diversionary attack at Gommecourt on 1st July. The German artillery at this point was well placed to fire into the British flank, and the aim of the diversion was to prevent this by occupying their defences. At 5am, Russell's battalion were in position in dug-outs near Hebuterne, and all ranks issued with hot pea-soup. There was considerable shelling of the assembly trenches, but no casualties. At 6:15am, guns of all calibres started an intensive bombardment of German lines, and an hour later, smoke was discharged. This was dense along the whole Division front when the first battalions moved forward just before 7:30am. The War Diary recorded, "Lines advanced steadily in excellent formation, and enemy opened barrage fire on all trenches. Our troops reached enemy trenches with comparatively small losses. Machine gun in Gommecourt Park opened fire. Enemy massed his parapet in places, but his fire was ineffective." An hour later, Germans appeared coming forward, hands up in surrender. The enemy barrage was still very intense, stopping reinforcements in No Man's Land. Soon after midday, the Germans launched a vigorous counter-attack, gradually forcing the British troops out of the third line. Having exhausted their own bombs, the battalion used German grenades they had found. Soon after this, the communication lines went down and messengers had to be sent across to get messages to the attackers. The British troops were being forced from the front line and coming back, but were ordered to attack again. 'C' Company, who were attacking on the right, were met by a heavy barrage, and machine gun fire from both flanks; they soon stopped, having lost all their officers. Many of them were killed, only fifty men survived, including wounded, crawling in after dark. 'D' Company tried to attack three times, but were stopped each time by artillery and machine gun fire. By 4pm, the enemy were seen to be advancing from Epte against the captured trenches, and three hours later, only seventy men remained in occupied territory. By 8:00pm, the last survivors were returning, and both sets of artillery had almost ceased firing by 10pm. Russell was one of the day's casualties, and is buried in Hebuterne Military Cemetery. Although he may not have lived in Crowthorne, an uncle resided in the village, and it was probably him who put Russell's name forward for the War Memorial.

FREDERICK L. DEANE

Frederick Llewellyn Deane was born in Crowthorne early in 1886, and baptised on 30th January. He was the middle of three sons. The family lived in Wellington Road, and his father worked as an accountant at Eton College. Although the family employed no servants, all three brothers were educated privately at St John's College, Hurstpierpoint, Sussex. Frederick went on to qualify as a solicitor, his younger brother became a banker, while elder brother Charles went on the stage. Frederick signed up under the Derby Scheme in late 1915, attesting in London, and joined the 15th (County of London) Battalion, a Territorial Battalion. It is not clear whether Frederick had joined the battalion by May 1916, when the Germans attacked Vimy Ridge, but he would have been involved in one of the phases of the Battle of the Somme which took place at Flers-Courcelette in September 1916. This was notable as tanks were used for the first time. Every single tank available was used, but this was only 49 along a front of 12 kilometres. Sir Winston Churchill, who had championed the development of the tank, complained "my poor land battleships have been let off prematurely on a petty scale." These early tanks proved notoriously unreliable. Weighing approximately 28 tons, they could only move forward at half-a-mile per hour. Although impervious to small arms fire, and to a lesser extent machine gun fire, shell fire could, and did, easily destroy a tank. Navigation and visibility were poor, and radio communication was not available until late in the war. The attack was preceded by an artillery bombardment designed to leave unshelled lanes open for the advance of the new mobile weapon. Seventeen tanks were unable to make it as far as the front line, and a further seven failed to work at Zero hour. Despite this, the launch of the tanks produced devastating effects upon German morale, and led to gains of over a mile within the first three days, something of an achievement at the time, and particularly during the Battle of the Somme. Led by tanks, the villages of Martinpuich, Flers and Courcelette fell to the Allies, as did the much sought-after High Wood. Frederick's battalion took part in the attack on the wood, and although 'A' Company, on the right, were successful, the other three companies were badly cut up by machine gun fire. At 11am, the German front line was bombarded with Stokes mortars, and soon after, the Germans surrendered. Around 250 other ranks were killed, wounded or missing after the attack; Frederick was one of those killed, and is buried in Flatiron Copse Cemetery, Mametz.

HORACE G. DICKER

The late Pte. H. DICKER, 1/4th Hants Regt., King's Road, Crowthorne.—Died in Mesopotamia.

Horace George Dicker was born at Crowthorne in 1890, and baptised 12th October. He was the middle child of three, with two sisters. His father worked as a domestic gardener, taking on groom duties as well. Horace worked as a blacksmith after leaving school, and also joined the 1/4th Battalion, Hampshire Regiment, a Territorial Regiment, attesting on Salisbury Plain. The battalion sailed for India on 9th October 1914, and remained there until the following March, when they moved Mesopotamia. The Regimental History records: "On arrival, the British had made some tactical moves to seize important or threatening points beyond Basra. After an early string of cheap successes, eyes increasingly fell on the Mesopotamian capital, Baghdad. The 6th (Poona) Division advanced, leaving a very thinly stretched supply line of hundreds of miles behind it, only to receive a bloody repulse at Ctesiphon. A ragged and dispiriting retreat back to Kut-al-Amara began. The Turks pursued the retreating Division to Kut, and soon surrounded and cut it off. British forces in Mesopotamia were now growing, and these formations were ordered to advance north along the Tigris to relieve Kut. They ran into strong and stoutly defended lines and suffered some hard knocks; although they got close to Kut, the garrison there was surrendered on 29 April 1916. It was an enormous blow to British prestige and a morale-booster for the Turkish Army." After the fall of Kut, a new British Commander was installed, who introduced new methods, culminating in a decisive defeat of the Turks in February 1917 and the capture of Baghdad in March. They continued to make gains, but no decisive victory, until the Turks signed an armistice on 1st October 1918. Like Gallipoli, conditions in Mesopotamia were difficult. Temperatures of 120 degrees were common, arid desert and regular flooding, flies, mosquitoes and other vermin, all led to very high levels of sickness and death through disease. Medical arrangements were also poor, with wounded men spending up to two weeks on boats before reaching any kind of hospital. Over 12,500 men died of sickness in the region, one of them being Horace on 2nd October 1918. By this time, many men were suffering from malaria, so it is likely this was the cause; he is buried in Tehran War Cemetery. Horace is unique in the Bracknell Forest area in having been awarded a medal from Serbia. This was the Order of Karageorge, Gold Medal, awarded in the autumn of 1916 by the King of Serbia, for an act of gallantry or bravery that did not reach the standard for a British award. Horace's name appeared in the London Gazette published on 15th February the following year; he was one of only five men in the Hampshire Regiment to receive this award. Both he and William Bell had joined the battalion together, bearing consecutive service numbers, but neither would return home to Crowthorne.

CHARLES EALES

Charles Eales was born at Shinfield in 1893. He was one of six children, a seventh dying in infancy. His father had a succession of labouring and farm jobs, with the family frequently moving, Charles's siblings being born in Stratfield Turgiss, Hampshire, Winnersh, and Bearwood. The family was living in Warfield Street at the time of the 1911 census. Charles by now had left school, and was working as a dairyman labourer in Wokingham. An address of Broadmoor is also recorded, but it is not clear whether Charles or his next-of-kin worked there, and it was probably on the hospital farm, rather than in the hospital itself. Charles joined the 2/4th Battalion, Royal Berkshire Regiment, a Territorial Battalion that had formed in 1914, attesting in Wokingham. Training was done on Salisbury Plain before going to France, landing at Le Havre in late May 1916. The battalion took part in the attack at Fromelles later that year, and operations on the Ancre in 1917. On 21st August 1917, the battalion moved into assembly trenches at Wieltje, northeast of Ypres, for an attack the following day. Their role was to follow close behind the leading platoons, assaulting each enemy strong point as it was reached, either taking or blockading it, allowing the leading battalions to continue their advance. Zero was at 4:45am. The first strong point was Pond Farm which resisted two attacks but finally fell in the afternoon. Hindu Cottage, the second strong point, was surrounded as marshy ground prevented a frontal attack. A private from 'A' Company, who had lost his own platoon, managed to get into the strong point, and held nineteen Germans prisoner for forty-eight hours until relieved by an Officer from the 2/6th Gloucestershires; he was awarded a Military Medal. A third strong point, Schuler, was also taken with the capture of 76 Germans, and although in an isolated position, was also held for forty-eight hours until relieved. Three further strong points could not be reached due to heavy machine gun fire from the right, but the position reached was consolidated and the battalion finally relieved on the night of the 23rd/24th. 32 men were killed in the attack, over one hundred wounded and around eighty missing; Charles was one of the latter, and his name is recorded on the Tyne Cot Memorial.

ERNEST ELMER

Ernest Elmer was born on 1st May 1886 at Sandhurst, but by 1891, the family had moved to Crowthorne. He was the youngest of seven surviving children, three more dying in infancy. His father worked as a carrier in north and east London before the family moved to Berkshire. Ernest worked as a farm labourer after leaving school, but decided to try a new life in Canada and emigrated in 1905, arriving in Montreal, bound for Toronto, on 13th October. He visited England briefly in 1908 before returning to Canada. On 22nd July 1915, he attested at Toronto, and joined the 60th Battalion of the Canadian Infantry, having served in the Territorial Army for nine years. He was only 5'3" inches tall, with brown eyes, brown hair, and a fair complexion; he also stated his date of birth as 1st May 1888, making him two years younger than his real age. The battalion had been formed two months earlier at Montreal, and trained at Valcartier until it sailed for England on 5th November with five officers and 250 other ranks. On arrival, they headed for Bramshott, near Liphook, Hampshire, and remained there for three months before proceeding to France. They took part in phases of the Battle of the Somme in the autumn. On the morning of 16th September, they received orders to be prepared to move at a moment's notice, which they did at 2pm, leaving Usna Hill, to march via La Boiselle to some chalk pits. On arrival, the men had a hot meal, and equipment was given out in preparation for an attack at 6:30pm. A few casualties were suffered from a heavy bombardment as they moved up in readiness. When they arrived, they found an earlier attack had failed, and the situation confused. Eventually they managed to lend support, but all units suffered heavy casualties in the fighting. Ernest was missing at the end of the day, and his name is recorded, along with over eleven thousand others, on the Vimy Memorial on the highest point of Vimy Ridge. Just over six months later, the battalion were in trenches at Vimy again. Soon after came the news the battalion might be disbanded; the decision was delayed, but on 24th April, the War Diary recorded, "Received intimation that the Battalion is to be disbanded." And on the 29th, an obviously disgruntled Adjutant wrote, "The disbanding of a force of 828 fighting men of all ranks, well trained, with a prefect organisation to carry it through the war, for Political reason, seems most unjust and shows little feeling or respect for the Officers, N.C.O.s, and men, who have been in the trenches for fourteen months, and to those who have made the supreme sacrifice with their lives, and who rest in named, and un-named graves throughout France and Belgium. If tried and efficient Battalions are to be broken up like this in the midst of a great war, and on the very battlefields, it will surely be more discouraging than encouraging, to further recruiting in Canada."

JAMES L. GILBERT

James Lewis Gilbert was born in 1873 at Avebury, Wiltshire, the elder of two boys. His father, an agricultural worker, died in 1894, by which time James had left school and was an apprentice carpenter. His mother remarried four years later to a man fifteen year her junior, but the couple were living apart by the 1911 census. After finishing his apprenticeship, James moved to Reading and then Sonning Common, where he married Alice Webb in 1903, and had three sons. Although officially too old for active service, James joined the Army Service Corps, which used his carpentry skills in the repair and making of wheels. He served with the 866th Horse Transport Company in Dublin, and died on 10th October 1918, officially at Navan, County Meath. His name is listed on the Hollybrook Memorial at Southampton which commemorates nearly two thousand servicemen and women of the Commonwealth land and air forces whose graves are not known. Another soldier from 886 Company, who died on the same day as Gilbert, is buried in Grangegorman Military Cemetery, Dublin, a casualty of the sinking of the RMS 'Leinster', which was sunk by a torpedo on this date. Gilbert's name does not appear on the list of casualties from this sinking, but as there is no complete passenger list for the Leinster, and there is also a military death registered 'at sea' for a J. Gilbert, it is likely this is how James died. As his widow was living in High Street, Crowthorne, when the Roll of Honour was being compiled, he is listed on the village war memorial, although he may not have ever lived there.

JOSEPH GILES

Joseph Giles was born on 31st March 1889 at Plaistow, east London. He was one of twelve children, one of whom died in infancy. His father, who had been born in Sandhurst, was a bricklayer and builder, and the family had moved to Crowthorne by 1911. Joseph worked as a labourer for a coal merchant in Canning Town after leaving school, before joining the 4th Battalion, Essex Regiment, a Territorial Battalion, attesting at Stratford, just before his seventeenth birthday, adding a year to his age to do so. Although he gave his real address, intriguingly he invented names for a brother and sister as next of kin. He was just 5'2" tall, weighed about eight stone, with blue eyes, brown hair and a fresh complexion, and had a scar over his left shoulder, and a tattoo on his left forearm. After a few weeks, he transferred to the 2nd Battalion, Northamptonshire Regiment, and was stationed in Malta in the 1911 census. It is not known when Joseph went to Canada, where he worked as a carpenter, but on 28th September 1914, he attested at Valcartier, and joined the 10th Battalion. Again, he was a little economical with the truth, claiming to have served with the Hampshire Regiment Territorials for three years previously. Army food had obviously suited Joseph, as by now he was nearly six feet tall. His next-of-kin is now listed as a wife, Amy Giles, but again, there is no record of the marriage. The battalion left Canada the following month, arriving at Plymouth on the 19th, and proceeding by train to Salisbury Plain to continue training. This started with physical training and battalion parades, with marching, squad and Company drills, musketry training, and lectures gradually being introduced. To break the routine, the men had half the day off on Saturday afternoons, and there were church parades on Sundays. The weather conditions were recorded every day, with the word 'rain' written against many entries. On 17th December, an entry records the departure of a Captain, the battalion "having no further use for his services," a veiled reference to a misdemeanour leading to his dismissal. On Christmas Day, divine service was held in the Y.M.C.A. hut, and later all men dined together. A few days later, the men were being put to use, building roads and sidewalks in the camp, presumably the wet weather causing problems. 1st January 1915 was another holiday, and a week later, five officers and over two hundred men were sent to Lark Hill Camp to form a working party. Orders were received on 7th February for them to move overseas, and they started out three days later, marching to Amesbury, Wiltshire, and then travelling to Avonmouth by train. The battalion sailed on the S.S. 'Kingstonian' at 5am on the 11th, dropping anchor at St. Nazaire two days later. But within two hours, the ship had drifted on to a sandbank, and it was almost 24 hours before she could be freed. After disembarkation, they marched to the railway station, and travelled via Le Mans to billets near the front. By the end of the month, they were in war routine, manning or digging trenches every day. On 14th April, they took over front line trenches from the French at Weltse where the Germans were very active, and the first notes on casualties start appearing in the War Diary. The Second Battle of Ypres started on the 22nd with a surprise attack by the German 4th Army. This attack witnessed the first use of a new German weapon on the Western Front, poisonous chlorine gas. It was carried on a gentle breeze towards French troops, and six thousand men died within ten minutes from the effects. The German infantry were able to make a significant advance into Allied territory within a few hours, but with the coming of darkness, and the lack of follow-up troops, they did not exploit the gap they had created in the Allied lines, and Canadian troops were able to put in a hasty defence by urinating into cloths and putting them to their faces to counter the effects of the gas. At Kitchener's Wood, Joseph's battalion, which had been in billets at the time, and had heard a heavy bombardment late in the afternoon, was ordered to counter-attack into the gap created by the gas attack. They formed up after 11:00 pm, and moved forward some forty-five minutes later. However, without prior reconnaissance, they ran into obstacles half way to the objective, and drew heavy automatic weapons fire from the Wood, prompting an impromptu bayonet charge. Their attack cleared the former oak plantation of Germans, but at a cost of 75 per cent casualties. The official records record that Company Serjeant Major Joseph Giles was killed in action on the 23rd near St Julien. His body was never found, and his name is listed on the Ypres (Menin Gate) Memorial. A British Officer would later write of that day, "Dusk was falling when, from the German trenches in front of the French line, rose that strange green cloud of death. The light north-easterly breeze wafted it toward them, and in a moment death had them by the throat. One cannot blame them that they broke and fled. In the gathering dark of that awful night, they fought with the terror, running blindly in the gas-cloud, and dropping with breasts, heaving in agony, and the slow poison of suffocation mantling their dark faces. Hundreds of them fell and died; others lay helpless, froth upon their agonized lips and their racked bodies powerfully sick, with tearing nausea at short intervals. They too would die later – a slow and lingering death of agony unspeakable. The whole air was tainted with the acrid smell of chlorine that caught at the back of men's throats and filled their mouths with its metallic taste." And a young private, arriving soon after, observed, "We knew there was something wrong. We started to march towards Ypres, but we couldn't get past on the road with refugees coming down the road. We went along the railway line to Ypres and there were people, civilians and soldiers, lying along the roadside in a terrible state. We heard them say it was gas. We didn't know what the Hell gas was. When we got to Ypres, we found a lot of Canadians lying there dead from gas the day before, poor devils, and it was quite a horrible sight for us young men. I was only twenty so it was quite traumatic and I've never forgotten, nor ever will forget it."

SAMUEL GODDARD

Samuel Goddard was born at Crowthorne in 1877. He was the eldest of ten children, two of whom died in infancy. His father was the manager at Broadmoor Gas Works, but suffered some sort of breakdown in 1890, and was admitted to the Moulsford Asylum at Cholsey, near Wallingford, where he died two years later. Soon after, Samuel went to live with relations in Blackheath, southeast London, later joining the Royal Field Artillery, attesting at Aldershot. In 1911, he was based at Jabulpore in India and was married, but it has not been possible to track down details of the marriage. During the war, he was with the 15th Brigade, part of the pre-war regular army, and went to France in August 1914. Initially with 52 Battery, he had been moved to 68 Battery in the 14th Brigade by September. On the 6th, Samuel's battery was supporting the 10th Infantry Brigade, south of Villers, guarding their left flank. Two days later, they started marching south, and around midday came into action, and engaged with the enemy. On the 13th, the battery advanced, and took up position southwest of Acy. At about 11am, they crossed the river Aisne, using a partially destroyed bridge at Venizel, and gained Bucy le Long by sections, although under shell fire. By 5pm, the battery was on some high ground north of Le Monvel, supporting the Rifle Brigade. Next morning, the battery was in action just north of Venezel bridge, when, at about 8am, they came under "very hot oblique fire." The Officer in charge of the battery was badly wounded, and two gunners killed, one of them being Samuel. After the war, his grave could not be located, and his name is now listed on the La Fert-Sous-Jouarre Memorial, one of 33 men from the Royal Field Artillery who lost their lives that day. His mother was still living in Crowthorne when names for the War Memorial were being collected, and it is probably her that made sure Samuel was remembered in the village.

JAMES L. GODWIN

James Lewis Godwin was born in Crowthorne in 1876, and baptised on 20th February. He was the youngest of four children. His father graduated from being a boot maker to running a shop in the village High Street, selling oil and newspapers. He died in 1896, and two years later, James's eldest brother died at the Moulsford Asylum at Cholsey, near Wallingford. His mother continued to run the business, adding ironmongery to the items stocked, and both James and his sister helped in the running of it. James did not serve overseas during the war, but at the 1st Reserve Mechanical Transport Depot of the Army Service Corps at Grove Park, Greenwich. This was a workhouse, taken over for the duration of the hostilities, and used as a tuberculosis hospital for South London after the war. The depot would have filled a variety of administrative, recruitment, induction, training and re-supply roles. James died on 1st February 1917 at Balgowan Hospital V.A.D. (Voluntary Aid Detachment, a voluntary organisation providing field nursing services), at Beckenham, Kent, and is buried at the east end of Crowthorne churchyard; his sister died in 1962, and is recorded on the same headstone. The Reading Mercury of 10th February 1917 contained a brief report of his burial: "The funeral of Mr James L. Godwin, the well-known newsagent of High Street, took place at Crowthorne on Tuesday …. many tradesmen and others were present …. Mr Godwin joined the Colours about five weeks ago, and contracted laryngitis; pneumonia followed, and heart failure, causing his death. He was in the 42nd year."

WILLIAM J. GOODCHILD

William James Goodchild, who had an elder brother, was born at Easthampstead in 1892, and baptised there on 22nd May. Although his father worked as a grocer when William was born, the family soon moved to Waterloo Road, Wokingham, with his father now listed as an estate forester, possibly at Easthampstead Park. After leaving school, William worked as a domestic gardener at Bill Hill, an estate just off the A321, north of Forest Road. He joined the 1st Battalion, Royal Berkshire Regiment under the Derby Scheme, attesting at Wokingham, and was mobilised in February 1916; a report on his death from the Reading Mercury stated, "the death of Private W. Goodchild brings to five the number of asylum staff killed in action," indicating he had have been working at Broadmoor before joining up. Until mid 1918, attendants at the hospital were exempt from service, and many men applied to work there to avoid serving in the forces. The War Diary only mentions a draft of new soldiers arriving in August, but William may well have been in France for the fighting on the Somme in 1916, as well as the Battle of Arras in the spring of the following year. At the beginning of April 1917, the battalion were training at Tangry, despite a heavy snowstorm for almost twenty-four hours. On the 7th, they marched to Orlencourt and Monchy Breton, and then to Etrun Huts, through frequent snow and hail showers, three days later. The following evening, they went into the front trenches opposite Roclincourt, and spent the next couple of days clearing them and burying the dead, before moving forward again as the Germans retreated to the Hindenburg Line. They were relieved overnight on the 16th/17th, and spent a week behind the lines before going forward again. They came under a very heavy bombardment on the 25th, with seven men being killed, and evacuated the front line the next morning in order that the Heavy Artillery could cut the wire in front of them. On the 28th, the 5th and 6th Brigades attacked the village of Oppy, and although the Berkshire were not involved, some of the men were called upon to assist the field ambulances evacuate the wounded; others were on standby to act as stretcher-bearers, but were not called upon. They moved forward again later for an attack at 4am the following morning, and captured part of the Oppy Line. However, the troops on their right failed to get forward, leaving that flank exposed. The Germans attacked, and after five hours the Berkshires were forced to withdraw, due to a shortage of bombs. The front line came under heavy shelling, machine gun, and rifle fire for the rest of the day. Sixty per cent of the 250 men were casualties, with William being one of almost fifty missing; his body was never recovered, and he is listed on the Arras Memorial.

CHARLES G. GOODRIDGE

Charles George Goodridge was born on 19th June 1887 near Blandford Forum, Dorset, and had a sister nine years his junior. His father was a gardener who worked at two different locations in Hampshire before the family moved to Crowthorne by the time of the 1901 census. After leaving school, Charles worked as a carpenter and joiner for a few years. With Canada keen to encourage young men, Charles crossed the Atlantic to start a new life, landing at Montreal on 17th May 1907, bound for Ottawa. He visited England three years later, and returned to Saskatoon, now working as a gardener, and was also in England for the 1911 census. On the penultimate day of 1914, he signed up for the Canadian Expeditionary Force, joining the 1st Canadian Mounted Rifles Battalion. He was almost 5'7" tall, with brown eyes, black hair, and an olive complexion, and recorded his religion as Wesleyan rather than Church of England. He claimed to have previously served in the Royal Hampshire Regiment for three years while in England, as well as the 29th Light Horse Regiment in Canada for a further four years. His previous military experience would enable him to rise to the rank of Company Quartermaster Sergeant. The battalion, which supported a brass and pipe band, left Montreal on 12th June 1915 for England, where they spent several months training. The War Diary starts in September 1915, by which time they were at South Shorncliffe, Folkestone, Kent, which they left on the 22nd for France, and headed for Ploegsteert. Conditions on the Western Front made its mounts more of a hindrance than a benefit, and on 1st January 1916, all six Canadian Mounted Regiments were dismounted, converted to infantry, and reorganized. The battalion then fought in most of the 3rd Canadian Division's engagements until the end of the war. On 2nd June 1916, when the Germans launched their assault at the outset of the Battle of Mount Sorrel, its positions were overrun, and eighty per cent of its members were killed, wounded or captured. The battalion were rebuilt over the summer, and was one of the first Canadian Corps units to attack when the corps shifted to the Somme. Charles was in England towards the end of 1917, when he married Nora Rosser, an Irish girl who worked as a domestic servant (she was at Shinfield in 1911, so they may have known each other for several years). By the end of September 1918, the battalion were in the Bullecourt area. At 8am on the 29th, they made an attack, but were soon forced to retire by the Allied artillery firing short. Enemy machine gun posts were still firing from the vicinity of the church and main street in the town of St Olle, and Charles was killed instantly by fire from one of them. Although progress was made, casualties were very heavy, with more than seventy men killed during the day. Charles was buried in Raillencourt Communal Cemetery Extension, along with 63 comrades, the village having been captured the previous day.

RICHARD C. GOULDING

Richard Cecil Goulding was born in October 1899 at Brading on the Isle of Wight. He was the eldest of four children (including a pair of twins), with a younger sister dying in infancy. His father worked away from home as a butler when Richard was born, but as the family grew, he took a job as a hotel waiter, and the family moved, first to Camberley, and then to Crowthorne, where he worked at the Waterloo Hotel. Richard attended Crowthorne School and Ranelagh

School in Bracknell, appearing on the Roll of Honour in both establishments, was a member of the Crowthorne Boy Scouts troop, and also sang in the village church choir. Not wanting to miss out on the 'excitement' of war, he joined the Guards Band of the King's Royal Rifles on 1st December 1914, attesting at Winchester, and claimed to be almost sixteen year old. He was just 5'2" tall, weighed less than seven stone, with blue eyes, fair hair, and a fresh complexion, and recorded his profession as musician. His young age was soon discovered, and a letter from his parents to the authorities the following June agreed to his serving in the band, although he would not be eligible to serve overseas until he reached the age of nineteen. In October 1916, he was transferred to the 5th Battalion, based at Sheerness, Kent, performing coastal defence and other home duties, where he remained until February 1918, although correspondence reveals there were still questions about his age, compounded by the pay office granting him proficiency pay before the due date, an error picked up and corrected by the Colonel of the Regiment. Richard served in France with the 13th Battalion until September 1918, when he was wounded and admitted to hospital for treatment, before rejoining his battalion on 19th October. On 4th November, they made an attack through the village of Louvignies-lez-Quesnoy at 6:15am. Although faced with a heavy enemy barrage, it mostly fell behind them, and caused little trouble. Enemy machine gun fire was troublesome from the orchards and hedges to the west of the village, but with the aid of a tank, they moved slowly forward, although it was not until dusk that they captured both the village and a nearby ridge, on which the Germans had made a determined stand. Richard, now with the Lewis Gun section, was one of the day's casualties, and is buried in Beaurain British Cemetery. In July the following year, his father wrote, asking if there were any personal effects to be returned, but only one letter was found, and forwarded to the grieving family.

WILLIAM C. GREENMAN

The late Pte. W. C. GREENMAN, High St., Crowthorne, late of Wellington College.—Killed in action. Aged 30.

William Charles Greenman was born in 1886 at Ablington, near Cirencester, Gloucestershire (this is confirmed by the birth registration and census returns, although SDGW states he was born in Lambourn, Berkshire). He was one of nine children, although three died in infancy. William grew up in Hampshire, where his father worked as a groom, initially near Odiham, and then at Fareham, where William worked alongside him after leaving school. By 1911, William was living at East Heath, south of Wokingham, and working as a brickyard labourer. He had married Daisy Bacon in Reading the previous year, although a son living with them was born six months before the marriage, so it is not clear whether William was the father. William joined the Army under the Derby Scheme, attesting at Wokingham, and joined the 3rd Battalion, Royal Berkshire Regiment for his training, being mobilised at the end of May 1916. He was then transferred to the 1st Battalion (the Commonwealth War Graves website records him as being in the 2nd Battalion, but this is not consistent with his date of death). The battalion took part in the Battle of the Ancre, the last large British attack of the year. On 13th November they were at Serre, and started moving forward in readiness for an attack the following day. They came under heavy artillery and machine gun fire all morning, as well as from mine-throwers, and snipers were active in the afternoon; nine men were killed during the course of the day, and more than twenty wounded. At 5am the following morning, the battalion advanced across No Man's Land, suffering casualties from machine gun fire as well as British artillery "shorts." These were especially heavy on the right, and there were insufficient men left when they reached the German trenches. Despite this, they managed to capture several prisoners, and captured part of Serre Trench, the objective. The following day, the Berkshires captured another fifty yards of trench. Enemy fire had been slight all day, but at dusk, their artillery started a heavy bombardment, which made the bringing up of rations, and the relief of the battalion, almost impossible. Two soldiers were killed in the bombardment, one of them being William. His body was never recovered, and his name is listed on the Thiepval Memorial. As his parents were by now living in Crowthorne, his name was put forward for the local War Memorial, and the records show that William was also living in the village when he joined up. His widow moved to London, where she eventually remarried in 1948, and died in 1964.

The late Sergt. W. GREENOUGH, Broadmoor Farm, Lower Broadmoor, Crowthorne.—Killed in action.

WILLIAM G. GREENOUGH

William George Greenough was born in 1896 at Blewbury, Berkshire. His mother died soon after he was born, so he spent the first few years of his life with his mother's parents, George and Mary Warner, at West Lockinge, near Wantage. Meanwhile, his father worked as a farm carter at Hurley, near Henley, and married Florence Bryant in 1901. The couple moved to Crowthorne, where William joined them, and two half-siblings were born later. William went into domestic service after leaving school, and was listed as a houseboy, aged fourteen, in the 1911 census. He had joined the 2/4th Battalion, Hampshire Regiment, a Territorial Battalion, at Yateley, which had formed a month after the outbreak of war, but William was one of more than seven hundred men who transferred to the 1/4th Battalion, and arrived in Mesopotamia on 18th March 1915. He rejoined his original unit when they moved to Egypt in 1917, and took part in the Third Battle of Gaza which started at the end of October. On 19th November, the battalion moved through Latrun, a strategic hilltop, to a Guard House in a pass on the Jerusalem Road. Next day, they cleared the enemy from the hills on the left of the road, before moving on to Kuryet El Enab, and carried White House, three men suffering wounds in the fighting. On the 21st, they were shelled in their bivouac area, which killed two men and injured another 23, before moving on to Biddu and supporting an attack on Neby Samwil on the 23rd. Here, they went into the front line at 2pm to support a battalion of Gurkhas. By the time they were relieved at midnight, the Hampshire had suffered just over one hundred casualties. William was one of fourteen men killed, and is buried in Jerusalem War Cemetery, Israel.

The late Bdr. MAURICE ("Buller") GROVE, M.M., Belmont Cottage, Owlsmoor.—Killed in action.

MAURICE B. GROVE

Maurice Buller Grove was born at Sandhurst early in 1897. He was the youngest of seven surviving children in a family where two others had died in infancy. His oldest brother, who had been a Private in the Yorkshire Regiment, died in 1904, and his father, a general labourer, six years later. Maurice worked as a butcher's errand boy after leaving school. Although officially still underage for overseas service, he volunteered, attesting at Camberley, joined the Royal Field Artillery, and arrived in France on 8th July 1915. This indicates he may have been part of the 15th (Scottish) Division for the duration of his time there, a Division that served with distinction, winning the regard of the enemy as one of the most formidable in the British army. Maurice also played his part, winning the Military Medal at some point in his career. The Division took part on the Battle of Loos in the autumn, and three phases of the Battle of the Somme the next year. Earlier in 1916, they had also faced a German gas attack at Hulluch at the end of April. The first few days in April 1917 were spent preparing for an attack at Arras. For two days, the batteries were firing to cut the enemy wire and bombarding the German's two front lines of trenches, and then practised a creeping barrage for the next two days. On the 8th, they concentrated on making the gaps in the enemy wire larger, and the attack began at 5:30am the following morning. The infantry assaulted the enemy front system, preceded by a creeping barrage supplied by 18 pounders. Meanwhile, 4.5 inch Howitzers and the Heavy Batteries systematically bombarded the enemy works behind the front system, and the attack was successful. One of the batteries of the 71st Brigade took a direct hit, but men from other guns were also killed during the action, including Maurice. He is buried in Beaurains Road Cemetery, Beaurains. His widowed mother was living in Owlsmoor when names for the Crowthorne War Memorial were being collected, so he is recorded on it as well in his native Sandhurst.

SIDNEY C. HALLETT

Sidney Cyril Hallett was born at Crowthorne in 1884, and baptised 30th March, one of six children. His father, who worked as a coachman, died when Sidney was only six years old, leaving his mother to work as a charwoman. His two eldest brothers were old enough to have left school, and were working as domestic gardeners. By 1901, Sidney had left school, and was living with an elder sister in Church Road, Crowthorne, and working at making and repairing boots and shoes. He married Matilda Taylor, from Barkham, in 1909, and they had four children within six years. He joined the army under the Derby Scheme, attesting at Wokingham, and joined the 2nd Battalion, Royal Berkshire Regiment, being mobilised at the end of May 1916. Sidney arrived in France after the battalion's involvement at the start of the Battle of the Somme, but took part in the Third Battle of Ypres the following year. For the last nine days of March 1918, the battalion were involved in heavy fighting against the German Spring Offensive, and the War Diary only records the phrase "took part in enemy offensive operations" for each day, as they fought desperately to halt the onslaught. The battalion had been billeted at St Martin-au-Lert for over a week, but on the 22nd, they proceeded to Guillaucourt by train, and then marched to Chaunes. At around midnight, they received orders to move to the left bank of the Somme, between Roncy-le-Grand and Pargny, which was done under heavy fire. All day on the 23rd, they remained in reserve, but on the 24th were in the front line. Early the next morning, the battalion were ordered to attack, but the Germans launched their own at 6:15am. The British line was thinly held, and a gap developed. By mid afternoon, the Berkshires had withdrawn to Omiecourt, having suffered heavy casualties. They continued to fall back over the next few days, mounting the occasional ineffectual counter-attack, until they were at Castel on the 31st. At 2:30pm came the news of a breach in the line at Moreuil Wood, and the Berkshires were sent to recover the situation by capturing an outlying copse, which they achieved. There was high ground in front, held by the enemy, making their position very dangerous, and with his men very wet and weary, Major Griffin requested his men be relieved, which was done under cover of darkness. Just over three hundred men from the battalion were casualties for this period, but it was two days later before the records were updated, so Sidney's date of death is recorded as 2nd April 1918. His body was never found, and he is listed on the Pozieres Memorial.

FREDERICK A. G. HARFIELD

Bandsman FRED HARFIELD, 2nd Batt. Yorkshire Regiment, Crowthorne.—Wounded and missing. [His brother was killed in action.]

Frederick Augustus George Harfield was born in Crowthorne in 1894, and baptised 10th June. He was the second of six children. His father, who came from the Isle of Wight, worked as an attendant at Broadmoor Asylum. Frederick joined the army as a young teenager, attesting at Reading, and appears in the 1911 census at Strensall Camp, just north of York. This had been set up by the War Office in 1884 for training troops, and Frederick is listed as a member of the Yorkshire Regiment. At the outbreak of war, he was a bandsman with the 2nd Battalion who were in Guernsey, and returned to the mainland at the end of August, before spending a few weeks in preparation, and crossing from Southampton to Zeebrugge, arriving on 6th October. The Battle of Ypres started on the 19th, continuing for over a month, bringing the advancing German army to a standstill. All units suffered grievous losses. On the 29th, the battalion were in reserve, and two companies were sent up to support the Royal Scots Fusiliers. The enemy had broken through on the left of the line, and the 21st Brigade was forced to withdraw, but were quickly reorganised, and an attack was mounted which was successful in driving the enemy back, and regaining the ground which had been previously lost. During the withdrawal, the casualties were heavy. Frederick died of wounds received in the fighting. After the war, his grave could not be found, so his name is listed on the Ypres (Menin Gate) Memorial.

WILLIAM H. C. D. HARFIELD

Sergt. HARRY HARFIELD, 2nd Batt. Yorkshire Regt.—Killed in action.

William Henry Charles Down Harfield was Frederick's elder brother, baptised on 13th March 1892, having been born earlier in the same year. By 1911, he was a Lance Sergeant in the 2nd Battalion, Yorkshire Regiment, based at the Infantry Barracks in York, having attested at Aldershot two years earlier. At the outbreak of war, the battalion were in Guernsey, returning to the mainland at the end of August, before spending a few weeks in preparation, and crossing from Southampton to Zeebrugge, arriving on 6th October. The Battle of Ypres started on the 19th, continuing for over a month, bringing advancing German army to a standstill. All units suffered grievous losses. On the 30th, the War Diary records the battalion occupied trenches on the right of the position of the assailant. "The Germans were seen running in front of our trenches behind a hedge, and appeared to be concentrating on the right. 2/Lieut. H. G. Brookebank, who was commanding a Platoon on the extreme right of the Battalion, reported (at about 1pm) that a large force of Germans, approximately five hundred had occupied trenches in front of him. He opened fire on them and caused a great deal of damage. It was impossible to reinforce him at the time. A message was received at 3:30pm ordering the Battalion to retire. The message had been delayed two hours on account of the Orderly having great difficulty in getting through the woods, owing to constant strafing and shrapnel. The Battalion were placed in a very awkward position owing to the delay, and also our Commanding Officer, Lieutenant Colonel C. A. C. King, having been killed. As our Second in Command had also been killed (Captain E. L Gruern), the command of the Battalion were taken over by Captain B. L. Spence Blundell, who had to make up his mind immediately whether to rush the retrenchment in daylight in heavy fire, or to risk the chance of being able to hold out until dusk. He decided on the former and withdrew his left Company first, leaving the Platoon on the right to hold back the enemy beforementioned till last. The result of this move was that he was able to withdraw his whole Battalion with the loss of only ten men. The casualties were heavy before retrenchment took place owing to some very accurate sniping." Lance Sergeant William Harfield was one those killed; his body was never recovered and his name is listed on the Ypres (Menin Gate) Memorial.

Lost on the "Leinster."

Lieut. BASIL HAYE, R. Berks Regt., the eldest son of Mr. and Mrs. George Haye, of Trevear, Wellington College, was on the R.M.S. Leinster, which sank by the German brutes, and was drowned. Lieut. Basil Haye, whose age was 24, joined the S.R. of officers, Royal Berks Regt., at the outbreak of war. He went to France in May, 1915, and led his company into action at Bois Grenier, October, 1915. He transferred from the S.R. to the Regular Army that year and served with the 2nd Battalion during all his period of service abroad. He was wounded severely on the Somme in July, 1916, recovered, and returned to France in January, 1917, and was dangerously wounded in the head on March 8th of that year. For some months he was with the 3rd Battalion at Dublin, and was then passed fit for general service again, and was under orders for France when drowned in the sinking of the Leinster on October 10th, 1918.

Lieut. ALEX. P. AVELINE, M.C., R. Berks Regt., only son of Mr. and Mrs. Sydney Aveline, of Wingham House, Reading, was in the water a long time before he was picked up by a destroyer. He was bruised but soon recovered from his terrible experience.

BASIL HAYE

Basil Haye was born on 23rd August 1894 at Wokingham, the second of five children. His father was a solicitor who could afford to employ a couple of servants to look after the house, a governess for the younger children, and a private education for his sons. Basil was educated at Wellington College as a day boy, and later as a boarder at St Bees School, near Whitehaven, Cumbria. He applied for a Commission four days after the outbreak of war, and joined the Special Reserve of Officers, Royal Berkshire Regiment. He was described as being 5'10" tall, weighing twelve stones, and able to ride. Although vision in his left eye was not perfect, he was able to read without glasses. He went to France in May 1915, joining the 2nd Battalion on the 25th at Neuve Chapelle. He led his own company into action at Bois Grenier later that year in October, a diversionary attack from the Battle of Loos that cost the lives of well over one hundred men of the battalion.

The War Diary records him going to hospital on 15th February 1916, and returning just over a month later, but gives no details of the cause, although the battalion had been in trenches near Croix Blanche for the three previous days, and five men were wounded. He was also admitted to hospital, along with two other men, at the end of April from the Divisional Reserve Camp at Henecourt Woods. He was severely wounded on the Somme on 1st July, while holding the rank of temporary Captain. The battalion had the objective of capturing the village of Ovillers, north of La Boisselle. After a night during which the trenches had been shelled by the Germans, at around 6:30am, the British barrage began. An hour later, the men climbed out of the trenches to start the attack, but immediately came under terrific rifle and machine gun fire from the German trenches in front of Ovillers, which prevented them from reaching the enemy line. A small group on the left did manage to get into the trench, but was eventually bombed out again. By 7:45am, the fire on the parapet of the British trench made it impossible for any more men to leave it. In less than three hours after the attack started, over half the battalion had been killed, while the regiments to the left and right had lost an even higher proportion of men. With such losses, it was clearly impossible to mount another attack, and the Brigade remained in their trenches until dark, when it withdrew to bivouacs at Long Valley. Private William Bond, himself wounded, gave an eye-witness account from Beaufort War Hospital just over a week later: "On July 3rd, at La Boiselle, about 550 yards from our lines, I saw Lt. Hayes of 6th Platoon, 'B' Company, Royal Berkshire Regiment, hit. This was about 3:30am. He fell but I do not know whether he was killed or not. He was on my left, about ten yards away." Although the date is at odds with the official documentation, it must be remembered that the soldiers were in the middle of fighting in the Battle of the Somme, and details were confused. On the 5th, Basil arrived back at Southampton, to be treated for a gunshot wound in his left shoulder. Medical reports indicate he was hit by shrapnel, causing a wound a few inches long from which debris was removed, and by mid December had fully recovered. Basil returned to France in

January the following year, but was wounded again on 5th March. A large attack had been planned for the previous day, and the battalion had been practising on a model while in rest billets the week before. The first objective was Pallas Trench, near the village of Bouchavesnes, which was captured without too much resistance. The second wave pushed on towards Fritz Trench, which ran parallel to it, but it had been so damaged by the bombardment from the British artillery, that they failed to recognise it in the darkness, and carried on Bremen Trench, but retreated when they realised their error. The Berkshires held the two captured trenches despite several counter-attacks, but were heavily bombarded in Pallas Trench at 4pm, and lost many men. Twelve hours later, the Germans recaptured part of Fritz Trench, and the remainder of the battalion were occupying a new trench, dug between the two, when they were relieved the following night. That day, a telegram was sent to his parents from 5th Clearing Station in Corbie, stating he had been admitted with "Gunshot wound, skull. Dangerously ill." Four days later, he was transferred to No. 8 General Hospital, Rouen, where his condition remained unchanged for a month before he started to show slight signs of improvement. Two weeks later, he was well enough to be returned to England again, for further treatment at Bodmin Military Hospital, Cornwall. The first report from the Medical Board, charting the progress of wounded soldiers, reported, "He was struck by a piece of shrapnel, which smashed his shrapnel helmet, and caused a scalp wound. He walked to Clearing Station and gradually became unconscious, a condition which lasted more or less a week. On 29th March, he had a sort of fit. He then had weakness of *the* left arm and was inclined to mumble and stammer. He also had photophobia. He has improved, but is still unable to concentrate and lacks self-confidence, *and* gets easily tired mentally." Recovery was slow, with frequent mentions of headaches and spells of giddiness. In September, he was allowed home on leave for three weeks, after which he reported to Victoria Barracks, Southsea, and considered fit enough to undertake light duties. Two months later, he was in Dublin, back with the Depot Battalion of the Royal Berkshire Regiment, but could still only manage light duties, and it was not until the following July that he was considered to have recovered enough to go back to France. At 9am on 18th October 1918, he boarded the R.M.S. 'Leinster' which left Dun Laoghaire, County Dublin, bound for Holyhead. On board were almost five hundred military personnel (from Ireland, Britain, Canada, the United States, New Zealand and Australia), 180 civilian passengers (men, women and children, most of them from Ireland and Britain), 22 postal sorters from Dublin Post Office (working in the ship's onboard postal sorting room), and a crew of 77 men. Shortly before 10am, about sixteen miles from Dun Laoghaire, a few people on the deck saw a torpedo approaching the port side of the ship. It missed the 'Leinster', passing in front of her. Soon afterwards, another torpedo struck where the postal sorting room was located; Postal Sorter John Higgins later recorded that the torpedo exploded, blowing a hole in the port side. The explosion travelled across the ship, also blowing a hole in the starboard side. In an attempt to return to port, the 'Leinster' turned 180 degrees, until it faced the direction from which it had come. With speed reduced and slowly sinking, the ship had sustained few casualties, and lifeboats were being launched. At this point, a second torpedo struck the ship on the starboard side, practically blowing it to pieces. The 'Leinster' sank soon afterwards, bow first. In the days that followed, bodies were recovered from the sea, Basil's being found on the 13th, the day after his parents had received a telegram reported him to be missing. Some of the dead were taken to Britain, Canada and the United States for burial, but 144 military casualties, including Basil, were buried in Grangegorman Military Cemetery in Dublin. No personal effects were available to return to his parents, but just over £4, found in his pockets was sent. The family had moved to Crowthorne by 1906, and Basil's name is on the Roll of Honour in the village, as well as at Wellington College.

PHILIP HAYE

Philip Haye was one of Basil's younger brothers, born at Wokingham on 25th October 1895. He attended Wellington College as a day boy, and Rossall Hall, Fleetwood, Lancashire. The school had opened in 1884 as a rival for Eton and Harrow; indeed it became known as "The Eton of the North." The school enjoyed close links to the British Armed Forces, and while there, Philip joined the Officer Training Corps. At the outbreak of war, he joined the 19th Battalion, Royal Fusiliers, formed in September 1914 at Epsom, and consisting mainly of young men from Public Schools and Universities. He was 5'5" tall, weighed almost ten stone, had hazel eyes, dark brown hair, a medium complexion, and claimed to be Church of England. The battalion moved to Clipstone Camp, near Mansfield, Nottinghamshire, in June 1915, and then to Tidworth Barracks, on the eastern edge of Salisbury Plain, two months later, before landing in France in November. But within a month, Philip was back home, suffering from trench foot, a not uncommon complaint from standing in cold, wet trenches for many hours at a time. It was late March 1916 before he returned to France, but a month later, the battalion were disbanded as many of the men had left to take a commission, with Philip being transferred briefly to the Machine Gun Corps. But he decided also to obtain one, achieved with the 3rd Battalion, Royal Berkshire Regiment in September, and attached to the 8th Battalion the following month. After five months with them, he was back in England, having sustained a superficial gunshot wound to the left hand that had turned septic and required an operation, from which he took two months to recover and heal satisfactorily. He was then attached to the 82nd Company, Machine Gun Corps, fighting in the Balkans, where he stayed until the beginning of the next year, when he was sent to Egypt for a training course. While there, he appears to have been out of action for a couple of months, although the reason is not given. He returned to Salonika in March. Although the fighting finished in November, there was still work to be done, and many men did not return home for a considerable period of time. Philip was posted to Russia, arriving in early January 1919. On 14th April, a telegram was received by his parents in Crowthorne, "Stationery Hospital, Tiflis (modern day Tblisi, the capital of Georgia) reports April 10th, dangerously ill, damage to kidney." Then a day later, a second arrived, reporting his death. This had actually occurred on 2nd April, a fact confirmed by the War Office, who had investigated the time delay in the news arriving home. A report was received into the circumstances of his death. "On the morning of April 2nd, he went to exercise his horse, when two sheep dogs set at his horse. He rose in his stirrups to frighten one away, but at the same minute, the other bit the horse, which bucked and threw his rider. He was taken at once to hospital, but died at 10pm from rupture of the kidney and spleen." Although he was buried in Tiflis British Cemetery, his name is also recorded on the Haidar Pasha Memorial in Turkey; this memorial commemorates servicemen who died in post Armistice operations in Russia and Transcaucasia. A long list of personal effects was returned to the family, most of them consisting of clothing or military equipment, but also included were a Russian visiting card, seven Turkish notes (total value "unknown"), an up-market fountain pen, and a cheque value £2 signed "Barbara Hartley" (possibly the wife of court room artist William Hartley from London).

WILLIAM A. HERMON

William Adams Hermon was born in 1894 at Wantage. He was one of four children, one of whom died in infancy. His father, a domestic groom, died in 1907. Soon after, William left school and moved to Crowthorne, lodging with a family in Pinewood Avenue. The wife ran a greengrocer business from the house, with William as an assistant, probably making deliveries. He volunteered for service, attesting at Camberley, and joined the 7th Battalion, Royal West Surrey Regiment. Most of his training was done at Colchester, but in May 1915, the battalion moved to Salisbury Plain, were inspected by the King the following month, and arrived in France in July. The battalion suffered appalling casualties on the Somme the following year, with five hundred men killed, wounded or missing on 1st July, over two hundred more at Trones Wood on the 13th, and almost four hundred in the assault on Schwaben Redoubt near Thiepval. At the start of November, the battalion had had a few days for rest, reorganisation and training at Albert, and recipients of awards since the beginning of July were awarded in the town square on the 1st. They were in and out of the front line for the first half of the month, but attacked and captured German trenches near Ovillers on the 18th. William was killed during this operation, one of almost ninety men of the battalion to lose their lives. His body was never recovered, and his name is listed on the Thiepval Memorial. His parents were still living in Wantage at the time of his death, so it may well have been his employer who put his name forward for the local War Memorial in Crowthorne.

HAROLD HEWITT

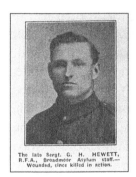

The late Sergt. G. H. HEWETT, R.F.A., Broadmoor Asylum staff.— Wounded, since killed in action.

Thomas George Harold Hewett, known as Harold to distinguish him from his father who was also named Thomas, was born in 1888 at Wantage. He was the eldest of five children, a further two dying in infancy. When Harold was born, his father worked as a labourer in a provisions store in East Hagbourne, near Didcot. But by 1901, the family had moved to Ascot and then Bulbrook, and would later live on the London Road in Wokingham when Thomas senior got a job as an insurance agent. Harold had left school by the age of twelve, and worked as a grocer's assistant, before joining the Royal Field Artillery, attesting at Aldershot. In the 1911 census, he was based at Bulford Barracks on Salisbury Plain. At the outbreak of war, Harold, now a sergeant, crossed the Channel with the 25th Brigade on 16th August 1914. A week later, they were involved in the Battle of Mons, the first major encounter with the advancing Germans. This was followed by the Battle of the Marne, and the Battle of the Aisne the following month. On 20th September, the Brigade moved to Frenchencourt and spent the next week in training. They then moved northwest, towards Bapaume, and bombarded Eaucourt l'Abbeye on the 29th. The next day, they concentrated on the Flers Line, cutting the wire in front of it, and bombarding the line itself for over an hour. The bombardment continued on 1st October, and the 141st Infantry Brigade successfully attacked both targets in the afternoon. From 6pm onwards, the new target was the front of the Warlencourt Line, and a slow rate of fire was kept up all night. It was during this day that Harold was killed; he is buried in Bazentin-le-Petit Communal Cemetery Extension. During his short time in France, Harold had been awarded the Military Medal.

CYRIL DE V. HINDE

Cyril de Villiers Hinde was born at Leeds on 8th July 1897, the youngest of four children. His father had served in the Royal Engineers, reaching the rank of Lieutenant Colonel, so the family were able to afford to employ three or four servants to help raise the children and look after the house. The family moved firstly to Sussex, where Cyril's elder attended preparatory school, and then to Crowthorne. Cyril attended Eagle House School, Sandhurst, from 1906 to 1910, and Wellington College, appearing on the Roll of Honour at both schools. He then went to the Royal Military College at Sandhurst, entering in 1914, and leaving with a commission the following year. He joined the 2nd Battalion, Royal Berkshire Regiment, but only arrived in France in July 1916. The delay was caused by a laceration to the leg, and although his Service Record does not indicate how or when it occurred, it was recorded as the cause when he appeared before a Medical Board at Winchester in October 1915. He was also reported to be convalescing in Alexandra Hospital, Cosham in April 1916, although is no further detail on this either. Cyril was in France, now with the 5th Battalion, Royal Berkshire Regiment, for less than a month when he sustained a slight gunshot wound to the left hand at Pozieres on 8th August, and admitted to No. 2 Red Cross Hospital, Rouen two days later. But the injury turned out to be more serious than at first thought, and he returned to England a week later for treatment at 3rd Southern General Hospital, Oxford. It was reported the injury had shattered the two terminal phalanges of the two middle fingers, which were subsequently amputated. This led to a loss of sensation in the palm and fingers, and a restriction of movement, in his left hand. It would be the end of February 1917 before he was considered well enough to return to the front, although it was noted "the grip of one hand is permanently weakened." He went back to the 2nd Battalion, but a week into April, he was in hospital in Rouen again, with a slight gunshot wound to the right arm. The injury occurred on the 4th, when the Berkshires were part of an attack on Metz-en-Couture in snowy conditions. For his part in this, Cyril was awarded the Military Cross; the citation reads, "For conspicuous gallantry and devotion to duty. He led out a patrol and inflicted heavy casualties on the enemy. Later, although wounded, he remained in command and successfully withdrew his men." He rejoined his unit on 23rd May, which was near Ypres by July. At 1am on the 11th, a raid was launched against the German trenches. The first line was reached without incident except for some men pushing forward too quickly and getting caught in their own barrage, and the second objective secured within fifteen minutes. However, in the dark, the entrances to some dug-outs in the first trench were missed, and Germans came out of one with a machine gun, firing on the Berkshire men from behind. Cyril was reported missing after the raid, but it was not until 9th October that a letter from the War Office reached his father: "The Military Secretary deeply regrets to inform Col. Hinde that the following information in respect of his son Lt. C. de V. Hinde, Royal Berkshire Regiment, appears on an official German list of dead which has been forwarded to the War Office by the Netherland Legation, Berlin." On 14th February 1918, there was "no record of body being recovered," and after the war was over, Cyril's name appeared on the Ypres (Menin Gate) Memorial, unveiled in 1927.

WILLIAM H. R. HINDE

William Henry Rousseau Hinde was Cyril's elder brother, born at Southsea, Portsmouth, on 27th May 1891. He was educated at a preparatory school in Brighton, Eagle House School,

Sandhurst (from 1901 to 1905), Wellington College (where he twice played in the school cricket team), and Oriel College, Oxford, where he obtained an M.A. He then worked as a solicitor's articled clerk at Bletchingley, Surrey. He played Minor Counties cricket for Berkshire on five occasions in 1913 and 1914, although not especially proficient with the bat. He had been a member of the Officer Training Corps at both Wellington College, where he had been Colour Sergeant, and Oxford University, where he was Company Quarter-Master Sergeant, and applied for a Commission in the Special Reserve a month after the outbreak of war. Due to a congenital cardiac defect which left him subject to "fatigue easily induced by exertion," he was considered "not fit for General Service," but accepted for Home Service in the Army Service Corps. He spent most of the war working at the Main Supply Depot in Leeds, where he was promoted to Captain. He was in the Northern General Hospital, Leeds in March 1918, suffering from mouth ulcers, from which he recovered, but died in a nursing home in Leeds on 22nd October the same year, from influenza and septic pneumonia. His name is listed on the Screen Wall at Lawns Wood Cemetery, Leeds, after his war service had been brought to the attention Secretary of State for War, presumably by his father, a former Lieutenant Colonel in the Royal Engineers.

HAROLD HOLDAWAY

Harold Holdaway was born in 1897 at Crowthorne, and baptised 24th October. He was one of seven children, but his mother died in 1904, giving birth to an eighth, and his father, an attendant at Broadmoor, remarried within two years. It is not known if Harold had a job after leaving school, but he joined the 1st Battalion, Leicestershire Regiment in 1913, attesting at Reading. The battalion were at Fermoy in Ireland when war was declared, moved to Cambridge a couple of weeks later, and landed at St Nazaire on 10th September. They would take part in actions on the Aisne Heights later the same year, at Hooge in 1915, phases of the Battle of the Somme in 1916, and the Battle at Hill 70 and Cambrai Operations in 1917. In the second half of March 1918, the battalion were in the Vaulx–Morchies Line. The War Diary describes the action in some detail. "After a quiet night, the morning of the 22nd dawned with a heavy fog, and as soon as it was light, the enemy put down a very heavy barrage. At 11am, the 2nd South Lancashire Regiment reported that the enemy had broken through. A request was sent to the 2nd Sherwood Foresters and 9th Norfolk Regiment to move up to cover *the* valley. Defensive flank for high ground east of Vaulx Wood regained by 2nd South Lancashire Regiment and bombing parties sent forward to recover lost trenches. Reinforcements asked for, for left of Brigade front. At 11.40am enemy reported massing. Officer Commanding 'C' Company, 11th Leicestershire Regiment, reported that he had only 37 men left, and that enemy were in Vaulx Wood. He was instructed to look after his left flank. 1 officer and 40 other ranks of 11th Leicestershire Regiment, who had come from Vaulx–Morchies line, reported at Battalion HQ's. At 2.00pm, 'B' Company reported that they had gained some ground in bombing up the Vaulx–Morchies line, and were continuing the bombing attack with the help of 1 officer and 60 other ranks of the 2nd South Lancashire Regiment. Maricourt Wood and the vicinity of Battalion HQ's were heavily shelled throughout the morning. At 2.30pm, heavy bombardment by both sides opened on the right of the Brigade front. At 3.15pm, enemy seen from Battalion HQ's pouring into Vaulx–Morchies line between Lagnicourt–Maricourt Wood Road and Vaulx Wood. At 3.45pm, the breach this time was effective, and the situation was becoming very grave. The withdrawal became somewhat disorderly, and the enemy came rapidly through Morchies.

A ridge was held by our machine gunners, and troops withdrawing were collected and an orderly withdrawal instituted to the partially consolidated line. Up to this time only one man (wounded, belonging to 'B' Company) of the Battalion had come back from the Vaulx–Morchies line. At 4.30pm, the enemy brought up his light machine guns with great rapidity, and was soon putting up a strong barrage with them along the valley and the ridges east and west of it. This valley and the heights were thickly held by troops of 25th Division. An immediate counter-attack was urgently required if the Vaulx–Morchies line was to be regained, but all the troops holding the new line had orders that they were on no account to move forward. Eventually, a number of Tanks (about 16) in the visible front came forward, and under very heavy shell and machine gun fire, advanced as far as the Vaulx–Morchies line with most of the enemy retiring before them. This Tank attack was not supported by infantry, and gradually petered out as the Tanks became casualties, or used up all their ammunition. At 9.00pm, the remnants of the 3 Battalions of the Brigade were:- 1st Leicestershire Regiment about 40 all ranks under Lieutenant Colonel F. Latham D.S.O. …. The night passed quietly. Casualties, other ranks 'A' Company: 6 killed, 14 wounded, 46 missing, 'B' Company: 3 killed, 14 wounded, 83 missing, 'C' Company: 6 killed, 21 wounded, 49 missing, 'D' Company: 1 killed, 12 wounded, 113 missing." Harold was one of those missing, and his name is listed on the Arras Memorial.

The late Lce.-Corpl. A. V. HOOK, Wellington Road. Crowthorne.—Killed in action. Aged 21.

VICTOR A. S. HOOK

Victor Albert Sidney Hook was born 25th July 1894 at Sandhurst, and baptised there on 16th September. He had a younger sister as well as two older half-sisters from his mother's first marriage. His father worked as a gate porter at Wellington College, and the family soon moved from Longdown Road to Crowthorne, living in Wellington Road. Victor worked as a grocer's apprentice after leaving school, before volunteering for service, attesting at Camberley, and joined the 7th Battalion, Royal West Surrey Regiment. His initial training took place in and around Colchester before moving to Salisbury Plain in May, with an inspection by the King the next month. Victor arrived in France with the battalion in July. There was no major action for them until the Battle of the Somme the following year. They were based near Montauban, a village in German hands, which it was their objective to capture. The days preceding the attack, in which the enemy positions were relentlessly bombarded, had mixed effects. In front of the West Surrey's, it was pretty effective; the enemy trenches were badly damaged and lightly held, and the Royal Flying Corps reported large explosions at the enemy dumps. Just before 7:30am on 1st July, two mines, laid by one of the Royal Engineer Tunnelling Companies were blown; they were the signals for the lead units to advance from the British front trenches. Units in the centre were held up by fire from a crater field in No Man's Land, the results of mine warfare in the area in May. The enemy had occupied the craters and had built some strong points, which survived the bombardment. Undamaged machine guns fired from these when the battalion began to advance. Gradually, as the day wore on, the enemy were driven back and the pressure on the battalion eased, but it was not until 5.15pm that Montauban Alley was taken. The enemy artillery, having been badly damaged in this area, did not greatly interfere with the work of evacuation of the wounded, the bringing up of supplies, and consolidation of the ground won, which now began in earnest. However, enemy shellfire falling on the area intensified and stayed heavy, causing many casualties, and making relief and re-supply very problematic.

174 men from the battalion were killed during the day, 284 wounded, and a further 56 were missing. Victor, a Lance Corporal, was one of the later; his body was never found and his name is recorded on the Thiepval Memorial.

JOSEPH C. JAMES

Joseph Conquest James was born at Beenham, between Thatcham and Theale, on 21st January 1876. He was the middle of three children, with two sisters. His father ran the original Wellington Hotel, near Crowthorne railway station, which was demolished in the late 1960s. Joe, as he was known, attended Reading School (beside the Royal Berks Hospital). He went to South Africa as a volunteer, and served in the South African Police for four years, and with Thorneycroft's Mounted Infantry for nearly eighteen months, and probably took part in the unsuccessful attempt to take Spion Kop from the Boers. He was discharged, at his own request, in March 1901, and returned to England. He married Annie Burnett in London in 1905, and together they took over the running of the Wellington Hotel, allowing his widowed father to retire to Wokingham. At the outbreak of war, he volunteered for a Territorial Unit of the Royal Horse Artillery, which provided artillery for the Berkshire Yeomanry, attesting on 7th September 1914 at Reading. His medical inspection records he was 5'10" tall, weighed over 11½ stone, with hazel eyes, dark brown hair, and a dark complexion. Three months later, while based at Saxthorpe, near Norwich, he applied for a commission, and served in England with the 9th Battalion, Royal Berkshire Regiment at Bovington Camp in Dorset. In 1916, James was then transferred to the 5th Battalion and went to France; the War Diary notes his arrival on 20th May, when the battalion had marched to Raimbert. Although they were not involved on the first day of the Battle of the Somme, the Berkshires were in the front trenches the following day, facing the village of Ovillers, with orders to capture it. A bombardment of the German trenches for an hour before Zero (at 3:15am on the 3rd), brought heavy fire in response, causing many casualties on the waiting men, and as they crossed No Man's Land. They reached and captured the German front trenches without much difficulty, and pushed on to the second and beyond. There was fierce fighting all day with the supply of bombs to the attackers being the critical factor, but in the end, they retreated to their start positions, being unable to hold the ground taken. When they were sent back to Albert that night, only about seventy men were left with Colonel Willan, although two Second Lieutenants and about sixty others turned up later, having dug themselves into No Man's Land in the interim. Back in Crowthorne, a telegram arrived at the Wellington Hotel on the 7th: "Capt J C James, Berks Regt. Dangerously ill. GSW (*gun shot wound*) left foot. In No. 14 General Hospital Boulogne. Admitted 4.7.16. Regret permission to visit cannot be granted." Five days passed with no further news, so John's wife sent a telegram, asking for an update. A response arrived the next day: "You are permitted to visit Capt J C James, Berks Regt. Dangerously ill at No. 14 General Hospital Boulogne." John died the following morning at 9:45am, and was buried in Wimereux Communal Cemetery three months later. He left a will, and the estate of over £16,000 was administered by solicitor William Henry Sergeant, whose two sons are listed on the memorial at Easthampstead Church.

GEORGE E. H. KEESEY

George Ernest Howard Keesey, known as Howard, was born on 19th June 1886 at Croydon, Surrey, the eldest of three brothers. His father was a Congregational minister, based for many years at Kennington, London, where he became known as "the Congregational bishop of East London." He later moved to Sandwich, Kent, before going to Natland, near Kendal, Cumbria. Howard attended Caterham Congregational School, before winning a scholarship to St Olave's School, Orpington, Kent, at fourteen, where he was school captain 1904-5. It was here that he gained the nickname "The Intellectual" for his 'maturity of manner and thought.' As a scholar at Downing College, Cambridge, he gained a B.A. in Natural Sciences with first class honours, and later an M.A. He then followed a career in teaching, firstly at Kendal Grammar School, and then at Wellington College as Science Master. He held a commission in the Territorial Force after serving in the Officer Training Corps at Wellington College, and began active service in October 1914 as a Lieutenant, attached to the 1st Battalion, Rifle Brigade, being promoted to Captain the following year. The referee in his application for a commission was Joseph Bevir, a master at Wellington, who would also lose a son in the fighting. It is not recorded when Howard went to France, but the battalion took part in the Battle of Messines in late autumn 1914, and the Second Battle of Ypres in spring the following year. On 1st July 1915, Howard received a slight gunshot wound to the right shoulder, requiring treatment at hospitals at Etaples and Brighton, but returned as a Company Commander, "the best in the battalion" according to the Colonel of the Unit, and served with the 8th Battalion, Rifle Brigade, apart from a brief spell with the 14th Battalion. On 7th August 1916, after a week's training near Doullens, the battalion arrived in the Somme area, and went into the line north of Longueval a week later. A limited attack on the 18th was successful; another on the 21st less so. On the 24th, Captain Keesey led his company on an operation, and he and his batman were found in a trench, apparently killed instantly by an exploding shell. Over the next month or so, several reports were collected, concerning the circumstances of his death; details varied, but the general account remained the same. "I have just been told by Col. Ross of the 8th Battalion that Capt. Keesey was killed by a shell at Delville Wood on 24th August last. His body was recovered two or three days afterwards." "I heard that Capt. Keesey's body had been found by the 7th Battalion, Rifle Brigade, and buried by them." "An Acting Corporal of 'A' Company, who I met in No. 5 General Hospital, Rouen, told me that Capt. Keesey had got back all right to battalion." "He was formerly 2nd Lieut. of XIII Platoon. I heard Capt. Barker-Mill tell Sergeant Mills that his body had been found; he was buried by shell the day before." "I heard a week before leaving the battalion that a digging party had found Capt. Keesey's body in the trench at Delville Wood." "He was buried by a shell in Delville Wood and afterwards his body was recovered and buried close by. I saw this happen." "He was blown to pieces by a shell and was found lying dead in the northeast corner of Delville Wood on 24th August. He was buried where they found him, and I wrote to tell his wife about a week ago." "He was found dead and buried in a trench on the right of Delville Wood." "I knew Capt. Keesey. He was in 'D' Company and was missing on 21st August after the attack on Guillemont. It come (sic) through the Orderly Room that he, and Rifleman Paine of 'D' Company, were found by some of the 7th Battalion the following day. They had been buried by a shell and then death was ascribed to shell shock. I understand Capt. Keesey was going to the C.O.'s quarters when he was hit." "He was my Company Commander. I think it was on Thursday 24th August, between 6-7pm, that we attacked the German positions south of Delville Wood, in front of Cuinchy. The Captain was buried by a shell just before we started in our own trench. We missed him after the attack, but it was being known where in the trench he was. Search was made there and his body was found." "He was killed in Delville Wood on 24th August, and his body was bought in." "I know Capt. Keesey, he was in 'D' Company and was missing about 24th August on the right of Delville Wood. He had been buried by a shell." "He was buried by a shell. This was in Delville Wood. We could not get out to look for him because of the shell fire." "He was buried by a shell at Guillemont, and as he was getting out, another shell came and buried him again. About three days later, the body, or parts of it, were found, and he was identified by his ring. He was buried in a small trench leading from the front line to the support." "After the attack at Delville Wood, I and others saw him lying in front of their trenches. I am certain he was dead. We never lost that ground." "On 24th August, he was buried by a shell in the communication trench, together with his orderly." "He was killed at the end of August, near Delville Wood. His runner, George Keeling, told witness Capt. Keesey had been buried by a shell during the bombardment and that his body had been recovered." "He was over 'D' Company was a good Captain, his men spoke well of him. He was killed on the right of Delville Wood with his batman; they were together in a small dugout." "At Delville Wood, in the latter end of August, he left us, telling us to take cover, and went over towards 20th Division through an unoccupied trench, and he did not return." "He was killed on the right of Delville Wood towards the end of August. He went along the trench with an orderly during a heavy bombardment in the afternoon of the day he was killed. We did not see him again. Men of the 7th Battalion relieved us there. They found his body the next day." "About 24th August, after we had been fighting in Delville Wood, I went to see a friend of mine in 'D' Company. While I was there, information was received that Capt. Keesey had been killed by a shell dropping near him. His body was afterwards found in our advanced trenches." "At Delville Wood on 18th August, he was killed by a shell and his body was buried by KRRC very near to place where he fell." "He was buried by a shell in our trenches just before Delville Wood. His body was recovered and buried by 7/KRRC out of Delville Wood with his servant and another man." "I knew Capt. Keesey, he was in charge of 'D' Company at Delville Wood at the end of August or beginning of September, and was killed in a bit of trench in the wood." Howard is now buried in Serre Road Cemetery No. 2. He had married Violet Swinglehurst in August 1913, and a son, who would die in World War Two, was born two years later. As well as the memorial in Crowthorne, his name is listed at Wellington College, and at Natland, Cumbria, where a memorial window was added in 1946, to the memory of the father and son.

RUPERT A. KETTLE

Rupert Arthur Kettle was born at Fleetwood, Lancashire in 1895, and baptised there on 2nd June. His father, a Lieutenant in the South Staffordshire Regiment, died in India in 1906 at the age of 37, and his mother married Cecil Lavie, a schoolmaster at Wellington College, three years later. Rupert was educated at Lambrook School, Winkfield, Wellington College (his name appears on the Roll of Honour at both schools), and the Royal Military Academy at Sandhurst from 1912 to 1914, obtaining a commission in the 3rd (King's Own) Hussars five days after the outbreak of war. The Hussars were stationed at Shorncliffe Camp near Folkestone, Kent, and landed at Rouen on 15th August; Rupert followed at the end of October, arriving in the midst of the First Battle of Ypres. A few days earlier, the 3rd Hussars had been heavily involved, suffering numerous casualties as the Germans repeatedly attempted to break through the line. During the early months of 1915, the Hussars moved continuously between various towns and villages located to the west of Bailleul, performing various duties. On 22nd April, the Second Battle of Ypres commenced with the Germans discharging chlorine gas in the areas between Pilckem and Langemarck in an attempt to seize strategically important high ground. This act, the first use of poison gas in the Great War, caused panic and heavy casualties to the Algerian and French

Divisions holding this part of the front line. The French abandoned their positions, resulting in a large gap of over four miles on the left flank of the 1st Canadian Division. The line was temporarily held, even when the defenders had no form of protection against the effects of the gas, but, due to the sheer weight of the enemy's attack, St. Julian was abandoned and a subsequent retirement was ordered, followed by a strategic withdrawal to a new defensive line. On 29th April, the Hussars moved to positions located near St. Julian which they occupied for just over a week, finally being withdrawn on 7th May to Rue Pruvost. At the end of the month, the Hussars were withdrawn from the Salient to billets located at Wallon-Cappel, west of Hazebrouck. The remainder of 1915 would see further movement in reserve positions to the west of Bethune, with the winter months being spent in billets at Bayenghem, northwest of St Omer. For several months, they performed the mundane task of providing labour. On 15th April 1916, the Hussars moved closer to Boulogne, and in early June spent a few days on the channel coast at the towns of Ambleteuse and Audresselles, before moving once again back to various towns and villages in the area around Hazebrouck and Bailleul. On 16th August, they moved to Morval, north of Combles. It had been anticipated that if the infantry succeeded in capturing the line from Combles to Gueudecourt in the north, the cavalry, who were held in reserve, could then push through to capture the high ground east of Bapaume. Despite the capture of areas of the line to the north, Combles was not to fall until 26th September, and any projected advance by the cavalry did not materialize. Consequently, during the month spent on the Somme, no offensive operations were mounted by the Hussars, who remained on routine labour duties. They were not involved in any major actions in 1916, but in the early months of the following year, the German Army began a gradual retirement to the Hindenburg Line. An Allied attack, aimed at breaking through the line in snowstorms in April, failed, and they were also involved in the Cambrai Operations in the autumn. The Hussars had been training in March 1918, when news arrived that an attack was expected on the 3rd Corps at any time. At 4:30am on the 21st, the enemy launched a heavy bombardment. As the day wore on, the retirement of British infantry units began. The 3rd Hussars, now fighting as a dismounted unit, were involved, although with only one man wounded on the first day. Rupert led a mounted Troop from the 3rd Hussars on the 23rd, which formed part of a defensive flank to the south of Ham, the enemy having entered it during the early morning. The War Diary records, with a somewhat melancholy tone, that later in the day, "all the band instruments of the Regiment had to be left at Grandru, owing to lack of transport, and *they* subsequently fell into the hands of the Germans." Things were becoming more critical on the 24th, as the enemy worked around both flanks, where the French had retired, passing through surrounding woodland. Although outnumbered, and coming under machine gun fire from the direction of Golancourt, the brigade charged the enemy with swords drawn. Although casualties to the enemy were heavy, it cost the brigade dearly, with about fifty per cent casualties being sustained to a force that initially numbered about 150 men. The mounted Troop of 3rd Hussars, under the command of Lieutenant Kettle, was still operating in the field on the 25th. The remnants of the fighting forces were reorganised into a Composite Regiment under a single commander. Along the whole length of the battle front, worrying gaps had developed between French and British units; if German forces could exploit these gaps, the road to Paris would be open. A snowstorm developed the next day. The troops marched towards Dive-le-Franc, southwest of Noyon, with orders to seize Mont Porquericourt to the northwest, but the Germans were already on the hill by the time they arrived. Reports of a gap in the British line proved false, but they continued to fall back, coming under fire from the advancing troops. By the end of the day, Rupert was recorded as missing. His body was later found, and he was buried in Noyon New British Cemetery. But information was not reaching the War Office, as six months after his death, the following letter was written: "Wounded and missing 26.3.18. No further official report has been received. Enquiries through the Netherland Legation have been without result. In view of the lapse of time since anything has been heard of this Officer, his name is put forward for presumption of death. The mother of this Officer wrote that she had heard from the German Red Cross that her son was dead, but unfortunately the letter seems to have been passed to accounts for regarding a matter of disposal of disc. No official report has yet come to hand." However, two months earlier, a report from the Geneva Red Cross read, "Fallen disc forwarded by Intelligence Officer. No further details." Executors of Rupert's will wrote in February 1919 to the authorities: "Shot while on patrol duty on or about 23rd or 24th March, somewhere near La Fere or St Quentin (require death certificate)," but received the response, "Death not officially accepted so no death certificate can be issued." It would be a further six months before his affairs could finally be settled.

VICTOR R. KIBBEY

The late Drummer V. R. KIBBEY, Grenadier Guards, Terlings Park, Harlow, Essex.—Killed in action.

Victor Reginald Kibbey was born in 1887 in London at Pimlico. He was one of six brothers, an elder sister dying as a small child. His father served as a Private in the Grenadier Guards until 1890, completing twenty-one years of service, including short spells in Egypt and Cyprus. However, most of his time was spent at home, with Victor's siblings being born in Bristol, Pontefract, Ireland and Windsor. He then worked for a brief spell as an attendant at Caterham Lunatic Asylum, one of the first institutions erected by the Metropolitan Asylums Board, set up in 1867, to administer care for certain categories of the sick poor in metropolitan London. Victor's mother also worked, as a laundress, and the family moved to Chepstow around the turn of the century, to run their own laundry business. After leaving school, Victor returned to London to join the 1st Battalion, Grenadier Guards as a drummer boy. He married Clementina Smith in 1909, who also worked as a laundress with her mother in Owlsmoor, with a son being born a few months later. Victor was in Wellington Barracks, London, when the 1911 census was taken, and the battalion were still in England when war broke out, landing at Zeebrugge on 7th October. However, Victor did not join them, until May the following year, missing the fighting at Ypres in 1914, when the battalion suffered heavy losses, and the Battle of Neuve Chapelle in March and April. The battalion also fought at Aubers and Festubert just after he arrived, the Battle of Loos in the autumn, and two phases of the Battle of the Somme in 1916. The Regimental history recorded, "It was not until the beginning of September that the Guards Division arrived in the Somme area, so it was not present at the first two phases of the battle. But in the attacks of September 15th and 25th, the men covered themselves with glory; their discipline and coolness under fire were magnificent, and they captured lines which had up to then been considered impregnable." On the latter date, at Zero hour (12:35pm), the 2nd Battalion, Scots Guards and 4th Battalion, Grenadier Guards, attacked, and captured the first and second objectives within two hours. Victor's battalion then came forward, and captured the third objective, taking less than an hour to do so. The battalion on the left, having been held up, they had to form a defensive flank on that side, but held the captured ground. The ten days of fighting had cost a total of around six hundred casualties in the 1st Battalion, Grenadier Guards alone. Victor was one of more than eighty whose bodies were never found, and his name is listed on the Thiepval Memorial.

FRANK LANGLEY

Jesse Frank Langley, known as Frank, was born in Crowthorne towards the end of 1891. He was the youngest of seven children, one of whom died in infancy. His father worked as a carter, and Frank worked with him after leaving school. He joined under the Derby Scheme, attesting at Reading, and initially joined the Berkshire Yeomanry, before transferring to the 2nd Battalion, Royal Berkshire Regiment. It is not known when Frank went to France, although it was probably in 1916. The War Diary records a draft arriving on 16th May 1916, another on 15th July; if Frank was with the former, he would have taken part on the first day of the Battle of the Somme when the battalion has as their objective the capture the village of Ovillers, but were met with very heavy rifle and machine gun fire as they left the trenches, and suffered well over four hundred casualties. The winter of 1916/17 was exceptionally cold with many cases of frostbite among the men. A large attack had been planned for 4th March, and the battalion had been practising on a model while in rest billets the week before. The first objective was Pallas Trench near the village of Bouchavesnes, which was captured without too much resistance. The second wave pushed on towards Fritz Trench, which ran parallel to it, but it had been so damaged by the bombardment from the British artillery that they failed to recognise it in the darkness and carried on Bremen Trench, but retreated when they realised their error. The Berkshires held the two captured trenches despite several counter-attacks, but were heavily bombarded in Pallas Trench at 4pm and lost many men. Twelve hours later, the Germans recaptured part of Fritz Trench, and the remainder of the battalion were occupying a new trench, dug between the two, when they were relieved the following night. Frank was killed during the German counter-attack; his body was never recovered, and his name is listed on the Thiepval Memorial.

Pte. A. J. LOVICK, of Crowthorne.— Wounded and mentioned in despatches.

ARCHIE J. LOVICK

Archibald James Lovick was born at Crowthorne in 1895, and baptised 16th June. He was one of six children, including a pair of younger twins. His father ran the Crowthorne Inn in the High Street, and also supplied horses, carriages and drivers for hire. Archie moved to Fulham after leaving school, to take up an engineering apprenticeship, before becoming a motor driver. He volunteered for service a month after war was declared, one of sixteen from the village who signed up that month, attesting at Camberley, and joined the 6th Battalion, Royal West Surrey Regiment. Although the battalion went to France at the end of May 1915, Archie remained in England until September the following year, possibly his driving skills were wanted at home. The War Diary records a draft of 169 men arriving on 1st October, which presumably included Archie. In the next four days in the trenches, eight men from the battalion were killed, and almost fifty wounded, a sobering start for any new recruit. There are several references to the wet weather in November, which caused parts of the trenches to collapse (and the need for rebuilding them), and for training being cancelled. They were in billets at Grand Rullecourt for Christmas and the start of 1917, before moving to Arras in lorries, and going into the trenches again in the middle of January. Two small parties of Germans were seen approaching in the early hours of 3rd February, and although they entered the sap head, they were driven out again. The battalion suffered one man missing, but only his steel helmet was found. On 9th April, they successfully attacked the German trenches and gaining ground, but with over a hundred casualties. A few days later, Archie left France with a gunshot wound to his left arm, which occurred during this attack. He was treated at No.18 General Hospital near Etaples, before being shipped back to England to Bradford War Hospital. It was probably at this time that his heart condition was first diagnosed, as rather than being sent back to France, he remained in England with the 301st Company of the Labour Corps, a Mechanical Transport Company. On 3rd October, he was interviewed at Thetford, Norfolk. The subsequent report records, "He states that he never knew he had heart trouble until after enlistment. This had no hospital treatment. He had a history of measles in childhood. He was in *the* signal section for some time, and did a good deal of cycling. His heart, he says, has been worse since. He states that he suffers small attacks of shortness of breath and giddiness." The conclusion was that his condition was caused by "Measles in childhood *and* aggravated by military service. Heart is slightly dilated, and he is unfit for any military duties." He was reckoned to be permanently incapacitated by forty per cent. He was described as being 5'6" tall, with grey eyes, dark hair and a fresh complexion; his military character had been exemplary, and he had been awarded the Military Medal. Two months later, he was discharged at Nottingham, and returned home to his parents at Crowthorne, where he died on 25th February 1919. He is buried just to the southwest of the church. The Reading Mercury of 8th March 1919 contains a report of the burial: "Much sympathy is felt for Mr and Mrs Charles Lovick in the death of their third son Archibald James at the early age of 23 years. He was one of the Crow's Nest (a group of sixteen youths who all joined together early in September 1914). He joined the Queen's Royal West Surreys, and was wounded at the Battle of Arras in April 1917, and was awarded the Military Medal."

The late Pte. HARRY LOVICK, Pinewood Avenue, Crowthorne.—Died of wounds.

HENRY LOVICK

Henry Lovick was born at Crowthorne in 1883, and baptised 19th June. He came from a family of seven children, three of whom had died in infancy, and was Archie's cousin. His father, a domestic gardener, died in 1908, and Henry followed a similar profession, and had married by 1911. Initially he joined the Berkshire Yeomanry, probably under the Derby Scheme, attesting at Wokingham, and was mobilised at the end of May 1916, but does not appear to have served overseas with them. He was later transferred to the 2/4th Battalion, Oxford and Bucks Light Infantry, a Territorial Battalion based at Parkhouse Camp on Salisbury Plain, before going to France. Before he got there, the battalion had been involved at the Battle of Fromelles, which was an unmitigated disaster for the Division, and they were not used again for the remainder of 1916, other than for holding trench lines. The following year, the Division was involved in operations on the Ancre, and captured Chaulnes and Bapaume in March as the Germans retreated to the Hindenberg Line. In August, they took part in the Battle of Langemarck, a phase of the Third Battle of Ypres, where both sides were hampered by heavy conditions underfoot from the rain that summer. The British revised their methods and main offensive effort, and gained three big successes in September and October. The 2/4th Oxfords were specially selected for an attack on Hill 35 on 9th September, a German stronghold that had already repulsed six attacks. The attack was postponed by 24 hours as the preceding day's bombardment from howitzers could not take place due to mist. The attack was to be launched from shell holes in No Man's Land, and the men were in place from dawn, sixteen hours ahead of Zero, and were to suffer from 'shorts' from the British artillery, as well as a gas attack from our own lines, believing them to be the enemy (the Company Commander's outrage at this mistake is all too evident in the Regimental History, although he excuses the artillery's incorrect range, putting it down to worn barrels of the guns). The day was hot and described thus: "The sun, which had displaced a morning mist, struck down with unrelenting rays till shrapnel helmets grew hot as oven-doors. Bluebottles (for had not six attempts failed to take the hill?) buzzed busily. The heat, our salt rations, the mud below, the brazen sky above, and the suspense of waiting for the particular minute of attack, vied for supremacy in the emotions." A creeping barrage started at 4pm, but the men were soon in trouble. "Our progress, at only a few dozen yards a minute, gave the Germans in their pill-boxes ample time to get their machine guns going, while correspondingly the barrage passed away from our advance in its successive lifts. Heavy firing commenced to enfilade our ranks. Long before the objective was approached, our enemies, who in some cases left the pill-boxes and manned positions outside, were masters of the situation. The seventh attempt had failed to struggle up the slopes of Hill 35." The battalion suffered over 270 casualties including Henry, who was wounded. He died a week later in one of the two hospitals adjacent to Abbeville Community Cemetery Extension, where he is buried.

LESLIE G. MARTIN

The late Pte. LESLIE MARTIN, Crowthorne.—Killed in action.

Leslie Gilbert Martin was born in 1898, at Westbury-on-Trym, northwest of Bristol. He was one of seven children, an eighth dying in infancy. Within two years, the family had moved to Crowthorne, where his parents ran a successful laundry business employing four girls, part of Wellington College. Although only seventeen years old, Leslie volunteered for service when war broke out, attesting at Camberley, and joined the 7th Battalion, Royal West Surrey Regiment. He may have been inspired by his elder brother Frederick, already a trumpeter with the Royal Field Artillery at the age of eighteen, and stationed in India in 1911. Leslie's battalion left Southampton for Le Havre on 26th July 1915, consisting of 971 men (all but about two hundred being privates), 31 horses, 42 mules, and three Lewis guns. Two of the companies were in the front trenches at Dernancourt on the 9th of the following month, receiving instruction in the art of trench warfare, with the other two companies replacing them four days later. In September, the Germans exploded a small mine close to the trench occupied by the battalion, and a report that a shelter had fallen in, burying several men was received at headquarters, Two officers were sent to assess the situation, but a bomb from a shell-mortar fell into the trench just as they arrived, killing both. "The report as to the shelter was much exaggerated," states the War Diary. Other than this, the battalion followed the routine, in and out of trenches, forming working parties, or resting in billets. There are several reports of mines being exploded by both sides, and seven men, attached to 55 Brigade Mining Section, were killed in October by the explosion of a German one. Frost and heavy rain had made conditions miserable by December, and thigh gumboots were worn by men in the trenches. They were in the front line on Christmas Day, with some artillery activity by both sides. The entry for 1st March, just after a thaw set in, records, "the health of the Battalion is very good in spite of very bad weather." Anything that broke the day-to-day tedium was recorded. Private Frederick Holgate was accidentally drowned on 5th May while washing in the river; vellum certificates were given to eight men, "Mentioned in Despatches for conspicuous and gallant conduct in the field" were awarded three days later.

From 22nd June, the German position was incessantly bombarded. The entry for 1st July looks quite bland. "At 7:30am, the Battalion assaulted the German front trenches on a front of about four hundred yards. After twelve hours' fighting, the objective, west of Montauban, was achieved and consolidated on a front of about 260 yards. Other ranks killed 174, wounded 284, missing 56." One of those killed was eighteen year old Leslie Gilbert Martin, son of Mr and Mrs A. B. Martin, of Wellington College, Berkshire. He is buried in Dantzig Alley British Cemetery, Mametz.

R. E. MARTIN

Richard Edward Martin was born at Yorktown in 1889. His father had served in the army for nearly twenty years, including spells in India and Afghanistan, before being invalided out with chronic rheumatism. He then worked for a time as a servant at the Royal Military College, and as a bricklayer, before the 1911 census records him as being unable to work. He fathered thirteen children, but only one survived from his days in India, Richard being one of six born back in England. Richard worked as a labourer after leaving school, before volunteering for service, attesting at Camberley, and joining the 6th Battalion, Dorsetshire Regiment. The battalion went to France in July 1915, but were not involved in any major actions before Richard was transferred to the 2nd Battalion, Hampshire Regiment, which had been fighting at Gallipoli before arriving in France in March the following year. The new unit took part in the Battle of the Somme in July, and by October were faced with a line of defences at Transloy Ridges. They had already attacked near Guidecourt on 12th October, suffering some 150 casualties in three days, followed by two days in support. On the evening of the 17th, they moved up again, to attack Grease Trench. Despite heavy fire, the two attacking battalions kept close to the barrage, and were quickly into the trench, overpowering its defenders, and repulsed all efforts to dislodge them. Despite heavy shelling and atrocious weather, they held it, the Regimental History calling it "among the 2nd Hampshire's most notable achievements." Richard's was one of 31 lives lost in its capture; his body was never found, and his name is listed on the Thiepval Memorial.

JAMES W. MAY

James William May was born at Owlsmoor in 1898, and baptised in Crowthorne Church on 29th May. He was one of eight children, one of whom died in infancy. His father, himself the son of a soldier and born in Burma, had also spent twelve years in the army, before working as a servant at the Royal Military College. James was only sixteen years old when war broke out, but volunteered immediately, lied about his age when attesting at Winchester, and was accepted into the 3rd Battalion, Hampshire Regiment, a depot/training unit. This battalion moved to Parkhurst, Isle of Wight, and to Gosport the following January for duty with the Portsmouth Garrison. James was transferred to the 2nd Battalion, who had left England for Gallipoli at the end of March, and was part of a draft that arrived in mid June. The Regimental History describes the action on the day James died. "In early August, after five days in the reserve line, the 88th Brigade took over the right sub-section of the Divisional line, east of Gully Ravine, in readiness for another attempt on the old objectives. The Turkish position had been considerably strengthened since the last attack and the Hampshires had the nastiest piece of the work, for their left had to tackle a formidable redoubt, while their right and centre had nearly three hundred yards of open ground to cross. The assaulting troops were in position at 8am on the 6th, but had to wait for six hours before the bombardment started. At 3:50pm, the infantry went forward, the Hampshire men attacking in four waves. A low crest of fifty yards was crossed almost without loss, but then machine guns opened up on all sides and mowed the attackers down wholesale before many of them had got any way across No Man's Land. The Hampshires suffered terribly, and with too few to maintain their foothold, they were overcome by numbers." James is one of many killed that day, listed on the Helles Memorial. The Regimental History called it "the worst day in the whole story of Cape Helles."

HAROLD V. MCEUNE

Harold Vernon McEune was born 15th June 1899 at Dover, and was one of seven children. His father was an army man, serving with the Mounted Military Police in the Boer War, with Harold's elder siblings being born at Farnham, Ash Vale, Aldershot and Farnborough. By 1904, his father had left the army, and the family moved to Owlsmoor for him to work as a groom at the Royal Military College, Sandhurst. Harold volunteered for service in late October 1915, despite being only sixteen years old, attesting at Camberley, and joined the Royal Army Medical Corps, stating his occupation as a footman. No doubt he saw this as his last chance to become a solider; with the looming introduction of the Derby Scheme, it would be another two years before he was eligible to fight overseas. He was barely five feet tall, weighed just under seven and a half stone, with blue eyes, brown hair, a fresh complexion, and had a scar over his left eyebrow. During his training, doubts were cast over his true age, and a letter was sent to his parents, asking for a copy of his birth certificate. Its receipt confirmed that Harold was under-age, and an internal military letter to the Officer in charge of South Camp, Ripon, dated 15th May 1916, read, "Please note that as this man, according to Birth Certificate, is under 17 years of age, his Discharge may be proceeded with." Harold was discharged, with a good reference, but as he had completed several months of training, was transferred to the 107th Provisional Battalion, based at Frinton, Essex, consisting of young soldiers and those whose medical condition precluded overseas service. On 1st January 1917, in a reorganisation, this became the 31st Battalion, County of London Battalion, and after reaching the requisite age, he was transferred to the 9th Battalion, and finally went to France. In the final year of the war, the battalion took part in both Battles of the Somme, involved in the fighting during March, April and the end of August. On 21st September, they marched to assembly positions east of Epehy, and were in position by 5am. Forty minutes later, under cover of an artillery barrage, the battalion attacked, but came under very heavy machine gun fire and was unable to advance beyond its first objective, Mule Trench. At 1pm, under cover of a very weak barrage, they again tried to push forward, but again, very heavy machine gun fire was opened, and no progress could be made. There were more than 280 casualties, Harold being one of those killed, and is buried in Epehy Wood Farm Cemetery, Epehy.

T. WILLIAM MOREN

Thomas William Moren, known by his second name, was born in 1893, probably in Owlsmoor as he was baptised in Crowthorne Church on 12th March. He was one of nine children. His father was a bricklayer, working away from home in Essex when the 1911 census was taken. William, by now, was in the army, having attested at Guildford earlier in the year, and was a member of the 4th Battalion, Rifle Brigade, based at Winchester. The battalion were at Dagshai, in India, when war broke out, and sailed from Bombay in October, arriving at Devonport on 18th November. From there, they made their way to Magdalen Hill Camp at Winchester, and a month later landed at Le Havre. The following year, they were involved in the Action of St. Eloi in March, a battle to recapture 'The Mound,' which was lost the previous day during the Battle of Neuve Chapelle, and the Second Battle of Ypres. At the beginning of May, after being relieved in the line, they made their way to Sanctuary Wood, where they spent the next two days digging trenches. The battalion then moved to Hooge to take over a new front-line system while the 27th Division evacuated the Polygon Wood salient. The Germans were seen following the next day, many of them wearing plundered British greatcoats. This misled the battalion into withholding fire, thinking they were British soldiers, until the reality of the situation was realised. It was now apparent that the greater part of the new position was commanded from the ground that had been given up. As an officer of the Battalion wrote, "The position of the companies for the next two days was not pleasant." The enemy hurried up his artillery and machine guns to little more than point-blank range. A sustained bombardment, reinforced by gas shells and heavy machine gun fire, to which for lack of ammunition, there could be little or no reply from the Royal Artillery, was rained upon the new line. In two days, the 4th Battalion lost nearly 150 men killed and more than two hundred wounded. On the 8th, the Battalion were in dug-outs behind Bellewaarde Lake, waiting to relieve the Princess Patricia's (Canadian Light Infantry). Early next morning, a bombardment began that was to be the prelude a general attack. By 10am, the Canadians were in dire straits, and two companies were sent to help them. The line on the left had been broken, and the bombardment was severe. By 11:30am, the enemy was working forward, but was stopped by the 4th Battalion's machine guns. Another attempt to advance was stopped, with 'D' Company meeting and breaking three separate attacks with rifle fire. They were relieved that night and marched back, with four men left from the original sixty. William was killed during the day's fighting; his body was never recovered, and his name is listed on the Ypres (Menin Gate) Memorial.

ROBERT W. NUNN

The late First Class Stoker ROBERT NUNN.—Killed through ship striking a mine.

Robert William Nunn was born on 18th January 1881 at King's Cross, north London, a few weeks after his parents' marriage, the eldest of five children. His father drove a horse-drawn vehicle, making deliveries and collection of goods for a railway company, but was out of work in 1911. After leaving school, Robert worked as a labourer until he joined the Royal Navy on 2nd February 1899, signing on for twelve years. He was 5'3" tall, with blue eyes, brown hair, a fresh complexion, and a scar on the right side of his face. Although the 1901 census records him as a sailor, his naval rank was stoker, working below decks to keep the engines running. During his time in the navy, he went to China, as well as patrolling in the English Channel and the Mediterranean. While on one of his stays on shore, he married Edith Wilkinson, and they had four children. Robert's naval service came to an end early in 1911, and he took a temporary job in a local pub, before the family moved to Crowthorne. All men who had served, whether in the army or navy, were placed on the reserve list after their term finished, from which they could be recalled if war broke out. In Robert's case, this was for six years, so he was recalled in August 1914, and sailed on HMS 'Birmingham'. On his first day on board, the 'Birmingham' spotted a U-boat on the surface in heavy fog, attempting repairs. The 'Birmingham' fired on her, missed the target, but rammed the U-boat, slicing it in two. It sank with all hands on board, the first U-boat to be lost in the war. She also took part in the Battle of Heligoland later the same month, and sank two German merchant ships that year. She took part in the Battle of Dogger Bank in January 1915, and the Battle of Jutland in the following year, where she sustained damage. Robert left the 'Birmingham' in September 1916, and then served on a series of ships patrolling the east coast of England from the River Humber. On 27th March 1918, the destroyers 'Exe', 'Kale' and 'Waveney' were sailing from the Humber to Portsmouth when, off the Suffolk coast, the trio steered six miles to the east of the swept channel into a British minefield. Both the 'Exe' and 'Kale' hit mines; the 'Exe' survived, but the 'Kale' was not so fortunate and sank. Robert was one of several men killed by the explosion; his name is listed on the screen wall at Islington Cemetery and Crematorium. There is also a note on his Navy service record to the effect: "If this man dies or is discharged ashore … Broadmoor Criminal Lunatic Asylum … to be informed," so he must have been working there, prior to being recalled from the reserve.

Pte. A. E. PARKER, King's Own Yorks L.I., son of Mr. and Mrs. Parker, Broadmoor Gas Works.—Wounded and frostbitten.

ALBERT E. PARKER

Albert Vernon Edward Parker, known as Edward, was born at Little Sandhurst in 1884. He was one of six children, one of whom died in infancy. His father drove a horse and cart, making deliveries, but then got a job at Broadmoor as a gas stoker, and the family moved to Crowthorne. Edward worked as a general labourer after leaving school, before joining the Coldstream Guards, attesting at Reading in 1899, adding three years to his age to do so. He was 5'7" tall, weighed nine and a half stone, with brown eyes, brown hair, and a fresh complexion. He signed on for three years, during which time he spent nine months overseas in South Africa. There is a veiled reference to a less than perfect disciplinary record, with the phrase "latterly good" written on his Service Record when he was discharged. By 1911, he was living just outside Doncaster, Yorkshire, working above ground at a coal colliery. At the outbreak of war, he joined the 2nd Battalion, Yorkshire Light Infantry, attesting at Pontefract, joining them in France at the start of October 1914, a couple of months after they had first arrived there. Edward took part in the First Battle of Ypres, as well as the Second, beginning in April the following year. The Reading Mercury reported he had suffered from frostbite as well as being wounded, but without supplying any more details. On 1st September 1915, the battalion went into the trenches at Carnoy, and stayed there until the 9th. They then went into billets at Bray and supplied digging parties. On the 14th, a German mine exploded in the vicinity of a mining gallery where Albert was working. He was overcome by its poisonous fumes before being able to escape, and although a Second Lieutenant from the South Staffordshire Regiment dashed in to rescue him, he too was overcome by the gas, and both men died. They are both buried in Albert Communal Cemetery Extension.

E. PARKER

George Edward Parker was born at Crowthorne in 1893, and baptised 19th March. A cousin of Albert, he had an elder brother, but his mother died when George was eleven years old. His father, a general labourer, remarried in 1909, and George soon gained a half-sister. After leaving school, he worked with the cattle on a local farm, before becoming a carter. The records have become confused as there was also a George Edward Parker, living in Burghfield, who served with the Machine Gun Corps, and who died within a fortnight of the Crowthorne man. But the local George Edward only ever served in England with the Army Service Corps. He was a little over 5'1" tall, with grey eyes and brown hair, when he attested at Wokingham on 19th July 1915, and joined the 54th Remount Squadron at Arborfield. Each Remount Squadron (there were four in the country) generally consisted of around two hundred men, responsible for obtaining and training five hundred horses at a time for use by the Army. Each horse took between two and three weeks to train, after which time they were sent to France No doubt his lack of height, and experience with horses, contributed to his posting. He later transferred to the Remount Depot at Shirehampton near Bristol, close to where horses from abroad arrived on ships docking at Avonmouth on the Bristol Channel. On 3rd January 1917, George was admitted to the Southern General Hospital at Bristol, having fractured his left kneecap in an accident. He was operated on, and the kneecap wired two days later, and was discharged at the end of March. A few weeks later, the wire was removed, but he was left with a knee that was frequently painful when walking, and he was often unable to flex the joint at all. As this left him unfit for military service, he was discharged on 5th September that year, and died in Staffordshire on 15th November 1918. He is buried in Crowthorne churchyard, just to the southwest of the church.

ARTHUR PEARCE

Arthur Pearce was born at Grazeley, just south of Reading, in 1893. He was one of seven children, all born in different places as his father, a coachman, moved between jobs until the family settled in Crowthorne in 1901. Arthur worked as an errand boy for a general draper after leaving school, and volunteered for service, attesting at Camberley, and joined the 7th Battalion, Royal West Surrey Regiment. His initial training was carried out in and around Colchester before moving to Salisbury Plain in May 1915, with an inspection by the King the next month. Embarkation for France began on 24th July, with William's draft arriving three days later. There was no major action for the battalion until the Battle of the Somme the following year. They were based near Montauban, a village in German hands, which it was their objective to capture. The days preceding the attack, in which the enemy positions were relentlessly bombarded, had mixed effects. In front of the West Surrey's, it was pretty effective; the enemy trenches were badly damaged and lightly held, and the Royal Flying Corps reported large explosions at the enemy dumps. Just before 7:30am on 1st July, two mines, laid by one of the Royal Engineer Tunnelling Companies were blown; they were the signals for the lead units to advance from the British front trenches. Units in the centre were held up by fire from a crater field in No Man's Land, the results of mine warfare in the area in May. The enemy had occupied the craters and had built some strong points which survived the bombardment. Undamaged machine guns fired from these when the battalion began to advance. Gradually, as the day wore on, the enemy were driven back and the pressure on the battalion eased, but it was not until 5.15pm that Montauban Alley was taken. The enemy artillery, having been badly damaged in this area, did not greatly interfere with the work of evacuation of wounded, bringing up of supplies and consolidation of the ground won, which now began in earnest. However, enemy shellfire falling on the area intensified and stayed heavy, causing many casualties and making relief and re-supply very problematic. They were relieved the following day. On the 11th, they were in the front line again, northwest of Maricourt. Two days later, they were ordered to attack the northern portion of Trones Wood, an area with which they were not familiar. The leading Company moved forward from Dublin Trench at 5:30pm. The battalion were greatly impeded by a relief moving up into Longueval Alley at the same time. At 8pm, they assaulted Trones Wood from northern extremity over a front of 750 yards. Men from another battalion, who were to assist in the assault, became disorganised owing to casualties from shell fire when moving up to the attack, and only about one and a half platoons arrived in time to partake in the assault. The advance was met by very heavy rifle, machine gun and shell fire, and checked. At 8:50pm, a message was received that northern portion of Trones Wood would be re-bombarded, and that the attack was not to be pressed if success seemed unlikely. At 9pm, the remaining men reorganised for defence of Longueval Alley, and some three hours later, instructions were received that the battalion might withdraw to the German old front line position if Longueval Alley was sufficiently held, which they did a couple of hours later. The attack had cost over two hundred casualties. Initially reported missing, Arthur was later confirmed killed, and is buried in Delville Wood Cemetery, Longueval.

Pte. F. PEARCE.—Wounded. He was the first in the Crowthorne " nest " to fall.

FREDERICK PEARCE

Frederick Pearce, known as Fred, was one of Arthur's two elder brothers, born at Calcot in 1890. After leaving school, he worked as a vanman, making deliveries in a horse-drawn van. Like his brother, he also volunteered for service, attesting at Camberley, and joined the 7th Battalion, Royal West Surrey Regiment, but was later transferred to the 10th Battalion. Both Fred and Arthur arrived in France together, but it is not known when Fred transferred; the 10th Battalion's War Diary, a thorough and well-kept document, makes no mention of men arriving. On 24th February 1917, the 10th Battalion took part in a raid on enemy lines at Hollandscheschuur Salient. Although an officer and more than fifty other Germans were taken prisoner, the operation cost over one hundred British casualties. Fred was one of 26 men killed, and is buried in Klein-Veerstraat British Cemetery.

LAUMANN S. W. PEARSON

Laumann (also spelt Laumarin in some records) Saxe William Pearson was born on 21st May 1892 at Golden Hill, on the edge of Stoke-on-Trent, Staffordshire. He came from a small family, only having a younger sister, born in central London. The children grew up in South London, with Laumann's father working as an accountant, but he also had links with Crowthorne, with cousins in the village (including Frederick Deane, also listed on the War Memorial). After school, Laumann worked as a stock jobber's clerk, recording the sale and purchase of stocks and shares. At the outbreak of war, he volunteered for service, attesting on 26th August 1914, and joined the 16th Battalion, London Regiment, going to France in the following January, two months after the first men from the battalion. On 17th February, he sustained a gunshot wound to the shoulder, and returned to England for treatment. His Service Record shows a typical route taken for dealing with serious injuries; 19th Field Ambulance on the 17th, No. 2 Clearing

Hospital, Bailleul, on the 18th, No. 14 General Hospital, Wimereux, on the 19th, and the hospital ship 'St Andrew' from Boulogne, a week later. The wound had healed by the end of March, and in July he was passed fit to return to service. While at Summerdown Convalescent Camp, Eastbourne, he applied for a commission. The Camp had opened in May, so Laumann was probably one of its first patients. Being almost six feet tall, he had a commanding presence, and was accepted, and promoted to Second Lieutenant in the 13th Battalion, Essex Regiment, passing to a School of Instruction in Chelmsford in September, before returning to France. Later, he was attached to the 10th Battalion, and fought with them in the Battle of the Somme. On 16th July, the battalion were at Billon Wood, with an attack on Delville Wood planned for the following day. It rained all the day, and the attack was postponed by twenty-four hours, and then put back again, as the conditions underfoot were too bad. Finally, at 3:30am on the 19th, they formed up in the rendezvous area, to the right of the Montuaban to Longueval road. Just over two hours later, they moved off, but immediately began to slow down and then stop; the road was badly congested, with many dead bodies lying in the way, and the Brigade was forced to move along it in single file. The War Diary notes, at 7am, "From the outset, nothing went according to the program, and it is impossible to give a full account of everything that happened." The 8th Battalion, Norfolk Regiment led the attack fifteen minutes later, without waiting for a further barrage. By 8:30am, they had entered Delville Wood but were held up by machine gun fire, delaying the Essex men from advancing to their forming-up position. A fresh barrage was put down on the wood at 9am, but at 10:30am, the Norfolks reported they were still held up, and asked for assistance; two platoons of No. 1 Company were sent up to help. By 12:30pm, two companies were in the wood, with a third moving up into position, but touch had not been made with the units on either flank; this was finally established at 3pm. Half an hour later, the Essex reported they had made three efforts to move forward from the Princes Street line, but these had been stopped by our own heavy artillery and enemy machine gun fire. Ten minutes later, a report was made to Brigade Headquarters that casualties to the Essex were very heavy, and that repeated applications for Stokes Guns had produced no result. At 5:10pm, orders were finally received to consolidate the line, and hold on for the night. Enemy machine guns continued to be very active through the hours of darkness. Laumann was killed during the day's fighting; his body was never recovered, and his name is listed on the Thiepval Memorial. After the war, his widowed mother was living in Crowthorne; Laumann's name is listed on both the local memorial, and on the Stock Exchange memorial in London, unveiled in 1922.

BENJAMIN PESCOD

Benjamin Pescod was born on 30th October 1887 at Brighton. He was the youngest survivor of nine children, a younger sister dying at the age of three. His father had run a hotel or restaurant business in Tunbridge Wells, but by 1891 was working as a travelling gas engineer. In 1901, Benjamin's mother was running a boarding house in Hove as his father's mind was "affected through illness," and he died later the same year. Unlike one of his brothers, who was a chorister at Arundel Cathedral, Benjamin worked as a waiter after leaving school, until he joined the Navy in 1904 as an officer's steward. He was just over 5'1" tall, with fair hair, blue eyes, and a fair complexion, and would later get tattoos on his right arm. After his initial training at Portsmouth, he served on several ships including the HMS 'King Edward', the Atlantic Fleet flagship, HMS 'Thunderer', the last (and largest) warship ever built on the

River Thames, and HMS 'Enchantress', the ship of the Lord Commissioners in peacetime. She was used by Winston Churchill, then Lord of the Admiralty, while Benjamin was on board, mainly in home waters, but also paid visits to Gibraltar, Italy, Malta and Tunisia. Benjamin's time with the Navy ended in March 1914, and he then worked as a chauffeur for nearly a year before volunteering for service in the Army, attesting at Reading on 15th February 1915, and joined the Army Service Corps. He had married Agnes Page three years earlier in Portsmouth, and by now had two children, with a third born in 1916, and they were living in Wellington Road, Crowthorne. Benjamin spent three months in Tidworth Military Hospital in Wiltshire in the spring and summer of 1915, suffering from pyelitis, an inflammation of the renal pelvis caused by E. coli, but was passed fit for overseas service in October. It was February of the following year when he sailed from Southampton for Boulogne, and attached to 641 Company. The company provided transport to haul the heavy guns and howitzers of the 57 Siege Battery, Royal Garrison Artillery, with their attendant equipment and ammunition, and operated the dumps, or stores, of ammunition. He was to later serve with five other companies, all providing the same service to different artillery batteries. His service record gives no details of any hospital admissions, but he did have six days of leave in September 1917. In April 1918, he was providing support services for the Australian Corps Heavy Artillery. On the 23rd, some German prisoners indicted that an attack might be expected. The War Diary records the attack on the following day: "We put down Counter Preparation at 3:45am. Enemy also opened a heavy bombardment on front and support lines with H.E. *(high explosives)* and gas, also neutralised a large number of heavy and field batteries. At 6:30am, III Corps were heavily attacked, Villers Bretonneux and Bois L'Abbe being occupied. Heavy fighting all day, and H.A. fired about 20,000 rounds of 6" How*itzer* and 60 pounder ammunition. At 10pm, two Australian Brigades and one British attacked under cover of a special barrage put down by Australian Corps H.A., and recaptured the village and ground lost. For practically the whole day, the H.A. barrage was the only protection to the infantry answering to the first rush of the enemy, having carried them through to the Bois L'Abbe. The field and heavy artillery of the III Corps had retired and were unable to cover their front. Heavy and Siege batteries carried out their tasks in heavy concentrations of gas and H.E., maintaining their accuracy, rates of fire, and ammunition supply. Casualties were heavy. One group of batteries maintained a slow barrage from 2pm 24.4.18 to 3:50am 25.4.18 without ceasing fire". For his part in this action, Benjamin was awarded the Military Medal. By late September, Benjamin's company was attached to X Corps Heavy Artillery, south of Ypres. On the 26th and 27th, they were mainly concerned with harassing the enemy, firing on hostile batteries, and shelling the roads that it was anticipated German reliefs would be using. The War Diary records one German battery was shelled with gas and "three explosions and two fires were caused." Needless to say, the Germans were doing precisely the same to the British. On the 28th, the infantry were active, pushing out patrols and engaging the enemy, and by 7:30am, had captured two farms, a cottage, and brickstacks, north of Wytschaete. The village had been shelled two hours earlier, and although the enemy response was "slight," there were troublesome machine guns to the south. During the day, all bridges over the Lys between Warneton and Deulement were "harassed heavily," and the roads and approaches were also heavily shelled, as was a suspected enemy headquarters, and German batteries. The War Diary is more concerned with recording the use of the guns than with men, but there were obviously casualties. Benjamin, now a Corporal, was killed on the 28th, and is buried in Westoutre British Cemetery.

FREDERICK PITHER

Frederick John Pither was born at Yateley in 1882, one of six children, one of whom died in infancy, and grew up on Cricketer's Hill. His father, who worked as a general labourer, died in 1898. Frederick, with two of his brothers and his widowed mother, moved to Crowthorne, where he worked as a bricklayer's labourer. He married Annie Eden in 1908, and had four sons. Frederick was conscripted in 1916, attesting at Wokingham, and joined the 7th Battalion, Northumberland Fusiliers. After training in Dorset, he went to France at the end of the year. The battalion took part in three phases of the Arras Offensive in 1917, and at the beginning of June were at Monchy au Bois, southwest of Arras. Here, they were camped in bivouacs near old German front line, carrying and training, but even this not a safe area, as Frederick was wounded on the 7th. The War Diary records the strength of the battalion at that time – 40 officers, 775 other ranks, 30 horses, 25 large mules, 16 Lewis guns, 145 transport vehicles (mainly carts and limbers, the latter being two-wheeled carts designed to support the trail of an artillery piece), and nine bicycles; the Commanding Officer also made a note that six trained signallers were required for the unit. The injury may have prevented Frederick from returning to the infantry, as by the time of his death he was serving in the 5th Field Survey Company, Royal Engineers. As movement in France stopped and the sides became deadlocked, the artillery found themselves firing at an invisible enemy. The Field Survey Companies surveyed the ground, created maps, and identified the German positions. On 27th October 1918, Frederick's unit moved to La Capelle and started work on a bridge for heavy vehicles at Pont de Buat. Two sections of the company were involved, with a third ready to give assistance when necessary. Most of the work was completed within 24 hours, and by the 29th, the bridge and adjacent screening, to give protection to those on it, had been finished. The War Diary also records some details on Sapper A. P. Davies. A month earlier, he had been sentenced to 90 days' Field Punishment No. 1 (this consisted of the convicted man being placed in restraints, and attached to a fixed object, such as a gun wheel, for up to two hours per day). A sentence of this length was often the result of going AWOL. The "unexpired portion of sentence *was* remitted for Gallantry and devotion to duty" the day before. The diary also gives monthly totals for casualties during September (eleven wounded, two gassed, three sick) and November (nine sick), but sadly, not for the month in between. Frederick was killed on 30th October, and is buried in Wassigny Communal Cemetery. One of Frederick's sons, who was about nine years old when his father was killed, wrote some important dates in a diary: "Dad joined the army on June 17th 1916, went to France on December 29th, he was wounded on the 7th June 1917, come (sic) home on February 1918, returned to France on 1st March 1918, lost his pack on 21st March 1918 *(this was at the start of the German Spring Offensive)*, Dad sent our knives on 4th April 1918, Dad was killed on the 30th October 1918."

J. ROBERT REID

James Robert Reid, known by his second name, was born in Edinburgh in 1896, the younger of two brothers. His father had worked in the Indian Civil Service before retiring, and the family were able to live in some comfort with four servants, including two nurses to look after Robert and his brother when they were young. His father died in 1908, and within three years, his mother had moved to Edgbarrow Lodge in Crowthorne. Robert attended Eagle House School at Sandhurst, and Marlborough College, before obtaining a commission at the Royal Military

College, Sandhurst, in 1914, and joining the 1st Battalion, Royal Berkshire Regiment. However, he did not go to France until March 1916. The battalion were not involved in the initial attacks of the Battle of The Somme, and it was late July before they were involved in a serious attack. The Berkshires had gone into the front line near Delville Wood on the 24th, and the attack started three days later with a bombardment at 6am, lasting just over an hour. Robert, now a Lieutenant, led 'D' Company, which covered the right flank. Two hundred yards of ground was gained and they dug in. At 8:10am, the advance resumed until they finally reached Princes Street, their objective, running east/west through the middle of the wood. They had encountered considerable rifle fire, but it was not very accurate and did little harm. However, enfilading machine gun fire caused some problems for the consolidating parties. This was followed by high-explosive-shell fire for the remainder of the day, preventing any supplies of food or water reaching the men. More shelling and fire continued the next day, and it was quite late before the battalion could be relieved. 'D' Company, being closest to the German lines, had to wait until after dark, before being relieved. 37 men were killed during the course of the two days, with a similar number missing. Robert was one of the two officers, initially reported missing. On 22nd March 1917, the War Office wrote to Robert's mother: "No further official report received. Enquiries the American Embassy have been without result. In view of the lapse of time since anything has been heard of this Officer, his name is put forward for presumption of death." In April, she wrote to the War Office to see if they had any further news, but their reply on the 17th confirmed that nothing further had been heard. Later, Private Arthur Neale, of 'D' Company, 1st Battalion, Royal Berkshire Regiment, who had been held as a Prisoner of War, but later repatriated, gave an eye-witness account of Robert's death: "I saw two Officers of the Regiment, whose names I did not know, killed by machine gun fire, and their bodies were left in No Man's Land. One belonged to 'D' Company, the other, I think, to 'B' Company. The latter had arrived with a draft on June 3rd." Robert's name is recorded on the Thiepval Memorial.

PERCY ROBINSON

The late Pte. P. ROBINSON, 1st Batt. East Surrey Regt., Crowthorne.— Killed in action. Aged 29.

Percy William Victor Robinson was born at Crowthorne in 1885, and baptised 26th August, one of eight children. His mother died in 1902, leaving one of his elder sisters to run the household. His father, an attendant at Broadmoor, died in 1909, and one of Percy's sisters also worked as a nurse with mental patients in East London. Percy worked as an errand boy after leaving school until he was old enough the join the army on 4th January 1905, attesting at Aldershot, and joined the 1st Battalion, East Surrey Regiment. Although his Service Record still exists, it is illegible in many places, giving tantalising glimpses of him. He was 5'7" tall, weighed just over nine stone, with green or grey eyes, and had a fair complexion. His military record was 'exemplary', gaining two badges for good conduct; he also expressed a desire to work in gentleman's service when his time in the army finished. In September the same year, Percy sailed with the battalion for India, and is recorded in barracks at Meiktila, Burma, in the 1911 census. The battalion were in Dublin when war was declared, and landed at Le Havre just eleven days later, although Percy did not join them until September (the War Diary records the arrival of nearly two hundred men on the 10th, just after the Battle of the Aisne). They also took part in the Battle of the Aisne and the First Battle of Ypres later that year.

The War Diary also records some details of events at the beginning of 1915. On 1st January, Private Charles Owen from London was blown to bits while digging out men from a collapsed trench. On the following day, eighty pairs of gumboots were issued to each company as the conditions in the trenches were so wet; they were found to be useful, but the mud was so deep, it often came over the top of them. A concert was held on the evening of the 6th, and two days later, there was a football match. Corporal Williams was recommended for the D.C.M. on the 18th for putting himself at risk, and being wounded, while going to the assistance of two fellow soldiers. By the 23rd, it had turned bitterly cold again, and cases of frost bite were recorded. Another concert was given on the 27th, and repeated the next evening. On 3rd February, the thatched roof of a barn being used by the battalion caught fire in the early hours, and it was daylight before it was brought under control and extinguished. On the 8th, they played the Royal Field Artillery at football, against the Devonshire Regiment two days later, and the 14th Field Ambulance on the 18th. In between, there were spells in the trenches, and patrols going out, with a steady stream of casualties. As winter melted into spring, fewer social activities are recorded, and the details of the fighting are more evident. By the end of March, there were suspicions from the injuries being seen, that the Germans were using some kind of expanding bullet. In early April the battalion marched to Ypres, taking over the front line on the 11th. Three men were killed next day, and on the 13th, shelling accounted for another three, one of them being Percy. Initially buried near to where he fell, his body was moved to Chester Farm Cemetery in 1921. Although several of Percy's siblings had left Crowthorne before the war, a brother and a sister still lived in the village, and they ensured his name was put on the village War Memorial.

D. SAXE

Dick Chapman Lindfield was born in 1891 at Billingshurst, Sussex. He was illegitimate and if his second name is the surname of the father, then it is one of two brothers from Horsham. His mother married John Saxe about eighteen months later, and young Dick took his step-father's surname. The couple had six more children, two of whom died in infancy. John Saxe had worked as a groom and gardener in Billingshurst, but between 1907 and 1911, the family moved to Binfield, and he worked at Marchfield House, Forest Road (near its junction with Binfield Road). Dick had left school, and was also working as a gardener by this time. He joined under the Derby Scheme, attesting at Camberley, and joined the Royal Berkshire Regiment; this suggests he may have been working in Sandhurst by the end of 1915. However, he was transferred to the 1st Battalion, Hampshire Regiment before leaving England. Just before he set off, he also married Susan Smith from Crowthorne, although the marriage took place in Devon. The battalion took part in phases of the Battles of Arras and Third Battle of Ypres in 1917 (including the First Battle of Passchendaele), and the first Battle of Arras and phases of the Battle of the Lys the following year. After four days of rest, the Hampshire relieved the 2nd Battalion, West Riding Regiment in the Pacaut Wood sector on 13th June 1918, two Companies being in the wood itself, and others on the bank of the adjacent canal. The General Officer Commanding had the idea that some musketry practise on the 17th would be a good idea, with each man by the canal firing five rounds rapidly at the opposite bank. The enemy retaliated with heavy shelling next evening, and again the following morning. This caused one casualty, Dick, who was killed, and is buried in Le Vertannoy British Cemetery, Hinges. He is also listed on the Binfield War Memorial.

W. HOWARD SCRIBBINS

William Howard Scribbins, known as Howard, was born in Crowthorne on 6th November 1899, the eldest of three children. His father worked as a clerk, and later steward, at Wellington College. By 1911, Howard was attending Ranelagh School in Bracknell, a co-educational, fee-paying grammar school, but only part time. He joined the Royal Flying Corps on 17th November 1917, and was based at Farnborough. He was appointed Flight Second Lieutenant at the end of July the following year. On 22nd August 1918, while flying an Avro RE8 from Number 1 Training Depot Station at Stamford, Lincolnshire (now RAF Wittering), Howard was killed in an aeroplane accident, and is buried in Crowthorne churchyard, on the north side of the church. The Reading Mercury of 31st August 1918 carried a report of his burial: "The death, the result of a flying accident, of Flight Lieutenant William Howard Scribbins, RAF, has occasioned much regret in Crowthorne, both he and his parents having been so very well known in the district. Much sympathy is felt for his parents, Mr and Mrs Scribbins of Wellington College, who had the sad experience of witnessing the accident that terminated their son's career. The decreased was only 18 years of age, and after passing through various courses in his training with continuous success, had recently been appointed instructor. He was buried with Military Honours in Crowthorne Churchyard on Monday." William is also listed on the Roll of Honour at Ranelagh School.

The late Pte. E. SEYMOUR, London Regt.—Killed in action.

ERNEST C. SEYMOUR

Ernest Charles Seymour was born in 1891 at Rotherfield, near Crowborough, Sussex, and was one of eleven children. His father worked with horses, driving a cart for hire. In about 1896, the family moved to Reading when he found a new job as a groom, and then to Crowthorne, where he worked as a coachman at Wellington College. Ernest worked as a gardener after leaving school, until he volunteered for service, attesting at Clapham, and joined the 1/23rd Battalion, London Regiment in September 1914. His training was done near St Albans, before going to France in mid March 1915. On 9th May, the battalion were involved in the fighting for Aubers Ridge, and suffered fifty casualties under heavy shrapnel fire. They were in the front line again at Givenchy on the 25th, and ordered to attack a German trench. 'A' Company were able to reach it "without great loss," but were unable to advance any further, and dug in. Telephone wire had been sent forward with the attackers, and the War Diary records that telephone contact was made within three minutes. There was great congestion in the communication trenches, so the support had to advance across open ground to join them. By 8pm, the whole battalion were in the captured trench, but less than an hour later, they found themselves enfiladed by rifle and machine gun fire from the left, which the British machine gun failed to stop, and the telephone line was broken. There was a severe bomb fight on their right flank at 9pm, and two counter-attacks were repulsed with rifle fire. There were many casualties overnight as the trench was enfiladed from both flanks. The Londons were digging communication trenches in the dark, but had to stop once it got light, although one of them was usable. The battalion continued to hold the captured ground, despite enemy sniping from a higher position on their right, and captured twenty Germans. At 7:30am, the trench was shelled very heavily, and it was under shell fire all afternoon as the Germans tried to recapture it. The battalion were relieved by 10pm that evening, but the two days had cost more than four hundred casualties. Ernest was one of almost one hundred men missing; his body was never found, and he is listed on the Le Touret Memorial. A few letters and photos were the only personal effects returned to Ernest's family.

FRANK SEYMOUR

Pte. F. SEYMOUR, Q.R.W. Surreys.—Wounded.

Frank Seymour was born at Reading in 1896, and was one of Ernest's younger brothers. The family lived just off the Oxford Road, not far from the football club's old ground at Elm Park. Frank worked as an errand boy after leaving school, but appears to have joined under the Derby Scheme, attesting at Camberley, and joined the 10th Battalion, Royal West Surrey Regiment. This was part of the 41st Division, and was inspected by both the King and Field Marshall Lord French at Aldershot at the end of April 1916. The first men sailed for France a few days later, but Frank left a couple of months afterwards, arriving at the end of July. Although not involved in the fighting on the first day of that month, the battalion were involved in later phases of the Battle of the Somme in the autumn, along with the Battle of Messines and phases of the Third Battle of Ypres in 1917. In mid November, they moved by train to Italy, and at the beginning of December, took over the front line northwest of Treviso. Here they spent the next three months before moving back to France, near Doullens and Mondicourt, although the journey was much delayed by bad weather. On 20th March 1918, the battalion entrained at Saulty, when news was heard that a large German offensive had begun and that many places many miles back had been shelled, and it was soon found their destination had been changed from Albert to Achiet-le-Grand. They arrived at 1:30am the following morning, and marched to Camp No. 12 at Favreuil. There is now a gap in the records as the battalion fought against the German Spring Offensive, only resuming at the end of March with a list of casualties for the month. While almost one hundred men were sick, twice that number were missing, 26 had been killed, and almost 150 wounded. Frank was one of those missing; his body was never found, and his name is listed on the Arras Memorial.

GEORGE H. SEYMOUR

Pte. G. SEYMOUR, Queen's (R.W.S. Regt).—Missing.

George Henry Seymour was another brother in the same family, being born at Rotherfield in 1892. After leaving school, he worked as a waiter at the East Berkshire Golf Club. Originally owned by Wellington College, the Club was then sold to Mr Palmer, a partner of Huntley and Palmer biscuit company in Reading, who leased it back to the College on favourable terms. George volunteered for service, attesting at Camberley, and joined the 7th Battalion, Royal West Surrey Regiment. After training at Colchester, the battalion moved to Salisbury Plain in May 1915, was inspected by the King on 24th June, and went to France at the end of July. The battalion fought in the Battle of Loos in September of that year. Men in parts of the line suffered from their own gas as the breeze failed to carry it over to the German lines, and on 10th October, some British miners were gassed when a German mine was exploded. Two weeks later, they were inspected near Ribemont by the King again, and by the French President, the Prince of Wales also being present. Steel helmets arrived the following month, but only enough for use by sentries, and in

December, thigh gumboots were being worn in the trenches, so bad were the conditions underfoot. Conditions became even worse the following spring when a thaw set in, although the health of the men was still reported as being good. From 22nd June, the German position was incessantly bombarded. The entry for 1st July looks quite bland. "At 7:30am, the Battalion assaulted the German front trenches on a front of about four hundred yards. After twelve hours' fighting, the objective, west of Montauban, was achieved and consolidated on a front of about 260 yards. Other ranks killed 174, wounded 284, missing 56." The battalion were relieved the next day and moved back to billets on the 3rd. On the 11th, they were in the front line again, northwest of Maricourt. Two days later, they were ordered to attack the northern portion of Trones Wood, an area with which they were not familiar. The leading Company moved forward from Dublin Trench at 5:30pm. The battalion were greatly impeded by a relief moving up into Longueval Alley at the same time. At 8pm, they assaulted Trones Wood from northern extremity over a front of 750 yards. Men from another battalion, who were to assist in the assault, became disorganised owing to casualties due to shell fire when moving up to the attack, and only about one and a half platoons arrived in time to partake in the assault. The advance was met by very heavy rifle, machine gun and shell fire, and checked. At 8:50pm, a message was received that northern portion of Trones Wood would be re-bombarded, and that the attack was not to be pressed if success seemed unlikely. At 9pm, the remaining men reorganised for defence of Longueval Alley in conjunction, and some three hours later, instructions were received that the battalion might withdraw to the German old front line position if Longueval Alley was sufficiently held, which they did a couple of hours later. The attack had cost over two hundred casualties, including George; his body was never recovered, and his name is listed on the Thiepval Memorial.

WILLIAM T. SEYMOUR

Dvr. W. T. SEYMOUR, A.S.C. M.T.— Died at Oxford from Blackwater fever after 2½ years' service at Salonika.

William Thomas Seymour was the fourth brother of the Seymour family to die as a result of the war. He too had been born at Rotherfield, in 1886, and worked as a groom, possibly also at Wellington College. William married Margaret Hill in 1911, and they had two daughters. He volunteered for service, attesting at Wokingham, and joined the Army Service Corps. William served with one of the Mechanical Transport Companies, transporting and hauling the heavy guns and howitzers of the Royal Garrison Artillery, along with their attendant equipment and ammunition. They also operated dumps, or stores, of ammunition. Having served in Salonika for over two years, William returned to England, suffering from the effects of malaria. In total, more than 162,000 men in that area would suffer from the disease, with over 20% being returned to England. William died in one of the Oxford hospitals on 10th November 1918, officially from Blackwater fever, a complication, in which the red blood cells burst in the bloodstream, causing chills, high fever, jaundice, vomiting, rapidly progressive anaemia, and dark urine. He is buried in the south-west part of Crowthorne (St John the Baptist) Churchyard. The Reading Mercury of 23rd November 1918 recorded the burial: "Mr and Mrs Seymour, who have lost three sons and two sons-in-law in the war, have now been further bereaved by the death from pneumonia, following influenza, of their second son, Driver W. T. Seymour, Army Service Corps. He has been invalided here from Salonika after two and a half years' service, and died in hospital at Oxford on November 10th."

CHARLES SHARPE

Charles Sharp (the surname is spelt both with and without the final 'e' in the records) was born in 1868 at Honey Hill, off Nine Mile Ride, although he grew up in Sandhurst. He was one of twelve children, his six elder siblings all being born in his father's home village of Waltham St Lawrence. His father worked as an agricultural labourer, but Charles worked as a bricklayer's labourer at Hartley Wintney after leaving school. He joined the army, attesting at Reading on 22nd May 1888, and joined the Royal Berkshire Regiment. He was 5'5" tall, with blue eyes, brown hair, a fresh complexion, and had a mole on his left calf. After spending nearly six months completing his training with the 3rd Battalion, he transferred to the Suffolk Regiment, and may have spent some time with them in India. He fought in the Boer War, was mentioned in Dispatches in 1901, and gained Long Service and Good Conduct Medals. Charles had married in about 1905, possibly in Gibraltar, his wife's birthplace, and settled in Bury St Edmunds, where the couple had three children, and is listed in the 1911 census as a Colour Sergeant. By now he was in the 3rd Battalion, Suffolk Regiment, the Reserve Battalion, but on the outbreak of war, was transferred to the 7th Battalion, formed in the town. No doubt as an old soldier, he trained the new recruits, crossing the English Channel with them in May 1915 as the Company Sergeant Major. In late June, the battalion were in the front line for the first time, holding trenches in a relatively quiet sector at Ploegsteert Wood. The Battle of Loos started on 25th September, and lasted more than three weeks. The Suffolks were in action on 13th October, having taken over the front trenches near the Hoenzolhern Redoubt the previous day. After an intensive bombardment of the German positions that lasted for two hours, 'B' Company attacked at 2pm under cover of smoke. However, the smoke lifted, and they came under very heavy machine gun fire, which prevented them from reaching their objective, and causing around seventy casualties. Both 'A' and 'C' Companies supported bombing parties from the 7th Battalion, Norfolk Regiment, both parties being held up, but the Suffolks rushed the German positions, and the bombers were able to advance until running out of bombs, when positions were consolidated. The battalion were relieved the following day, and retired to the old British line to rest and re-organise. After a light shelling early in the morning, 19th October was a quiet day. At 5:30pm, orders were received ordering the battalion into support as an attack on a newly-dug trench was expected. The attack came half an hour later, before the Suffolks were in position, but by 6:15pm, they were able to help repulse it. At 9pm, leaving one party forward, they withdrew, spending the rest of the night forming working parties, until relieved at 2am the following morning. At some point during the action, Charles was wounded; he succumbed to his injuries on the 20th, and is buried in Lillers Communal Cemetery. Several of Charles's siblings still lived in Crowthorne, and they ensured his name was included on the village War Memorial.

WILLIAM A. SHARP

William Arthur Sharp was born on 30th June 1886 near the village of Hooton, near Ellesmere Port, Cheshire. He was one of four children, having three sisters. His father was a commercial bookkeeper, but the family were able to afford a servant as his mother probably inherited money from her own father, a ship-owner. The family had moved to Hanwell, Middlesex, by 1901, but then William disappears from the records until 1914, when he volunteered for the Canadian Expeditionary Force, attesting on 8th December 1914 at Victoria, British Columbia, and joined the 2nd Canadian Mounted Rifles Battalion. He was 5'7" tall, with grey eyes, brown hair, a fresh complexion, and had a scar on his nose. The War Diary commences in September 1915, by which time the battalion were already at Shorncliffe Camp, near Folkestone, Kent. The 9th was obviously a red letter day as the issue of identity discs, up-to-date rifles and webbing was mentioned, along with maps of France for the Squadron Commanders on the following day. They left England on the 22nd, arriving at Boulogne the same evening. The King's message for Christmas 1915 is recorded in full in the War Diary: "Another Christmas finds all the resources of the Empire still engaged in war, and I desire to convey on my own behalf and on behalf of the Queen, a heartfelt Christmas greeting and our good wishes for the New Year to all who on sea and land are upholding the honour of the British name. In the officers and men of my Navy on whom the security of the Empire depends I repose, in common with all my subjects, a trust that is absolute. On the officers and men of my Armies, whether now in France, in the East, or in other fields, I rely with an equal faith, confident that their devotion, their valour and their self-sacrifice will, under God's guidance, lead to victory and honourable peace. There are many comrades now, alas, in hospital and to these brave men also I desire with the Queen to express our deep gratitude and our earnest prayers for their recovery. Officers and men of the Navy and of the Army, another year is drawing to a close as it begun, in toil, bloodshed and suffering, and I rejoice to know that the goal to which you are striving draws nearer into sight. May God bless you and your undertakings." On New Year's Eve, the court Martial of Trooper Keith "for using the Official Gum Envelope for an Improper Purpose" was mentioned, but no more details of the case, nor the outcome, were recorded (this may be Private Neil Keith, originally from Scotland, killed on 1st October 1916). By March 1916, the battalion were at Bourse Farm. 'B' Company reported a "slight epidemic of diarrhoea" on the 3rd, and training for them was cancelled. Three days later, it snowed (the weather is recorded with almost fanatical detail in many of the Canadian War Diaries). Drafts of men arrived during the next few days, as the weather turned "warm and bright." There was "heavy snowfall" on the 24th, and casualties were occurring daily from heavy shelling. Five men were killed on the 25th, two on the 26th, and another two on the 27th. One of these last two was William; according to the records, he was killed in trenches at Hooge. He is buried in Menin Road South Military Cemetery. By now, his parents were living in Crowthorne, so although William probably never set eyes on the village, his name is included on the War Memorial.

GEORGE W. SLYFIELD

George William Slyfield was born at Crowthorne in 1897, the eldest of six children. His father was an attendant at Broadmoor Hospital. It is not known what George did after leaving school, but he volunteered for service, attesting at Denham, Buckinghamshire, and joined the 16th Battalion, King's Royal Rifle Corps. The battalion were initially formed from current and previous members of the Church Lads Brigade, and after several moves, went to France in November 1915. But George does not appear to have been with them, his record suggesting he arrived in France the following year, on reaching the age required for overseas service. The battalion were near Cuinchy for the first day of the Battle of the Somme. The artillery bombardment was continuing, and just after midnight, mines were exploded at Mine Point and Railway Point, as well as east of Twin Craters, and smoke bombs fired. A raiding party went out just before 1am, but got caught in machine gun fire from both flanks at the German wire. They managed to get into a German trench, but then ran out of bombs. Three-quarters of the small party were casualties. George was one of eleven wounded and missing; his body was never recovered, and he is listed on the Loos Memorial.

The late Corpl. A. H. SMITH, of Wexford Cottage, Broadmoor Road, Crowthorne.—Wounded and died of pneumonia in France.

ALBERT H. SMITH

Albert Henry Smith was born in 1894 at Brightwalton, between Newbury and Wantage. He was the youngest of four surviving children, a fifth dying in infancy. His father worked as a carter on local farms, and although Albert started farm work after leaving school, he had moved to Crowthorne, and was an attendant at Broadmoor by 1911. This was a protected profession until late into the conflict, and men doing it were exempt from conscription until 1918. Albert's service number shows he was not called up until February of that year, and joined the 2nd Battalion, Grenadier Guards. He arrived in France after the German Spring Offensive, but the battalion fought in the Second Battle of Ypres later the same year, as well as the Battles of the Hindenburg Line in September and October as the Allies advanced. The battalion were in the vicinity of Maubeuge at the Armistice, but Albert was in a Casualty Clearing Station near the village of Beugny, and died five days later from a combination of his wounds and pneumonia. He is buried in Delsaux Farm Cemetery, Beugny.

STANLEY A. SMITH

Stanley Arthur Smith was born in 1899 at either Ascot or Egham (both places are given in the records), and had an elder sister, a third child dying in infancy. His early years were spent in London Road, Sunninghill, where his father worked as the manager of a shop selling fish and poultry. But by 1911, the family had moved to Crowthorne, where his father ran his own grocery business, Central Stores, in the High Street. Stanley was conscripted into one of the Training Reserve Battalions in the 8th Reserve Brigade. These battalions replaced the system of Regimental Reserve Battalions in September 1916, to cope with the larger number of men needing to be trained once conscription started. The local nature of recruitment for infantry regiments was abandoned, and the entire system centralised. Once basic training had been completed, men were allocated to any regiment, not necessarily their local one, and Stanley went to the 1/4th Battalion, Shropshire Light Infantry. He probably joined the battalion around the time of the German Spring Offensive in March 1918. At the beginning of May, the battalion went into the front line near Dickebusch for forty-eight hours. During this period, he was wounded, dying on the 7th, and is buried in Arneke British Cemetery.

Pte. VICTOR SMITH, Crowthorne.—Invalided with rheumatism and frostbite.

VICTOR R. SMITH

Victor Robert Smith was born at Sandhurst in 1895. He was the youngest of eight children, one of whom died in infancy. His father worked for many years as a domestic groom, before starting to lose his hearing. By 1901, the family had moved to Owlsmoor, and he worked as a bricklayer's labourer, and later became a jobbing gardener. Victor, by now, had left school, and was working as a man-servant at Wellington College, but had been lucky to survive a childhood accident in 1904 when a spirit lamp exploded, injuring him. He volunteered for service, attesting at Wokingham, joined the Royal Berkshire Regiment, and went to France at the end of November 1914. This was a very early date for a man with no previous military experience, so it is possible he went as the personal servant with one of the young officers from Wellington College. A report in the Berkshire Mercury, when he was invalided suffering from rheumatism and frostbite, records him as being in the 1st Battalion, but the military records state he was in the 2nd Battalion at the time of his death. He was with them at Bois Grenier when they went into the front line on 24th September 1915, with an attack scheduled for the following day. The British trenches formed a semi-circle while the German trenches ran more or less in a straight line. At their closest, the opposing sides were one hundred yards apart, but five times that distance in the centre. However, there were old fire trenches in the intervening distance, and the Berkshires assembled in these for the attack which started at 4:30am after a heavy bombardment of the enemy. 'A' Company, on the right, had the worst of it. The wire in front of them was imperfectly cut, a German searchlight picked them out, and the Germans here seemed more ready for them. Consequently, only a few men reached the German trench and they were not sufficient to hold on. 'B' Company in the centre were most successful, but 'C' Company on the left suffered from an enemy machine gun and, in the dark, they missed some German dug-outs and their occupants were able to fire on the rear of the troops who had passed. The fight developed into a bombing tit-for-tat, although further back, 'D' Company, in reserve in the assembly trench, were hit by shells, causing more casualties. By the end of the day, all the attackers had withdrawn back to their starting positions. 130 men were killed, over 200 wounded, and sixty were missing. Victor was one of the latter and his name is recorded on the Ploegsteert Memorial. One of Victor's sisters married Victor Kibbey, who is also listed in the lych gate at Crowthorne.

EDWARD W. SMITHERS

The late Sglr. EDWARD WILLIAM SMITHERS, Crowthorne.—Lost at sea in torpedo boat. Aged 34.

Edward William Smithers was born on 16th November 1880 at Shinfield. He was one of six children, two of whom died in infancy. His father worked as a coachman, and the family had moved to Reading by 1891. Edward worked as a telegraph boy after leaving school, before joining the Navy just before his sixteenth birthday, signing up for twelve years' service. He was 5'10" tall, with hazel eyes, dark brown hair, and a fresh complexion. He spent the first two years in training, off the Devon coast near Torquay, and at Portland, Dorset. He was officially engaged on his eighteenth birthday, and served as a signalman on HMS 'Icarus' for nearly four years, sailing to a base at the southern end of Vancouver Island, Canada, and patrolling in the Pacific; at the time of the 1901 census, the ship was at Honolulu, Hawaii. He then had spells on HMS 'Andromache' in the Fleet Reserve, and the cruisers HMS 'Hawke' and HMS 'Dido', interspersed with training, before sailing on HMS 'Encounter', part of the Royal Navy Australia Squadron, which patrolled the waters around the self-governing British colony. Throughout his naval career, Edward had an unblemished record, and when his term finished in late 1910, he was able to get a job as assistant attendant at Broadmoor. He married Olive Bosley in 1913, with a son being born later the same year. He was recalled to the Navy in December 1914, and served on torpedo boats, based at Sheerness, Kent. These were small vessels, typically fifty to one hundred feet long, capable of travelling at speeds of up to fifty knots, and carrying two to four torpedoes, and several machine guns. On 10th June 1915, the boat carrying Edward and his crewmates was lost, possibly sunk by a German destroyer. His body was not recovered, and his name is listed on the Chatham Naval Memorial.

FRANCIS W. SPEAR

Francis William Spear was born at Camberley in 1896, the eldest of four children. His father was a builder, and the family lived in Fleet for a time, before moving back to Crowthorne, where both Francis's parents had been born. Francis joined the 2/4th Battalion, Hampshire Regiment, a Territorial Battalion, attesting at Winchester. The battalion left for India just before Christmas 1914, but Francis did not leave England until after 1915; he may have joined them in India, or in Egypt which they reached in mid May 1917. Finally, the battalion went to France in June 1918. The Second Battle of the Marne, starting the following month, was the last major German offensive of the war on the Western Front, which failed when an Allied counterattack, led by French forces and including several hundred tanks, overwhelmed them. The battle started on the 15th, stalled two days later, and by the 20th, the Germans were retreating. Francis's battalion made a long march in great heat on the 19th, bringing them to the Forest of Courtagnon in the Ardre valley, down which the British were to attack the next day. The valley, whose steep sides were thickly wooded, was open, but crops of corn concealed the German defences, especially the machine gun posts. Heavy fire, largely from machine guns which were hard to locate, met the attackers, inflicting heavy casualties, and progress was slow. The supporting battalions, which included the 2/4th Hampshire, suffered almost as severely from both artillery and machine gun fire. Francis was one of those killed, and is buried in Marfaux British Cemetery.

The late Pte. F. J. SPICER, Worcestershire Regt.—Died of wounds.

FREDERICK J. SPICER

Frederick James Spicer was born in Crowthorne in 1899, the middle of three children, and baptised 1st September. His mother died when he was only two years old, and a maiden aunt came to live with the family and act as housekeeper. Frederick's father worked as an attendant at Broadmoor, but it is not known what work Frederick did after leaving school. He was conscripted into the 3rd Battalion, Worcestershire Regiment, attesting at Wokingham. Although men were being called up at the age of eighteen, the age at which recruits were being sent to France had fallen to eighteen and a half, often with barely three months' training (this reverted to nineteen years in July 1918). Frederick may well have been shipped out in response to the German Spring Offensive at the end of March 1918. On 5th August, Frederick's battalion marched eastwards from Auchel to Chocques, "a dirty mining village half in ruins". The next evening they took over the trenches in front of Avelette. A quiet day followed. That night came word that the enemy had withdrawn; patrols were sent out, and reported on their return that they had advanced some eight hundred yards without encountering any opposition. Arrangements were made for an immediate advance. By 7am on the 8th, the leading platoons had advanced half way to Locon, and later were able to push on to the outskirts of the village. There they encountered the enemy's rearguard, and there was intermittent sniping throughout that night. At some point during the day, Frederick was wounded, and died the following day from his injuries. He is buried in Pernes British Cemetery.

ERNEST STRATFORD

The late Lieut. E. P. STRATFORD, R.A.M.C., Crowthorne.—Died of wounds received in rescuing wounded soldier from shelled house.

Ernest Stratford Pipkin was born on 24th June 1876 at Dulwich, South London. He had an elder sister, but his mother died a few months after Ernest was born. His father, who worked as an auditor for an insurance company, and would later become its General Manager, moved in with his two young children, and lived as a boarder with a schoolmistress at Hendon College, marrying her in 1882. Ernest was privately educated at Marlborough College and St Paul's School, London (co-incidentally, the school was evacuated to Easthampstead Park during World War II). Many boys from the school won entrance awards to Oxford and Cambridge Universities, and Ernest successful graduated in medicine from the latter in 1900. He then served in the South Africa War, in Bethune's Mounted Infantry, in which he attained the rank of Captain, but was invalided home after the relief of Ladysmith. After this, he trained at St Thomas's and St Mary's Hospitals in London, going on to gain M.R.C.S. (Membership of the Royal College of Surgeons) and L.R.C.P. (Licentiate of the Royal College of Physicians) qualifications in 1908, afterwards acting as resident medical officer to the West Ham Hospital for Diseases of the Nervous System. He married Amy Rose in 1910, and the couple were living in Crowthorne by the following year. While at University, he reversed his second and third names (Stratford being his late mother's maiden name) - perhaps Ernest Stratford carried more gravitas than Ernest Pipkin – but intriguingly, under place of birth in the 1911 census, he has listed 'at sea.' At the outbreak of war, he took a temporary commission as a Lieutenant in the Royal Army Medical Corps on 16th September 1914, and after serving for three months as a surgeon at Netley Hospital, a large military hospital near Southampton, and at Bournemouth, went to the front in February 1915, attached to No. 8 British Field Ambulance in the Labour Division of the Indian Expeditionary Force. While rescuing a wounded soldier at Neuve Chapelle on 17th March 1917, he was himself wounded by an exploding shell. For a short time, he was in hospital at Dieppe, from which he was invalided home, and died at Bourne End on 20th April from septicaemia. He is buried in Wokingham (All Saints) Churchyard. His death was reported in The Times on 22nd April 1915. Ernest's widow remarried the following year, and died in 1964.

FRANK SUTTON

Frank Sutton was born on 25th January 1891 at Hawton, near Newark, Nottinghamshire, one of four children. His mother died when he was only two years old, giving birth to his younger sister, and a maiden aunt came to live with the family and act as housekeeper. His father worked as a domestic gardener, and the family had moved to Burghfield by 1901. While there, Frank's father married the local schoolmistress, and later moved to Crowthorne, where his new wife had gained a head teacher position. After leaving school, Frank worked in service, and appears in the 1911 census as a footman working at Leigh House, Chard, Somerset. The following year, he sailed from Liverpool, arriving at Quebec on 26th May, bound for Winnipeg, where he intended to get a job in the motor trade. Instead, he finished working for an electrician, which was his occupation when he joined the 100th Winnipeg Grenadiers at the end of 1915. The unit had been authorized a week earlier, and left Canada for England in September 1916, and then provided reinforcements to the Canadian Corps in the field. Frank was 5'8" tall, with green eyes, fair hair, and a ruddy complexion, and gave his religion as Church of England. He fought in France with the 78th Battalion of the Canadian Infantry, although it is not known precisely when he joined them. While many of the British War Diaries are quite terse, the Canadian ones often add a little more background information as to what was happening at the time. For example, in Frank's battalion, the following entries have been found: 11th October 1916: "Court Martial of Lieutenants Hegan, Qua, and Robinson held …." (although what they had done to be court martialled, and the outcome, are not recorded). 14th October: "Reports show eight killed, 25 wounded, and one Officer missing, believed killed. On reports received, some misunderstanding must have arisen between Engineers and guides, as several parties were practically lost." The following day: "Trouble arisen through guides not being familiar with rendezvous locations." The Engineers would have been given the task of marking out areas with tape, from which the next attacks would take place; the guides would then take the troops to their correct place at the appropriate time. 10th November: "Pte Kennedy, W.S. given thirty days forfeit pay for self-inflicted wound. Verdict: negligence" (William Scott Kennedy, an American who had attested exactly one year previously). 26th November: "A German wandered over into our lines and gave himself up. In bad condition, taken to dressing station." 28th November: "Battalion had great difficulty getting out of the line owing to muddy condition. Men wandered in during the night and early morning in ones and twos …. billets bad, unfit for habitation." 3rd December (after a day's march): "Quite a few stragglers due to bad feet and poor road." There were no special celebrations to mark Christmas Day, but on 1st January 1917: "We ushered in the New Year by putting over a shoot in the Hun's rear area directly opposite our point, sharp on the strike of twelve midnight. Trench system in very bad condition – very muddy, no bath mats." Later in the month are comments about insufficient billets, especially for the Officers, and a shortage of fuel, considering how cold the weather was. On the 27th: "Kaiser's birthday today. We expected a strafe, but the Hun was quiet." 2nd February: "Paraded in afternoon to hear promulgation of sentence on Kemers, C. He was sentenced to serve ten years penal servitude" (Christian Henry Kremers, another American, had joined twelve months before in Winnipeg. Again, there are no details of the offence). 19th February: "New crater eighty feet in diameter and twenty feet deep caused by a mine explosion. The mobile charge, which caused its creation, was thrown by Sergeant Lloyd, who unfortunately was buried under several tons of earth." In April, all four divisions of the Canadian Expeditionary Force participated in a battle together for the first time, as they attacked Vimy Ridge. The attack commenced on the 9th, with most of the ridge being captured during the first day, and completed by the 12th. Historians attribute the success of the Canadian Corps in capturing the ridge to a mixture of technical and tactical innovation, meticulous planning, powerful artillery support, and extensive training. It had been very cold, with snow at the start of the month, but the weather had improved by the eve of the attack, only to turn bad again. This helped the attackers, as the snow was blowing into the faces of the German defenders. Zero was at 5:30am. After a brief pause after the preliminary bombardment, which had lasted through the night, all guns of the Canadian Artillery began firing again, and mines were exploded under No Man's Land and the German front trenches. Initially the German Artillery held their own, but as the Canadians advanced, they were overwhelmed as the horses to pull them back had been killed in the initial gas attack. Three of the Canadian Divisions reached their first objective within the first hour, and the second later in the morning. The 4th Division were held up by hostile machine gun fire, but eventually fought their way up too. By midnight on the 12th, the Canadians had lost almost 3600 men killed, and another seven thousand wounded. Frank was killed during the first day of the fighting; his body was never found, and his name is listed on the Vimy Memorial.

BERTIE THIEMANN

Albert Frederick Max Thiemann, known as Bertie, was born at Finchampstead in 1894, the eldest of five children. His father had been born in Germany but was a British subject, and worked as a nurseryman and florist. Bertie was fourteen years old when his father died, and may have gone to live with relatives in Germany as he, and two of his siblings, are missing from the 1911 census. By April 1913, he was back in England, living in West Ealing, when he joined the 2nd Battalion, King's Royal Rifle Corps, attesting at Hounslow. The battalion were at Blackdown Barracks at Deepcut, Surrey, when war broke out, and landed at Le Havre just nine days later. They took part in the Battle of Mons two weeks later, and the Battle of the Marne and the Battle of the Aisne in early September. The War Diary records their actions later in the month. September 20th: "We marched at 1am and heard a considerable amount of firing as we dropped down the hill towards Bourg. We reached Pargnan at 4:45am and went into some very dirty billets, but nothing mattered and all slept well. There was a great deal of writing of letters by the men, and their censorship took a great deal of time. A reconnaissance to site defensive works was carried out in the evening. There was no release from shell fire, as our own and French batteries were in action on the high ground above Pargnan to which the enemy's artillery made continual reply". September 21st: "Commenced consolidating the position chosen the day before and worked at it all day. A few shells from the German heavy guns came along, but they were nothing to bother about despite hostile aeroplane reconnaissance, which was not countered by our own aircraft." September 22nd: "Digging again and construction of obstacles, the barbed wire being taken from farm fences and gardens. The men were sent down to baths, a platoon at a time. "Black Marias" (*German shells which issued black smoke*) arrived, and one went through the roof of a farmhouse in which 'B' Company's Headquarters were; luckily the officers were away at luncheon, as the shell knocked the house down, but some men were unfortunately wounded, and Major Jelf's mare 'Sheila' was killed. Field Marshal Sir John French arrived in the afternoon and walked down through the village, paying visits to the billets, and personally thanking the men of the 2nd Brigade for what they had done. His visit was much appreciated. Prince Arthur of Connaught came to see us about 2pm, and went on the high ground above the village. He afterwards had tea with us in the priest's house." September 23rd: "On the 23rd the Brigade was ordered out early in the morning to occupy the ridge just to the north of Moulins in support of the French. Cover was found for most of the men in caves at the top of the ridge, but we were hardly shelled at all. Two batteries in the valley were heavily shelled all day, but although one gun was smashed by a direct hit, not one man was hit, and the batteries only ceased fire at intervals when the shelling became especially unpleasant. We returned to Pargnan that evening. Next day we heard the 1st Battalion were resting at Oeuilly, and some of us went down to see them. At that time they had lost 65 officers wounded but not one killed." There is no entry for the 24th, but on the following day: "On the 25th, we relived the 18th Brigade in the old line about Troyon. They had suffered very badly in a German attack soon after they had relieved us. For the next three or four weeks we remained in the same position, carrying out reliefs as a rule every four days. The time was spent in improving the trenches and making better shelter for officers and men. We were constantly shelled and lost a good many officers and men, both from this cause and from rifle fire in the trenches. There were frequent 'alarms' and warnings of German attacks, but we were never seriously attacked, and it is doubtful if the enemy ever left their trenches except for sniping. During this time we filled up with drafts from home, and by the middle of October were nearly up to strength." There are no more entries until the middle of October, but Bertie would not live until then, having died of wounds on September 29th. He is buried in Terlincthun British Cemetery, Wimille.

A. E. VAUGHAN

Albert Edgar Ody Vaughan was born at Bagshot in 1894. He was the younger of two children, having a sister seventeen years older. His father worked as a tailor, and Albert worked with him after leaving school. He enlisted under the Derby Scheme, attesting at Wokingham on 8th December 1915, and joined the 9th Battalion, Royal Berkshire Regiment, a training battalion based near Wareham in Dorset, and later transferred to the 1st Battalion, Royal West Kent Regiment. The battalion, part of the 5th Division, was having a rest in July 1916, after a spell in the front line near Arras earlier in the year, and missed the beginning of the Battle of the Somme. However, they were involved in later phases, and also took part in phases of the Battle of Arras and Third Battle of Ypres the following year. After the Second Battle of Passchendaele, the 5th Division moved to Italy late in 1917. This was a strategic and political move, agreed by the British Government at the request of the Allied Supreme War Council, as an effort to stiffen Italian resistance to enemy attack after a recent disaster at Caporetto. Many private diaries at this time, written by men who had witnessed the slaughter in the floods of Passchendaele, talk of the move and Italy as being "like another world." Much work was done preparing to move into the mountainous area of the Brenta, but eventually the Division was instead moved to the line along the River Piave, taking up positions in late January 1918. Unfortunately this pleasant period was not to last; the Division was hurriedly recalled to France once the enemy had made an attack in overwhelming strength on 21st March. The Regimental History records "On January 22nd, the battalion … set out for the Piave by march-route … and on the 29th, it went into the front line again. This consisted of trenches running down to the river bank …. The enemy's lines were three quarters of a mile distant, and during the 1st Battalion's stay on the Piave, his infantry were extraordinarily inactive …. Patrolling …. and the activity of the enemy's aircraft were the chief features of this time, nearly two months in all …. About the middle of March, the Division was relieved by the Italians and withdrew to billets at Visnadello …. Casualties had been extremely low, under twenty for the whole period." But Albert was one of the casualties, being killed on 26th February 1918, and is buried in Giavera British Cemetery, Arcade.

FRANK E. WALL

Frank Edgar Wall was born 13th December 1882 at Battersea, London, one of four children. His father worked as an iron moulder, and by 1891 the family had moved to the north of England, initially to Stockon-on-Tees, and then close to Sheffield, where he died in 1905. Frank also worked in the iron trade after leaving school, making moulds for the production of castings, but had sailed for Canada earlier in 1905, arriving at St John, New Brunswick on 15th April, bound for Prince Albert, Saskatchewan. The 1911 Canadian census records him living in lodgings in Strathcona, Alberta (later to become part of the city of Edmonton), where he worked as a bar tender. Later, his mother and younger sister moved to Edmonton too. At the outbreak of war, Frank volunteered, attesting at Valcartier on 23rd September 1914, and joined the Fort Garry Horse Regiment, part of the Canadian Cavalry. He was 5'9" tall, with brown eyes, brown hair and a fresh complexion, but with a tendency to varicose veins, and had a mole left side of his back. The regiment had already arrived in England and were based at Lark Hill, near Stonehenge, by the time entries start in the Regimental Diary in January 1915, but soon moved to Tidworth and then Shorncliffe in Kent. They sailed from Southampton to Le Havre at the end of February 1916, and continued training at St Blimont and Vaudricourt. A month later, a few horses began to show signs of glanders, an infectious bacterial disease, usually contracted through contaminated food or water, and had to be destroyed. In the days following, men began to trickle into hospital, suffering from typhoid. They saw their first action at Ville sous Corbie on 14th July, when five men and ten horses were wounded. Despite a program of inoculation, horses and men were still being taken ill, and the first deaths due to enemy action occurred at the start of August, along with eight cases of shell shock. As a relief, sports were held at the end of the month, but most entries in the diary record training, exercise rides, horses being struck off or arriving, and men being admitted to, or discharged from, hospital with a variety of illnesses including pleurisy, lumbago, rheumatism, sciatica, injury to ribs, infected feet, burns, and venereal disease. January 1917 contains references to machine gun training on Belgian ranges. They were in action again on 24th March, capturing the village of Ytres, some twenty miles from Arras; the diary proudly notes this was the first village captured by British Cavalry since October 1914, and continued fighting until being relieved four days later. Another attack was made at Vadencourt at the end of May, and completed successfully in less than half an hour. Diary entries are now also regularly entered on aircraft activity, although most entries record "below normal", and any attempting to fly over the lines were driven off. Two entries the following month reported some good news. Corporal Johnson, previously thought to have been killed three months earlier, was reported alive, albeit a prisoner of war, while Sergeant MacDonald of Manitoba was awarded the D.C.M., with another three men receiving the Military Medal, and three officers the Military Cross. Another successful raid took place on 8th July, with the capture of over thirty Germans, and more decorations awarded to members of the regiment later in the month and again in August. A Corps Horse Show was held on 1st September. Sixty men and 140 horses were casualties in November in support of an advance which encountered heavy resistance, but it is apparent just how little action the unit was involved in, although details of patrols and their personnel are recorded, something not mentioned so frequently in British diaries. Private A. J. McDonald, a persistent offender against the regulated life in the military, including drunkenness, missing from parades, breaking out of camp, being in Le Havre without a pass, contracting venereal disease, losing Government property (his kit), escaping from the Guard Room while in confinement, and desertion, was sentenced to penal servitude for life in January 1918 (this was later commuted to ten years' hard labour). At the end of March, they faced the German Spring Offensive, losing almost half of a Corps of 150 men on the 24th, but capturing around one hundred Germans, and injuring some seventy more with sabres, giving "renewed confidence" to the retreating British infantry. The retreat was halted and the tide began to turn a week later. In the middle of April, reinforcements arrived, but they were mainly from infantry regiments, and unable to ride. Despite being heavily shelled for much of the day, the regiment held a tent-pegging contest in the evening of 19th May. Bombs were dropped by enemy aircraft during the next two nights, but no casualties resulted. A month later, in a break from routine, there were sports for the entire day, and a concert party in the evening. On 27th July, representatives from the Canadian press visited for a few hours to write reports on their country's fighting men – it would be fascinating to know what was in their articles! In August, they moved to Amiens and started to move forward until checked two days later. In September, they were in support of another attack, but saw practically no action. The unconditional surrender of the Bulgarians at the end of the month was recorded (without comment). The following night, they were bivouacked at Caulaincourt, where they were bombed by German aircraft, but escaped casualties although the Royal Canadian Dragoons suffered several. Eight days later, on 9th October, they went into action, capturing the villages of Maurois and Haumont, but that night, a high explosive shell burst near the Regimental Headquarters, killed three men and wounding another eight; Frank was one of the latter, dying from his wounds the same day, and is buried in Roisel Communal Cemetery Extension. Frank had been in England in the summer of 1917, and married Louise Packer. Originally from Swindon, she was living with her married sister in Crowthorne in 1911; this is Frank's link with the village, and why his name appears on the list of names in the lych gate.

A. WARWICK

Alfred William Warwick was born on 9th February 1894 at Magg's Green, Swallowfield Road, Arborfield, and was one of nine children. His father had been born near Wallingford, and served in the Suffolk Regiment, deserting twice, but later obtaining two medals for Good Conduct. After almost ten years of service, he had been discharged medically unfit, having sustained an injury that caused wasting of his left leg, and had also contracted malaria and hepatitis while in India. The Staff Officer of Pensions, Royal Hospital, Chelsea had written on his record, "This man's pension has been made permanent as I am convinced he will never be fit for much," noting that he was capable of "no certain employment, holding horses and doing odd jobs, earning about four shillings per week". The pension was paid for over fifty years until his death in 1925. His physical handicap may also explain why he moved between farms in the area for work, at Hurst, Sindlesham, Henley and Arborfield. Alfred's mother, who was illiterate, died in 1910, by which time Alfred was also working as a farm labourer, living with his married sister and her young family at Farley Hill. He joined the Royal Berkshire Regiment as a Special Reservist, attesting at Reading. This entailed three weeks' training each year, with an instant call-up in the case of war. He joined the 1st Battalion, who were at Aldershot when war was declared, and went to France on 12th September, arriving in a draft of almost one hundred men recorded in the War Diary on the 21st. By the time he arrived, the German advance had been halted and trench warfare on the Western Front began. The next major incident occurred on 24th October when the battalion, now northeast of Ypres, were ordered to drive some Germans out of the area around Westhoek. The attack began in mid-afternoon and, despite coming under heavy rifle and shell fire, was successful, and a ridge running from Zonnebeke to Bekelaere captured. The enemy attempted to deceive them by sounding the British "Retire" and representing themselves as Belgians, but "failed ignominiously". During the next two days, the trenches were heavily shelled, and Alfred was killed during this period; his body was never recovered, and his name is listed on the Ypres (Menin Gate) Memorial.

The late Motor Mechanic H. L. WATSON, Broadmoor, Crowthorne.— Killed on one of H.M. ships.

LESLIE WATSON

Harold Leslie Watson, known by his second name, was born on 9th January 1899 at Crowthorne, and baptised 26th February. His father worked as a plumber on the Broadmoor estate, only moving from Devon with his wife and two children a year or so before Leslie was born; a fourth child was born in the village four years later. It is not known what work Leslie did after leaving school, but he joined the Royal Naval Volunteer Reserve on

29th January 1917, and served as a motor mechanic. He served on HMS 'Hermione', a protected (rather than armoured) cruiser, built just before the turn of the century to protect trade vessels. In mid June, he transferred to HMS 'Prize', a three-masted topsail schooner that was sailing under the German flag when it was seized in 1914, and converted to a Q-ship in early 1917. These were merchant ships, crewed by Navy personnel, and bearing hidden weaponry. When attacked by U-boats, a portion of the ship's crew (referred to as a panic party) would appear to evacuate the vessel, sometimes setting smoke fires to simulate damage. This would encourage the attacker to approach, and when the U-boat was close enough, the Q-ship's guns would become operational and open fire, hopefully destroying the submarine. The 'Prize' was captained by William Sanders, the only New Zealander to win a Victoria Cross, and there is a suggestion the ship was a marked vessel, as she had already accounted for several German submarines. The 'Prize' had already been badly damaged in the Atlantic in an attack in April 1917, and had also taken part in patrols in both May and June. It was on its fourth patrol when, on 14th August, it was spotted by the U-43, which fired two torpedoes into the sailing ship, blowing her to pieces. Rescue craft were unable to find a trace of her crew, numbering twenty-seven men, when they arrived in the area. Leslie's name is recorded on the Portsmouth Naval Memorial.

SIDNEY W. WATTS

The late Pte. S. WATTS, Oxford and Bucks L.I., son-in-law.—Killed in action.

Sidney William Watts was born at Wokingham in 1878, the youngest of eleven children. His father worked as a shoemaker, but within three years of Sidney's birth, he was admitted to the Berkshire County Moulsford Asylum at Cholsey, where he died in 1890. Sidney's mother struggled to support the family, working as a charwoman, but was admitted to Easthampstead Union Workhouse in the first decade of the twentieth century, dying there in 1915. Sidney worked as a butcher in Crowthorne after leaving school, living with an elder brother, before marrying Emily Seymour in 1906. He signed up under the Derby Scheme, attesting at Reading, and joined the Royal Berkshire Regiment, later being transferred to the 2nd Battalion, Oxford and Bucks Light Infantry. The battalion had been in the vicinity of Ovillers, but moved to Aveluy on 14th February 1917, and provided working parties for the next few days. Later that month, they went back into the trenches, and there were some casualties on the 27th, from both German shelling, and our own artillery firing 'shorts'. Casualties for the month were seven killed and fourteen wounded. They were in the front line on 1st March, and relieved after dark by the 24th Battalion, Royal Fusiliers, a relief that was effected quickly and without incident. The diary records that one man was killed; that man was Sidney. His body was not recovered, and his name is listed on the Thiepval Memorial. As well as her husband, Sidney's wife lost four brothers in the conflict; she died in 1976.

H. C. WEST

H. C. WEST.

Henry Cave West was born in 1881 at Chiselhurst, Kent, and had two younger sisters. His father was a barrister, and the family lived comfortably, looked after by two or three servants. Henry attended Wellington College from 1896 to 1900, and was Head of School in 1899. Following this, he went to Balliol College, Oxford, where he played both rugby and hockey for the College, and graduated in 1902. At the end of the same year, Henry obtained a commission in the Royal Horse Artillery, and spent much of the next twelve years in India. He married in Scotland in 1911. He was with 'S' Battery in India when war broke out, and they remained there until March 1915, when they moved to Mesopotamia. Henry was awarded the Military Cross for his quick-thinking at Nukhaila on 3rd March. In mid afternoon, the Turks attacked, just as the guns were being limbered. The Regimental History records the action: "Seeing the guns of 'S' Battery in danger, a squadron of 33rd Cavalry, led by Lieutenant Colonel Stack, charged right into the enemy, and that gallant officer was wounded. But the enemy got into the Battery, whose officers fought hard with swords and pistols and severe hand-to-hand fighting developed; in thick dust and sand, the figures of wildly galloping horsemen could be seen, bullets whistling in every direction. The Arabs, clearly after a gun, shot at the horses of 'A' sub-section. Captain H. C. West, the Section Commander, and Major J. Renny-Tailyour, dashed across to the gun and, with some gunners, defended it with revolvers and rifles, keeping the enemy at bay." He was also Mentioned in Despatches. In November, they were at El Kutunie, southeast of Baghdad, in modern-day Iraq. There was daily reconnaissance, but very little to report, and any enemy encountered turned tail and fled as soon as the British and Indians opened fire. The Division marched to Zeur on the 19th, and to Levy the following day. A column, consisting of the Cavalry Brigade, the 76th Punjabis, and the Maxim Battery left again at 7:45pm, to march and get into position for an attack on Ctesiphon the next day, arriving at 3am. Six hours later, the column was attacked from the rear by a large body of Arab Cavalry, but they again fled as soon as the guns opened fire. They were then fired on by Turkish infantry from concealed trenches over half a mile away. It took the British guns half an hour to get their range, but then about four thousand Turks were seen retiring from the trenches and vanished over the ridge, with the 76th Punjabis in pursuit. Later, they came under heavy artillery fire from the west, and a Turkish counter-attack, in which the Cavalry Brigade suffered heavily. Henry, a Captain, was the only Officer killed, caused by an exploding shell; more horses sustained injury than men. After the war, Henry's grave could not be located, and his name is now listed on the Basra Memorial.

Tpr. F. WESTLAKE, Havelock Road, Wokingham.—Wounded.

FREDERICK T. WESTLAKE

Frederick Thomas Westlake was born in Wokingham in 1886, and grew up in Havelock Road near the railway station. He was one of six brothers, a sister dying in infancy. His father worked as a carpenter, but none of his sons followed the same trade. After leaving school, Frederick worked as a baker for George Pigg, who ran a shop in Broad Street, Wokingham, before joining the Royal Berkshire Regiment, attesting in Reading on 20th September 1903. He was 5'8" tall, weighed just over eight stones, with brown eyes, brown hair, a sallow complexion, and scars on his left knee and right shoulder. After nine months' training with the 3rd Battalion, he became a regular solider, and was in Chakrata, India, with the 2nd Battalion at the time of the 1911 census. After completing his time with the Colours, Frederick worked as an attendant at Broadmoor; this is his link with Crowthorne as all his family remained in Wokingham. At the outbreak of war, he was recalled and served with the 1st Battalion. The battalion were at Aldershot when war was declared, and were ready to leave a week later when they were inspected by King George V and Queen Mary. They left Farnborough by train the next day, and crossed the Channel from Southampton to Rouen overnight. They were in trenches for the first time on the 23rd at Villereuile-le-Sec, about five miles southeast of Mons and, although coming under heavy shelling for four hours, played no part in the attack that day. For the next two weeks, the British were in retreat, but the tables turned on 8th September, and they started to advance again. By the middle of the month, the advance was halted and trench warfare on the Western Front began. The next major incident occurred on 24th October when the battalion, now northeast of Ypres, were ordered to drive some Germans out of the area around Westhoek. The attack began in mid-afternoon and, despite coming under heavy rifle and shell fire, was successful and a ridge running from Zonnebeke to Bekelaere captured. The enemy attempted to deceive them by sounding the British "Retire" and representing themselves as Belgians, but "failed ignominiously". It was probably during this attack that Frederick was wounded. He died in a hospital at Boulogne on the 29th, and is buried in Boulogne Eastern Cemetery. He is also listed on the War Memorial at Wokingham Town Hall, in Wokingham.

EDWARD A. WHITE

Edward Albert White was born at Sandhurst on 6th May 1886 and baptised there two months later. His father, a coal porter, died when Edward was only eight years old, and the family moved to Crowthorne with his mother working as a laundress and domestic servant to support the family of seven children. Edward worked a telegraph messenger boy after leaving school, before joining the 1st Battalion, Hampshire Regiment in 1905. As he attested at Blackwater, it is likely he was a member of a Territorial Battalion before becoming a regular soldier. In the 1911 census, he was in South Africa with the 2nd Battalion. He was back with the 1st Battalion at Colchester at the outbreak of war, and as part of the 4th Division, it was initially planned to be part of the original British Expeditionary Force, but was held back in England at the last minute, to counter any German landing. A decision was soon taken to despatch it to France, and it arrived at Le Havre before the end of August, just in time to play a valuable part at the Battle of Le Cateau. The battalion also took part in the Battle of the Marne, the Battle of the Aisne and the Battle of Messines in the same year, as well as the Second Battle of Ypres in 1915. It was during this that the Hampshires moved into the front line on 10th May, and faced a German attack three days later. A heavy bombardment, lasting some three hours, started at daybreak, with the whole the whole trench disappearing in a cloud of yellow smoke. At 7am, the German infantry began to advance across the three hundred yards of No Man's Land, but neither this nor two subsequent attacks succeeded, and heavy casualties were inflicted on the attackers. To the disappointment of the defenders, who even stood up and challenged them to try again, the Germans abandoned their effort and let their gunners resume the bombardment, which raged until early in the afternoon. The day had cost the Hampshires some ninety casualties, including Edward who was killed. His body was never recovered, and his name is listed on the Ypres (Menin Gate) Memorial.

FREDERICK WHITE

The late Sergt. FRED WHITE, Royal Irish Rifles, Crowthorne.—Killed in action. Aged 24.

Frederick White was Edward's younger brother, born on 4th December 1890 at Sandhurst, and baptised there on 22nd February the following year. He too joined the Army, choosing the 2nd Battalion, Royal Irish Rifles, attesting at Aldershot in 1909, and is listed with them at the Citadel Barracks, Dover, in the census taken two years later. On the outbreak of war, the battalion were at Tidworth Barracks on the edge of Salisbury Plain, and landed at Rouen just over a week later. They took part in the Battle of Mons, the Battle of the Marne and the Battle of the Aisne that year. On 14th October, the battalion moved forward and re-occupied an old position just south of Crois Barbee. Soon after dark, heavy firing broke out on the right, and extended along the whole front, both sides firing heavily for two to three hours. Subsequently, it was ascertained this originated from a French attack on Vermelles. Five men were killed during the night, one of them being Serjeant Frederick White. His grave could not be located after the war, and his name is listed on the Le Touret Memorial.

W. HORACE WICKS

William Horace Wicks, known by his second name, was born at Hydrabad, India, in 1896, the eldest of three brothers. His father, a soldier in the Wiltshire Regiment, died in about 1900. His mother returned to England with her three young sons to live in her home town of York Town, but further misfortune overtook her when her youngest son died the following year. She remarried in 1903, and four more children were born over the course of the next decade. It is not known what work Horace did after leaving school, but he was conscripted into the 1st Battalion, Bedfordshire Regiment at the beginning of 1917, attesting at Camberley. It is difficult to know precisely when he joined the battalion in France, but a draft of eight men arrived on 27th May while they were in a camp south of Roclincourt. If Horace was in this draft, he would have watched 13 Platoon, 'D' Company win the inter platoon football final the following day, 'D' Company taking on the rest of the battalion on the 29th, and the battalion lose to the 11th Battalion, East Lancashire Regiment on the 31st. Two more drafts arrived on the first two days of June, and their first experience in the front line occurred a fortnight later, with the successful capture of trenches at Oppy Wood at the end of the month. The King visited the area on 11th July, for which they lined the road. They took part in the Battle of Poellcapelle, part of the Third Battle of Ypres, on 9th October, attacking Polderhoek Chateau, but the attack failed and they withdrew to their start positions. Having been under heavy shelling for a week, they were withdrawn to Ridge Wood, and spent time recovering and preparing for the next attack. The Second Battle of Passchendaele would start on 26th October, and on the previous day, the Bedfordshires were stationed at Stirling Castle, near Sanctuary Wood in the Ypres Salient. Here they were heavily shelled at intervals, and it appears that Horace was killed by one of the shells. His body was never found, and his name is listed on the Tyne Cot Memorial.

P. JOHN WILDMAN-LUSHINGTON

Percy John Wildman-Lushington was born on 1st November 1888 at Camberley, one of seven children. His father was an Army Captain who had met his wife while stationed in Ireland. After he retired in the 1890s, the family moved to Crowthorne, where his sons attended Wellington College as day boys. It is not known what Percy did after finishing his education, and is missing from the 1911 census, but he married Agnes Gaynor on 2nd September 1912 in Vancouver, Canada. He joined the Canadian Battalion, Royal Irish Fusiliers there on 2nd March 1913, but left at his own request a week before Christmas to return to England with his wife and a young daughter. His brother, Gilbert, who had been Winston Churchill's flying instructor, had been killed in a flying accident at the beginning of the month. Percy volunteered for service when war broke out, and was stationed at Hawick, just over the Scottish border, with the King's

Own Scottish Borderers. In April 1915, he applied for a commission which was immediately granted, and went to France in October the same year, attached to the 6th Battalion. He suffered a slight head wound from a piece of shell at the end of January 1916, which required hospital treatment at Etaples. The battalion fought in several phases of the Battle of the Somme later that year, and in the Arras Offensive during the spring of 1917. On 2nd May, the Borderers were in Obermayer, and moved up to the line during the evening, for an attack at 3:45am the following morning. Although they were successful in reaching their objective, the battalions on either side of them failed, leaving them "in the air." Eventually, it was decided they should retire to the original line, but found it very difficult as the intervening ground was swept by machine gun fire. Casualties were very heavy, with over four hundred casualties among the other ranks. Thirteen of the fifteen Officers failed to return, including Percy, who was listed as missing. Letters were sent between the War Office and the Red Cross in Geneva from June onwards, trying to establish his whereabouts. An unofficial report had been received eight days after the failed attack: "*He was killed to the right of Oppy Wood about 4am on 3rd May, and informant saw it.*" A month later, another report surfaced, from Lance Corporal Edward McCann in Etaples Hospital: "On the night on May 3/4th, Pte Powell, 19111 in 'A' Coy, and another man came in. They had been in a shell hole all day as the attack was not a success. Pte Powell told me that he had seen an Officer lying dead, and he felt almost sure it was Mr Lushington. Powell was a Lewis gunner in Mr Lushington's platoon, so he would know him well, though he told me he could not be absolutely certain it was the Lieutenant. This was to the left of the chemical works, and on the right of Gavrelle." This report was marked 'Not Sufficient,' and probably never reached his family. An eye-witness report was filed on 15th June. The informant was Private James Cannon, in hospital in Paisley, Glasgow: "I saw Lt. Lushington killed in action in an attack on the right of Oppy Wood at 4 o'clock in the morning of 3rd May. I was wounded in the same attack, so do not know what happened to his body. He was dark, tall, broad, and clean-shaven." The same man was interviewed four weeks later, when he stated he "saw Lt. Lushington wounded, and that he saw him fall, but that he himself was wounded immediately afterwards, and he saw nothing further of Lt. Lushington." On 22nd November, the War Office wrote to Percy's widow to state they had received no news, including from Prisoner of War lists, and her husband was presumed dead. Just over a week later, the War Council considered his case, and his death was officially notified to the waiting family on 13th December. At the end of the year, another report, from Private James Branigan, was received: "I heard Pte D. Graham say, when I was behind the line, that Lt. Lushingon was killed," but by March the following year, he had changed his story: "Killed at Gavrelle on 3rd May 1917. I saw him killed myself." Percy's body was never found, and his name is listed on the Arras Memorial. His widow, now with two small children, received just under £600. Percy's medals came up at auction in 2011.

Pte. W. WILLOUGHBY, Broadmoor, Crowthorne.—Prisoner of war.

WILLIAM C. WILLOUGHBY

William Charles Willoughby was born at Reading in 1887, the eldest of three brothers. His father worked as a clerk at Huntley and Palmer's biscuit factory, dying in 1912. But William joined the Royal Scots Fusiliers in 1903 at the age of sixteen, attesting at Reading. After serving in the army, he took a job at Crowthorne as an assistant attendant at Broadmoor Hospital, and married Florence Woods, a laundry maid at the hospital, in 1913. Recalled at the outbreak of war, he arrived in Le

Havre with the Royal Scots Fusiliers on 14th August, just ten days after war was declared. Eight days later, they crossed the border into Belgium, arriving at Ghlin, near Mons, around 1pm, having moved north in stages by train and marching. The weather had been very hot and dry, and the Medical Officer sent back 23 men who had been unable to cope with the marches. A hasty medical inspection of Reservists suggested that periodic inspections would be necessary to assess their physical fitness. The battalion took up a position on the south bank of a canal, running from Jemappes to Mons, guarding four crossings. At 11am next morning, the Germans attacked in force at the two western crossings. The Scots Fusiliers held on until they were informed the units on both flanks had withdrawn, and retired to the north edge of Flamieres at about 3pm. Before the withdrawal, all the bridges were blown and boats sunk to impede the Germans' advance. There were fifty casualties from this first encounter with the enemy; William was missing, presumed dead, and his name is listed on the La Ferte-sous-Jouarre Memorial. The Reading Mercury published his photograph, listing him as a Prisoner of War, but there is no other evidence to support this. His wife gave birth to a son a few months after his death.

DOUGLAS R. WOLFE

Douglas Robert Wolfe was born at Hawkhurst, Kent, in 1894, and was one of ten children. His father worked on the railways as a porter and warehouseman, but was not in work at the time of the 1911 census when visiting his son, who was by now working at Crowthorne as a telegraph boy. One of Douglas's elder brothers was also in the village, making deliveries for a grocer. At the outbreak of war, Douglas, who had moved to Bracknell, volunteered for service, attesting at Wokingham, and joined the 2nd Battalion, Royal Berkshire Regiment. He arrived in France in mid March 1915 when the battalion were fighting at Neuve Chapelle, and was probably in the draft of three hundred men who joined on the 21st, just after the battle. The battalion took part in the Battle of Aubers in May, and at Bois Grenier in September. The latter was a diversionary attack, coinciding with the Battle of Loos, designed to capture a section of the German front line. Three companies of the Berkshires were in the centre of the line, with one coming under fire as they formed up prior to the attack, having been picked up by a searchlight. The attack was mainly successful except for one section of trench, from which the Germans eventually pushed back all the attackers. The battalion took part on the first day of the Battle of the Somme in 1916. Their objective was to capture the village of Ovillers, but they were met with very heavy rifle and machine gun fire as they left the trenches, and suffered well over four hundred casualties. The winter of 1916/17 was exceptionally cold with many cases of frostbite among the men. A large attack had been planned for 4th March, and the battalion had been practising on a model while in rest billets the week before. The first objective was Pallas Trench near the village of Bouchavesnes, which was captured without too much resistance. The second wave pushed on towards Fritz Trench, which ran parallel to it, but it had been so damaged by the bombardment from the British artillery that they failed to recognise it in the darkness and carried on Bremen Trench, but retreated when they realised their error. The Berkshires held the two captured trenches despite several counter-attacks, but were heavily bombarded in Pallas Trench at 4pm and lost many men. Twelve hours later, the Germans recaptured part of Fritz Trench, and the remainder of the battalion were occupying a new trench, dug between the two, when they were relieved the following night. Frank was killed during the German counter-attack; his body was never recovered, and his name is listed on the Thiepval Memorial. He is also listed on the War Memorial in his home village of Hawkhurst.

The late Sergt. F. WRIGHT, 1st Batt.
Royal Irish Rifles, Crowthorne.—Killed
in action.

FRANK WRIGHT

Francis William Wright was born in Crowthorne in 1887, but grew up in Kingston-upon-Thames, Surrey. He and his twin brother Charles were the eldest of nine children. Their mother died in 1905, and their father remarried the following year, with two further children being born. Frank's father worked as a print compositor, but Frank joined the army in 1903, not long after his sixteenth birthday, attesting at Kingston, and joined the 1st Battalion, Royal Irish Rifles. The 1911 census lists him at Alexandra Barracks in Maymyo, Burma. The town had begun as a military outpost, but became a permanent military post in 1896, and the summer capital of British Burma (when Rangoon became too hot and humid). It was considered a very desirable army posting, as well as a pleasant refuge for colonialists for whom daily trainloads arrived, carrying bulky furniture, silver teas services and pianos! There was a polo ground, and a golf course. Even the surrounding jungle had been carved up with walks, rides and avenues cut through it. The battalion were in Aden when war was declared, returning to England in October, and arriving in France on 6th November. Nine days later, they were marching to the trenches from Tilleloy to Laventie at 4:30pm, and came under fire for the first time, although it appeared to be targeted on a nearby British battery rather than them. There were also sounds of heavy firing coming from their right. By 9pm, they were in the trenches, although two men were mortally wounded during this changeover. The War Diary describes the 15th as a "baptism of fire in this war." The next six days were spent improving and deepening the trenches. Several men were hit by snipers, and 'A' Company, at the extreme right of their position, suffered from fire from high explosive shells. This company was so far from battalion headquarters that, without telephone communications in place, messages were taking an hour and half to arrive in either direction. The Germans made some "minor attacks …. but without vigour." Officer patrols visited the German trenches at intervals during the hours of darkness to obtain information, the most valuable of which was that the Germans kept very few men in front trenches at night. During these six days, the battalion suffered around forty casualties, including ten deaths. Frank was one of these, and is buried in the Royal Irish Rifles Graveyard, Laventie. His twin brother Charles survived the war, and died in 1959.

DENNISTOUN H. YATMAN

Dennistoun Hamilton Yatman was born at Weymouth, Dorset, on 22nd August 1898, and baptised there a month later. His father served with the Northumberland Fusiliers, rising to Brigadier General, and was awarded the D.S.O. during the Boer War, a conflict in which he was taken prisoner-of-war for forty-eight hours. Dennistoun spent some of his early childhood living in Jersey with his maternal grandparents, and attended Eagle House School at Sandhurst from 1907 to 1912, where he appears on the Roll of Honour in the school chapel, Marlborough College, and the Royal Military College, Sandhurst, leaving with a commission in his father's regiment in 1916. He served with the 1st Battalion, probably arriving in France to take part in some of the phases of the Battle of the Somme. The battalion also took part in phases of the

Battle of Arras, the Third Battle of Ypres, as well as the Battle of Cambrai in 1917, and faced the German offensive in the spring of 1918. On 10th April, the Northumberlands moved to a position near Le Hamel, east of Corbie, and by mid afternoon were in support to the 15th Battalion, Yorkshire Light Infantry, in shell holes in front of the village. Two companies went into the front line in the evening, with the other two also occupying the front trenches the next day. Although there is no mention of incident that caused his death, the War Diary records that Dennistoun was killed on the 11th; the most likely cause being a sniper's bullet. He is buried in Canadian Cemetery No 2, Neuville-St, Vaast.

CROWTHORNE SCHOOL

The Roll of Honour, containing the names of 46 former pupils of Crowthorne Church of England School on Dukes Ride, was unveiled on 9th May 1921.

H. ANNETTS
Harry George Annetts – see main Crowthorne listing

S. BARRETT
Sidney L Barratt – see main Crowthorne listing

W. BARTLETT
William Bartlett – see main Crowthorne listing

W. BELL
William W Bell – see main Crowthorne listing

A. BROWN
Charles Alan Brown – see main Crowthorne listing

G. COX
George Harry Cox – see main Crowthorne listing

F. L. DEANE
Frederick Llewellyn Deane – see main Crowthorne listing

H. C. DICKER
Horace George Dicker – see main Crowthorne listing

E. ELMER
Ernest Elmer – see main Crowthorne listing

S. GODDARD

Samuel Goddard – see main Crowthorne listing

J. GODWIN

James Lewis Godwin – see main Crowthorne listing

R. C. GOULDING

Richard Cecil Goulding – see main Crowthorne listing

S. HALLETT

Sidney Cyril Hallett – see main Crowthorne listing

F. HARFIELD

Frederick Augustus George Harfield – see main Crowthorne listing

H. HARFIELD

William Henry Charles Down Harfield – see main Crowthorne listing

F. LANGLEY

Frank Langley – see main Crowthorne listing

A. LOVICK

Archibald J Lovick – see main Crowthorne listing

H. LOVICK

Henry Lovick – see main Crowthorne listing

C. MARTIN

Charles William Martin was born in Crowthorne in 1893, the youngest of three boys. By 1901, the family had moved to the Paddington area of London, where his father worked as a gas and hot water fitter. After leaving school, Charles worked as a garden boy in Bromley before joining the 1st Battalion, Grenadier Guards, in 1912. The battalion were already in London when war was declared, and after a brief spell in the New Forest, went to Zeebrugge in early October with orders to defend Antwerp against the advancing German army. However, by the time they arrived, the city was already falling, and instead they held certain important bridges and other places that would help the westward evacuation of the Belgian army. After this, they moved westwards and entrenched in front of Ypres. The Regimental history describes the fighting over the next few days: "A violent attack was made by the enemy on 24th October on the salient formed by the British line. After some desperate fighting, the Wiltshire Regiment was driven in, and the Germans got possession of Polygon Wood. In the evening, news arrived that the First Corps was attacking the enemy on the left, and this somewhat relieved the situation.

The following day, the Germans were reported to be concentrating all along the southern front and opposite Zandvoorde. About sunset, the Grenadiers were attacked, and one platoon from No. 2 Company, under Lieutenant Lambert, became isolated, the enemy having taken the trench on its right and also the houses behind it. Three messengers were sent back to Battalion Headquarters for help, but only one got through, and he was wounded. Another attack developed later that night, and a mass of men were seen advancing on the left. A voice called out, 'Don't shoot! We are the South Staffords.' But the German helmets could be distinctly seen against the glow from a burning farm; a heavy fire was opened on them, and slowly they disappeared. In the morning, forty or fifty dead Germans were counted in front of the platoon under Lieutenant Lambert. Before dawn, Charles's Company took over the fire trenches. A terrific shelling of the trenches began early in the morning, and reached such a pitch that the men counted as many as sixty shells a minute on each small trench. The men held on, in spite of the fact that again and again, the shells blew in the trenches and buried half-a-dozen men at a time, all of whom had to be dug out with shovels. Some of them had as much as three feet of earth on top of them, and many were suffocated before they could be rescued. So violent were these attacks that by mid-day, the Germans had broken through the line held by two companies of the South Staffords, which had been sent to relieve the Border Regiment. By 2:30pm, the enemy had gone through the gap, and had managed to get in rear of two companies of the Scots Guards, which suddenly found themselves surrounded and fired at from all directions. Although the Scots Guards still fought on, they were captured by degrees in small parties, and the survivors were finally made prisoners. Finding his flank exposed, Lieut.-Colonel Earle at once gave orders to the Grenadiers to retire, but his order did not reach the fire trenches for a long time, and was never received by the King's Company at all. By now, the Germans had got round both flanks, and the rest of the Battalion were retiring. The isolated platoons continued to fight on until they were overwhelmed by the advancing German masses." Charles and his colleagues were killed; his body was never recovered after the fighting, and his name is recorded on the Ypres (Menin Gate) Memorial.

F. MARTIN

Frank Herbert Martin was an elder brother of Charles, born in 1892. He was still living with his parents by the time of the 1911 census. By now, they had moved to Bromley Common in Kent, where his father worked as a farrier and general smith; Frank was recorded as a "house boy domestic." By January 1915, he gave an address in Kingston Road, Wimbledon, and was working as a ship's steward. He volunteered for service, and joined the 9th Battalion, Royal Berkshire Regiment at the Reading depot in Oxford Road. He was described as almost 5'8" tall, with "much hair on chest and top of shoulder blades." After completing his training, he went to France at the end of July. Early the following year he reported sick, complained of diarrhoea, and it was noticed he was losing weight. He was invalided home on 20th February, still suffering from diarrhoea, and tuberculosis was diagnosed in his sputum. He was discharged from the Army on 24th March with tuberculosis of the lung, not the result of, but aggravated by, active service, and died a few months later.

L. MARTIN
Leslie Gilbert Martin – see main Crowthorne listing

A. MCCABE

The late Second Lieut. A. P. McCABE, formerly of Crowthorne.—Killed in action. Aged 27.

Albert Peter Patrick McCabe was born at Crowthorne in 1886. His parents were both Irish and had fourteen children, ten of whom survived. The family soon moved to Sandhurst where Albert's father worked as a gymnastic instructor at the Royal Military Academy. Albert joined the 2nd Battalion, Royal West Surrey Regiment, on 4th May 1905, attesting at Guildford, not being in work at the time, and was based at Stoughton Barracks, to the north of the town. He soon became a physical training instructor like his father, qualifying in 1906, and adding the additional subject of swimming two years later. He had signed on for ten years, and risen to the rank of Company Sergeant Major by the time he applied to extend the period to 21 years in 1914, and was transferred to the Royal Military Academy at Sandhurst as an instructor. After the outbreak of war, he applied for a commission just before Christmas, and went to France as a Second Lieutenant in the middle of January 1915, although the War Diary does not record his arrival. At the beginning of February, as a relief to the task of fighting, the battalion played the Royal Fusiliers at football, but were soundly beaten by six goals to nil. On the 14th, they were placed on instant readiness as a German attack was anticipated, but it never materialised. Men were going to, and returning from, hospital all month, probably suffering the effects of trench foot. At the beginning of March, the battalion moved from Fleurbaix to Laventie, and entered a new set of trenches. Next day, a German practically walked into the trench, and was taken prisoner. Not much is recorded in the War Diary for the rest of the month, or for April. Late in the evening on 8th May, the battalion marched up to the support trenches for an attack the next day, designed to capture Aubers Ridge. The attack made little progress, and they remained in support all day, being shelled intermittently, before returning to the trenches for the night, and returned to billets in Essars 24 hours later. On the 16th, it was their turn to lead the attack. The distance between British and German lines was less than two hundred yards, but the intervening ground was very uneven and difficult, consisting of ditches and long grass. The attack started at 3:15am, but was immediately met with intense rifle fire, the Germans not seeming to have been affected by the preceding artillery bombardment. A second bombardment was asked for, and this was more successful, and the German trench captured by 6am. Throughout the day, the enemy heavily shelled the original British line and captured German first line, and at 3:30pm, the British found themselves subject to enfilade high explosive shell fire from both flanks. "The battalion had done what was asked of it but at great cost," recorded the War Diary. Albert, who was Mentioned in Despatches, was one of those killed, although there was some confusion on the actual date of his death, but it was finally recorded as 16th May. He is buried in Guards Cemetery, Windy Corner, Cuinchy.

A. E. PARKER

Albert Edward Parker – see main Crowthorne listing

G. PARKER

George Edward Parker – see main Crowthorne listing

A. PEARCE

Arthur Pearce – see main Crowthorne listing

F. PEARCE

Frederick Pearce – see main Crowthorne listing

F. PITHER

Frederick John Pither – see main Crowthorne listing

P. ROBINSON

Percy Robinson – see main Crowthorne listing

The late Pte. CHAS. ROSE, 1st Batt. Hants Regiment, formerly a servant at Wellington College and at the Royal Military College, Sandhurst.—Killed in action. Aged 28.

C. ROSE

Charles Rose was born at Chobham, Surrey in 1885. He was the youngest of eight children, but his mother died when he was only three years old. His father, a police constable, remarried in 1893, and another four children were born. But his second wife also died, and he married for a third time in 1900, with a further seven children being born, three of whom died in infancy. His father had by now retired from the Police Force, and was working as a farm labourer near St Sebastian's church on Nine Mile Ride. Charles joined one of the Territorial Battalions of the Hampshire Regiment at Blackwater, and transferred to the 1st Battalion in 1905. The battalion were at Colchester when war was declared, and landed at Le Havre less than three weeks later. They were soon in action at Le Cateau where, although heavily outnumbered, the British held the Germans at bay and inflicted heavy losses, before making a retreat. On September 12th, after three hours in billets at Septments, the Hampshires led the way down to the river Vesle. About midnight, they started to cross the river, using a damaged bridge. It was a tedious business, the main girders having been cut through; men could only cross in single file, while ammunition carts had to be unloaded, taken across empty, and then reloaded on the far side. No opposition was encountered, and they found Bucy de Long unoccupied. The Hampshires reached the foot of the nearby heights just as day was breaking, sweeping up them, the battalion established itself on the crest. A German outpost, completely surprised, retired in haste. Unluckily, the position had serious tactical defects, above all, the difficulty of finding good artillery positions north of the river. When, early on 13th September, the Germans started a heavy bombardment, little reply could be made and the men could only hang on despite the shell-fire and do their best with their 'grubbers' to improve their position. This lack of artillery support effectively prevented any advance during the three weeks the Hampshires spent on the Aisne. Charles was killed two days later, and is commemorated by a Special Memorial in Crouy-Vauxrot French National Cemetery, Crouy, which marks several unidentified men brought in after the armistice.

W. H. SCRIBBINS

William Howard Scribbins – see main Crowthorne listing

R. SEDMAN

Richard Henry Sedman was born at Catford, Kent, on 29th May 1892, and had an elder brother. His father had been in the army for eight years, serving in the Hussars and Army Service Corps, before working as a commercial traveller, while his mother, a Wokingham native, was an elementary school teacher. In the 1901 census, the family were recorded as living in Station Road, Crowthorne (presumably Duke's Ride). After leaving school, Richard worked as a messenger boy, before joining the Army Service Corps, signing for twelve years' service at Woolwich on 29th August 1907, at the age of just fifteen. He was just five feet tall, and weighed six stone, with brown eyes, dark brown hair, a dark complexion, a scar on his cheek, and moles below the right shoulder, right buttocks, and left of his navel. He continued to study, gaining Third Class and then Second Class education certificates within six months. There are no further entries on his service record to record any overseas service, nor any details of the cause of his discharge, on the grounds of misconduct, on 8th December 1911. Whatever happened, Richard decided to make a new start, and the following year left England and sailed to Australia, arriving at Sydney in October. Although he had been employed as a chauffeur after leaving the army, he worked as a farm labourer in his new home, and applied for naturalisation. Soon after war broke out, he enlisted for the Australian Forces, attesting at Sydney on 27th August. By now, he was 5'10" tall, and weighed ten and a half stone. He joined the 3rd Battalion, which had formed at Randwick, six miles from Sydney, two weeks earlier. By 3rd September, the battalion were at full strength. The following day, the War Diary bemoaned the slackness of the rank and file in saluting the officers. Inspections were held, those not already vaccinated were duly inoculated, feet were inspected(!), Church parades were held (and a list of Methodists compiled), and all leave cancelled. There were route marches, instruction and lectures, musketry practise, trench digging, and drills. On 19th October, trams took the men to the quayside, where they boarded the Transport Ship 'Euripides' which sailed the following day. Training for signallers and machine-gunners started at once. A week later, they arrived at Albany, having had calm seas for the voyage so far. No leave was allowed, and no visitors allowed to visit those on board. All gambling and dice games were also banned. The transport fleet left Albany on 1st November, with lectures and training continuing. Instructions were ordered that nothing was to be thrown overboard; this was an on-going problem as the same instructions are recorded in the War Diary at regular intervals. On the 7th, the alarm sounded when a German vessel was sighted, but nothing happened. The first casualty occurred two days later, although it is not recorded as to what caused the death, and the body was buried at sea. Concern was noted about the amount of water being used, and it was only to be made available during certain hours. Activities were suspended in the afternoons on account of the heat. On the 13th, there was a ceremony on board as they crossed the equator, and three days later, they reached Columbo. Eighteen hours later, they were on their way again, reaching Aden on the 25th, Alexandria on 3rd December, and proceeded to Mena Camp, next to the pyramids at Cairo. At the entrance of the camp, a whole township had risen almost overnight, which was dedicated to serving the troops at Mena. Everything was on sale: foods, coffee, liquor, postcards, as well as four cinemas that featured the very latest of Hollywood releases, even before they reached Australia. The buildings were constructed from any available materials, such as hessian and corrugated iron, as well as stone. The streets and alleyways were filled with the sounds of the vendors touting for business, while different aromas "gave the nose a range of sensations from enjoyment to disgust, all in the space of a minute." The seemingly mandatory activity, that every soldier participated in, was getting a picture taken of them on a camel by the Pyramids. Catching the last tram back to Mena Camp in the evenings was always precarious for everyone. The tramways were not designed to carry such large numbers, and to cope with the sheer volume, men were compelled to sit on the roof of the carriage, causing bemusement to the local Egyptians. Less entertaining was the desire of tram conductors to check every ticket, regardless of the time it took to perform or the crowded state of the trams. This caused great tension between both the tram conductors and the men, and there were many cases occurring of angry Australian soldiers taking out their frustrations on particularly officious and lugubrious conductors. Late arrival back at camp would have meant punishment. Many complaints were lodged at Mena Camp Headquarters by conductors who were assaulted for carrying out their duties. Another Australian was to write home later, "I had no chance to go to Cairo or any other large town to get the lace you want, although I don't remember seeing any native lace in Cairo. There is a terrible lot of fancy stuff sold there, mostly alleged silk shawls etc. synthetic silk I think – it does not appear to me to be genuine - of course the best shops have the real article, but they want high prices. Anyway nearly all of those sort of goods are not Egyptian, but are imported from France and England. The natives seem incapable of making anything but shoddy stuff, even the antiques are faked and are not worth having." Training continued with many night operations. Christmas was marked with "divine services". To break the routine, a field firing competition was held. Finally in early April, they left Cairo by train and embarked at Alexandria, although one man deserted. The voyage to the Greek island of Lemnos took two days, and although the sea was described as 'calm', many of the men were seasick. A contemporary wrote his impressions on arrival at Lemnos: "Shortly after breakfast, we swung round and headed up a broad harbour. The entrance was well mined, leaving only a small channel in the middle for the ships to pass through. A few large troopships were anchored outside the mined area. On the sides of the hills, all round the harbour, were numberless camps, like little white villages of canvas. At the far end of the harbour could be seen villages and farms with cultivated lands. We moved on, through channels and around islets and peninsulas, till we came out into a nice bay which was full of vessels of all sizes and descriptions, hundreds and hundreds of them. There were large grey ominous-looking battle-ships, cruisers, destroyers, gunboats, and trawlers, large troopships, cargo vessels, hospital ships, motor launches, and sailing skiffs. Shortly after we anchored, a submarine appeared in the distance, coming into the bay. She came fairly close to us, so that we got a good view of her. It was the first submarine I have seen." They remained at Lemnos for three weeks, during which time there were more lectures (subjects included 'Co-operation of the Artillery when the Infantry are Advancing', 'Fire Direction and Control', 'First Aid', 'International Law', 'Field Entrenchments', 'Outposts', 'Notes on the Turkish Army', and 'Enemy's Ruses and Espionage'), as well as training in boat drill, and embarkation and disembarkation over the side of the ship. They left Lemnos on 24th April, arriving at Gallipoli next morning. They managed to get ashore at Anzac Cove within three hours, although under heavy fire from the enemy who held all the high ground overlooking the landing site, and by evening had captured and occupied some trenches. These were heavily shelled until the navy knocked out the guns firing on them. Heavy fighting continued for the next few days, with the accuracy of the enemy's infantry being noted as a problem. They remained in the firing line for four days until relieved. The fighting so far had cost forty lives, with a further 69 men missing, and 150 wounded. Probably due to his previous experience in the army, Richard had initially been appointed Company bugler, but was promoted to Corporal and then Lance Sergeant in quick succession. A general pattern began to emerge of quiet days, during which the trenches and defences were improved or repaired, followed by bombardment and attacks from the enemy during the nights, but there were no changes in the positions of the front lines. The Turks mounted a serious attack on 19th May, inflicting many casualties, but sustaining heavy losses themselves. A temporary ceasefire was arranged (by flags) the next day in order that the dead and wounded could be collected, but it was felt the Turks were taking advantage of the truce to obtain information about the Allied positions, and a bombardment was resumed. The enemy retaliated on the 21st, and Richard was one of several men wounded, although in his case, it was 'slight.' The War Diary also records "sightseers", men from other units, who left the beach and wandered around the countryside, exposing themselves to fire from both sides, so sentries were posted to prevent them straying into dangerous areas. In October, another letter home recorded, "Our trenches are all captured from the Turks and are swarming with vermin. It is impossible to keep them out of our clothes and blankets. Every morning the boys take off their shirts and have a kill. Raiding their shirts they call it. It is very amusing to see them, sometimes they bet each other also who will kill the most. The Turks are good fighters, all the fighting is done at night time and very early morning. I got one the other morning about day break. We are at present having a spell on the island of Lemnos, the capital town Castro is too far away to visit, but there are some small villages close by which we visit and buy things, the prices of course are very high, exorbitant in fact. Eggs are six for a shilling, butter cannot be got, tinned fruit is two shillings a tin, the cheapest things are grapes. We get about three and a half pounds for sixpence." But Richard was not involved in this advance. On 1st August, he had been admitted to hospital, although it is not clear whether this was for diarrhoea, as recorded in his Service Record, or more likely he was one of the twenty men wounded that day. After four days, he was transferred to Malta, where he was treated for a further three weeks, before being put on a ship back to England, and taken to the 1st Southern General Hospital at Birmingham, based at the city's university. He was discharged from hospital on 3rd December, but spent the next ten months recovering at Number 2 Depot, Weymouth, which accommodated those Anzacs not expected to be fit for duty within six months. In late October 1916, he was taken on a permanent posting there to make up the staff, and was made a temporary Sergeant, where he remained until the following April. He then went to the Command Depot at Perham Downs on Salisbury Plain for three weeks, before rejoining the 3rd Battalion, who were now in France at Burire, near Tincourt. He spent six weeks there, training, marching and parading, before attending the Anzac Corps School at Aveluy for a further five weeks. At this time, the Australian Imperial Force was undergoing a period of expansion, and experienced men were needed as cadre for new battalions that were being raised. But he returned to the 3rd Battalion, who were now at Sec Bois, north of Merville. It was mid September before they would be in the front line again, at Dickebusch. Here they faced shelling, machine-gun fire, and enemy snipers, suffering over one hundred casualties in four days. October saw them at Anzac Ridge, taking over the front line on the 3rd, ready for an attack at 6am the next morning. The enemy artillery had been in action for thirty minutes before this, but fired on the trenches rather than the assembly position in front of it, so no-one was hit. This eased as the Allied artillery opened up, and the Australians advanced behind the barrage. They were held up at a line of German pill boxes, but after some fierce fighting, these were taken. The rest of the day was taken up with consolidating the new line. But at the end of the day, Richard was reported missing, later confirmed as killed. Soon afterwards, the Australian Red Cross Society was dealing with correspondence from worried family and friends. On 5th November, a Miss H. Beeston from Ealing, wrote, "I am writing to ask if you could find out any information for me concerning: 485 Sgt. R. H. Sedman, 3rd Batt. A.I.F. France. We had a notification from the Australian Hd. Qtrs. on Oct. 29th to the effect that he had been missing since Oct. 5th." Four day later, his brother wrote, "I am writing to ask if you could kindly obtain information of my brother Sergeant R. H. Sedman N. 485 3rd Battalion, Australian Imperial Forces, France, posted missing since Oct. 5th. This information reached me Oct. 29th from the Administrative Dept. Westminster, but since this date a registered letter posted by my mother to him was returned bearing mark 'Killed in action Oct. 10', but a parcel despatched after this letter was returned two days later than former marked 'Wounded'. I should very much like some definite information, which the Australian Administrative Dept. appears not to be able to furnish, to put an end to the suspense. Though not reported officially as killed, his allotment to my mother has been stopped." Before an official response could be assembled, his mother wrote, three days into the new year, "I beg to inform you that Sergt. R. H. Sedman 485, 3rd Battn. Aus. Inf. is now reported killed (officially) 5.10.17. I must thank you for all your efforts in trying to trace him, but now must accept the official news received today. I shall try and show my gratitude to the splendid work you do, by forwarding a small donation to the funds in a few days." On the 15th, the news was confirmed, "I very deeply regret to have to inform you of an unofficial report about Pte. R. H. Sedman 485 3rd Battn though we cannot vouch for its accuracy. The informant is Lieut. C. Champion 'A' Coy., 3rd Battn. He states that Private Sedman was a Gallipoli man, an original member of the Battalion. He was Sergeant of No. 1 Platoon 'A' Company, and was also Sergeant Bugler. On October 4th, Lieut. Champion reported him missing. He disappeared during the attack. He saw him leave the tape at 6am at Molenaarelsthoek at the bottom of Passchendaele Ridge, and he was never seen afterwards. Half of the platoon fell from machine-gun fire, and witness is satisfied he must have been killed for it was most improbable any prisoners were taken as the enemy were on the run. We are continuing our enquiries and hope to get you more definite information. Our most sincere sympathy is with you in your loss." A series of eye-witness accounts of Richard's death were also assembled and passed to his relatives. "I knew him personally. He was Sergeant of my platoon. He was in the attack of Oct. 4th 1917, and to my knowledge was last seen at the beginning of the attack at Broodseinde. Eight men from the platoon reached the objective, one of these Frank Charts and Geo. Matick, same platoon, asked me if I had seen anything since the opening of the attack. He was well liked by his men. He had been away from Battalion since Gallipoli." "R. H. Sedman, No. 1 Platoon, "A" Company, 3rd Battalion, were (sic) my platoon sergeant. He was with the platoon at the commencement of the attack, east of Ypres on the 4th October. I was wounded very early in the attack, but was not carried away for 36 hours. Just before being carried away, one of my mates in the same platoon, Pte F. Charters, was brought down wounded to the dressing station (advanced) where I was, by two other men of the platoon, Pte George Matich and another. They asked me if I had seen Sgt. Sedman as none of the remaining men of the platoon had seen him since the opening of the attack. Knowing the nature of the fighting it is, in my opinion, extremely unlikely that Sgt Sedman was taken prisoner, also the heavy raids of the following days would make it very difficult for the searchers to find the men killed in action." "I remember he was reported missing on the 5.10.17, and apart from that I have heard nothing regarding him. I left the Battalion myself on the 7.10.17 wounded, and since them have heard very little concerning them. However should I happen to find out anything regarding him I shall let you know at once. P.S. General description of above – height 5' 8", slight build, complexion dark. Also has few teeth missing in front." "He was killed by a shell near Anzac Ridge, and death was instantaneous, but I myself did not see the casualty. Refer to Sgt. Nixon, 3rd Battalion, for he was Pioneer Sergeant, and put a cross on the grave, near Anzac Ridge." "Sedman was a Sergeant in 'B' Company, 3rd Battalion. A shell burst, and I saw Sedman killed on the morning of 5th Oct. 1917 at Paschendaele (sic). Death was instantaneous. Sedman was tall and of dark complexion, and very popular among the boys. He was buried about a mile to the north of Anzac Ridge." Richard's death was officially recorded for 5th October 1917. After the armistice and the subsequent search for the dead and missing, his grave could not be found; consequently, his name is listed on the Ypres (Menin Gate) Memorial.

E. C. SEYMOUR

Ernest Charles Seymour – see main Crowthorne listing

F. SEYMOUR

Frank Seymour – see main Crowthorne listing

G. H. SEYMOUR

George Henry Seymour – see main Crowthorne listing

F. SLYFIELD

Frank Ernest Slyfield was born at Crowthorne in 1892, a younger brother of George (see main Crowthorne listing). He died in Ireland in 1919, aged just sixteen, so it is probable he had been conscripted into the 3ʳᵈ Battalion, Royal Berkshire Regiment, a training battalion, who were based in Dublin, and died of the Spanish flu that swept through Europe, and beyond, after the war. He did not see active service.

G. SLYFIELD

George William Slyfield – see main Crowthorne listing

S. A. SMITH

Stanley Arthur Smith – see main Crowthorne listing

The late Second Lieut. S. A. SMITH, 10th Batt. Hants Regt.—Killed in action, August 10th, 1915.

S. SMITH

Sydney Arthur Smith was born at Crowthorne on 27ᵗʰ September 1885, the second of seven children. His father worked as an attendant at Broadmoor, but had retired by 1911, and later moved to South Farnborough. Sydney attended St Alfred's Grammar School at Wantage until the age of fifteen, and then for a brief spell, lived with relatives in Farnham, Surrey, who ran the 'Royal Oak' pub, working as a bar assistant. Sydney then joined the Army Service Corps, attesting at Aldershot on 18ᵗʰ July 1900, adding just over three months to his age to do so. He was described as being almost 5'3" tall, weighed seven stone, with blue eyes, dark brown hair, and a fresh complexion. He served for twelve years, leaving with the rank of 2ⁿᵈ Corporal. After his period of service finished, Sydney moved back to live with his parents, working as a clerk in the Commandant's Office at the Royal Military Academy at Sandhurst. At the outbreak of war, Sydney re-enlisted on 5ᵗʰ September 1914, attesting at Camberley, and joined the 7ᵗʰ Battalion, Royal West Surrey Regiment. Because of his previous military experience, he was promoted to Orderly Room Sergeant within a week, and applied for a commission in December. The Assistant Commander, of the R.M.C. gave him a glowing reference, stating, "I have a high opinion of him, both as a man and a solider." He was accepted, although the Lieutenant Colonel of the battalion requested a "posting not to 7/Queen's, in the interest of Sgt Smith"; Sydney was posted to the 10th Battalion. The battalion spent several months in Ireland before returning to Basingstoke, and sailed from Liverpool on 7th July 1915. Going via Mudros, they landed at Gallipoli overnight on the 5th/6th August, where they dug in, with ten men wounded on the first day. The Regimental History records what happened during the next few days: "The 10th Hampshire had spent the early hours of August 7th in a futile move up another gully, north of Russell's Top, only to be sent back again to Shrapnel Gully, and to spend the day there inactively, hearing all sort of rumours. Starting off again at 10am the next day, they filed along the great sap, running northward up the coast to the Fisherman's Hut, where they remained until evening. Advancing again, they found the seaward end of the Chailak Dere being shelled, and had to rush across in small parties, and then struggle along in single file along the narrow gully, choked with wounded making their way down it. Progress was slow and tiring, touch was hard to keep, halts and delays were frequent, and the column had barely settled down in a bivouac before, about 10pm, orders were received to push on. The guides then went wrong and led the column to the foot of a precipice. This meant turning round and retracing the route .... By the time (6am) *the* battalions could start their advance ... the Turks were ready and well placed..... Major Pilleau, with 'A' Company and half *of* 'D', now went forward up a gully ... at its head, however, they came under heavy fire, mainly machine-guns with some shrapnel, and could advance no further .... About 2pm, Captain Hicks took half 'B' Company to reinforce the New Zealanders on Rhododendron Spur, but was sent back as the Brigadier was unable to use the party, which thus incurred a good many casualties and was quite exhausted to no purpose before it got back to battalion headquarters .... Further to the left, a vigorous counter-attack against our troops on Damakjelik Bair had been repulsed with heavy losses, but no forward move could be developed on that flank to assist the troops on the bare slopes of Chunik Bair. They had to lie out, exposed without shelter to a scorching sun, with a mere mouthful of water, while every attempt to advance or move instantly drew fire, and as the troops had little to fire at, their own casualties, though not heavy, were the more noticeable. No more counter-attacks were attempted during the night, but with dawn (August 10th) the Turks came forward in great force, pressing hardest against the troops on Chunuk Bair and driving them back upon Rhododendron Spur." There were many moves and counter-moves recorded during the day; the British and their allies seemed to be in the most desperate positions but managed to hold on, albeit at a high cost. "As far as could be ascertained .... 2/Lt. S. A. Smith *was* killed or missing," concludes the Regimental History. Sydney's body was never found, and his name is recorded on the Helles Memorial. Although Sydney had not made a will, there was an insurance policy with the Pearl Insurance Company, although they would not pay out until a death certificate had been produced, a situation that took several months to resolve due to the lack of his body ever being found. His father also had to write to the War Office for the War Gratuity to be increased, as they had failed to pay the amount due to an officer.

V. SMITH
Victor Robert Smith – see main Crowthorne listing

F. E. SPICER
Frederick James Spicer – see main Crowthorne listing

F. SUTTON
Frank Sutton – see main Crowthorne listing

B. THIEMANN
Albert Frederick Max Thiemann – see main Crowthorne listing

A. E. VAUGHAN
Albert Edgar Vaughan – see main Crowthorne listing

E. A. WHITE
Edward Albert White – see main Crowthorne listing

F. WHITE
Frederick White – see main Crowthorne listing

D. WOLFE
Douglas Robert Wolfe – see main Crowthorne listing

F. WRIGHT
Frank Wright – see main Crowthorne listing

Other Graves

There are three other graves in the churchyard of men who were on the Army lists, but who are not listed on the list of names in the lych gate.

John McAllister Cameron

John McAllister Cameron was born at Lowestoft, Suffolk, in 1881, and was an only child. His father was a Customs Officer, and would have moved from post to post every few years; this was common practise to avoid potential 'convenient arrangements' between them and the local populace. As well as Lowestoft, John grew up in King's Lynn and Yarmouth. He did not serve overseas in the war, but joined the staff at Wellington College as a teacher, and took a commission for service with the Junior Division, Officer Training Corps at the beginning of in 1918. He died on 11th November 1919, and at the end of the year, the College magazine contained a tribute to him: "John McAlister Cameron, who came here in Michaelmas Term, 1915, fell ill at the end of last Summer Term, but as he had never enjoyed good health no-one suspected the gravity of the case, or guessed that the loyal help he had given unsparingly to College was to be withdrawn, and that his work at Wellington was finished. Our consciousness of the wideness of his interests contributes in no small degree to our sense of loss. A classical scholar of long residence in France and Germany, he taught a variety of subjects with great efficiency. As Quartermaster in the Corps, he gave invaluable assistance during a difficult period of transition. As a violinist, he was the mainstay of the Orchestra, and his sitting-room became the recognised resort of the struggling amateur musician. His mordant wit and readiness to oblige endeared him to his colleagues, and it was the latter trait in his character which made him so good an under-Tutor in 'the Murray,' who have lost in him one of their truest friends. True friends are most readily recognisable in moments of crisis, and it was perhaps not until the influenza epidemic of last year that we really appreciated the possibilities of Mr Cameron's usefulness as a friend in need. Something of his capacities for service had already been recognised. Here was seen at its best the quality underlying those capacities – unselfishness. For this quality we shall chiefly remember him; for its loss among us we shall chiefly mourn his death." He is buried in the southwest part of Crowthorne (St John the Baptist) Churchyard.

Rupert Edward Holden Lockley

Rupert Edward Holden Lockley was born in 1878 at Chilton, near Sudbury, Suffolk. His father, a Captain in the West Yorkshire Light Infantry, died in 1890, and his mother remarried four years later. Along with his younger brother, Rupert was educated at King William's College on the Isle of Man, and then obtained a commission in the Lothian Regiment in 1896. He fought in the Boer War with the Gordon Highlanders, returning in 1902 on board a ship with General Viscount Kitchener (later to become Lord Kitchener, Secretary of State for War), and Sir John French (who would be given command of the British Expeditionary Force in 1914). In 1905, he married Fanny Heslewood in London, after which they both went to live in Africa. He transferred to the West African Frontier Force, a field force formed in 1900 due to concerns over French colonisation in the area, to garrison Nigeria, Gold Coast (now Ghana), Sierra Leone and Gambia. He returned to England in September 1913, obtaining special permission to bring his dogs back with him, before returning to Sierra Leone until June the following year. By now, he had risen to the rank of temporary Major. He does not appear to have fought overseas during the conflict, and died on 20th October 1915. Rupert is buried in the churchyard, east of Crowthorne Church, along with his wife, who died a month and one day later.

H. E. STOKES

Herbert Edward Stokes was born at Crowthorne in 1891, one of five children. His father, an attendant at Broadmoor, died in 1899, so his mother took to running a tobacconist and confectionery shop in the High Street, later assisted by one of her daughters, but Herbert worked as a hairdresser. He married Nora Higgs in 1913, with three sons being born, one of whom died within a few days. Herbert stayed in England during the war, serving in the 12th Battalion, Royal Berkshire Regiment. When conscription started, men were classified as to their fitness and those fit for labouring service but unfit for general service, were formed into companies that later became part of Labour Battalions, and then incorporated into the Labour Corps. These were either infantry, agricultural, or labour works companies. The agricultural companies were sent to work on farms, the labour companies were used to build defences in the Portsmouth area, and the infantry works companies were allocated to the camps on Salisbury Plain to do all the odd jobs and heavy work. Herbert's unit was one of these labour battalions, formed in June 1916. On 16th November 1918, five days after the Armistice, the Reading Mercury reported, "The village *(of Crowthorne)* is in the throes of influenza, and in some houses whole families are laid up. Both Broadmoor and Crowthorne schools are closed." Two weeks later, it was reported, "The influenza epidemic is still raging in the neighbourhood. At Wellington College, there are four hundred cases, and there are also many cases at Mr Lockhart's School *(Eagle House)* and at Broadmoor and in the village. Both Broadmoor and Crowthorne schools remain closed. The majority of cases are slight." Herbert was a victim of the outbreak, and is buried near Crowthorne Church. The Reading Mercury of 23rd November 1918 contained a report of the burial: "Mr H. E. Stokes, who carried on business at a newsagent in Crowthorne High Street, died on November 16th from pneumonia, following influenza. At the time he caught the complaint, his wife and two children were ill with influenza. Deceased, who was only 27 years of age, was the second son of the late Mr John Stokes and Mrs Stokes of Chiswick House. He had been employed in the woods on national work for some time. The funeral took place on Tuesday …. four of the deceased's fellow workmen from the woods acted as bearers."

SANDHURST

ST MICHAEL'S CHURCH

The original Roll of Honour, consisting of 75 names, was located in the local branch of the British Legion, and was unveiled early in 1922. When the Club closed, the memorial passed to Sandhurst Council who displayed it in a wooden building. The building burnt down in 1978, when it was realised no transcript of the names had been made. The list in Sandhurst Church was an attempt at a reconstruction of the original list, but contains a few errors and omissions, that have come to light during my research.

H. ACKRILL

The late Pte. H. R. ACKRILL, Royal Warwicks, Sunny Rest Cottage, Sandhurst.—Died of dysentery in France.

Harold Richard Ackrill was born in 1899 at Crowthorne. He was the second of four brothers, another dying in infancy. His parents were both from Oxfordshire, moving to Berkshire with his father's job as a domestic coachman. Harold was conscripted into the 2/7th Battalion, Royal Warwickshire Regiment, attesting at Wokingham. It is not clear precisely when Harold joined the Warwickshires in France, but the battalion were in the forward zone of defences, in the area northwest of Saint Quentin, when the German Spring Offensive started in March 1918. Although vastly outnumbered, the South Midland Division only began to retire on the afternoon of 22nd March, due to the enemy's progress in other parts of the line. They were also involved in action in the River Lys valley and Flemish hills in April. The War Dairy records a lot of sickness in the battalion from July onwards, including 37 men on 2nd July. Harold was one of 68 men taken ill in October, dying on the 9th; he is buried in Terlincthun British Cemetery, Wimille.

A. ANDERSON

Alexander Hay Anderson was born on 5th December 1881 at Sandhurst, and baptised 8th January the following year. He was one of six brothers; a sister dying in infancy. His youngest brother was born in 1894, but by 1901, his mother had been admitted to a lunatic asylum near Wallingford, where she remained until her death in 1926. His father was born in Scotland, and served in the Army, before working at the Royal Military Academy, initially as a valet, and later as a gardener. After leaving school, Alexander also worked as a jobbing gardener. He married Eleanor Phipps in 1907, a daughter being born the following year, and a son six years later. Alexander volunteered for service, attesting at Reading, and joined the 2nd Battalion, Royal Berkshire Regiment. He went to France on the last day of June 1915, and would have gone into the front line a couple of weeks later, when the battalion were taking its turn defending trenches at Bois Grenier. Here they remained, apart from the last two weeks of August when they were in Divisional Reserve at Bac St Maur. On 24th September, they went into the trenches again for an attack the following day. The British trenches formed a semi-circle while the German trenches ran more or less in a straight line. At their closest, the opposing sides were one hundred yards apart, but five times that distance in the centre. However, there were old fire trenches in the intervening distance, and the Berkshires assembled in these for the attack which started at 4:30am after a heavy bombardment of the enemy. 'A' Company, on the right, had the worst of it. The wire in front of them was imperfectly cut, a German searchlight picked them out, and the Germans here seemed more ready for them. Consequently, only a few men reached the German trench and they were not sufficient to hold on. 'B' Company in the centre were most successful, but 'C' Company on the left suffered from an enemy machine gun and, in the dark, they missed some German dug-outs, and their occupants were able to fire on the rear of the troops who had passed. The fight developed into a bombing tit-for-tat, although further back, 'D' Company, in reserve in the assembly trench, were hit by shells, causing more casualties. By the end of the day, all the attackers had withdrawn back to their starting positions. 130 men were killed, over 200 wounded, and sixty were missing. Alexander was one of the latter and his name is recorded on the Ploegsteert Memorial.

E. ANDERSON

Edward Louis Anderson was a younger brother of Alexander, born 30th September 1891, and baptised 8th November. After leaving school, he worked as a butcher's labourer in Sandhurst High Street, living with an elder brother who worked at the same establishment. Edward was already a member of the 2/4th Battalion, Hampshire Regiment, a Territorial Battalion that left for India in December 1914. But he remained in England, transferred to the 1/4th Battalion, who had already gone to Mesopotamia in March 1915, and joined them in October of that year. The Regimental History describes the situation: "Earlier in the year, the British had made some tactical moves to seize important or threatening points beyond Basra. After an early string of cheap successes, eyes increasingly fell on the Mesopotamian capital, Baghdad. The 6th (Poona) Division advanced, leaving a very thinly stretched supply line of hundreds of miles behind it, only to receive a bloody repulse at Ctesiphon. A ragged and dispiriting retreat back to Kut-al-Amara began. The Turks pursued the retreating Division to Kut, and soon surrounded and cut it off. British forces in Mesopotamia were now growing, and these formations were ordered to advance north along the Tigris to relieve Kut. They ran into strong and stoutly defended lines and suffered some hard knocks; although they got close to Kut, the garrison there was surrendered on 29th April 1916." The Battalion Headquarters and one Company of the Hampshires were in the town when it fell. Starting the next day, the captured garrison were forced marched some 1200 miles from Kut to Smyra, over desert, mountains and by river, in searing summer temperatures, where they were placed in Prisoner of War Camps. Already weakened by the long siege, the garrison were in no fit state to undertake the trek, and many died from beri-beri, scurvy, dysentery and malaria during the forced march. Conditions in the destination camps were no better, where the survivors received insufficient food, and faced epidemics of dysentery, cholera, and malaria. Edward was one of those who died during the march, with an official date of 5th February 1917. His name is listed on the Basra Memorial.

J. ANDERSON

James Hay Anderson was born in 1879, and baptised 3rd August, the eldest brother of Alexander and Edward. In the 1901 census, his job is recorded as postman, but ten years later, he was living with his brother Alexander and his young family, working as a jobbing gardener. He volunteered for service, attesting at Kingston-on-Thames, and initially joined the 3rd Battalion, East Surrey Regiment, a training/depot battalion. He was transferred to the 1st Battalion, Border Regiment, and fought in Gallipoli for a couple of months at the end of 1915, before being evacuated to Egypt, and then moved to France, arriving in March the following year. On 1st July, the battalion were just south of Beamont Hamel. The 2nd Battalion, South Wales Borderers, whose objective was the first two German lines, were wiped out by machine gun fire in our own wire. The 1st Battalion, Border Regiment then went over the top from the support line, and met with heavy losses. Despite this, the men formed up as ordered outside our wire, made a right incline, and advanced into No Man's Land at a slow walk, as ordered. The advance was continued until only little groups of half-a-dozen men were left here and there and these, finding that no reinforcements were in sight, took cover in shell holes or wherever they could. By 8am, the advance had been brought entirely to a standstill, and fifteen minutes later, the enemy restarted their bombardment. At 10:30am, any men remaining were ordered back to the Reserve Line, and any attempt to advance in this sector was abandoned. Of the eight hundred men of the battalion who started the advance, over half were wounded, 150 were missing, and around fifty killed. James was one of the latter, and is buried in Hawthorn Ridge Cemetery No 2, Auchonvillers.

F. BANKS

Frampton Joseph Banks was born in 1882 at Lower Wraxall, a few miles northwest of Dorchester, Dorset. His unusual first name was his mother's maiden name. He was one of four children, his mother having died giving birth to his younger sister when he was just four years old. With his father working as a blacksmith, his maternal grandmother lived with the family, to keep house, until her death in 1895. After leaving school, Frampton worked as a labourer near Bridport, Dorset, before joining the Army Special Reserve on 5th November 1900, attesting at Dorchester, and joined the 3rd Battalion of the local regiment. After his initial six months' training, he returned to work, with a period of annual training every year until 1906, when his period of engagement ended. On signing up, he was only 5'1" tall, weighed eight stone, with brown eyes, brown hair, and a fresh complexion. However, he had a particularly well-developed chest, and the note, "Good chest and well-formed recruit" was written on the paperwork at his medical inspection. In 1911, he was working as a domestic groom at Evershott, only a couple of miles from his childhood home. He married Edith Smallbone in 1913, before being recalled to the army at Dorchester at the outbreak of war, joining the 1st Battalion, Duke of Cornwall's Light Infantry, and going to France in early May 1915. Within two months, he had promoted to Lance Corporal, and transferred to the 1st Battalion, Dorsetshire Regiment. On 5th July, the Dorsets were in Ypres Hill 60 sector. At 3pm, one of the trenches was suddenly violently bombarded, with three minenwerfer (short range mortars) quickly following. Soon after, the bombardment was extended to other positions held by the battalion, and the War Diary records the minenwerfer shooting was very accurate, each one followed by four field gun shells. Two machine gun emplacements were destroyed and the trenches badly damaged, but repairs soon made good the damage after the firing stopped. There were eighteen men killed by the firing, five missing, and more than thirty wounded; eight men were also recorded to be suffering from shock. Frampton was one of those killed, and is buried in Larch Wood (Railway Cutting) Cemetery. His wife had moved to Sandhurst by 1916, and a son was born, named after the father he never saw. Although Frampton never lived in the town, he is named on the War Memorial, his name being put forward by his widow.

R. BAREFOOT

The late Pte. REGINALD O. BAREFOOT, the " White Swan," Sandhurst.—Killed in action. Aged 21.

Reginald Osbert Barefoot was born at Englefield, west of Reading, in 1894, and had an elder sister. His father worked as a journeyman carpenter before becoming the publican of The White Swan in Sandhurst. Although his elder sister helped in the pub, Reginald worked as a tailor's assistant after leaving school. He volunteered for service soon after the outbreak of war, attesting at Reading, and joined the 1st Battalion, Royal Berkshire Regiment, arriving in France with a draft on 23rd November 1914; the War Diary records them joining the battalion at Caestre a week later. The battalion marched to Meteren three days later, and was inspected by the King and the Prince of Wales. They remained in billets at Caestre until 18th December, although poor weather prevented much training. Bathing facilities were arranged at the town hall, where men were able to have hot baths twice a week, and concerts and football matches were arranged weekly. They left on the 22nd, travelling to Bethune by bus, marched to Beuvry, and took over part of the line near Givenchy. The trenches were very wet and muddy, and needed much work to improve them, and hard frosts made life even more uncomfortable. Christmas Day was spent digging new trenches toward the German lines. A human note is recorded in the War Diary for January 9th. Ten shells pitched near the Battalion Headquarters around midday, where the Adjutant was playing a song on the piano called "Goodbye." There was little to disturb the routine of trench warfare early in the year, with not all casualties being noted. On 6th March, after a quiet morning, the battalion were ordered to make a "demonstration" at 3pm, to provide a distraction as the French were about to make an attack at Notre Dame de Lorette. Rifle and artillery fire was matched by rifle fire and shelling from the Germans. At one point, a German mortar destroyed part of the front line trench, killing Reginald and another man; they are both buried in Guards Cemetery, Windy Corner, Cuinchy.

E. BATT

The late Pte. E. H. BATT, Devon Regt., Oak Cottage, Little Sandhurst.—Killed in action. Aged 23.

Edward Harry Batt was born at Sandhurst on 28th December 1891, and baptised 28th February the following year. He was one of seven children, two of whom died in infancy. Edward grew up in Little Sandhurst, where his father and two elder brothers worked as carpenters. Edward probably enjoyed sport, as by 1911 he was in lodgings off Oxford Road in Reading, employed as a golf club maker. At the outbreak of war, he volunteered for service, travelling to Canterbury to attest, and joined the 8th Battalion, Devonshire Regiment (the Devonshires were recruiting in Kent at the time). It is not known why Edward travelled there, but many men travelled large distances to attest, especially if they wanted to join a particular unit. He went to France with the Devonshires on 25th July 1915, as an orderly to Major Carden. The 60 year-old Major, who had won the D.S.O. in South Africa in 1901, had come out of retirement and appointed Second- in-Command of the Battalion, and Edward would have been his right-hand man, transmitting his orders, etc., and been with him in the field at all times. In September, they were at Vermelles, and went into the trenches the previous evening, ready for an attack early the next morning. As soon as the British guns started their intense bombardment, the German guns replied with heavy and light artillery and caused some casualties. On the signal being given, 'C', 'A' and 'D' Companies seemed to all go forward together in one line, probably because 'A' and 'D' Companies started too soon. The result was great crowding towards gaps in the wire and a consequent increase in casualties. The German trenches were captured quite readily, the Germans surrendering as soon as the attackers reached them. The attack pushed on, coming to a halt at crossroads west of the village of Hulluch due, in part, to a lack of support. At 6:15pm, ration parties went back to get supplies, but were intercepted on their return by some of the enemy who had got behind the forward positions. The Devons were forced to retreat, suffering many casualties from rifle fire and bombing from the enemy, but also from rifle and machine gun fire from a Bedfordshire battalion in Gun Trench who, in the dark, mistook friend for foe. Another Private in the battalion wrote a letter home describing the day's events. "We had a terrible time starting on the 25th September. We lost over six hundred men and all the officers that went with us. I never felt more proud of Devonshire men than I do today. When we were all lined up waiting for the word to charge (of course we were in the first line of trenches all night, it was 6.20am when we got the order to charge), not a man failed. When we got over the parapet, we were met with a terrible rifle and shell fire, gas, and barbed wire. The enemy seemed to know what we were going to do. My orders were to stick with the Second-in-Command, Major Carden. He also had an orderly, Private Batt. We had to go with him wherever he went. I regret to say Major Carden and Batt got killed near the wire, just past the gas. It was terrible just at this point; I am sorry to say scores got killed just here. I had to go on. I was very lucky. I got to the farthest point of the advance with the few that were left to our regiment, under Captain Gwynn, who, I am sorry to say, got badly wounded soon afterwards. He has been awarded the D.S.O., which he thoroughly deserved. We were now left without any officers. We were only a few, so we got on very well. I was again very lucky. I got hit on the left side of my right knee. I only lost a little blood and a bit of my trousers. When we got back, about four days later, I got it bandaged." Neither Edward nor Major Carden's bodies were recovered; both are among the 20,000 names listed on the Loos Memorial.

S. BEDFORD

James Sydney Bedford, known as Sydney, was born at Wokingham in 1888. He was the youngest of eleven children, six of whom failed to live more than a few years. The family lived on London Road, opposite All Saints Church, and Sydney's father worked as a bricklayer until his death in 1902. The family then moved to New Wokingham Road, Crowthorne, where his mother took in laundry, assisted by two of her daughters, while Sydney worked as a hair dresser. He joined the 1st Battalion, Royal West Surrey Regiment, possibly under the Derby Scheme, attesting at Wokingham. The War Diary records a draft of 154 men arriving on 31st May, which probably included James, but comments, "First batch of Derby recruits among them; rather a poor lot physically." However, it has been impossible to find a medal card for James, which would include information on when he went to France. The battalion took part in the Arras Offensive and Third Battle of Ypres in 1917, and the Battle of Hazebrouck in 1918. On the night of 11th/12th April, they were billeted in huts near Meteren, which was shelled heavily all night. The camp was hit by a shell the following day, just as orders were being given to the Company Commanders, wounding eight men. Although the high ground they were to occupy was held by Germans with machine guns, they captured it with very few casualties. They held the positions all day, no troops succeeded in joining up on either flank, and they came under machine gun and rifle fire, as well as shelling, but held firm. An attack was beaten off early the following morning, but three outposts of 'B' Company were later overwhelmed, forcing that company to withdraw. A general withdrawal was ordered for 1pm which was accomplished, although under heavy machine gun fire from the right and shrapnel from field guns. There was continued heavy fighting all day, and a slow withdrawal of the battalion as the Germans succeeded in getting better positions and firing on them. Sydney was wounded at some time during these two days of action, and died of his wounds on 13th April; he is buried in Lijssenthoek Military Cemetery. James's name also appears on the Rolls of Honour at both Crowthorne and Wokingham St Sebastian's.

B. BENFELL

Bernard Benfell was born on 6th March 1897 at Dover. He was one of twelve children, one of whom died at the age of two. His father may have served in the army, as some of his children were also born at Woolwich, but by 1911, he was running the Town Hall Tavern in Chertsey. Bernard joined the Navy straight from school, aged just fifteen, and served on HMS 'Black Prince' from April 1914. At the end of that year, he was described as being 5'4" tall, with grey eyes, auburn hair, and a fresh complexion. The ship was stationed in the Mediterranean at the outbreak of war, and her first action was to pursue two German cruisers until they reached the haven of Ottoman waters. She then proceeded to the Red Sea, in mid-August, to protect troop convoys arriving from India, and to search for German merchant ships, capturing two. On 6th November, she was ordered to Gibraltar to join a squadron of French and British ships to search for German warships still at sea off the African coast, but this was cancelled two weeks later after the location of the German East Africa Squadron was revealed by survivors of the Battle of Coronel. Her guns were modified in March 1916, as a result of lessons learnt from this battle, and she took part in the Battle of Jutland two months later, where she was sunk with the loss of all aboard. As no-one had seen her sink, the last sighting being at around 5:45pm, stories started to circulate about the cause of her disappearance. The last contact had been three hours later, when she reported sighting a submarine. One story that gained credence at the time, angering relatives of the lost crew, was that the ship had been hit and the Captain, ordered to return home, had refused, wanting to stay and fight. After the war, when historians were able to access German records, the real story became known. The 'Black Prince' briefly engaged the German battleship 'Rheinland' at about 11:35pm, scoring two hits. Separated from the rest of the British fleet, she approached the German lines half an hour later, but turned away too late. The battleship 'Thuringen' opened fire, and several others joined in the bombardment, with return fire from 'Black Prince' being ineffective. She was hit by at least twelve heavy shells and several smaller ones, and sank within fifteen minutes, and all 857 of her crew were drowned. The bodies were never recovered, and their names are listed on the Portsmouth Naval Memorial. By the time he died, Bernard's parents had moved to Longdown Road, Sandhurst.

D. BENFELL

David Benfell was born in 1893 at Acton, Middlesex. He was one of Bernard's three older brothers, and worked as a grocer's assistant after leaving school. He joined the Army in January 1916, one of the first group of conscripts, attesting at Reading, and joined the East Surrey Regiment (possibly the 13th Battalion), but was transferred to the Machine Gun Corps before he left England. He probably arrived in France in June 1916, just in time to be involved in phases of The Battle of the Somme. The Division was also heavily involved in the Third Battle of Ypres in 1917, including both the First and Second Battles of Passchendaele. On 26th March 1918, during the German Spring Offensive, 'B' Company of David's battalion, comprising eight guns, was moved to a position near Proyart. The War Diary records that thee men were wounded, and a further nine missing at the end of the day. David was one of the former, dying of his wounds later the same day, and is buried in Honnechy British Cemetery.

A. E. BINFIELD

Albert Edward Binfield was born at Sandhurst on 21st March 1894, and baptised 3rd June. The family, with six children, lived at Rose Cottage, High Street, and in 1911, a sister-in-law, a niece and a boarder joined Albert and the rest of the family. His father worked as a printer, and Albert followed a related trade of bookbinder after leaving school, being an apprentice when the 1911 census was taken. He joined the 3rd Battalion, Royal Berkshire Regiment under the Derby Scheme, attesting at Wokingham on 21st January 1916, and on completion of his training, transferred to the 2nd Battalion. The War Diary records a new draft arriving in the middle of May; if this included Albert, he had arrived in France in time to take part in the Battle of the Somme, when the battalion suffered over four hundred casualties. In the middle of November, they suffered badly from the effect of gas shells with more than fifty men being affected in one week. The enemy retreated to the Hindenburg Line in March 1917, and there were only nine casualties in the battalion for the entire month. At the Battle of Pilkem at the end of July, the Berkshires were in reserve. The 25th Brigade were not involved until six hours after the start of the attack, but still suffered from German shelling, and later from machine gun fire. On 15th August, the battalion moved to assembly positions at Westhoek Ridge for an attack the following day. The advance started at 4:45am and went well, with the capture of fifty prisoners. The troops on the right were not so far forward, and despite 'C' Company being deputed to guard this flank, the battalion came under heavy machine gun enfilading fire. 'A' and 'B' Companies continued to press forward, capturing the greater part of Iron Cross Redoubt and land beyond it, but they were now exposed on both flanks. When a counter-attack came at 10:30am, they were pushed right back to the assembly position, suffering heavy losses. A considerable number of wounded men had to be left behind to fall into enemy hands. Another German attack came at 3pm, which was slowed by the British artillery, but a shortage of ammunition limited the effectiveness of the Berkshires, although they caused enough delay for troops on their right to retire. Many more lives were lost, the one bright event of the day being the claim of having shot down a German aircraft with rifle fire. One third of the 360 casualties during the day were missing men, Albert being one of these. His body was never found, and he is listed on the Tyne Cot Memorial.

H. BIRCH

Henry Birch was born at Sandhurst on 2nd September 1896 and baptised three days later. The hasty baptism may indicate he was a sickly baby, and thought unlikely to survive. His father had come to the area from Amersham, initially to work as an assistant gardener, and then as a farm labourer. Henry was one of ten children, four of whom died young. He also worked as a farm labourer after leaving school, and joined the 1/4th Battalion, Hampshire Regiment, a Territorial Battalion before the war, attesting at Yateley. Although the battalion had sailed for India in 1914, before returning to Basra in March the following year, Henry was not with the first draft, and only arrived in October 1915, having reached the age of nineteen, necessary for overseas service. The Regimental History describes the situation: "Earlier in the year, the British had made some tactical moves to seize important or threatening points beyond Basra. After an early string of cheap successes, eyes increasingly fell on the Mesopotamian capital, Baghdad. The 6th (Poona) Division advanced, leaving a very thinly stretched supply line of hundreds of miles behind it, only to receive a bloody repulse at Ctesiphon. A ragged and dispiriting retreat back to Kut-al-Amara began. The Turks pursued the retreating Division to Kut, and soon surrounded and cut it off. British forces in Mesopotamia were now growing, and these formations were ordered to advance north along the Tigris to relieve Kut. They ran into strong and stoutly defended lines and suffered some hard knocks; although they got close to Kut, the garrison there was surrendered on 29th April 1916. It was an enormous blow to British prestige and a morale-booster for the Turkish Army. An attack on El Hanna, on 21st January, was part of this advance. 'Zero' was fixed for 6:30am, but a mirage prevented the gunners from seeing their targets, so the attack had to be postponed till 7:45am, by which time the Turks had fully realised what was coming. The Hampshires had been under fairly heavy long-range rifle fire even before 'Zero', and had had a few men hit. The fire was heavy, and the battalion had a long stretch to cover, even to gain our old front trench. With no support coming up and heavy casualties, the advance was held up short of the Turkish line. On the extreme left, some men managed to join Black Watch in the Turkish trenches and lend a hand in a struggle which they maintained for over an hour against heavy odds, though no more support reached them. Eventually, they were overwhelmed, only a few survivors regaining our lines. Meanwhile, the rest of the battalion could merely hang on behind such cover as they could scrape together with their entrenching tools and wait till darkness allowed them to move and to try to assist the wounded. A pelting rain and bitter cold added to the trials to be endured, and stamina and endurance were severely taxed." Well over half the attacking infantry were casualties, including Henry's battalion, who lost almost 250 men. Henry was killed in the fighting; his body was never recovered, and his name is listed on the Basra Memorial.

Pte. ARTHUR BOYDE, 7th Batt. Royal Sussex Regt.

A. BOYDE

Arthur Boyde was born at Sandhurst in 1893. He was one of seven children, another two dying in infancy. His father, a local man from Finchampstead, worked as a night watchman at Wellington College for well over twenty years, and the family lived on Wokingham Road, and later on Addiscombe Road. Arthur went into domestic service after leaving school, and in the 1911 census, held a position of footman at an address in West London. However, he may well have been working in Sussex at the outbreak of war, as he immediately volunteered, attesting at Bexhill-on-Sea Town Hall on 19th August 1914, and joined the 7th Battalion, Royal Sussex Regiment. He was only 5'4" tall, but weighed just over ten stone, with grey eyes, light brown hair, and a fresh complexion. His initial training was done in the Folkestone area, before the battalion moved to Aldershot in March the following year, and crossed the Channel to Boulogne at the end of May. They were involved in the Battle of Loos in September, and although in a 'quiet area' from mid December to mid January, still suffered heavy casualties. A month later, they were moved to the area round Hohenzollern Redoubt, where underground mine warfare was very active. Four mines were exploded under the Redoubt on 2nd March 1916, allowing the infantry to capture the craters, giving them important observation over enemy lines. Severe fighting continued in this area for several weeks, and although Arthur was wounded on the 21st March, he remained on duty. He was granted a few days' leave in England the following month, but soon returned and was involved in the Battle of the Somme. On 7th July, the battalion were in trenches near Ovillers, and attacked after an intense bombardment. At 8:28am, the front line crawled out of trenches to get in line on top of ground. For the previous few minutes, a heavy German barrage had been put on to the new assembly trench and over the old front line trenches. At 8:30am, the whole Brigade advanced in line. Arthur's battalion got a good share of machine gun fire, and were heavily shrapnelled by whizz bang (high velocity shell) guns and Jack Johnsons (German shells which burst with black smoke). On reaching the line, they got enfilade machine gun fire, and found the Germans either decamping, or in their deep dug-outs. The clearing-up process then started, under machine gun fire from the southeast. Germans were in groups, some fighting, some surrendering, and there was a good deal of individual sniping, and some bomb throwing. Although each man had to carry over twenty bombs in sandbags, many of them were dropped and the supply had to be saved, even after collecting German bombs, of which there were a number in the dug-outs, but no dump could be found. Up to this time, no communication could be obtained; several messengers volunteered, but none of them ever reached Brigade Headquarters. Rain began to fall and continued throughout day, making the trenches into a kind of porridge mud. After 6pm, men from the Essex Regiment came up, and supplemented the line. There are no casualty figures in the War Diary for this period, but one can assume the losses were heavy. Arthur was one of those killed, and he is buried in Ovillers Military Cemetery. He is also recorded on the War Memorial at Crowthorne.

G. BOYDE

Cpl. GEORGE BOYDE, Oxford and Bucks L.I.

George Boyde was born in Sandhurst in 1888, and was an elder brother of Arthur's. He too worked in domestic service, and is listed as first footman at a house in Shrewsbury in the 1911 census. He also volunteered for service, attesting at Woking, and joined the 7th Battalion, Oxford and Bucks Light Infantry. The battalion went to France in September 1915, with George marrying Kathrine Widdows in Oxfordshire, a few months before he sailed. The battalion were only in France for a couple of months before sailing for Salonika. Just after Christmas, units began moving from Lembet to Happy Valley Camp, and were all in place by early February 1916. In August, the Division took part in the capture of Horseshoe Hill, and fought in both the Battles of Dorian the following year, the second occurring on 8th to 9th May. George's battalion were involved during the night, and the War Diary contains a report on the action: "The assaulting Companies, 'A' and 'B', left our lines, reaching the north side of Jumeaux Ravine with very few casualties. As they were forming up in wave formation, they were apparently seen, as trench mortar fire was opened, Major Homan, two Company Commanders, and one Company Sergeant Major all being badly wounded by it. Except for one gun firing high explosives into the left of our left assaulting company, and causing about ten casualties, our barrage was very accurate, so that our first wave was able to creep within about twenty yards of the enemy's trench before assaulting. The wire was no obstacle at all. Our first wave met with practically no resistance, there being about ten dead Bulgars and a few live ones, who were easily disposed of. Parties of bombers were sent along the trench, while the first wave of the left company manned the enemy's parados, preparatory to forming for the advance. The crossing of the Jumeaux had been made so easily that our first three companies suffered quite considerable casualties while waiting 45 minutes in the preparatory position for the assault. An effort was made to alter the time of assault, but this proved impossible. The following fifteen minutes' wait in the first line trench, till the barrage was to make its second lift, cost us heavy casualties, especially in the left company. 2/Lieut. Kelly, 'B' Company, had been badly wounded in the leg just before the assault, and 2/Lieut. Hutchins, the only officer left of the company, was wounded in the leg by shrapnel. The supporting company, 'C' Company, now seems to have been engaged, although no intimation to that effect reached the Battalion H.Q. 2/Lieut. Garland, 'C' Company, hearing that 'B' Company had lost all its officers, took charge of 'B' Company, bringing up one platoon on the left, as 'B' Company had been held up by trench mortar fire. The third and fourth waves failed to carry the attack on. Lieut. Steels, although already wounded, now took a platoon of his supporting company to fill in the gap between 'A' and 'B' Companies. I cannot sya what ultimately happened to the rest of 'C Company, as all its officers. and most of its N.C.O.s, are missing. 'D' Company, who were in reserve, reached Green Pan with very few casualties about 0300 hours. Trench mortar and artillery fire continued very heavy all over the captured position. While 'B' Company was held up, 'A' Company, on the right, easily attained their objectives, and began consolidation. About a quarter of an hour after their arrival, about two hundred enemy counter-attacked from Deep Ravine. They were easily repulsed by our artillery and Lewis gun fire, suffering very heavy casualties. Matters were critical, as our left could make no further advance. In addition to their bad mauling by the enemy's fire, it appeared certain that one of our heavy guns was still firing on to our left. 2/Lieut. Hutchins actually saw four of his men killed by the shells from this gun." By the time the battalion came back after the fighting to bivouacs in Vladaja Ravine, fifteen officers and nearly 450 men were casualties; only 45 remaining on duty. Corporal George Boyde was missing; his body was never found, and his name is listed on the Doiran Memorial. He is also recorded on the War Memorial at Crowthorne.

Pte. WALTER BOYDE,
7th Batt. Oxford and Bucks L.I.

W. BOYDE

Walter Boyde was a brother of Arthur and George, born at Sandhurst in 1892. Unlike his two older siblings, he was still living at home in 1911, and was working as an assistant at the East Berkshire Golf Club, founded some eight years earlier by masters of Wellington College. He too volunteered for service, attesting at Woking, and joined the 7th Battalion, Oxford and Bucks Light Infantry at the same time as George; they have consecutive service numbers. It is not known whether they fought side by side, but one can only imagine his feelings when his brother was killed. At the beginning of 1918, the Allied troops in Salonika were prepared for a major offensive, intended to end the war in the Balkans. The Greek

Army had been reorganised and joined the Allied force. The offensive began in July, but the British contingent did not play a significant part until early September, when they attacked a series of fortified hills. The final assault began along the whole front on 15th September, the British being engaged in the Lake Doiran area. This battle was a disaster for the British Divisions, who had to frontally assault Pip Ridge, a two thousand foot high, heavily defended mountain ridge, with fortresses built on some of the higher mountains, notably Grand Couronne. This was what the Bulgarians had been working on in the first months of 1916 and early 1917. They sustained very heavy casualties, and a report from a Staff Officer of the 28th Division called it "a futile massacre." By the end of the month, they were pursuing the enemy, crossing the Serbian-Bulgarian boundary on the 25th; hostilities with Bulgaria ceasing two days later. The Division advanced towards Adrianople, the war with Turkey still being underway, but this too was to stop soon. The 26th Division had suffered just over eight thousand men casualties during the war, but a much larger number had been sick with malaria, dysentery and other diseases rife in the Salonika theatre. Walter succumbed to disease on 14th January 1919, one of almost forty men in the battalion to suffer that month, and is listed on the addenda panel of the Haidar Pasha Memorial. This panel was added to the memorial at a later date, to commemorate some 170 men, buried in cemeteries whose graves can no longer be maintained by the Commonwealth War Graves Commission. Walter is buried in Batoum British Cemetery in Georgia. He is also recorded on the War Memorial at Crowthorne.

H. BRENNAN

Harry Brennan was born at Sandhurst in 1891. His father, an Irishman from County Kildare, was an ex-soldier, with his eldest children being born while he was still serving, in Ireland, Kent, Colchester, and Yorkshire. However by 1891, he had left the army, and was working as a servant at the Royal Military Academy. Harry was one of seven children, and was already working as a labourer when his father died in 1910. He joined the 1st Battalion, Hampshire Regiment before the war, attesting at Winchester in 1913. The battalion were at Colchester at the outbreak of war, but were in France within three weeks, and took part in the Battle of the Marne, the Battle of the Aisne, and the Battle of Messines in 1914. On 25th April 1915, they were north of the outskirts of Ypres, which was being shelled, while wounded and stragglers were coming back and congesting the road. The situation was confused; guides failed to turn up, telephone lines were cut, and there were no trenches in the position the battalion had been ordered to fill. It was 2am, but fortunately a misty morning allowed trenches to be dug before the enemy caught sight and could open fire. Directly the mist really lifted, a tremendous bombardment of heavy shells started, coming down at the rate of fifty a minute. The German tactics were to drench the ground with shells, and then push infantry forward, thinking to take easy possession of a destroyed line. All day, the rain of projectiles went on, but the Hampshire stuck to their line, effectively preventing repeated efforts to turn the left flank of the Royal Fusiliers, or to penetrate into the large gap on the left, but at a cost. Almost sixty men were killed or missing; Harry was one of the latter, and his name is listed on the Ypres (Menin Gate) Memorial.

T. BRENNAN

Thomas Brennan was Harry's youngest brother, born at Sandhurst in 1896. After leaving school, he worked as a baker's errand boy. He volunteered for service, and joined the

8th Battalion, Royal West Surrey Regiment, attesting at Camberley. Early training was done near Shoreham in Kent. As with many new battalions, raised at the outbreak of hostilities, the early days were somewhat chaotic, and short of officers to lead the training, billets, equipment and facilities. It was not until the following March that makeshift uniforms were available, and rifles were not issued until July. They moved to Aldershot in June 1915 for final training, where they were inspected by Lord Kitchener and the King on successive days. Thomas was part of a draft that arrived in France towards the end of September, missing the fighting at Loos by a few days. The battalion would take part in the Battles of Delville Wood and Guillemont in 1916, as well as those at Vimy Ridge, Messines and Langemarck the following year. On 21st March 1918, they were at the village of Le Verguier. The War Diary reports that the Germans were very quiet for two days, although the British artillery was very active. But on the 23rd, things changed dramatically. Starting at 4:30am, an intense bombardment began which lasted for eight hours, and included shells of all calibres, including a high proportion of gas shells. Telephone lines were cut soon after the bombardment started, and messengers sent to warn the front line Commander lost direction in the foggy conditions. They arrived only a few minutes before the enemy. The Germans managed to get forward on both flanks, effectively cutting the front company off, and although a few men did eventually manage to get back, most were never heard from again. It is probable that Thomas was part of this company, as he went missing on this day. His body was never found, and his name is listed on the Pozieres Memorial. This was the start of the German Spring Offensive, and for the rest of the month, the British were on the back foot and retreated, before stabilising the situation again.

N. BRUCE-LOCKHART

Norman Douglas Stewart Bruce-Lockhart was born on 28th November 1894 at Beith, Ayrshire, a few miles east of Dundee, one of six children. His father, a Canadian, was the first headmaster of Spier's School at Beith, a co-educational day school opened in 1888, and later held a similar position at Eagle House School, Sandhurst. Norman was educated at Eagle House, Marlborough College (where he played rugby for the school and spent three years in the Officer Training Corps), and Corpus Christi College, Cambridge, where he spent two years. One of his brothers also recalls he showed promise as a fast bowler as a boy, and "if ever he began to lag could nearly always be roused to fresh energy by my fierce shout of 'get fizzy.'" At the outbreak of war, he obtained a commission in the 7th Battalion, Seaforth Highlanders in September 1914, and after training at Aldershot and Borden, landed at Boulogne on 9th May 1915. Three weeks later, he was writing home. "May 29th, Dear old Rufus, Just a few lines to say that I've already made the acquaintance of the Hun. On Monday the 26th, we left B---- and marched to A., a town within range of artillery fire. We spent the day there and in the evening we marched off for the trenches. We were with a regular Regiment who, having been in their trenches for six months, had got very casual - they were Irishmen. A little way out of the town, we began to see the star shells and to hear the bullets. The Hun's rifle has a much sharper crack than ours. It was a bright moonlight night but we just strolled along the road - never used the communication trenches. It was rather an 'eerie' experience. However we got into our trench, and carried out our relief with complete success. The Huns' line ran about 300 yards to our front, across a flat meadow. At night the sentries fire at their leisure (i) to keep awake (ii) to remind the Hun that he is awake (iii) on the off-chance of hitting one of the Huns. It is extraordinary how many rounds are fired without doing any damage, but as soon as it's light, all this changes, and the sentries can only look through steel plate loopholes or periscopes. Tuesday was a brilliant day. The trenches were very roomy and comfortable, and we amused ourselves watching the aeroplanes being shelled. First you see a wee flash in the air, then a beautiful ball of white smoke. There were no hits on either side. Towards evening, a curious thing happened. All our aeroplanes seemed to have gone off to tea, and a fine big Hun biplane came sailing toward us - he had made two attempts earlier in the day but was chased off. This time, however, he crossed our line and sailed along it, till right above us. Then our machine guns opened fire on it hard, and drove him off. However, he returned again and again; a furious fire opened on him. This seemed to annoy the Huns in the trenches opposite us, who had been sleeping and sniping all day. They started shelling our line on our left with 'Little Willie's whizz-bangs' *(three inch field guns)*, and bombs from trench mortars. Our line was like this *(drawing of a line rather like a rising wave)*. My Company was at 'B', and at 'A', there was a house held by us - a great bone of contention. They shelled this from 'C', and the nose-caps of the shells weighing about 1½ lbs came shizzing along the top and back of our trench; it was most exciting; after about forty rounds by them, during which time we sat very quiet, we phoned to our artillery who suddenly opened fire on' C'. The Huns replied at once, and we could hear all the shells go screeching high over us. Now we looked out over our parapet, and could see our shells bursting - it was all very exciting, and though several shells hit our trenches at 'A', no-one was hit. We left the trenches at 1.30am on Wednesday; stray bullets flew all round us at one point, and you could hear them strike the banks of the road. The impressions I formed of the trench warfare were 1) The comparative safety on a clear night, and the great need for care by day, also the extraordinary way in which we and the Germans have been able to build up (our breastworks are about four feet high), these great warrens within a few hundred yards of each other 2) The extraordinary way in which these great lines of trenches go on through everything. They cross fields, streams, road, railways, houses, gardens, etc. It is so impossible to believe one is at war, although I took a shot at the Hun myself. The weather is great, and I wish I were at home, spending a summer term at Cambridge University. Everyone longs for peace, but we are all as keen as possible and in the pink of condition. The more one sees of other regiments, the more we realise the better type that our boys belong to. Well, old boy, I wish we were all at home again enjoying this great weather. Cheer-ho & good luck. Write as often as possible. Love from Norman." The first major action the battalion would see was the Battle of Loos, commencing on 25th September. On the previous day, the battalion marched to three front lines of trenches, east of Vermelles, arriving at 1:00pm. They were in the section immediately opposite Hohenzollern Redoubt, which had been bombarded for four days. There were two schemes for the attack, depending on the wind conditions, and it was only at midnight when one was chosen, when it was described as "light winds in our favour." At 5:30am, gas was turned on in the advance trench for nearly an hour, with a brief break for smoke candles to be lit at 6:00am. Just before 6:30am, the men climbed out of the trenches and advanced behind the smoke screen. They were met by machine gun and rifle fire, but most of it was inaccurate. Several officers were killed at the Redoubt first trench, but the battalion continued up the communication trench, bombing as they went, until they reached the German trenches. They also made good some miners' cottages on the left, but the Cameronians on this flank had not managed to get forward, and they came under "murderous fire" from this wing until the Royal Fusiliers got forward and stopped it. By 9:00am, the Seaforths were making good the trenches captured, although still suffering many casualties from enemy shrapnel. They were relieved at midnight, but soon after, the Germans counter-attacked and recaptured the trench, so "two

Officers and some men" returned to force them out. There were two eye-witness accounts of Norman's death. "On September 25th 1915, at the Hohenzollern Redoubt, Lieut. Lockhart was shot through the head about a quarter of an hour after the attack had commenced, and before the German lines were reached. I was the third man from him when he fell, and saw a man trying to give him a drink of water but he was already dead. Lieut. Lockhart was the first man in the Platoon to fall." (Pte J. Strughters, 4798 C Coy. Seaforth Highlanders). "We made a charge at Vermelles on the Hohenzollern Redoubt, and Lieut. Lockhart was shot and died instantly without any pain. We took the Redoubt, and reinforcements came and relieved us, and then they lost the trench we took when the Germans made a counter-attack, and we had to charge again on the 27th, and then held the position. Lieut. Lockhart was probably buried, because his body was lying on the ground we finally gained, but I cannot tell you about this." (C.Q.M. Sergt. Syme, 7th Seaforth Highlanders). A later report from Sergeant Davidson, 8th Battalion, Gordon Highlanders said, "I didn't see Mr Lockett (sic) killed, but I was out on the night of Sunday, September 26th on the Hehenzollern. Our battalion supplied a burying party to the Brigade, and we came across Mr Bruce-Lockhart's body. It was quite dark, so we could not see how he had been hit, but we buried him, just on the right of the Redoubt. There was no time to put up a cross or anything else, as the Germans started shelling us. We would not have known who he was but for a bible I found on him and gave to some of the Seaforth officers." But a relative recalls, "A letter from one of his N.C.O.s said that he had been shot when returning to No Man's Land, to try to bring back one of his men who had been wounded." Norman had been promoted to Lieutenant shortly before his death. As the grave was not found after the Armistice, Norman's name is listed on the Loos Memorial. A week after Norman's death, his father had to ask a master to read out his message to the rest of the school: "If I had been able, I should like to have said a few words to you to-day. When I spoke to you last Sunday, I had no idea that my own dear son was dead on the field of battle; but even if I had known, I would not have chosen any other message to have given you than the one I spoke of then. Is not this the blood of the men that went in jeopardy of their lives?" He then paid tribute to his son, of Norman's love for his home and family, his schools, University, and Regiment, of his character and religion, of the letters of condolence from the Master of Corpus and the Master of Marlborough, telling of the affection he inspired and the blameless life he lived. "But I feel that what I want to say to you to-day is of the sacrifice that he, and so many others, have made at the call of Duty, for us, for you and me, that we may live here in safety and freedom; that we should not, must not use our lives, the price of men's blood, for our mere personal and selfish ends. When we hear of the terrible death of our dearest and best, we are all ready to cry out, 'How can God permit such things?' But if we consider, we may see that God may be, as it were, branding on our hearts with a hot iron a lesson which we all need, but will not learn." A list of effects, returned to his family, included two oilskin bags in a waterproof case, a cheque book, note book, purse containing one half sovereign and thirty centimes, a book, protractor, whistle, pouch, and wristwatch (broken). He had also left an unpaid mess bill of £1 which was deducted from the money later sent to his father. A month after his death, the War Office received a letter written from John Stuart in Wigan Infirmary, who had been Norman's servant, stating he was owed fifteen shillings in pay. By the time a reply was sent, he had left the hospital, but was eventually tracked down at the Seaforth Highlanders Depot near Inverness, from where he was discharged from the army towards the end of 1916, on account of the wounds he had received, although he does not appear to have received a pension.

F. CASTELL

Frederick Charles Castell was born at Crowthorne in 1899, and baptised there on 15th October. He was the eldest of nine children, three of whom died young. His father worked at various labouring jobs, but later got a job as a carter, and the family had moved to Yorktown Road by 1911. It is not known what work Frederick did after leaving school, but he was conscripted into the Royal Warwickshire Regiment, attesting at Reading, but later transferred to the 12th Battalion, Royal Irish Rifles. During the German Spring Offensive in March 1918, the main defences consisted of a number of isolated redoubts, in which the Ulstermen held on for several hours while under bombardment, but were ultimately surrounded and cut off. Frederick's transfer may have taken place after this, or possibly a month earlier when the Division was reorganised. They were involved in phases of the First Battle of the Somme and the Battle of the Lys that year. On 3rd June, the battalion were relieved in the front line by Belgians, and marched to Penton Camp, near Proven, northwest of Poperinghe. They spent the next few days training, and providing working parties at Brielen, and another location, south of the Ypres to Poperinghe road. The War Diary records 'D' Company suffered 37 casualties on the 6th; Frederick died of wounds on the 7th, so was probably caught up in this incident. He is buried in Esquelbecq Military Cemetery.

The late Pte. O. J. CHAMPION, Imperial Camel Brigade, Little Sandhurst. Killed in action.

O. CHAMPION

Oliver James Champion was born on 24th September 1896 at Little Sandhurst, and baptised 1st November. He was one of nine children, a tenth having died in infancy. His father worked as a bricklayer, but Oliver started work as a garden boy after leaving school. He volunteered for service, attesting at Camberley, and joined the 2/5th Battalion, Royal West Surrey Regiment, a Territorial Battalion formed at Guildford in September 1914. In May the following year, around four hundred men, including Oliver, were attached to the 2/4th Battalion, and in mid July, they sailed from Devonport, bound for the Greek island of Lemnos, going via Alexandria. In the early hours of 9th August, they landed at Suvla Bay on the Gallipoli peninsula, three days after the initial landings. Soon after 6:30am, they were ordered to move forward to support the 31st Brigade, which was then in action, and came under shell and rifle fire, and had sustained several casualties. By midday, the Hampshires had suffered more than 250 casualties, while all around them, the scrub was on fire. They fell back to Turkish Trench and, in the absence of orders, held on and strengthened their position, and remained there until relieved three days later. It would be mid September before they got some rest. Most of October was spent digging trenches by day, and on garrison duty by night; November was similarly occupied, but heavy rain, and blizzards towards the end of the month made life miserable, and on 14th December, they sailed for Mudros and on to Alexandria as troops were evacuated. The War Diary is rather sparse for this period as, when the battalion baggage arrived at Beni Salama Camp, where they were stationed, it was found that many packages had been rifled, including the Orderly Room stationery box which had contained them. On the plus side, the men were able to recover from the harsh weather and fighting, and sickness was much reduced, although the drinking water had to be boiled as it was full of insects. Much training and physical exercise was carried out, and by the end of March, every man in the battalion had passed a test in musketry.

On 12th May, the War Diary records, "It has been noticed that during the past few weeks, the natives have been decidedly more insolent in demeanour," and with a few cases of clasp knives being stolen, an armed patrol was posted to prevent further incidents. At the end of May, they moved to Ismailia, to help defend the Suez Canal, although diarrhoea, septic cuts, and the heat still caused some problems. In August, they moved to Kantara, but it was so hot that work was limited to two hours in the morning and a further hour later in the day "except on urgent matters." They moved again in September, to Moascar, but apart from providing guard duty for Ismailia, there was little to do. Three months later, they were on the move again, heading for Bir-El-Abd in northern Sinai, with further moves in January and February. At the end of March, the battalion took part in the First Battle of Gaza, the first attempt to invade the southern region of the Ottoman Empire. The Allies were on the point of capturing Gaza when they were withdrawn, among concern over large Ottoman reinforcements approaching. The Second Battle of Gaza, the following month, also resulted in a defeat. By now, diphtheria and scarlet fever cases were also being seen among the men. At the beginning of August, they were just outside Sheikh Ajlin, on the Mediterranean coast. Two companies frequently supplied men for working on coastal defences during the evenings, and gun emplacements for the Royal Field Artillery during the day. Although there are no records of casualties during this period in the War Diary, a summary at the end of the month records the loss of 65 men to the strength of the battalion. Oliver died on the 12th, and is buried in Gaza War Cemetery. Although the records state he was killed in action, the only other death for that month was from illness, so it is possible he was a victim of disease, rather than of the enemy.

E. COLLINS

EDWARD COLLINS, Sandhurst.— Wounded.

Edward Collins was born in 1887 at Crowthorne, and baptised in the parish church on 28th August. He was from a large family with eleven children, three of whom died young. His father worked as a domestic gardener, while Edward started as a grocer's errand boy after leaving school, before becoming a general labourer. He joined the 3rd Battalion, Royal Berkshire Regiment, attesting on 7th February 1905 at York Town, and after seven weeks' training, transferred to the 1st Battalion, Royal West Surrey Regiment. Edward married Harriett Puttick in 1908, and was working as a general labourer in 1911, he and his wife living with his parents. The battalion were in India until 1909, and spent some time in Aden before returning to England, but it is not known whether Edward went overseas with them. They were at Bordon Camp in Hampshire at the outbreak of war, when George would have been recalled, and landed at Le Havre just nine days later. During the remainder of the year, they were involved in the Battle of Mons, the Battle of the Marne, the Battle of the Aisne, and the First Battle of Ypres. The Battle of Aubers and the Battle of Loos followed in 1915, and the Battle of the Somme in 1916. On the 23rd August, the battalion were in trenches, west of Delville Wood. The Germans shelled the front and support lines continuously all day and all night, and orders were issued for an assault on the enemy line the following afternoon. The morning was quiet as the plan was explained to the Companies. 'Zero' was at 5:45pm, with the assault by the Surreys commencing just over an hour later. All the objectives were successfully taken, and by 8:30pm, consolidation was in progress and reinforcements requested. Messages were received back from the front line that officer casualties had been heavy, mostly due to shell fire prior to the assault. In total,

23 men were killed, and more than eighty wounded during the day. Lance Corporal Edward Collins was one of those killed; his body was never recovered, and his name is listed on the Thiepval Memorial. His widow moved to Wiltshire, and remarried in 1919.

F. COLLINS

Frank Collins was born on born 30th January 1895 at Sandhurst, and baptised there on 17th March. He was Edward's youngest brother, and worked as a farm labourer after leaving school, supplementing his income as a bell ringer at Sandhurst church. He married Millie Cotsford in 1913, and volunteered for service as soon as war was declared, attesting at Reading, and joined the 2nd Battalion, Royal Berkshire Regiment. The battalion had been in India at the outbreak of war, but returned to England, and went to France at the start of November 1914; Frank was in a draft that went out at the end of the same month. The battalion took part on the Battle of Neuve Chapelle and the Battle of Aubers in 1915, as well as action at Bois Grenier, a diversionary attack, coinciding with the Battle of Loos. They took part on the first day of the Battle of the Somme, and suffered over four hundred casualties, facing rifle and machine gun fire as soon as the attack had started. They also took part in the Battle of Langemarck in August 1917. An entry in the War Diary for 30th September lists the honours and awards given for fighting near Ypres in the middle of the preceding month, among them being Private F. Collins, who received the Military Medal (he was later promoted to Lance Corporal). At the beginning of December, they were just north of Passchendaele, with an attack scheduled for the early hours of the 2nd. There were problems just in getting into position in the dark, with 'A' Company losing its way, and the others having to negotiate marshy ground via duck-boards, which had been destroyed in some places, while under shell fire. The attack started at 1:55am. This was unobserved for about ten minutes, and even the fire that did then come from the enemy was, for the most part, ill-directed. Two platoons reached the Southern redoubt, and were engaged in bayonet and bomb fighting, with many casualties on both sides. Elsewhere, the advance did not get so far forward, due in part to moving to the left to keep touch with the 2nd Battalion, Lincolnshire Regiment, who had also gone too far left. The attack cost 150 casualties, including 35 killed and a similar number missing. Frank was one of the latter, and his name is listed on the Tyne Cot Memorial. After his death, his widow moved back to her parents in Surrey, and remarried in 1923.

GEORGE COLLINS, Albion Cottages, Sandhurst.—Missing.

G. COLLINS

George Collins was a brother of Edward and Frank, born at Sandhurst on 14th September 1891, and baptised 29th November. After leaving school, he worked as a domestic gardener, and appears at Haslemere, Surrey, in the 1911 census. He too was supplementing his income as a bell ringer at Sandhurst church before moving away. He volunteered for service as soon as war was declared, attesting at Reading, and joined the 2nd Battalion, Royal Berkshire Regiment a few days before his brother Frank. The battalion had been in India at the outbreak of war, but returned to England, and went to France at the beginning of November. George was part of a daft that arrived towards the end of the following month. The battalion took part in the Battle of Neuve Chapelle in March, suffering over three hundred casualties. At 11pm on

8th May, they moved into the assembly trenches at Laventie for an attack on the German position the following day. After a forty minute bombardment, the 2nd Battalion, Rifle Brigade started to attack at 5:40am, with 'C' and 'D' Companies of the Berkshires due to move up to the breastwork in support, the other two companies being in reserve. As the Rifle Brigade advanced, they were met by tremendous rifle and machine gun fire, killing many. The Berkshires found the front trench full of men, who claimed they had been ordered back. Even when they started to move forward, they encountered attackers falling back, and it was never established where the orders to withdraw had come from. Some of 'A' Company, following up, managed to get into the German trenches, but were either killed or taken prisoner. The battalion suffered almost three hundred casualties in the confusion, George being one of around forty men missing by the end of the day. His name is listed on the Ploegsteert Memorial.

A. R. COOPER

Arthur Ralph Cooper was born on 1st October 1889 at Sevenoaks, Kent, the eldest of five children. His father had worked a grocer's assistant in Sandhurst before his marriage. By 1897, the family had moved back to Sandhurst, and he took over his father's small business as a coal merchant, his father dying two years later. Arthur's mother died in 1905, his father remarried four years later, and Arthur became one of an increasing family, with six half-siblings. After leaving school, he worked as a carter boy until joining the Navy on 15th August 1905, signing up to serve for twelve years. He was barely 5'4" tall, with grey eyes, brown hair, and a fresh complexion, with scars on the left side of his face, beside his right eyebrow and on the inside of his upper left arm. His training took place at Shotley, near Felixstowe, Suffolk, until April, but was discontinued due to an inverted hernia, and he was discharged. But he enlisted again at Southampton in January the following year, having worked as a general labourer in the interim. This time, his initial training took place at Deal, Kent, and included infantry and field training, musketry, and sea gunnery. He served briefly on HMS 'Essex' in 1908, a ship with a reputation of "un-natural practises," before spending over two years with HMS 'Hermes', based in Cape Town. His Service Record contains an entry "eager for Hermes," implying he joined the ship a full month before she sailed. His service on the 'Hermes' finished just before Christmas 1910, and after a brief spell on HMS 'Hawke', and a spell ashore, he spent the next three years as a crew member on the Royal Yacht 'Alexandra', a posting that was ended by the outbreak of war. At this point, the Navy had more men, including reserves, than they needed to man their fighting ships, with the surplus serving in the Royal Marine Light Infantry, either on board, or as part of the Royal Naval Division that landed on Belgium 1914 to help defend Antwerp. Arthur found himself in this group, who initially landed at Ostend on 27th August, but were withdrawn four days later. They landed again on 19th September, and returned the following month; those that failed to get back crossed the Dutch border, and were interned in the Netherlands. There then followed a refit and retraining, during which time Arthur volunteered for the Royal Marine Cyclist Company, whose main tasks would include communications and despatch carrying. They sailed aboard the HMT 'Somali' for the Dardanelles at the end of February 1915, but by May were being used to reinforce the Royal Marine Battalions in the firing line at Cape Helles. Later still, they converted into the 'Divisional Bombers', with the personnel being trained in the use of catapults, bomb guns, and trench mortars. The bombs used were known as "Tickler's Bombs," made from empty tins of Tickler's jam. There was an acute shortage of hand grenades, and the troops were forced to improvise with jam tins, stuffed with explosive and barbed wire, cut up to act as shrapnel in the bomb. They were fired from a catapult which suffered from the elastic constantly breaking. All this wonderful improvisation was just another indication of an ill-prepared invasion force. Arthur was wounded in the leg on 14th August but recovered; the cyclists suffered remarkably few casualties, despite serving at Cape Helles for the entire Gallipoli campaign. It has been suggested the Cyclists were selected as being more intelligent than the average run-of-the-mill man in the RMLI ranks, but with their role now at an end, many were transferred to the new Trench Mortar Batteries, attached to the Marine Battalions. During May, the Division moved to Marseilles and on to the Western Front, taking part in the Battle of the Ancre in November, and phases of the Arras Offensive the following year. Arthur had already earned to Good Conduct badges, and was now promoted to Corporal in October 1916. It appears that Arthur was attached to the 63rd Medium Trench Mortar Battery in the 21st Division; this Division took part in two phases of the Arras offensive in the first half of 1917. On 20th July, a raid was carried out near Oppy Gavrelle at 1am. The purpose was three-fold – to kill and capture as many Germans as possible, to identify which units the Germans were part of, and to cause as much damage as possible to the enemy trenches. The Trench Mortars opened up at 'Zero' hour, and immediately, the German artillery turned their fire on the guns. The Medium Trench Battery War Diary reads "Corporal Townsend & Corporal-Acting Sargent Cooper both killed at their guns." Arthur is buried in Bailleul Road East Cemetery, St Laurent-Blangy.

C. COOPER

Charles Cooper was born at Sevenoaks in 1891, and may have been Arthur's oldest brother. However, he grew up living with his maternal grandmother, who ran a grocery shop in Little Sandhurst, near the 'Bird In Hand' pub, never living with his supposed parents and siblings. It is possible he was illegitimate, and was Arthur's cousin, rather than his brother. Charles worked as a carpenter after leaving school until being conscripted, and joined the 102nd Field Company, Royal Engineers, attesting at Camberley. As well as performing construction and maintenance work, the Field Companies, which were attached to the fighting portions of a Division, also saw action and took part in the fighting. Many kinds of trade were required in the army, and Field Companies would typically contain farriers, shoeing smiths, trumpeters, blacksmiths, bricklayers, carpenters, clerks, masons, painters, plumbers, surveyors, draughtsmen, wheelwrights, engine drivers, sappers, and batmen. The Division remained in France until November 1917, when it moved to Italy, where it remained until the end of the war. At the end of October 1918, they were involved in the Battle of Vittorio Veneto, including the crossing of the Piave on the 26th to 28th. On the 24th, Charles's unit marched from San Pelagio to Catena to take part in an attack, but it was postponed and they had to march back again. The following day was spent in training before a return to Catena, and a night in bivouacs. On the 28th, they marched to Salletuol, and began work on a pontoon bridge over the Piave at 2:30am, completing it by 6am next day. After crossing the river, they continued to Palazzon, where transport was waiting to take them to Salletuol. Here, part of a bridge had to be built before the transport could get across, and they finally arrived at billets in Bibano di Sotto at 4pm on the 31st. It is not clear how much of this involved Charles; the War Diary records that 19 drivers had been sent to hospital by the 21st. He died of illness on 1st November, and is buried in Staglieno Cemetery, Genoa, a city containing three War Hospitals, but well away from where his unit were in action.

E. COOPER

Ernest Cooper was one of Arthur's brothers, born at Sevenoaks in 1892. On leaving school, he worked alongside his father as a coal merchant, until volunteering for service, attesting at Reading in September 1914, and joined the 5th Battalion, Royal Berkshire Regiment. However, he remained in England until November 1916, when he was transferred to the Hertfordshire Regiment, which contained Territorial Battalions, most of which stayed this side of the Channel. Ernest's failure to serve in France in the early stages of the war was probably due to health grounds, but as the need for men for fighting increased, the criteria were relaxed, and Ernest was transferred to the 6th Battalion, Bedfordshire Regiment, and crossed to France at some point from March 1917 onwards. The Bedfordshires were involved in the Arras Offensive in the spring of that year, and the Third Battle of Ypres in October. From the last week of March 1918, the battalion were facing the German Spring Offensive. On 8th April, they were in the trenches at Mondicourt. The War Diary gives no details, but records heavy casualties for the day, with nine men killed, one dying of wounds, and another eight wounded; it is possible a section of trench took a direct hit. Ernest was one of those killed, and is buried in Gommecourt British Cemetery No 2, Hebuterne.

W. V. DICKINSON

William Vicris Dickinson was born on 28th April 1856 at Llandefailog Fach, a few miles north of Brecon, South Wales. His father had been a Colonel in the Brecon Militia. Although one of eight children, he grew up in a life of money and privilege; in the 1861 census, the family home of Glan Honddu was run by eleven servants. He was educated at home by a Governess, before attending a preparatory school on Jersey, Cheltenham College, and the Royal Military College, Sandhurst, and was commissioned a Second Lieutenant in the 2nd Battalion, Welsh Regiment in 1877. He reached the rank of Lieutenant Colonel before retiring in 1906, having served abroad in Gibraltar, South Africa (twice), Mauritius, Egypt and India (twice). He was commandant of the Wellington Depot for two years from 1896 to 1898, and held a similar position in South Africa for a year in 1903. He was also present at the Delhi Durbar, held in the same year to celebrate the coronation King Edward VII and Queen Alexandra. On the outbreak of war, William was appointed Assistant Adjutant-General at the 3rd Echelon of General Headquarters in Rouen, and died there, of illness, on 28th October 1917 and is buried in St Sever Cemetery, Rouen. He was Mentioned in Despatches three times for his work in France, and was also awarded The Order of St Michael and St George. He was well respected for his work, with General Graham writing to his widow, "Your husband had worked so devotedly and loyally for me ever since this war began, and I was hoping that in the New Year's Honours Gazette he would have seen how much I appreciated his services." Colonel Gough added, "He stood alone and above everyone else in the affection of all who came into contact with him. In the hustle and hurry of official business, friction and bickerings must have their place, but with him it was impossible. There was no-one who ever had a fault to find with him and his methods; he was straight and sympathetic, and a real friend to all," and another officer, "The Colonel was to me like my own father (whose guidance I never enjoyed, being only seven years old at his death), and his loving and smiling personality endeared him to me, and, in fact, to every one of us here. I shall miss my much revered 'friend' in a way that is impossible for me to express. There is the one comfort, if it can be called such, that he fell in his battle harness, serving his dearly loved native land, the personification of one of whose greatest gentlemen he was the embodiment." William had married Mary Ambrose in Mauritius in 1885, and they had two sons, Douglas and William, both of whom had distinguished careers in the Army. He is also listed on the War Memorial at Fawkham Green, near Swanley, Kent, but it is not known what his connection is with either that village, or with Sandhurst.

The late Sergt. A. DOE, Primrose Cottage, Finchampstead.—Killed in action.

A. DOE

Arthur Doe was born at Sandhurst in 1887. He was one of four brothers, one of whom died at the age of six. When Arthur was born, his father had a job making deliveries with a horse and cart, but later became a domestic gardener. Later still, the family moved to Finchampstead, where he had a new position, combining the posts of both gardener and groom. Arthur also worked as a gardener after leaving school, before joined the Royal Berkshire Regiment in March 1905, attesting at Yorktown. When war broke out, he was a member of the 1st Battalion who went to France later in August 1914, but was later transferred to the 2nd Battalion. This battalion was in India when war was declared, arriving in Le Havre on 5th November, and were in the front line trenches Fauquissart on the 14th. The British trenches were in low-lying ground and needed constant pumping to keep them more or less clear of water, but conditions were still miserable and the first cases of "trench foot" were seen. Of course, there was some relief on Christmas Day; the War Diary records, "Men got up on parapet and advanced half way towards German trenches and in some cases conversed with them. Orders given at 11am prohibiting men from going beyond parapet. Much work done in improving trenches during this day, the enemy protested against barb (sic) wire being repaired and we stopped enemy from repairing theirs." They were relieved at 5pm on the 26th, going back into the front line four days later; more men were recorded as going to hospital, due to the conditions of the trenches during this period, than were being killed or wounded. By the end of the month, the trenches were unusable, and a breastwork with shelters was constructed above ground-level; this offered less protection, and an increase in the number of casualties. One man, an N.C.O., was recorded as being killed on 1st January in the War Diary, the first fatality since before Christmas. This was Arthur, now a Corporal, and he is buried in Fauquissart Military Cemetery, Laventie.

A. DORSET

Albert Dorset was born at Frimley at 1899. His father had spent six years in India with the Highland Light Infantry, and then worked as a storeman at the Royal Military College, Sandhurst. He had married in 1891, just after finishing his service, but his wife died five years later. He then married his wife's niece, who gave birth to Albert and two daughters, but died giving birth to a third. His father then married a sister of his first wife, with another boy being born; Albert also had a half-sister from the first marriage. By now, the family had moved to Camberley where his father was working as a domestic gardener. Young Albert managed to get into the army underage, attesting at Camberley, and joined the 7th Battalion, Royal Sussex Regiment, but did not go to France until 1916. The battalion had suffered many casualties earlier in the year at the Hohenzollern Craters, and would have received new drafts before fighting at Ovillers in the Battle of the Somme. On 3rd August, after two days of shelling, the

5th Battalion, Royal Fusiliers attacked and captured most of Ration Trench, north of Pozieres, in the evening. A few hours later, the Sussex men were ordered forward to assist with mixed results, although by the end of the day, practically all the trench was captured and consolidated. Some platoons had come under heavy machine gun fire, while others had been driven back by an enemy counter-attack. 21 men from the battalion were killed during the two days of fighting, with almost thirty more missing and over one hundred wounded. Albert was one of those killed, and his body is buried in Courcelette British Cemetery.

A. DRAYCOTT

Albert George Nethercliffe Draycott was born in 1894 at Blackwater, Surrey, one of nine children. The family also used the surname Nethercliffe (Albert's paternal grandmother lived for several years with a William Draycott in Wokingham without marrying him). Albert's father worked as a waiter in the Officer's Mess at the Royal Military College, having met his wife while previously working at Brookwood Asylum, where she was on the staff, working as a nurse. Albert is merely listed as a "worker" in the 1911 census, before joining the 2nd Battalion, Highland Light Infantry a year before the war started, attesting at Aldershot. The battalion were still there when war was declared, and crossed the Channel to Boulogne ten days later. They took part in the Battle of Mons, the Battle of the Marne, the Battle of the Aisne, and the First Battle of Ypres in 1914, as well as the Battle of Festubert and the Battle of Loos the following year. On 13th June 1916, the Highlanders were at Camblain l'Abbe. A memorial service was held in the local theatre for Lord Kitchener, who had died eight days earlier on HMS 'Hampshire' which had exploded in mysterious circumstances, at which the battalion were "well represented." They went into the line the next day. It rained heavily for nearly sixty hours, leaving the trenches in "very bad condition." For two days, both sides were very quiet, then the enemy started shelling the British positions. There was a gas alert on the 17th, and the battalion were relieved on the following day. At some point during the shelling, Albert was wounded; he died on the 19th, and is buried in Barlin Communal Cemetery Extension.

F. FINAL

Frederick Richard Final was born at Sandhurst on 7th September 1894, and baptised 28th October. He was one of ten children, supported by his father who worked as a domestic servant at the Royal Military College. Frederick worked as a cowman with dairy cows at a local farm after leaving school until volunteering for service, attesting at Guildford, and joined the Royal Field Artillery. He served with the 37th Division Trench Mortar Battery, and arrived in France on 1st August 1915, having been inspected by the King on Salisbury Plain five weeks earlier. Trench mortars were used in a variety of defensive and offensive roles, from the suppression of an enemy machine gun, sniper post or other local feature, to the co-ordinated firing of barrages. Larger mortars were sometimes used for cutting barbed wire, especially where field artillery could not be used, either because of the danger of hitting British troops or where the effect of the fire could not be observed. The Division took part in the Battle of the Ancre in November 1916, the Arras Offensive and Third Battle of Ypres in 1917, as well as fighting around Ypres, and on the Hindenburg Line, in 1918. On 27th October, they were at Saleschas near Le Quesnoy, and were called upon by the infantry to engage some German machine guns that were holding them up on a road. But the enemy retaliated very heavily, and no further action could be taken, and the men retired to their billets. Those containing the men of the Trench Mortar Batteries were shelled the next day, killing four, and wounding another sixteen. Frederick was one those killed, and is buried in Romeries Communal Cemetery Extension.

A. GOSWELL

Private ALBERT GOSWELL, 1/4th Batt. Hants Regt.

Albert Goswell was born at Sandhurst on 11th July 1892, and baptised 9th February the following year. He was one of twelve children, all but one of whom survived. After leaving school, Albert worked as a domestic gardener, unlike his father and eldest brother who were both bricklayers. He was a member of the 1/4th Battalion, Hampshire Regiment, a Territorial Battalion, attesting at Winchester. The battalion sailed for India in October 1914, but then moved to Basra, landing on 18th March 1915. The Regimental History records the situation there: "On arrival, the British made some tactical moves to seize important or threatening points beyond Basra. After an early string of cheap successes, eyes increasingly fell on the Mesopotamian capital, Baghdad. The 6th (Poona) Division advanced, leaving a very thinly-stretched supply line of hundreds of miles behind it, only to receive a bloody repulse at Ctesiphon. A ragged and dispiriting retreat back to Kut-al-Amara began. The Turks pursued the retreating Division to Kut, and soon surrounded and cut it off. British forces in Mesopotamia were now growing, and these formations were ordered to advance north along the Tigris to relieve Kut. They ran into strong and stoutly defended lines and suffered some hard knocks; although they got close to Kut, the garrison there was surrendered on 29th April 1916. It was an enormous blow to British prestige, and a morale-booster for the Turkish Army. An attack on El Hanna, on January 21st was part of this advance. 'Zero' was fixed for 6:30am, but a mirage prevented the gunners from seeing their targets, so the attack had to be postponed till 7:45am, by which time the Turks had fully realised what was coming. The Hampshires had been under fairly heavy long-range rifle fire even before 'Zero', and had had a few men hit. The fire was heavy, and the battalion had a long stretch to cover even to gain our old front trench. With no support coming up and heavy casualties, the advance was held up short of the Turkish line. On the extreme left, some men managed to join Black Watch in the Turkish trenches and lend a hand in a struggle, which they maintained for over an hour, against heavy odds, though no more support reached them. Eventually, they were overwhelmed, only a few survivors regaining our lines. Meanwhile, the rest of the battalion could merely hang on behind such cover as they could scrape together with their entrenching tools, and wait till darkness allowed them to move and to try to assist the wounded. A pelting rain and bitter cold added to the trials to be endured, and stamina and endurance were severely taxed." Well over half the attacking infantry were casualties, including Albert's battalion who lost almost 250 men. Albert was killed in the fighting; his body was never recovered, and his name is listed on the Basra Memorial.

C. GRAINGER

Charles Henry Grainger was born at Sandhurst on 11th July 1893, the middle of three children. His father, who also had two step-children from his wife's first marriage, worked as a bricklayer.

Charles attended Sandhurst Wesleyan School until the age of fourteen, but is not known what work he did after leaving. However, on 13th November 1908, he appeared in front of the Petty Divisional Session at Wokingham, accused of stealing fish to the value of one shilling from a fishmonger in Reading. He was found guilty, and it being his second offence, he was sent to Kingswood Reformatory School at Bristol, to be held until he was nineteen years of age. Opened in 1852, Kingswood preceded the legislation bringing Reformed Schools into being, but its principles were the same. The schools were for offenders under the age of sixteen, and were very tough places, with stiff discipline, enforced by frequent beatings. Those admitted were there for a few years, away from the influence of family and friends, and were given a basic education and taught a trade. On entry, Charles was described as being just under five feet tall, with brown eyes, light brown hair, scars on his left cheek and top lip, and the letter 'C' tattooed on his right arm; in addition his character was described as "indifferent." While there, he was interviewed twice. In December 1908, it was reported, "A quick bright boy. Wants to be a carpenter," and a year later, "Slack and prefers indoor work, either as a carpenter or a tailor." He was released on 10th July 1912. Charles returned to Sandhurst, later volunteering for service, attesting at Wokingham, and joined the 2nd Battalion, Royal Berkshire Regiment, landing in France in July 1915. Toward the end of September, he would have been involved in an attack at Bois Grenier which ran into difficulties, with well over one hundred men killed. After this, the battalion continued in and out of the trenches for two months before a long rest period, during which they received more training and some divisional manoeuvres. They went back in the trenches from mid January until late March the following year, when they moved to the Somme area; they must have been glad to finally get out of permanently water-logged trenches in a wet part of the country. On 1st July, they were involved in the first day of the Battle of the Somme. The battalion had the objective of capturing the village of Ovillers, north of La Boisselle. After a night during which the trenches had been shelled by the Germans, at around 6:30am, the British barrage began. An hour later, the men climbed out of the trenches to start the attack, but immediately came under terrific rifle and machine gun fire from the German trenches in front of Ovillers, which prevented them from reaching the enemy line. A small group on the left did manage to get into the trench, but was eventually bombed out again. By 7:45am, the fire on the parapet of the British trench made it impossible for any more men to leave it. In less than three hours after the attack started, over half the battalion had been killed, while the regiments to the left and right had lost an even higher proportion of men. With such losses, it was clearly impossible to mount another attack, and the Brigade remained in their trenches until dark when it withdrew to bivouacs at Long Valley. Charles was one of those killed, and is buried in Ovillers Military Cemetery.

The late Bdr. MAURICE ("Buller") GROVE, M.M., Belmont Cottage, Owlsmoor.—Killed in action.

M. GROVE

Maurice Buller Grove was born at Sandhurst early in 1897. He was the youngest of seven surviving children in a family where two others had died in infancy. His oldest brother, who had been a Private in the Yorkshire Regiment, died in 1904, and his father, a general labourer, six years later. Maurice worked as a butcher's errand boy after leaving school. Although officially still underage for overseas service, he volunteered, attesting at Camberley, joined the Royal Field Artillery, and arrived in France on 8th July 1915. This indicates he may have been part of the 15th (Scottish) Division for the duration of his time there, a Division that served with distinction, winning the regard of the enemy as one of the most formidable in the British army. Maurice also played his part, winning the Military Medal at some point in his career. They took part on the Battle of Loos in the autumn, and three phases of the Battle of the Somme the next year. Earlier in 1916, they had also faced a German gas attack at Hulluch at the end of April. The first few days in April 1917 were spent preparing for an attack at Arras. For two days, the batteries were firing to cut the enemy wire and bombarding the German's two front lines of trenches, and then practised a creeping barrage for the next two days. On the 8th, they concentrated on making the gaps in the enemy wire larger, and the attack began at 5:30am the following morning. The infantry assaulted the enemy front system, preceded by a creeping barrage supplied by 18 pounders. Meanwhile, 4.5 inch Howitzers and the Heavy Batteries systematically bombarded the enemy works behind the front system, and the attack was successful. One of the batteries of the 71st Brigade took a direct hit, but men from other guns were also killed during the action, including Maurice. He is buried in Beaurains Road Cemetery, Beaurains. His widowed mother was living in Owlsmoor when names for the Crowthorne War Memorial were being collected, so he is recorded on it as well in his native Sandhurst.

H. HOLLAND

The late Pte. HARRY W. HOLLAND, Fern Cottage, Sandhurst.—Died of wounds.

Henry William Holland, known as Harry, was born at Sandhurst on 14th January 1891, and baptised 1st March. He was the second youngest of eight children, and was only eight years old when his father, a general labourer, died. His mother struggled on with two of her children, but Harry was placed in the Royal Albert Orphanage, located between Bagshot and Camberley. Although the orphanage has been demolished, the tree outside it, planted by Queen Victoria when she opened the facility, and which boys would punch on leaving for the last time, still stands near Portsmouth Road. However, after his mother's death in 1911, Harry's eldest sister managed to reassemble a household with three other sisters and Harry in Little Sandhurst, with the girls doing laundry work, and Harry providing income as a domestic gardener. He married Maud Caryer from Kent in 1913, although it is not clear from the records whether he had moved away from Sandhurst by this time. He joined the Army under the Derby Scheme, attesting at Camberley, and joined the 3rd Battalion, Royal Berkshire Regiment to be trained, and then transferred to the 8th Battalion. The battalion were not involved in the fighting on the first day of the Battle of the Somme, but went into the front trenches at Albert nine days later, and gained ground on the 12th and 13th, although an attack on the 14th was cancelled (the message did not reach the Berkshires who moved forward and captured a German trench, but then had to retire when a counter-attack was mounted). By mid August, they were on the north edge of Mamtetz Wood, and went into the front line near Bazentin-le-Petit at midday on the 18th. An earlier attack had failed, and the Berkshires were to repeat it. Unfortunately, one gun of the British artillery bombardment was firing 'short', dropping shells into their trench, damaging it and burying some men. This, along with smoke blowing across the line, hampered their forward movement, but they got to within one hundred yards of their objective before being halted by the German barrage and machine gun fire. They dug in, but were later forced back to their start position, with more than 160 casualties incurred. Henry was wounded in this attack and died two day later. He is buried in Heilly Station Cemetery at Mericourt-L'Abbe.

A. G. Hudson (Royal Berkshire Regiment)

Despite extensive research of census entries, places of attestment, death registrations, voters' lists, and the Royal Berkshire Regiment Roll of Honour, it has not been possible to identify this man. None of the nine men named Hudson from the latter list appear to have any connection with the area, apart from a Thomas Hudson who is listed on the War Memorial in Ascot High Street (he was the eldest son of the family, and signed on underage, dying in 1915 at the age of seventeen). As the original Roll of Honour for Sandhurst was lost in a fire in 1978, the list in Sandhurst Church was compiled from memory and a few errors have been found; it is believed this name is one such error.

A. G. Hudson (Coldstream Guards)

Arthur James Hudson was born at Wallingford, now part of Oxfordshire, in 1880, the second eldest of five brothers. His father worked at labouring jobs in the area, but by 1901, the family had moved to Sandhurst. His father now turned his hand to transporting goods by horse-drawn vehicle, a business which thrived as ten years later, he was regularly plying a trade between Sandhurst and Reading, with two of his sons assisting him, while a third did a similar job, operating from Sandhurst station. Arthur helped his father after leaving school until 1906, when he married Lilian Purvey and moved to Reading, where he worked as the manager in a grocer's shop. He was conscripted into the 1st Battalion, Coldstream Guards towards the end of 1916, attesting at Camberley. The battalion were heavily involved in the Third Battle of Ypres in the second half of 1917, including fighting at Passchendaele. On 27th November, the battalion were to attack the ground up to the Cambrai-Arras railway between the wood and Fontaine. The Regimental History describes the action of the day: "The advance was to be made with fourteen tanks, and was to be covered by a creeping barrage, moving one hundred yards every five minutes. The tanks arrived late, and their assistance was not available until later in the day. By zero hour, the snow had ceased to fall, and the forward movement was made in the half light and in a drizzle of rain. Almost at once the whole of our line, advancing in the open against an unshaken enemy, came under heavy machine gun and rifle fire, which caused very serious losses. The Germans concealed in houses, and in the sunken roads and sandpits that abounded, were able to make a stubborn resistance and to take our men in enfilade. No. 4 Company, diverted in this way from its proper direction to meet a hot fire in flank, lost touch with the centre company and was almost isolated; pressing on, however, it finally reached the objective and captured some fifty prisoners, though only about forty men remained effective. No. 2 Company, having lost all its Officers except its commander, as well as the senior N.C.O.s, was held up by a strong point on its front, but managed by bombing to clear a way for its advance, taking three machine guns and over two hundred prisoners; pushing on, it overcame the resistance of the enemy in another sunken road, with more prisoners to its credit, and arrived at the railway cutting, the objective, where, however, the position was enfiladed from ground lying to the north and where no touch could be obtained with No. 4 Company. The right Company, No. 3, after a severe struggle and subjected to sharp enfilade, drove the Germans out of their trench on the west side of Fontaine, and got into the outskirts of the village. It then surged onwards, bombing the cellars, but one platoon was not sufficient to 'mop up' properly and hostile snipers, left behind, caused a good deal of trouble. The Company then forced a way to the railway, seizing the line and the station, and taking three field guns, two machine guns, and yet more prisoners;

touch, moreover, was obtained with No. 2 Company and with the 3rd Battalion Grenadier Guards on the right, who had successfully penetrated far into the village. All the battalions engaged in the attack made good progress, and were able to report at 8:30am that they had got to their first objective, but their strength had been so much reduced that reinforcements were urgently needed, They had also captured a large number of prisoners, and at one moment over a thousand were in their hands, of which the 1st Coldstream took more than half; but owing to the serious losses and the consequent impossibility of providing proper escorts, many escaped and only some 550 were secured in the divisional cage. The enemy put down a heavy barrage to prevent the arrival of reinforcements, and counter-attacks immediately developed, with the situation becoming serious. One of these was directed against the remnants of No. 4 Company who were isolated and with both flanks exposed. At 9:30am, the small party, after losing heavily, was driven from the railway. Only one Officer and fifteen men of the Company managed to get back. A severe struggle was meanwhile raging near the railway station; we lost it, then we regained it, and the fight was still in progress when the enemy, massing for a counter-attack, threatened to cut off not only the two companies but also the Irish Guards, who were heavily engaged in Bourlon Wood and whose left was insecurely defended. Then yet another powerful blow was struck on the right flank from the direction of La Folie which endangered the line, as the advance south of the Cambrai road was held up. The Brigadier then ordered the battalions to withdraw and fall back to the line from which they started; this was done at about 10:40am, not, however, before the captured guns that could not be removed, were destroyed by bombs and rendered unserviceable. The enemy's pursuit was speedily dispersed by machine and Lewis gun fire, the prisoners being employed to carry back the wounded. The approximate strength of the attacking battalions was low at the moment when they returned, testifying to the severity of the struggle. The 1st Coldstream only had about 180 men remaining. During the remainder of the day, the enemy persistently shelled our front line and the ground south of Bourlon Wood." During the fighting, Arthur was fatally wounded, but it was not possible to recover his body, and his name is listed on the Cambrai Memorial at Louverval.

The late Pte. F. S. JAMES, 1, The Broadway, Sandhurst. Killed in action. Aged 19.

F. JAMES

Francis Sydney James was born at Sandhurst on born 25th September 1896, and baptised 8th November. He came from a small family, being the eldest of three boys. His father worked at the Royal Military Academy, waiting on table in the mess. On leaving school, Francis worked as a messenger boy for a rate collector until he volunteered soon after war was declared, attesting at Reading, and joined the 1st Battalion, Royal Berkshire Regiment. Although he was a year short of the official joining age of nineteen, he added twelve months and was accepted, crossing the Channel on the fourth day of 1915. The War Diary records the arrival of new drafts on the 19th and 25th of January, one of which would have included Francis. In April, the battalion were at Cuinchy, an area of mine warfare. On the 3rd, the Colonel-in-Chief of the Regiment arrived for an inspection, with less than two hours' notice. The War Diary records, "This caused intense pleasure …. Although the men had only come from the trenches in the morning, and had had little or no sleep the previous night, they were all shaved and well turned out." One can only speculate whether the men were as enthusiastic about the visit as the diary's author. In mid May, a twice-postponed attack took place with heavy casualties, due to the Berkshires and the battalion on their right leaving a gap, from which the Germans could enfilade both. It was three weeks before the battalion were in a state to fight again. On 28th September, they made an attack on quarries near Tulloch. This was made at 2:30am on a bright, moonlit night, and they were fired on while still some four hundred yards short of their objective. The action was notable for Second Lieutenant Arthur Turner single-handedly captured 150 yards of a German communication trench before being fatally wounded, an effort that earned him the Victoria Cross. He was one of eighteen men killed that day, with almost 150 missing, and well over a hundred wounded. Francis was one of those killed, and he is buried in Vermelles British Cemetery.

E. JARVIS

Edward Thomas Jarvis was born at Sandhurst on 30th March 1891, and baptised on 17th May (the spelling of the surname is Jarvoice in some of the earlier records). He came from a large family of fourteen children, twelve of whom survived. His father was a carpenter, working at the Royal Military College, and Edward's eldest brother also worked there. After leaving school, Edward worked as a bricklayer labourer until he volunteered for service, attesting at Camberley, and joined the Royal Field Artillery. At the time of his death, he was with the 70th Brigade, part of the 15th Division. Edward had arrived in France on 8th July 1915, a date when the 15th Division were crossing the Channel, so may have served with that unit for his entire war experience. The Division were involved in the Battle of Loos in September that year, several phases of the Battle of the Somme in 1916, the Arras Offensive in the spring of 1917, as well as the start of the Third Battle of Ypres later that year. Although the War Diary for the period of July and August 1917 is missing, it is possible to piece together the action from the diaries of other units in the Division. Fighting was taking place at Vlammertinge and Winnezeele, east of Ypres, from 31st July until 4th August. At this point, the infantry was withdrawn for further training, but the artillery were left in forward positions, to continue shelling the enemy. Edward's unit had already suffered 25 casualties in the fighting, and he became another fatality, being killed five days later, and is buried in Brandhoek New Military Cemetery.

Pte. W. F. JEANS, Wellington Villa, Sandhurst.—Missing since October 13th, 1915, believed killed. Aged 24.

W. JEANS

William Frederick Jeans was born in 1891 at Kegworth, near Loughborough, Leicestershire, and was one of four children. His father was employed as a brass worker, but by 1901 was working as a domestic gardener, and the family had moved, initially to Sussex, and then to Sandhurst. Both William and his younger brother also worked as gardeners after leaving school. He volunteered for service, attesting at Reading, and joined the 5th Battalion, Royal Berkshire Regiment, going to France at the end of May 1915. In the middle of June, the battalion received instruction on the "mysteries" of trench warfare, and held the front trenches on their own account on 4th July at Ploegsteert Wood. They continued in and out of trenches here until late September, when they moved to the area east of Loos. Here the trenches were only two feet deep and overlooked by the enemy, so much work was done under cover of darkness to improve the situation. On 12th October, they relieved the Coldstream Guards in the support trenches for an attack on the Hulluch Quarries the next day. They were called upon early in the afternoon, having put on their smoke helmets about four hours earlier. 'A' Company were despatched to assist the 7th Battalion, Norfolk Regiment, who had led the attack but suffered many casualties. Immediately, they came under heavy machine gun fire from a trench, thought to be hold by the Norfolks, but which was still occupied by the Germans. The battalion also supplied four bombing parties, under orders from the Brigade Bombing Officer, and operating completely independently from the rest of the battalion on this day. Although the first two bombing parties reached the German trenches, getting bombs to them proved difficult, and they were eventually forced back, sustaining many casualties during the day. William was one of those missing by the end of the day; his body was never found, and his name is listed on the Loos Memorial.

J. JONES

William James Jones was born at Tilford, near Farnham, Surrey, in 1882, the youngest of five children. His father, a police constable, died when William was only a few months old, forcing his mother to work as a nurse. After leaving school, William worked as a general labourer, living in lodgings at Godalming in the 1901 census. He married Charlotte Cree in London in 1907, and moved to Frimley Green, where he worked as a domestic gardener. A daughter was born the following year. As he does not appear to have seen active service (no medals have been awarded for overseas service), it is difficult to find any more details on him. The Roll of Honour in Sandhurst Church lists him as being in the Loyal North Lancashire Regiment, and there is a death recorded in Lancashire early in 1915 of a man of the right age. Why did he join a northern regiment rather than a local one? Had he left his wife and child? William's story has several unanswered questions.

L. JONES

George Leonard Jones (unrelated to William James Jones) was born at Frimley in 1894. He was known by his second name to distinguish him from his father, George William Jones, a tailor. Leonard was the second of six children, two of whom died in infancy. At the age of sixteen, he joined the 2nd Battalion, Royal Lancashire Regiment as a "boy", attesting at Guildford, and appears in the 1911 census at Fort Regent, Jersey. From 1876, boys could be enlisted from the age of fourteen as musicians, drummers, tailors, shoemakers, artificers (whose job was to repair military equipment) or clerks, but the matter was being reviewed in 1911. As recruiting sergeants were paid for each man they enlisted, it was often easy for under-age boys to join up. The battalion were in India when war was declared, and returned to England three days before Christmas, landing at Le Havre three and a half weeks later. As part of the 2nd Battle of Ypres, starting in the second half of April, the battalion took over some incomplete trenches in front of Frezenberg on 4th May. The enemy shelled them intermittently for three days, but then the intensity increased, blowing the trenches in, and making them untenable. They then advanced against the front line and, having captured it, pushed on against the Support Line, but were held in check at 10am, when some two hundred yards away. The Germans were then observed moving to the west on both flanks, and an hour and a half later, the battalion were ordered to return to Potijze. Leonard was killed in the shelling on the 8th; his body was never found, and he is listed on the Ypres (Menin Gate) Memorial.

R. MANNERING

Richard Reginald Mannering was born in 1894 at Camberley. His parents both worked in service, and married a few months before he was born. He had three younger sisters, but his father died when Richard was only five years old, and his mother remarried in 1900, having already had a child by Richard's stepfather; Richard would eventually have three half-siblings. The new family set up home in Sandhurst, where his stepfather worked as a house painter. After leaving school, Richard worked as a stonemason before joining the 1st Battalion, Hampshire Regiment in January 1913, attesting at Aldershot. The battalion were at Colchester when war was declared, and landed at Le Havre less than three weeks later. They took part in the Battle of Cateau at the end of August, and the Battles of the Marne and the Aisne. On 16th September, the battalion were in trenches, described as "very trying" at La Montage Farm. The Germans brought up heavy guns, reported to be 8.5" mortars, and with the aid of aeroplane observers, fired them "with amazing accuracy, and caused a good deal of loss in our trenches." By the following day, the Hampshires had dropped back to Bucy Le Long, but were still "heavily shelled by enemy heavy guns, which caused considerable damage." Over the two days, eleven men were killed and more than fifty wounded, all by the artillery fire coming from the Germans. Richard was one of those who lost his life on the first day; his body was never recovered, and his name is one of ten listed on a Special Memorial in Crouy-Vauxrot French National Cemetery, Crouy.

R. MILLS

Mark Mills was born in 1882 at East Worldham, near Alton, Hampshire, and was one of ten children. His father was an agricultural labourer, but the family moved frequently, with Mark's siblings being variously born at Easthampstead, Maidenhead, Bisley and Yateley, while the 1881 census records the family living in a barn at Heckfield! His parents obviously lost track with such a large family, as various census entries give his birthplace as Maidenhead as well as York Town, Surrey. His father died in 1898, by which time Mark had left school and was working as a general labourer, living with the rest of the family in Hawley at first, before going into lodgings in York Town. He married Ethel Marshall in 1915, before joining up under the Derby Scheme later the same year, attesting at Camberley, although by then he was living in Reading, and joined the 1st Battalion, Royal Berkshire Regiment. He was mobilised in March 1916, but there is no reference in the War Diary, to indicate when he would have arrived at the front. The battalion were not involved in the Battle of the Somme which started on 1st July, and started an inter-platoon football tournament on the 3rd! Their fighting resumed on the 27th at Delville Wood, where there were more than 260 casualties. They were not called on to fight again until 13th November, by which time they were at Serre, and started moving forward in readiness for an attack the following day. They came under heavy artillery and machine gun fire all morning as well as from mine-throwers, and snipers were active in the afternoon; nine men were killed during the course of the day and more than twenty wounded. At 5am the following morning, they advanced across No Man's Land, suffering casualties from machine gun fire as well as British artillery "shorts." These were especially heavy on the right, and there were insufficient men left when they reached the German trenches. Despite this, they managed to capture several prisoners, and captured part of Serre Trench, the objective. Almost half the battalion were casualties on the day; Mark was one of those killed, and is buried in New Munich Trench British Cemetery, Beaumont-Hamel.

C. J. MOTH

Christopher Job Moth was born at Egham in 1898, one of six children. His father worked as a bricklayer, but presumably whatever work was in the Egham area dried up, as by 1910, the family had moved to Sandhurst, and he was recorded as a general labourer in the census taken the following year. Christopher was a member of the 1/4th Battalion, Hampshire Regiment, a Territorial Battalion, having joined at Yateley. The battalion had been in India since the previous November, before sailing to Basra where they landed in the middle of March. On arrival, the British made some tactical moves to seize important or threatening points beyond Basra. After an early string of cheap successes, eyes increasingly fell on the Mesopotamian capital, Baghdad. Christopher arrived in Mesopotamia in October 1915, and presumably had lied about his age, being only seventeen, as nineteen was the age at which men were eligible for overseas service. An attack on El Hanna, on 21st January the following year, was part of the planned advance. The Regimental History describes the situation: "'Zero' was fixed for 6:30am, but a mirage prevented the gunners from seeing their targets, so the attack had to be postponed till 7:45am, by which time the Turks had fully realised what was coming. The Hampshires had been under fairly heavy long-range rifle fire even before 'Zero', and had had a few men hit. The fire was heavy, and the battalion had a long stretch to cover even to gain our old front trench. With no support coming up and heavy casualties, the advance was held up short of the Turkish line. On the extreme left, some men managed to join Black Watch in the Turkish trenches and lend a hand in a struggle which they maintained for over an hour against heavy odds, though no more support reached them. Eventually, they were overwhelmed, only a few survivors regaining our lines. Meanwhile, the rest of the battalion could merely hang on behind such cover as they could scrape together with their entrenching tools, and wait till darkness allowed them to move, and to try to assist the wounded. A pelting rain and bitter cold added to the trials to be endured, and stamina and endurance were severely taxed." Well over half the attacking infantry were casualties, including Christopher's battalion who lost almost 250 men. Christopher was killed in the fighting; his body was never recovered, and his name is listed on the Basra Memorial.

E. NASH

Ernest Seymour Nash was born at Sandhurst on 21st November 1891, and baptised 7th February the following year. He was one of eight children, two of whom had died by 1911. The family lived near The White Swan public house, and his father worked as a domestic coachman. Ernest worked as an engine cleaner after leaving school until he joined the 1st Battalion, Royal Berkshire Regiment in February 1909, attesting at Reading. He was 5'6" tall, weighted almost nine stone, had blue eyes, brown hair, and a fresh complexion, and circular scars on the back of his neck. The battalion were at Reading when war was declared, and ready to leave a week later, when they was inspected by King George V and Queen Mary. They left Farnborough by train the next day, and crossed the Channel from Southampton to Rouen overnight. The battalion were involved in the Battle of Mons, the

Battle of the Marne, the Battle of the Aisne, and the First Battle of Ypres in 1914, and the Battle of Festubert in May 1915. On 6th June, they had been in trenches at Grenay and were relieved overnight, and marched to Noeux-les-Mines and went into billets. The following evening, they marched to Verquieneul where the War Diary reports the billets were "bad and the men crowded, as a good number of French artillery men were also billeted in the village." Here they remained for three days of training, during which time Ernest was accidentally shot in the foot. After a week of treatment, he was sent back to England for further attention where he remained for five months. In 1916, the battalion took part in the Battle of Delville Wood and the Battle of the Ancre, both phases of the Somme fighting. The latter took place in November in trenches full of liquid mud. On the 14th, the battalion moved into trenches captured the previous day. Half the men then attempted to capture Munich Trench, but suffered heavy casualties and were too weak to make any impression when they reached it. Ernest was one of more than seventy men wounded, sustaining a gunshot wound to his left knee. He spent over a month being treated in France before coming back to England again, just after Christmas. On 22nd February the following year, he married Jessie Sloper at Earley, although a son born at the beginning of 1918, died after a few days. Ernest's wound prevented him returning to France, and he spent the rest of his time in the army at the Royal Berkshire Regiment Depot in Reading, probably training new conscripts. By now he had been promoted to the rank of sergeant. He was discharged, "no longer physically fit for war service" on 14th September 1918, and died 4th January the following year, and is buried in Sandhurst (St Michael) Churchyard. His widow remarried in Reading in 1921, and died in 1973.

G. Over

Gilbert William Over was born at Yorktown in 1897. He was one of the four sons of John Over, draper, outfitter, boot repairer and house furnisher, and the family could afford to employ one servant to help at home. The family business started on the London Road, opposite the old York Town School (now an Islamic Centre), and continued to trade in Camberley for over 120 years. Although underage, Gilbert volunteered for service, attesting at Camberley, and joined the 7th Battalion, Royal West Surrey Regiment. The first men from the battalion went to France in late July 1915, but Gilbert was part of a draft that arrived two months later. The War Diary records details of the first arrivals – as well as the officers (who are named), there were 47 Sergeants, 43 Corporals, 51 Lance Corporals, 773 Privates, 23 horses, 42 mules and three Lewis guns. They went into trenches for the first time on 9th August, and a Lieutenant and an N.C.O. became the first casualties, both being wounded in the right arm by the same bullet. The first death occurred four days later, when eighteen-year old Private Vokes was killed by the accidental discharge of a rifle. The battalion were involved in the Battle of Delville Wood, the Battle of Thiepval Ridge, and the Battle of the Ancre in 1916, and the Arras Offensive in spring the following year. The records state that Gilbert died in Germany, which indicates he was captured and treated as a Prisoner of War, possibly dying in a German hospital. There is a reference in the War Diary on 10th August 1917 to missing men when the battalion were fighting in the vicinity of Chateau Segard, near Dickebusch, so this may have been when he was captured. The death of Lance Corporal G. Over is officially recorded on 4th January 1918, and he is buried in Niederzwehren Cemetery, one of four cemeteries in Germany where the Commonwealth War Graves have been concentrated.

The late Pte. FRANK PAYNE, 1/5th Batt., Victoria Cottages, Little Sandhurst.—Died of cholera. Aged 21.

F. PAYNE

Frank Payne was born at Sandhurst on 4th July 1895, and baptised 15th September, the youngest of seven children. His mother died in 1907, and his father, who worked as a dormitory servant at Wellington College, remarried two years later with another child being born in 1910. Frank, by now, was living with one of his elder brothers in Little Sandhurst, working alongside him as a house decorator. He volunteered for service, attesting at Camberley, and joined the 1/5th Battalion, Royal West Surrey Regiment. The battalion had gone to India at the end of October 1914, remaining there for a little over twelve months before sailing for Mesopotamia. Frank was part of a draft that joined them there, a couple of weeks before Christmas 1915. The author of the War Diary at this period is full of complaints about delays, red tape, the work the men were having to do, poor food, overcrowding, stampeding mules, and untrained camels! But he was happier when they started fighting on 14th January: "The troops throughout were very steady, fire control and discipline were excellent," although the facilities for attending to the wounded came in for more criticism. Equipment and clothing was inadequate, in a poor state, or missing, and poor weather, coupled with exhaustion, led to a few deaths. A full issue of rum restored spirits. Signs of lice were found in all the Companies, which were blamed on the Indian regiments who had previously occupied the camp. 69 tins of plum pudding and 86 parcels of comforts arrived from the ladies of Bombay and Calcutta on 8th February – no complaints about that! Similarly welcomed was a large gift of books received a week later. Red tape continued to be a problem, leading to excessive clerical work. In March, a Captain was appointed sanitary officer, and immediately shut the camp bazaar, "no medical precautions were being taken as regards the food and drink being sold there." In addition, they had taken over the soda water factory and the ice-making plant. All this was set against a background of marching, improving roads and defences around the camps, building bunds to prevent the river flooding the camp, training, and occasional skirmishes with the enemy. There were more complaints in mid March, when a new draft arrived with inadequate paperwork, some untrained men, and others who had been wounded or suffered from disease in France. A few days later, the Arabs who had been paid to do some of the construction work, refused to turn up the following day, and were dismissed, the work falling on the men in the battalion. But then the Arabs had only managed to build one hut in two days (the intimation being that they did not work very well). "Thirty men per Company were put at Lieut. Mountford's disposal to construct the huts, and made good progress." The telegraph line was interrupted, in the same place, for the second time in a few days, so the nearby village was shelled. On 12th April, a firing party was made up to execute a Turkish Officer proved guilty of espionage. Later in the month, it was noted that the loading of camels had been improved and accomplished quicker, due to earlier training. The general health of the battalion "continued good," with only fifteen men in hospital. "After a few cases of insubordination from members of the (latest) draft, the number of minor offences very considerably decreased toward the end of the month." By May, the weather had turned much hotter, and the hours the men spent working were adjusted accordingly. The river also started to rise rapidly, causing much work on the bunds, but eventually it breached, flooding one of the camps. On the 15th, one death occurred from drowning when a Private, who could not swim, stepped off a ledge into deep water, and was carried away. Two days later, the first three cases of cholera were recorded. By the end of the month, the river level started to drop. Another case of cholera was recorded on 5th June, and those who shared a hut with him were isolated from the rest of the camp. More changes in red tape meant an even heavier workload of paperwork. On Whit Monday, Regimental sports were held in the afternoon, and the following day, the men who had been put in isolation were allowed to rejoin the rest of the camp, no new cases having occurred. The entry of 20th June starts with the record: "2361 Pte F. J. Payne, 'B' Company and machine gunner, having died of cholera on the 17th inst, was buried at 6:30am." A number of cemeteries were used in and around Basra during the war, subsequently two existing cemeteries were expanded and merged to form the Basra War Cemetery, and more than a thousand other graves were brought in. Frank is buried here along with two and half thousand other men who died.

C. POOLEY

Augustus Charles Pooley, who never used his first name in the records, was born near St Pancras, London in 1873, the eldest of five children. His father worked for a time in the police force, before taking on driving jobs around the city with a horse and cart. After leaving school, Charles worked as a clerk, before joining the army, adding one year to his age when attesting at the beginning of 1890, and joined the 5th Dragoon Guards, a cavalry regiment. He was described as having blue eyes, brown hair, and a fair complexion, and by 1902 was 5'9" tall, and weighed nine stone. He spent eight weeks in Cambridge Hospital a year after joining, with an unspecified injury, before returning to service. Charles had signed on for seven years, and been promoted to Sergeant by the end of his term. He married Kate Ashdown in 1897, and extended his service for a further twelve years. A month later, the regiment went to India, taking families with them, and the first of their six children was born soon after. However, Charles suffered with the climate, and required treatment on three occasions for the extreme heat. In October 1899, the Dragoons were posted to South Africa and fought in the Boer War, where Charles was promoted to Sergeant in the Quartermasters stores. He had already extended his service again by the time the regiment returned to India in April 1904 for twelve months, before moving to South Africa again. This time, the families came with them, Charles and Kate taking a second, newly-born son as well. Three more children were born before they returned to England at the end of 1908, and then moved to Dublin. The following year, he was promoted again to Regimental Sergeant Major, and allowed to extend his service beyond the normal twenty-one years, his Service Record continually recording his character as "exemplary." Charles received a commission in 1913. In July 1914, he spent a week in hospital with bruising to his back, after being thrown from a horse. He told the Court of Enquiry, held at the beginning of August, "At Ash Ranges on 7.7.14, I was on parade for field firing, and was galloping with a message when my horse fell on a piece of rough ground. I was thrown over the horse's head and hurt my back. I was taken to hospital the same day." Captain Pankhurst, who witnessed the incident said, "I was on duty at Ash Ranges on 7.7.14. I saw Mr Pooley's horse fall and found Mr Pooley had hurt his back. He was removed to hospital at once." The presiding officer concluded, "I consider this Warrant Officer was on duty and in no way to blame. I therefore recommend remission of full hospital stoppage." At the outbreak of war, the 5th Dragoons were at Aldershot, and arrived in France within two weeks, and took part in all the battles of the first year; Charles was Mentioned in Dispatches after the Battle of the Aisne, and was also awarded the Military Cross and the French "Medaille Militaire" for action during the First Battle of Ypres. 1915 saw him awarded the Belgian "Ordre de Leopold (Chevalier)" in March, take part in the Second Battle of Ypres later in the spring, and was promoted to the rank of Lieutenant. More action followed on the Somme (1916), in the Arras Offensive and Cambrai Operations (1917), and at the Somme again in March 1918. He also received another award from Belgium, the "Croix de Guerre" at the beginning of the same month. On 8th August, the Dragoons, including Charles, who had been promoted again to the rank of Captain, were near Vauvillers, and moved off at 10am. Moving forward, they were able to report the village of Harbonnieres and a nearby wood unoccupied by the enemy, but after capturing their third objective, were met with heavy opposition, which prevented further gains. At 5am the following morning, they moved to the Brigade Concentration areas near Guillacourt, and set off again at six in the evening, and assembled two miles west of Rosieres. Four hours later, the Brigade was bombed by a German aircraft and suffered a few casualties which included Charles, who was buried in De Luce British Cemetery. The list of personal belongings returned to his family included photos, two pocket books, a bible in a case, a waterproof leather case, a cap badge and six collar badges for the regiment, three Gilt stars and six cotton stars, an envelope of various medal ribbons and two brooches for them, eight overseas stripes, an envelope containing newspaper cuttings, a wrist watch, an English/French military dictionary and a French dictionary (published by Cassells), shaving apparatus, an electric torch, bulb and refill, and two Red Staff cap bands. He left the sum of just over £1200, out of which his widow agreed to pay £10, owed to her late husband's groom, who had survived the war, only to fall victim to the Spanish flu in February 1919. Several months after the conclusion of the fighting, Charles' widow, now living on York Town Road, Sandhurst, received the following letter: "Dear Mrs Pooley, I am writing with reference already sent to you regarding the place of burial of Capt. C. Pooley, M.C.. I am to inform you that in accordance with the agreement with the French and Belgian governments to remove all scattered graves and all cemeteries of less than 40 graves, also certain other cemeteries which were situated in places unsuitable for permanent retention, it has been found necessary to exhume the bodies buried in certain areas. The body of Capt. C. Pooley, M.C. has therefore been removed from De Luce British Cemetery and reburied in Caix New British Cemetery, northeast of Moreuil. I am to add that the necessity for the removal is much regretted, but was unavoidable for the reasons given above. You may rest assured that the work of reburial has been carried out carefully and reverently, special arrangements having been made for the appropriate religious service to be held." The original burial place was a small cemetery, close to the north bank of the nearby river, and contained thirty war graves. A letter to his sister in October 1919, also confirmed all the military awards given to him during the conflict.

The late Pte. J. PROVINS, Ambarrow Lodge, Sandhurst.—Killed in action. Aged 21.

J. PROVINS

Raymond Provins, known as Jack, was born at Sandhurst on 5th September 1894, and baptised 30th December. He was one of eight children in a family living at the lodge of the now demolished Ambarrow Court, where his father worked as a coachman. Jack also worked there as a groom after leaving school. He volunteered for service, attesting at Reading, and joined the 6th Battalion, Royal Berkshire Regiment. Training was done at Colchester until May 1915, and then on Salisbury Plain, before they arrived in France on 24th July, and were in trenches at Bouzincourt, near Albert, just over a week later. They stayed in the area until mid September before marching to Albert. Here there was a great deal of mining from both sides, and the battalion had over one hundred men, working four six-hours shifts every day, on mining fatigues, removing and disposing of over three thousand bags of chalk each day, without the enemy being aware of what was happening. Later in the month, the War Diary records the effect of gas from exploding mines on the men as being like that of alcohol, making them violent at first, and then sleepy. It was mid October before they went into billets at Buire and were able to enjoy such entertainments as a cinema. The rest of the autumn, winter and following spring followed a regular pattern of trenches and rest periods, although from March, training started in readiness for the coming Battle of the Somme. On 25th June, they moved to Grove Town in readiness for the attack. The British bombardment was in full swing for the advance, which was scheduled for the 29th but postponed due to wet weather. The following day, five men were killed and 42 wounded by the German artillery response, largely due to the inadequacy of the dug-outs. The battalion moved into its assembly positions at 3am on 1st July, leaving the third trench empty after it was observed this was where the majority of the enemy's shells were falling. They were opposite Mine Trench, the most advanced of the enemy's defences, at the west end of which was Casino Point. A huge mine was exploded under this at 7:27am (a few men of the battalion were hit by debris) but when the advance started three minutes later, Germans came out with their hands up to surrender. Mine Trench was captured in the first rush, Bund Support Trench was in the Berkshire's hands by 7:50am, and they were moving on to Pommiers Trench. Through the rest of the day, they continued to win ground, albeit at high cost. Trenches on a front over a mile long had been captured, but over sixty officers and men had been killed, almost 250 wounded, and a further 46 were missing. Jack was one of the latter; his name is recorded on the Thiepval Memorial.

R. REPTON

Richard Repton was born in 1898 near Lewisham, southeast London. He was one of ten children, all but one of whom survived. Richard grew up in the Manor Park and Leyton areas of London, where his father worked as a carpenter. He was conscripted into the 1st Battalion, Lincolnshire Regiment, attesting at Leyton. At the end of 1917, the battalion were involved in the operations at Cambrai. An initial British success was followed by losses when the Germans counter-attacked. On 17th December, the battalion were at Hedicourt. At 4am, the enemy raided a forward left post through a gap in the wire with a party of some twenty men, which was held by a similar number of 'A' Company. The night was very dark and there was also a snowstorm, and the attack came from flanks as well as the rear. Six men were wounded by grenades. Some of the enemy got into the British trench, but were thrown out, although not before taking two prisoners-of-war. The battalion were relieved at 6pm, but suffered six casualties from shelling. Richard was one of those killed, and is buried in Gouzeaucourt New British Cemetery. His parents were by now living in Sandhurst, and although it is not clear if Richard himself ever lived here, he is listed on the Roll of Honour in Sandhurst church.

R. ROBSON

Charles Alexander Burleigh Robson, who used both the names Charles and Alexander at various times, was born in about 1880 at Newcastle-upon-Tyne. It has not been possible to positively identify him in the census records, but he may have been one of a family of nine children fathered by Francis Robson, who worked on a tug boat on the River Tyne. The first definitive record for Alexander occurred on 3rd May 1898, when he joined the Northumberland Fusiliers, attesting at Newcastle. He was described as being 5'5" tall, weighed just over eight stone, with grey eyes, light brown hair, and a fresh complexion. He had previously been working as a labourer for Lord Armstrong, a fellow Northumbrian, who was an inventor, arms manufacturer, and shipping magnate. As well as designing and building swing-bridges, such as the one over the River Tyne at Newcastle, he took an active interest in politics, education, archaeology and landscaping. He was also important as a benefactor, making large donations and bequests to Newcastle's Royal Victoria Infirmary and Natural History Museum. In later years, he not only lived at Cragside, near Rothbury, Northumberland, but also bought and restored Bamburgh Castle. Unusually, a check was carried out at the address given by Alexander by a recruiting sergeant who reported, "I certify that I visited the address of the man named …. and found it correct. I also enquired of the Police as to his Character and they have nothing against him." Alexander's initial training lasted three months, and in November the following year, the battalion moved to South Africa for a little over twelve months. He was to later have a second brief spell in South Africa, as well as longer postings to Mauritius and India. There were also blemishes on his Service Record; twice he was absent from a tattoo (the second time for over a week until apprehended by the police), attempting to obtain a furlough under false pretences, "conduct prejudicial to good order and discipline" (for which he received the relatively lenient sentence of 28 days' hard labour), and irregular conduct on the Rifle Range. Despite these misdemeanours, he applied for, and received, an extension to his period of service. He married Alice Heaver at Gravesend, Kent, in 1906, with four children born in the next eight years (one of whom, born in India, died). The following year, Alexander's battalion were disbanded as a part of the reorganisation of reserve forces, and he transferred to the 1st Battalion, Royal Irish Fusiliers. Already a Lance Corporal, he was promoted to Cook Sergeant in 1908, having qualified at Aldershot two years previously. Another two years, and another black mark appeared in his Service Record: "Neglect of duty – not preparing the Battalion breakfast in the proper manner. Severely reprimanded," and the following month, "reverted to Duty Sergeant due to inefficiency as Cook Sergeant." Other breaches in army discipline followed; neglect of duty when in charge of a section, having an untidy bunk, having a dirty rifle, disregarding Battalion orders, absent from his Company overnight, absent from parade for Garrison piquet, and neglect of duty, reporting an incorrect number on parade to Sergeant Major. His medical record contains many entries as well, including treatment for primary syphilis, debility, phlebitis, a leg ulcer that required three spells in hospital, thrombosis (twice), and compassionate leave to look after his wife and children, who were suffering from an acute streptococcus bacterial infection while in Quetta, India. Despite all this, he left Karachi with a reference that described him as "hardworking and reliable." By now, he was with the 2nd Battalion, who were in India when war was declared, and returned to England in November, crossing the Channel to Le Havre a week before Christmas, missing the birth of a son by seven days. The battalion were involved in the action at St Eloi in March 1915. The previous day, Alexander had been appointed Acting Colour Sergeant. The promotion had an immediate effect, as his actions the following day earned him the Distinguished Conduct Medal; only the Victoria Cross is a higher award. The citation reads: "When almost encircled by the enemy, he held the trench against superior numbers with marked ability, and by his determination and example, greatly contributed to the complete success which was eventually attained." His promotion was confirmed two months later, during the Second Battle of Ypres. Towards the end of the year, the battalion left France and sailed for Salonika, arriving on 11th December. Two Brigades had been sent, at the request of the Greek Prime Minister, in order to help the Serbs in their fight against Bulgarian aggression. The expedition arrived too late, the Serbs having been beaten before they landed, but it was decided to keep the force in place for future operations. There was little action to occupy them, and they spent much of the time digging defences and putting up barbed wire. In July 1916, Alexander was promoted to 2nd Lieutenant, and a physical description in his file records he had now had several tattoos on his left forearm, including the initials J.R., those of his eldest child, Joyce Robson. He passed a signalling course the following spring, and was given two weeks' leave to see his family back in England. In September, the Battalion left Salonika and moved to Egypt for service in Palestine. The Ottoman Army held a line from Gaza to Beersheba, but the Egyptian Expeditionary Force began to drive them back at the Battle of Beersheba on the last day of October, followed by more success in the Third Battle of Gaza thirty-six hours later. Only Hariera, ten miles east of Beersheba, held out, and the Royal Irish Fusiliers were part of an attack on the 6th to capture it. They were in position by 9am, and the attack began three hours later. The War Diary gives no details of the fighting, but states "the battalion occupied enemy trenches by 4pm, and started consolidation. 10 prisoners captured and much war material." There were around fifty casualties, most of them wounded. At 6:30am the following morning, 'B' and 'C' Companies, along with a battalion from each of the Royal Irish Fusiliers and Inniskilling Fusiliers, attacked the Hareira Redoubt. As the gunnery horses were away being watering, the battalion's transport took the Howitzer battery into action for supporting fire. This was urgently required, as the attackers had to cross an open plain for three thousand yards under very heavy rifle and machine gun fire. By 4:30pm, they had occupied the enemy trench system, and half an hour later, the Redoubt was captured as well. The battalion lost 21 men killed, with a further 36 missing, and five officers wounded. Alexander was one of them, having been shot in the abdomen, and eventually sent to Alexandria for treatment, where he died in the 65th Clearing Station on 8th November 1917, and buried in Amara Military Cemetery. His wife received a telegram with the news of his death two days later. The list of effects eventually returned to her included his revolver, holster and lanyard, two leather belts, a Kodak camera, cheque book with six unused cheques, pouch, corkscrew, two discs, and a valise containing a waterproof coat, ankle boots, pyjama suits, gloves, breeches, trousers and braces, shirts, collar and ties, slippers, socks, underpants, a handkerchief, a pocket book containing photos, a packet of postcards, spurs, a cap and badge, map case, pillow, mirror, shaving stick and brush, towel, a tin of Vaseline, and a pair of sunglasses in their case. She had been living back in Gravesend since her return from India, but the house was not far from the sewage works and, with her children's health suffering, she moved to College Town, Sandhurst. As part of the optimisation and consolidation of graves after the conflict had ended, Alexander's body was moved and reburied in Beersheba Military Cemetery in October 1919. The final postscript to Alexander's story was his widow's attempt to track down her late husband's relatives, but a letter to the authorities in 1922 yielded the reply that none had been recorded in his file. His origins remain a mystery.

F. ROGERS

The late Pte. F. ROGERS, late of "Prince of Wales," Sandhurst.—Died of wounds.

Frederick Rogers was born at Sandhurst in 1879, and baptised on 27th April. He came from a large family of fourteen children, all of whom survived to adulthood. His father ran the Prince of Wales public house in Little Sandhurst for over twenty years. After leaving school, Frederick worked at labouring jobs, including bricklaying and farm work. He volunteered for service, attesting at Wokingham, and joined the 2nd Battalion, Royal Berkshire Regiment. The battalion had been in India at the outbreak of war, but returned to England, and went to France at the start of November 1914; Frederick was in a draft that went out at the beginning of May the following year. The battalion took part on the first day of the Battle of the Somme, and suffered over four hundred casualties, facing rifle and machine gun fire as soon as the attack had started. They also took part in the Battle of Langemarck in August 1917. At the beginning of December, they were just north of Passchendaele, with an attack scheduled for the early hours of the 2nd. There were problems just in getting into position in the dark, with 'A' Company losing its way, and the others having to negotiate marshy ground via duck-boards which had been destroyed in some places, while under shell fire. The attack started at 1:55am. This was unobserved for about ten minutes, and even the fire that did then come from the enemy was, for the most part, ill-directed. Two platoons reached the Southern Redoubt, and were engaged in bayonet and bomb fighting, with many casualties on both sides. Elsewhere, the advance did not get so far forward, due in part to moving to the left to keep touch with the 2nd Battalion, Lincolnshire Regiment, who had also gone too far left. The attack cost 150 casualties, including 35 killed and a similar number missing. Frederick was one of those wounded, dying two days later, and is buried in Lijssenthoek Military Cemetery.

A. SEEBY

Alfred Francis Osborne Seeby was born at Crowthorne in 1895, and baptised there on 9th June. He was one of seven children, one of whom died in infancy. His father worked as a florist in Crowthorne, but by 1911, the family had moved to College Town where Alfred worked alongside his father who now ran his own market gardening business. Alfred was conscripted into the Army early in 1916, attesting at Wokingham, and initially joined the Royal Field Artillery, but was transferred to the Machine Gun Corps before he went abroad. He would probably have been involved in some of the phase of the Battle of the Somme that year, as well as operations on the Ancre in 1917. The Battle of Arras, a British offensive, started on 9th April. When it officially ended just over five weeks later, British troops had made significant advances, but had been unable to achieve a breakthrough. Alfred's Company was in the line, and assisted in the operations carried out to capture the Oppy Line and Arleux Switch. The infantry made an assault on the enemy's line at 4:45am, "and 25 minutes later, 'A' Section, with four guns, moved forward from our Support lines in artillery formation. When passing over our front line, they encountered strong hostile barrage, which caused several casualties, and put two guns out of action. Upon arrival at *the* enemy front line, wire was found to be very thick, but a few good gaps were seen and made use of, and eventually we took up positions at strong points. Owing to troops of right flank of our Brigade being held up on *their* first objective by hostile machine gun and rifle fire, 'A' and 'D' Sections were unable to move to strong points allotted to them, but at 5:45am, 'D' Section moved forward to *a* position in our old front line, so as to protect the front line in case of a counter-attack. Some two hours later, 'B' Section, who had remained in our old front line, sustaining heavy casualties, moved forward with two guns (the other two having been put out of action) to *a* strong point on *the* right flank of our first objective, and through *the* rest of *the* day, we held on to our positions in spite of heavy hostile shelling, sniping, and machine gun fire. From Zero (4:45am) to 6am, 'C' Section, with four guns, and eight guns from 99 Machine Gun Company, carried out continuous barrage fire on *the* enemy trenches." Five of the machine gunners were killed, and two wounded, during the fighting. Alfred was one of the former, and as his body was not recovered, his name is listed on the Arras Memorial.

E. SHEPHERD

Edwin Roland Shepherd was born on the last day of April, 1899, at Broughton, Hampshire, midway between Salisbury and Winchester. Within two years, the family had moved to Sandhurst, where his father worked as a domestic gardener. A younger brother was born in 1909. On leaving school, Edwin joined the navy as a fourteen year old boy, and spent the first few months training at Devonport. He then transferred to the wireless telegraphy school at Portchester Creek, before spending time at the Portsmouth depot. In March 1915, he was finally assigned to a ship, HMS 'Vanguard', based at Scarpa Flow. In May the following year, the 'Vanguard' took part in the Battle of Jutland, but is not thought to have scored any hits on German vessels, or taken any hits herself. She returned to Scarpa Flow and was not involved in any subsequent actions. On the afternoon of 9th July 1917, the ship's crew had been exercising, practising the routine for abandoning ship. She anchored in the northern part of Scapa Flow at about 6:30pm. Just before midnight, the ship suddenly blew up, taking over eight hundred of her crew down with her. The explosion took place in one of the two magazines which served the amidships turrets. The most likely cause was a fire in an adjacent compartment which smouldered away undetected, long enough for some cordite near the adjoining bulkhead to overheat to dangerous levels. One eyewitness account stated: "I was on watch on HMS 'Marlborough' between 8pm and midnight, and was facing HMS 'Vanguard'. I saw her start to explode, first aft, second midships, and third in the foc'sle, and then one huge explosion." And another: "A great explosion occurred in the midst of the Grand Fleet, a terrible detonation took place lighting the whole fleet as if it were daylight. There was a crash and one of the big boats went sky high with a crew of nine hundred men. All searchlights were switched on immediately, but not a thing was to be seen. A trawler, which was close by, got smothered in blood and pieces of human flesh, and afterwards picked up half the body of a marine, the only body recovered up to date. I happened to be on watch and saw nearly everything; no-one knows how she went up, but seeing she had a new ship's company, it is surmised that it was the work of German spies." A court of inquiry heard accounts from many witnesses on nearby ships. They accepted the consensus that there had been a small explosion with a white glare between the foremast and 'A' turret, followed after a brief interval, by two much larger explosions. It also heard that some of the cordite on board, which had been temporarily offloaded in December 1916 and catalogued at that time, was past its stated safe life. The possibility of spontaneous detonation was raised, but could not be proved. It was also noted that a number of ship's boilers were still in use, and some watertight doors, which should have been closed in war-time, were open as the ship was in port. It was suggested that this might contribute to their being a dangerously high temperature in the magazines. The final conclusion of the board was that a fire started in a 4-inch magazine, perhaps when a raised temperature caused spontaneous ignition of cordite, spreading to one or the other main magazines, which then exploded. None of the bodies were recovered, and Edwin's name is listed on the Portsmouth Naval Memorial. His parents later moved to Stoke Poges, Buckinghamshire, and Edwin's name also appears on the memorial at the village church there.

H. Sheppard

Henry Bracey Sheppard was born on 29th August 1886 at Sandhurst. He was the second youngest of eight surviving children, two more dying in infancy. His father served as a bugler at the Royal Military College for over 25 years, having joined at the age of sixteen, and still listed his profession as a musician, as well as tailor. In later censuses, his occupation was recorded as clerk for a Friendly Society of Army Pensioners. Before modern insurance and the welfare state, Friendly Societies provided financial and social services to individuals, often according to their religious, political, or trade affiliations. Henry worked as a carpenter after leaving school, as well as being a member of the 1/5th Battalion, Hampshire Regiment, a Territorial Battalion, for four years. He married Florence Weston in 1911, and two years later, they decided to emigrate to Canada for a new life. He sailed from Liverpool on the 'Empress of Britain,' arriving at St John, New Brunswick on 12th April 1913, before travelling on to Toronto by train; his wife followed on the 'Virginian' five months later. Although Canadian men, especially those with close ties or who had recently arrived from Britain, had been volunteering to fight from the outbreak of war, conscription in Canada was not introduced until 1917. But Henry, although not joining the initial rush, volunteered in 1916, attesting on 29th March in Toronto, and joined the 21st Battalion, Canadian Expeditionary Force. He was described as being almost 5'10" tall, with blue eyes, light brown hair, with a fair complexion, and had moles on his right cheek and the right side of his neck, and a scar on his right index finger. It is not known when Henry joined his battalion in France, but a fellow Canadian, who had joined a month earlier, wrote home from the front in June: "My Dear Wife: Just a few lines to let you know I am well, and I hope you and the children are the same and enjoying good health. Well, I have been six days in the front line, and it was six days I will not forget, for we had it pretty warm. On the left of us, the Germans got through a week ago, and it had to be got back again. So when the time came, we were ordered to repeat fire, and when we did both the artillery and Germans started, and it was a perfect hell. You would wonder how a human person could live in such a place, but we all stuck to our posts. And I must add that the old boys of the 21st Battalion showed us new arrivals a good example. For being cool and brave is half the battle to new men in the trenches, and that was the main thing. The next night or so, the Huns came back and tried to regain them. They made two attacks and were driven back. It was a terrible battle, but our losses were not heavy. Some of the draft that came with me were among them, but they did their duty and fought like heroes." The battalion took part in phases of the Battle of the Somme, including Flers-Courcelette where tanks were used for the first time, in the Arras Offensive, including the Battle of Vimy Ridge where all four Canadian Divisions fought alongside each other and captured the high ground held by the Germans, but suffered over ten thousand casualties, at the Second Battle of Passchendaele in the autumn of 1917, and at Amiens in August 1918. On the morning of the 6th, the battalion moved forward of Villers Bretonneux to occupy new positions. While they were passing an ammunition dump, it was hit by an enemy shell, causing a big explosion which killed nineteen men, including Henry. He is buried in Longueau British Cemetery. His widow returned to England, arriving at Liverpool two days before Christmas in 1918. She remarried in 1930, and died in 1976.

R. Sheppard

Reginald Bracy Sheppard was born at Sandhurst in 1888, and was Henry's younger brother. He worked as a bricklayer after leaving school until volunteering for service, attesting at

Camberley, and joined the Royal Engineers. His unit arrived in France in mid July 1915. At the time of his death, Reginald was a Corporal in the 78th Field Company, 17th (Northern) Division. As well as performing construction and maintenance work, the Field Companies, which were attached to the fighting portions of a Division, also saw action and took part in the fighting. Many kinds of trade were required in the army, and Field Companies would typically contain farriers, shoeing smiths, trumpeters, blacksmiths, bricklayers, carpenters, clerks, masons, painters, plumbers, surveyors, draughtsmen, wheelwrights, engine drivers, sappers, and batmen. Early in 1918, Reginald married Avis Weston, a younger sister of his brother Henry's wife. The Weston family lived locally, and both sisters were working in domestic service in Camberley at the time of the 1911 census. He then returned to France. On 12th and 13th September, two sections of men were repairing huts at Rocquigny, while the remainder were resting. The next four days were spent training, before moving forward to billets east of Fins, and then to a position north of Gauhle Wood. There, they spent two days, constructing a strong point, and digging a new communication trench. On the 20th, the Germans made a small attack, using a flammenwefer (flamethrower), which was beaten off, but at a cost of ten lives. Reginald was one of those killed, and is buried in Gouzeaucourt New British Cemetery.

A. SLAUGHTER

The late Pte. A. W. SLAUGHTER, K.O.Y.L.I., Drummore, College Town, Camberley.—Killed in action.

Arthur William Slaughter was born early in 1889 in Binfield, and baptised there on 24th February, one of four children. The family lived on Wokingham Road near its junction with Beehive Road, and his father worked as a labourer at the brickyard adjacent to the current footbridge over the railway and A329 (M). Arthur worked as a baker after leaving school until he was conscripted into the Royal Garrison Artillery, attesting at Reading. He was then transferred to the 10th Battalion, King's Own Yorkshire Light Infantry before going to France. It is not known when Arthur went to France, but he was probably took part in some of the phases of the Battle of the Somme as the battalion were involved until October 1916. It also took part in the Arras Offensive during April and the beginning of May the following year. By the middle of September, the battalion were billeted near Hendeghem, and began intensive training for an attack the following month. On 1st October, they moved up into Brigade Reserve, south-west of Zillebeke Lake. Three days later, at 6am, they had formed up behind the 9th Battalion, in readiness. The back area was heavily shelled all the time, so the rations and rum were late arriving, but the carrying party pushed up "with great determination." The 9th attacked and had captured their objective within two hours, although strung out on the right, owing to the failure of troops on that flank to get forward. The 10th followed close behind, and when the leading battalion were checked, found themselves mingling with them. They pushed on, and the right company, although only being in support, actually got to their objective first by taking a circuitous route to avoid a swamp. As all the officers had been killed or wounded, the most senior man left decided to stop and dig in after advancing another 150 yards. A more complete line of defence was dug under cover of darkness during the night. But the attack was at the expense of over three hundred casualties. Arthur was one of the forty or so men missing, and his name is listed on the Tyne Cot Memorial.

T. SMITH

Thomas Smith was born at Tregare, between Monmouth and Abergavenny in South Wales, in 1889, and had two older brothers. The three boys were brought up by their grandparents on a farm four miles from Monmouth after their parents moved to Derbyshire (his father worked in the coal mines there). By the age of twelve, Thomas was only attending school part time, and was working as a servant on a farm near Chepstow. By 1911, he had moved to Surbiton, Surrey, where he worked as a hairdresser's assistant. He married Alice Green in 1915 in the Easthampstead registration district, and enlisted under the Derby Scheme at about the same time, attesting at Camberley, and joined the 1st Battalion, Royal Berkshire Regiment. He was mobilised in February 1916, and would probably have joined the battalion in France in May. There is no reference in the War Diary as to when the new draft arrived, but they managed to avoid an outbreak of German measles, recorded on the 13th May while training was taking place at Callonne Ricouart. Soon after the battalion arrived at Hersin on the 21st, the Germans began to shell the town and there were reports of gas being released, and although the gas cloud could be seen, no effects from it were felt. The next day they travelled by bus to Gouy and Servins, with orders to retake a trench taken by the Germans the previous day, but the enemy bombardment prevented them reaching the assembly positions, and the attack was postponed for 24 hours, and then cancelled. Instead, they relieved the 22nd Battalion, Royal Fusiliers in the front line, and set about improving the trenches which were very shallow. Although there is no mention of casualties for the next few days, and the situation was "quiet," Thomas was killed on the 26th, the only death for the battalion recorded on that day. He is buried in Cabaret-Rouge British Cemetery, Souchez. At the time of his death, both his parents and his widow were recorded as living in Little Sandhurst.

The late Pte. MARK SPARKS, a native of Sandhurst.—Killed in action.

M. SPARKES

Mark Sparkes was born at Sandhurst on 8th December 1890, and baptised 22nd February the following year. He was the youngest of eleven children, but was twenty years old when his father, a general labourer, died. After leaving school, Mark worked at Mill Farm, Yateley, as an assistant dairyman. He enlisted under the Derby Scheme, attesting at Lewisham, and joined the 22nd Battalion, London Regiment, and later transferred to the 10th Battalion, King's Royal Rifle Corps. By the spring of 1917, they were following the Germans who were retreating to the Hindenburg Line. On 3rd April, the battalion were suddenly relieved from the front trenches and camped overnight in Dessart Wood. The War Diary recorded, "Miserable accommodation for night, and rain. Awful day, snowed nearly whole time." They were also told they were to attack the enemy rearguard positions east and southeast of the nearby village of Metz on the following day. The attack started at 2pm in heavy snow. There were no problems at first, but within fifteen minutes, they came under heavy machine gun fire from nearby high ground. Casualties were incurred, but the advance continued steadily. The companies on the left pushed on into Metz itself, but the right companies were held up at a sunken road on the right flank. This road was eventually cleared, but more Germans counter-attacked from the southeast, inflicting heavy casualties, and drove them out of the second line. A company from the Rifle Brigade was brought up to help, but by then the Germans had either retreated or surrendered. Meanwhile, all the objectives had been taken, along with around thirty prisoners, and the "useful capture of Tommy's cookers, solidified spirits, and food and drink." The former were tins, containing wax and a wick, used to heat water for making tea, and to cook Maconochie stew, a mixture containing sliced turnips and carrots or beans, with a piece of pork fat on the top. Food in the trenches was not good, and there were many complaints about it, although it was often better than they were used to at home, and feeding the vast numbers involved was a huge logistics achievement. The casualties were "unfortunately heavy," with 27 men (including five officers) killed, and 150 wounded or missing. Mark was one of the former, and is buried in Gouzeaucourt New British Cemetery. The War Diary concludes, "Attack was a surprise to enemy, possibly due to snowstorm …. Behaviour of last new draft, joined three days ago, beyond praise."

R. SPARKES

Lce.-Corpl. RANDALL SPARKS, Royal Berks Regt.—Missing.

Randal Sparkes, and his twin brother Victor, were born at Sandhurst on 5th January 1886, and baptised on the 7th of the following month. They were part of a family of eleven children (Mark was the youngest), and their father did various labouring jobs. After leaving school, Randal went straight to Aldershot and joined the Royal Regiment of Artillery, attesting on 14th February 1901. He was 5'3" tall, weighed just over seven stone, and had blue eyes, brown hair, a fresh complexion, and three vaccination marks still evident on his left arm. By the age of eighteen, he had grown a further three inches in height. Not long after his nineteenth birthday, his service record reports he was "Awaiting trial," and a few days later, "Tried and imprisoned;" he returned to duty eight weeks later. In June 1905, the battalion went to South Africa, returning at the beginning of 1908. While there, he went through the same procedure twice, and on 5th February 1908, he was "Discharged with ignomy." The reasons for his trials and subsequent dismissal from the army are not recorded. Randal returned to domestic life, working as an assistant gardener, and living in lodgings in Easthampstead Road, Wokingham. Six days after war was declared, Randal attested at Reading, and joined the 2nd Battalion, Royal Berkshire Regiment, signing for six years as a Special Reservist. Given his earlier experience with the army, he used his brother Victor's name! On completion of his training, he arrived in France on 2nd February the following year, already having just been promoted to Lance Corporal. On 19th March, the battalion took part in the Battle of Neuve Chapelle. Although the German trenches and first objective were captured without too much opposition, there were several casualties caused by the British artillery firing "shorts". Two days later, they were twice called up in support of another attack, but this was twice postponed and then finally cancelled. At 11pm on 8th May, they moved into the assembly trenches at Laventie for an attack on the German position the following day. After a forty minute bombardment, the 2nd Battalion, Rifle Brigade started to attack at 5:40am, with 'C' and 'D' Companies of the Berkshires due to move up to the breastwork in support, the other two companies being in reserve. As the Rifle Brigade advanced, they were met by tremendous rifle and machine gun fire, killing many. The Berkshires found the front trench full of men, who claimed they had been ordered back. Even when they started to move forward, they encountered attackers falling back, and it was never established where the orders to withdraw had come from. Some of 'A' Company, following up, managed to get into the German trenches, but were either killed or taken prisoner. The battalion suffered almost three hundred casualties in the confusion. Starting in late June, the battalion spent the best part of three months defending the trenches at Bois Grenier. On 24th September, they went into the trenches again for an attack the following day. The British trenches formed a semi-circle while the German trenches ran more or less in a straight line. At their closest, the opposing sides were one hundred yards apart, but five times that distance in the centre. However, there were old fire trenches in the intervening distance, and the Berkshires assembled in these for the attack which started at 4:30am after a heavy bombardment of the enemy. 'A' Company, on the right, had the worst of it. The wire in front of them was imperfectly cut, a German searchlight picked them out, and the Germans here seemed more ready for them. Consequently, only a few men reached the German trench and they were not sufficient to hold on. 'B' Company in the centre were most successful, but 'C' Company on the left suffered from an enemy machine gun and, in the dark, they missed some German dug-outs and their occupants were able to fire on the rear of the troops who had passed. The fight developed into a bombing tit-for-tat, although further back, 'D' Company, in reserve in the assembly trench, were hit by shells, causing more casualties. By the end of the day, all the attackers had withdrawn back to their starting positions. 130 men were killed, over two hundred wounded, and sixty were missing. Randal was one of the latter and his name is recorded on the Ploegsteert Memorial. The final paperwork in his service file, when returning his personal belongings to his mother, records he used the name Victor as an alias. His brother Victor did not serve overseas (or may not have served at all). Given his experience with horses (he had worked as a domestic groom), he may have stayed in England and been involved with training the thousands of animals sent overseas. He died in 1968.

W. Sparkes

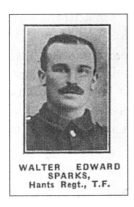

WALTER EDWARD SPARKS, Hants Regt., T.F.

Walter Edward Frank Sparkes is the third brother from the family to be listed on the Roll of Honour inside Sandhurst church. He too was born at Sandhurst on 26th February 1889, and baptised on 14th April. By 1911, he was the only one of the family still living at home, working as a baker. He was a member of the 1/4th Battalion, Hampshire Regiment, a Territorial Battalion, which he had joined at Winchester. Some of the battalion had sailed for India in October 1914, but were only there for three months before sailing again to Basra in Mesopotamia. Walter did not join them until October 1915. The Regimental History summaries the position: "Earlier in the year, the British had made some tactical moves to seize important or threatening points beyond Basra. After an early string of cheap successes, eyes increasingly fell on the Mesopotamian capital, Baghdad. The 6th (Poona) Division advanced, leaving a very thinly stretched supply line of hundreds of miles behind it, only to receive a bloody repulse at Ctesiphon. A ragged and dispiriting retreat back to Kut-al-Amara began. The Turks pursued the retreating Division to Kut, and soon surrounded and cut it off. British forces in Mesopotamia were now growing, and these formations were ordered to advance north along the Tigris to relieve Kut. They ran into strong and stoutly defended lines and suffered some hard knocks; although they got close to Kut, the garrison there was surrendered on 29 April 1916. It was an enormous blow to British prestige and a morale-booster for the Turkish Army." After the fall of Kut, a new British Commander was installed, who introduced new methods, culminating in a decisive defeat of the Turks in February 1917 and the capture of Baghdad in March. They continued to make gains, but no decisive victory, until the Turks signed an armistice on 1st October 1918. Like Gallipoli, conditions in Mesopotamia were difficult. Temperature of

120 degrees were common, arid desert and regular flooding, flies, mosquitoes and other vermin, all led to very high levels of sickness and death through disease. Medical arrangements were also poor, with wounded men spending up to two weeks on boats before reaching any kind of hospital. Over 12,500 men died of sickness in the region, one of them being Walter on 2nd October 1918. He is buried in Tehran War Cemetery.

E. SULLIVAN

Ernest Sullivan was born at Sandhurst in 1878, and baptised on 28th February the following year. He was the youngest survivor of eight children, three of whom died young. His father was a private in the Hussars, who died in Jamaica in 1881. By 1901, Ernest was the only sibling still living with his widowed mother, and was working as a general labourer. He volunteered for service, attesting at Camberley, and joined the 9th Battalion, East Surrey Regiment. Training was done at Shoreham in Sussex, the battalion initially being in billets at Worthing until wooden huts had been built as the training area turned into a quagmire in the rain. Arthur Goodchild, an under-age recruit with defective hearing, in the Suffolk Regiment, at Shoreham at the same time as Ernest, wrote a series of letters home. The following extracts give a feel for the time there. 1st October 1914: "They have given me an army shirt, it is a thick one and I shall not want my other vest. I have not got a coat yet but I think they will give me one tonight, they have given some out. We are not forced to be inoculated but I am going to be done. We all caught colds the first night but mine is nearly better now. We are going to be in tents about another month and then we are going in huts they are now building. We may get a short holiday at Xmas. If the war went on well for our side I feel sure we should. All this week we have been for a route march every morning before breakfast. I like that better than drilling. We have got some old rifles and are learning to handle them, but we are not going to shoot with them. We shall have new ones in about a month. There are nearly 20,000 soldiers here, and in the town last night there was the most people that ever I saw in my life. Every shop and pub was full and outside was just the same. We have been down to the beach to bathe twice, the first time was last Thursday week, it was a bit cold that day but on Wednesday it was hot and I stripped and went in. The beach here is not like Felixstowe, you can walk half a mile into the water before you are up to your neck. They are strict here, they don't like us to smoke fags but they don't mind pipes. I bought a pipe but I can't stick to it, so am sending it home for father." 10th October: "I have got over the first inoculation. I had letter from George *(his brother)* yesterday, he says the second time is worse than the first. I hope it is not much worse for the first was bad enough. My arm was useless for two days. I could not even get it in my pocket, but it's all right now and I feel as well as ever I did. We have to practise our eyesight and hearing the same as George did in the dark. We had an hour of it last night and are going to have four hours next week. We drill by signals now instead of speaking to us. They blow a low whistle and we look round and they signal by the arm. We still go for a route march every morn before breakfast. When we go for a route march they let us sing and play mouth organs, smoke pipes but not cigarettes. They say that the paper poison us. I smoke fags when I am off parade. I have since had my uniform, it's a blue one with black buttons and a red stripe on the cap. I will have my photo taken and send you one and then you will see what I look like. I sleep warmer of a night now. I used to lay one of my blankets down and cover myself up with the other, and I used to wake up as cold as ice. But now three of us put our blankets together, lay two down and cover ourselves up with four, and it's just as warm as a bed then. We have all we can eat. There's 14 in our tent now and we have 7 loaves of bread a day, plenty of cheese, butter and jam. We have hot sausages for breakfast, sometimes bacon. We have hot beef and potatoes for dinner. We have not had a cold dinner only once, and that was when we come from Ipswich. We had some good cake last Sunday for tea, and I always have all the tea I can drink. I eat more here than I did at home. The corporals used to be all in one tent, but now they are with the privates. In some tents they used to use bad language at night (but not our tent), so the corporals were put there to keep them quiet. There's one corporal in our tent." 15th October: "I meant to have told in my first letter that I get on quite well about hearing for I knew you would wonder about me. They took me to be stupid at first, but after a week they said my old head was screwed on right and so it is. They have not noticed me in the ranks for they all speak plain. I have had several messages whispered to me to pass along and have heard them the first time, so I know I shall get on alright about that so don't worry. In my company we have all got three good blankets each and a good overcoat each. Mine is an extra good one, it is thick and warm. I will not volunteer for any service abroad or anything of the kind. I don't intend to go out of England, but I may be forced, for I can see a very serious time coming for our country. I have not seen any Belgian refugees but I've heard there are some at Folkestone and Brighton. I feel sorry for the poor people, their country is ruined sure enough. I didn't come here with the intention of liking the drill, but it's better than hard work. The way to get on is to do what you are told, they don't find fault with me but some of the others are very awkward and stupid. Some don't try, they have discharged some of the extra awkward ones. The officers do have a lot to think about, I shouldn't like to be one." 19th October: "Ned, me and Sutton went to Brighton yesterday and had our photos taken. We all come out well I think. We are all inclined to laugh. There was an old man standing at the side of camera, he made us laugh. I thought I should get on alright about hearing but they have noticed this last week. They were calling out names for kitbags on Saturday, and I didn't hear mine the first time, they called it the second and then the sergeant asked me if I was deaf and I told him no. I should have heard only I was looking round the other way with my right ear to him. They have noticed me more in my tent too. I believe I shall get my discharge but I am not sure. I shall not mind if I do and I don't expect you will either." 24th October: "I don't think I shall get discharged after all. They have only noticed me in my tent, but as I told you before, the Sergt Major noticed me on Saturday (last) when he called my name out for my kitbag. He asked me if I was deaf but I told no, and he didn't take any more notice. The day after I got your postcard, saying you would like me to come home, I went to the orderly Corporal of 'A' Company and told him I was a little deaf, so I had to go to the doctor's tent. They syringed my right ear and tested my hearing with a watch, but the syringing didn't do any good, and they asked me if ever I had been sent off parade. I hadn't, so I had to tell them no. When I came out they gave me a paper, it said on it (Medical Duty) that meant if I didn't get any worse I was fit for the service. I asked the Corporal in our tent if he thought I would get discharged, he said no, they won't discharge such a chap as you. You are sound everywhere except your hearing, and you are only slightly deaf. They are more particular about eyesight and our feet and legs. I know one way how I could get out of it, by playing the fool, but I shan't do that for I should have to go through a lot of trouble and then get a bad character. I suppose I shall have to stick to it, and make the best of it, same as I always have done. You mustn't mind, for I don't think it will be for long. The papers have had better reports in them lately. They didn't look very well a little while back. The huts they are building for us will soon be ready. Some will be ready in a week but some won't be ready for a month. They have carted nearly all the timber. There were 9 or 10 traction engines going for nearly a fortnight, Sundays and all, so were the carpenters at work on Sunday, there are fifty or sixty horses still carting wood and about 300 men employed on the building. It's being done by a contractor from London. These huts are built of all wood roofs and all, so if they were to catch fire they would very soon be down." 28th October: "I feel strong and well, the army is making a man of me. I have learnt what rough life is, I shan't know how to feel when I sleep in a bed again and have my meals off a table, after sleeping on the floor and having my blankets for a chair and my knees or the floor for a table. You would laugh to see us sitting round the tent, laughing and talking, all as happy as can be. I have got used to the men in our tent, they seem like old friends now, three of them (old soldiers) went to Felixstowe last Saturday, but we have got three more in their places. We didn't take any harm last Sunday although it rained all the afternoon and until about ten at night. The water ran in our tents but it didn't wet our clothes. Some of us were afraid it might rain again so we carried our blankets and slept in the recreation tent, it was dry in there. The next day we had boards to put in our tents and they gave us half a day to put them in. It was an easy job for the boards were in four pieces and we had only to lay them down. We can keep our clothes and blankets cleaner, and if it rain a lot the water can run under the boards so we shan't take any harm. I like route marches for we see about the country and it's a nice change for us, they tell us to sing and they like them to play mouth organs. We sing all kinds of songs but 'Tipperary' is the favourite. The people cheer us when they pass and the women come out to the gates to look at us. I expect they think Germany could never conquer England, well, we know they can't, but there will be a rare hard struggle and a lot of lives lost, for the honour of country." 3rd November: "I was on sentry duty last Sunday and Sunday night, from 10am to 11am on Monday. There was 9 of us altogether and 3 posts to guard, so we had 2 hours on sentry and 4 hours off. The different battalions take it in turn. It was the Suffolks turn on Sunday and the Norfolks on Monday. It came my turn to go on sentry at 12 o'clock at night till 2. It rained pouring at 1 o'clock until about half past 2 but I did not get wet for I have a good coat and we have a sentry box each. We had to halt everyone we saw after 10 pm. I never saw anyone only the sergeant, he came up to me about half past one. I halted him as soon as I saw him, it was moonlight. We were not allowed to go to sleep in our 4 hours rest, we had to be ready any moment. It was a rare job for me to keep awake between 2 am and 6. I layed (sic) down flat once and the old sergeant told me if I went to sleep he would make me stand up all night. The other chaps were just as bad as me, they couldn't hardly keep their eyes open. We were relieved at 10am but had to go to the orderly room to be inspected so we didn't get off much before 11. There was just time to wash and change our shirts and pants and socks before dinner, and in the afternoon we had to go on parade again at six o'clock but I slipped away, but I didn't let anyone know though. I felt very sleepy, I went to the recreation tent and started reading a book but fell asleep. I woke again about 8.30 and then went to my tent and you may be sure I had a good night's rest. It was the first time in my life that I had been up all night. I can't say I liked that sentry job, I may not get it at Shoreham again, well, I hope I shan't, but a soldier must do as he's told. There's one chap here who's got himself into trouble. He said he didn't care about anyone in the whole British Army, and he would not do as he was told. He done anything wrong he could think of. He told an officer that he didn't care if he was shot. They put him in a tent and it's guarded night and day and he has got a lot of punishment to go through. He is tied down for 4 hours a day, and if he doesn't soon alter they are going to flog him. I expect he wish he had behaved himself now, he has soon found his master. I soon found that out the first week I was here. I done something wrong (I won't tell you what it was) and I got 5 nights, that is, I had to go to the police tent and answer my name 5 times every night at 6,7,8,9 and 10. I was not allowed to leave the camp. I was glad when that was over. I have been very careful since. We have not started firing yet, we have not got our new rifles. There is no range at Shoreham but there's one at Portslade about 2 miles off, we shall start in a week or two. We have learnt to stand and fire, and lay and fire, and kneel and fire, and we learn something fresh every day. Yesterday we were told how to clean our new rifles when we get them. As you know, my left big toe nail grew in. One Sunday morning before 7 o'clock I was going to clip it out, so I lit the candle for it was not quite light, one man (an old soldier) blew it out, he said I didn't want to burn the candle when it was daylight. I got a piece of my own out of my pocket and lit that, another chap threw a towel over it and put it out. I picked the candle up and threw it at his head and hit him. He got up to strike me but I was ready for him and struck him and knocked him to the other side of the tent. The bottom of the tent was rolled up so when he got up he was outside. He walked round slowly to [the] opening and never said another word, but during the day I noticed him cast several dark looks at me. It was that wet Sunday night and I went to sleep in the recreation tent. He came too and asked me if I would share my blankets with him. I said yes so we slept together that night and he's alright to me now. We have Jim Nastic's (sic) drill every morning for an hour, there is an instructor in every battalion, it will do us all good. I like it, we have had it for a week now and we have it a little different now. This morning we had to jump over some poles laid 7 feet apart and we have to run and walk as quick as we can, walk on our toes and do all sorts of physical things. If anyone was not strong they wouldn't be able to do it. We live better than we used to, we always have plenty of good cake for Sunday and sometimes during the week. We have salmon, baked beef, kippers, fried fish, bacon, plenty of butter, cheese, jam and bread. We have all we like to eat. We have got 8 or 9 loaves of bread in our tent and will have 6 more on the morning." 6th November: "The aeroplanes hadn't been up lately until today, the weather hadn't been good enough, but this afternoon they have been going up into the clouds, out of sight. We could hear them, they make a lot of noise just like a motor. I forget if I told you I had been close to them when they start and helped to pull them out of the shed. They are not at all heavy, they are made of wire, thin splines of wood and canvas, and the engine is at the front. The men are not strapped in them as I thought but sit in a long tin box with just their heads out. Sometimes two go up at a time. It's a funny thing when they start, they nearly blow you down. They move a crowd of people back a yard. I know it's right because I have stood by the side of them myself. When they start they run along the ground for about 100 yards at about 80 miles an hour and then begin to rise as steady as a bird. They are wonderful things if one come to think about them." 10th November: "We had to take our boards up from the bottom of our tents today to air them, they were mouldy underneath. B, C and D [Companies] had to take their tents down too, besides taking up the boards. The latest news about us going away from here is that the huts they have built are condemned and so are the tents, and that we are going away in 10 days' time, but I cannot say that's right. We have heard so many rumours lately and they have turned out to be lies, but we shall soon go out of tents. It's not fit for men to be under canvas in November, but the weather has been a little better lately, the mud have dried up in most places." 13th November: "We are getting forward with our drill now but have not started firing yet because our new rifles are not ready and there is no range at Shoreham but there is one at Portslade about 9 miles off and there is a lot of soldiers at Portslade of the R.F.A. (*Royal Field Artillery*) and Royal Engineers, so I don't think there would be room for us at that range. We have not been for a Battalion route march lately, but go for a short march every morning before breakfast, and back again before it's properly light. We always have to be on parade at 6.30 and sometimes before. We are called at 5.30 and should have our blankets rolled up by 6 o'clock and we must not be a minute late on parade. I have not been late since I have had my watch. They have given us two blacking brushes and a tin of dubbin each. We have to keep our boots clean and keep our clothes clean and our tents have to be kept perfectly clean. There must not be a piece of paper laying about and the boards of our tents have to be washed every morning. We take in turns to be orderly, the orderly has to wash up the breakfast dinner and tea things and fetch all the food away from the cookhouse and keep the tent tidy. Our tents are inspected twice a week. We have all we like to eat and we have good food too, we have tinned herring, pickles, pineapples, sardines, kippers, tinned beef and greens for dinner, and plum pudding and cake three times a week. We have jam, golden syrup, cheese, butter and biscuits and tea before we go on parade in the morning, and I think we are going to have half a day on Saturdays now. Lord Kitchener say he want his new army to have it, and it will only be fair to us, won't it? We went trench digging last Wednesday and have been again this morning. It take a long time to dig a trench here, for when we get down a foot we come to solid chalk, and we have to pick it up. We go about three miles inland to dig the trenches, and when we got there this morning it rained pouring. We worked for half an hour and then started back but we didn't take any harm for most of us had brought our coats. I think the war is going on very well for our side, but it won't be over yet, they still want more recruits, and if the men won't enlist they will make it compulsory." 27th November: "We have heard nothing about shifting yet. I doubt whether we shall get in the huts before December, they are not quite ready yet, the stoves are not fixed. They would have been ready weeks ago, only the carpenters went on strike. They started again this week and they are making roads round the huts, a lot of engines and horses carting stones and clinkers. They are making the roads in Shoreham and round about in a rare state. There are holes about a foot deep in some places, the weather is rather wet and rough too, and plenty of slush about. We are learning bayonet fighting, I dare say that come awkward for George because he is left-handed." 3rd December: "I am very pleased to say we are out of the rotten tents and into the huts, they are a lot better. There's plenty of room in them and they are dry and clean. They are 20 yards long and 7 yards wide. There is supposed to be 40 men in each but there are 36 in mine. We have 3 boards of two stands each so we are about 5 inches off the floor, and we are going to have straw mattresses and table in a day or two. We have got seats, we had to go and fetch them ourselves today and I expect we shall get the tables tomorrow. It's a treat to be in these huts after what we have been used to, it's just as good as being in a house, well, rather better because we are more to ourselves and have more room and we don't have to be quite so particular as we would in a house. There is a stove in each hut, so we shall be warm when the weather gets colder, but we shan't want fires yet for the weather is not very cold at present. We are going to have field training this month. It will be more messing about at night I reckon. We have not had much of that lately and don't want. I have wrote this in Southwick Town Hall, it is open to all soldiers as a reading and writing and recreation room, and there is a concert in here every night. Young women come and sing to us and there is a good gramophone too, it's been playing nearly all the time I have been writing, but I don't think I have made many mistakes." 16th December: "We have heard today that we are to be billeted out at Kemp Town (the other side of Brighton) by Saturday. I don't know if that's right but I think it is. We don't know what to believe, we have heard so many tales and they have turned out to be lies, but will send a card if we do move. Have you seen today's paper? In one paper I saw that the Germans have been shelling Hartlepool and Scarborough this morning, and that a big naval battle was expected. Our fleet have been doing well lately haven't they? But our people will do the Germans on the water, their navy can't touch ours. I have seen several big ships go along the Channel today but we couldn't see what they were for they were a long way out." 19th December: "Did you get my last letter saying we were going to Kemp Town Thursday, we didn't go, the order was cancelled, but we are going tomorrow. I am sure it's right, but I am not quite sure whether we shall go to Brighton or Kemp Town, will let you have my address as soon as possible, so don't write till you hear from me again. The reason why we are to be billeted is because the huts are draughty and the rain come in at the windows and under the doors. They are going to put match boarding inside our huts while we are away and finish them altogether so I expect we shall be out of them about a month. What do you think of those German ships bombarding Scarborough and Hartlepool and Whitby. I think it was a foolish and cowardly thing, killing innocent women and others, and as soon as they caught sight of our ships slipped off. They are afraid to fight our navy fair but I don't think they will get so close to our coast any more, our ships will be more on the alert. They don't seem to be getting on very fast with the war. It looks like lasting a long time. Our people have gained ground in places and lost it in others. They don't seem to me to be any forwarder than they were four months ago, but I hope there will soon be a change for the better. I don't think Italy and USA will be able to remain neutral no longer than February, and I saw in a paper that Norway Sweden and Denmark are going to have their Ministers of War meet on the 21st of this month." 11th January 1915: "I think we are going to stop at Brighton for a time. They are not repairing those huts at Shoreham and we have started shooting here. I saw the King and Queen on Saturday, they came here to visit the Indian wounded, there are several 1,000 wounded here now. We had to stand up one side of the street to keep the crowd of people back, and mounted police kept them back the other side. We had to stand there nearly an hour waiting for him. There are a lot of Indians here now, nearly recovered from their wounds. Some can speak a little English. I have spoken to some of them, they seem very pleased to be here, and it's very amusing to hear some of them talk." 21st January: "I am very comfortable and happy here. I know my way nearly all over the town now. We had Battalion drill again last Tuesday on Holingbury Park, but we ('A' Company) mostly parade on Preston Park, it is not so large as the former. We have not been firing lately, but are training very sharp in the bayonet fighting. We parade five hours a day on the average, and still have Saturday afternoons off. There are new rifles and equipment for the Battalion and khaki too up at Shoreham, I expect we shall all have khaki in a short time. We get quite used to the Indians, they are allowed to go about by themselves now, they dress in their native clothes, wrappers round their heads, some have never had their haircut nor a shave yet, they all look like brothers. We are training rather harder now. We went 14 miles yesterday over the hills and fields in extended order, and didn't get back to dinner before 2.30. We were very hungry and tired you may be sure. There are a lot of Belgium wounded here too. There is plenty of amusement about here, I went to a play last Friday night. I had a shilling ticket given me and last night I went to a concert, I had a 2s (shilling) ticket given me for that. It is very dark here at night now, not a single lamp alight in the whole town, not even on the trams. It is very awkward and rather dangerous for there's a lot of traffic and it is not safe to walk off the pavement. But putting the lights out is about the best thing they can do, it's for the safety of the town." 19th February: "They haven't made me hear any better, but I don't think they will send me 'sick' any more. I was on guard last Sunday night in a college, it is the Battalion's orderly room. I didn't mind that guard, I wasn't sentry only 3 hours and we had a nice fire to sit by and we could go to sleep if we liked. We have been shooting again, I am one of the best shots in the Company, if not the best of the lot. Some are very bad shots, the worst of them have been firing 14 or 15 times, but I haven't been only 3 times. They want to keep us regular, so we all shoot alike. We saw an airship the other day, almost the same make as the German Zeppelins. It was the first I had seen of that kind. I dare say USA and Italy will join the Allies against the Germans before long. I hope they will, it would end all the sooner then. Now food has got dearer it is good pay isn't it?" 2nd March: "They want to operate on me tomorrow mother, but I refuse to let them, one doctor says there is something in my ear and it's got to come out and an operation is necessary. Was there anything put in my ear when I was operated on before? The doctor put an instrument in my ear and scratched something, it is hard, I wondered if it was put in my ear for some reason when the other operation was performed. I am writing to ask if you agree to me being operated on. I am not willing myself and I don't think you will be either. I will copy the note what one doctor sent from one hospital to the other, it is as follows: 'this man has a concoction or foreign body in his ear. He must be kept in and operated on. Will you send him up tomorrow to be admitted.' I am afraid that the thing the doctor scratched is something that was put in my ear when I was little. I am making the worst of my hearing, when I do hear what they say I don't take any notice. I hope I shall get discharged. This doctor is a young fellow and I think he wants to experiment on me." The next letter is obviously written by the lady in whose house he was billeted: "Dear Mrs Goodchild, Many thanks for your nice letter and to tell you not to worry about Arthur, but I am afraid I must tell you that I think it was through me that they commenced on his ears, but Arthur knows I done it with the best of intentions, as I found the poor boy was always getting punished in some way or other for every little trifling thing he done. He seemed as though they made a special mark of him, and I thought if they knew he was deaf they would make allowances for him. I am sure the others I have had here, if they had their deserts they would be punished far more than he has, but you need not worry any more as I told him if he was my son I should not allow an operation and I was sure you would not allow one either, and I told him to be firm and not let them persuade him to be operated on, so it has all passed over. But I am sorry to say he will not be here after next Wednesday as they are going back to Shoreham. I wish for his sake only he was able to stay, I must say that if it was not for me he would have had a rough time even with the others in my house, only I put my foot down, and my children and I would take him out to concerts with us and picture palaces, and they have been jealous of him all the time, and even today I have had awful insults thrown in my face, although I have nursed and mothered every one of them, and now my husband has taken their influenza and is very ill with inflammation of the lungs following on the influenza, and because I will not allow them to stay out until 11 or 12 at night, before my husband was ill they had their supper and was in bed at 10 o'clock, and since he took to his bed, knowing I am up half the night with him, they stopped out later and I tell Arthur he is welcome to come and spend his Sundays with us, but I think he will soon get his discharge, if not, be transferred to another regiment, so cheer up as long as he is anywhere near us, we will do our best to make him happy. He will never go to the front, only at home in England, owing to his deafness, so I have done a little good for him after all." Then the boy's letters resume, 6th March: "I have been to the hospital this morning (and I told them that there is no cure for my deafness) and have got to go again on Monday. I think that will be the last time as we are going back to Shoreham on Wednesday. I will let you know as soon as possible about me getting discharged." 10th March: "I am leaving this battalion on Monday, to come to Suffolk to join the 3rd Battalion as I am only fit for home service. I think the 3rd is stationed at Felixstowe *(where it was used to defend Harwich)*, so I shan't be very far from home and will perhaps be able to get home for the weekend, there is 14 more beside me that are coming to Suffolk too, 3 out of 'A' Company. We came back to Shoreham today. I got into trouble for refusing to go into the hospital, I got 5 days C.B. *(confined to barracks)*." Meanwhile, Ernest and his battalion moved to Aldershot in June, and sailed for France on the last day of August, where they were met by Leopold Martin, their interpreter. The War Diary records their progress during the next few days. On the 2nd, they are in billets in farm buildings and cattle sheds, "very dirty and little space." On the 5th, "no shooting of game" was ordered. Two days later, a Captain and the Adjutant were suspended when four N.C.O.s, to be collected for training, were two hours late; this was rescinded the following day. "Officers who pay for food for the interpreter out of their own pocket cannot get it refunded." On the 9th: "Two civilians driving around in car endeavouring to obtain information from troops. Car shabby and old Roi de Belge open touring probably Darracq but with Darracq badge removed from radiator. Colour dark, radiator brass, car noisy. Individual 1. Oldish, grey to white scrubby beard, appearance French, speaks French; last seen, dark cap, brown suit. Individual 2. Well built. 5'10". 40 years, pasty face, fairly heavy black moustache. Units warned to instruct guards on roads to stop and arrest individuals." Instructions are detailed, men are sent on courses, one heavy draught horse died from over-eating. All cameras must be returned to England. Instances of drunkenness and absence are recorded and dealt with, a suspected case of spotted fever (menengitis) occurred, but this turned out to be a false alarm. By the 25th, they had advanced through Vermelles, and on towards Anny and Pont a Vedin. The next day, they were ordered to attack the enemy's position at Hulloch, but as the wire had not been cut, this was not achieved, "although several fruitless attempts were made." The positions were shelled for the rest of the day, and casualties were heavy. Ernest was killed at some point and as his body was not recovered, his name is listed on the Loos Memorial.

W. SUMPSTER

William John Sumpster was born at Sandhurst in 1882, but baptised at Crowthorne on Christmas Eve. He was the youngest of three children, having two elder sisters. His father, an agricultural labourer, died when William was eight years old. William continued to live with his mother after he left school, working firstly as a shop porter in Crowthorne, and then as a baker in Little Sandhurst. He joined the Army under the Derby Scheme, attesting at Camberley, and joined the 2nd Battalion, Royal Berkshire Regiment. He was mobilised in March 1916, and would have gone to France after 1st July, when the battalion suffered over four hundred casualties at the Battle of the Somme. The first major fighting William experienced was in October, supporting the 2nd Battalion, Lincolnshire Regiment in an attack on Zurich Trench, near Doullens on the 23rd. The initial attack failed owing to the strong reinforcement of the trench by defenders, and the Berkshires made a fresh attack early the following morning, which also failed under heavy machine gun and rifle fire from the trench. Fifty men were killed. The following month, they suffered badly from gas-shelling during a six day period whilst in the front trenches. Much of the winter months were spent in reorganising, training, and then practising for an attack on Pallas Trench, near St Pierre Vaast Wood. The attack, and subsequent counter-attacks, lasted two days, and although successful, there were around 250 casualties. Later that month, the Germans retreated to the Hindenburg Line. In August, the Berkshires were involved in the Battles of Pilkem and Langemarck, suffering badly in the latter. In March 1918, the Germans started their spring offensive. The battalion had been billeted at St Martin-au-Lert for over a week, but on the 22nd, they proceeded to Guillaucourt by train and then marched to Chaunes. At around midnight, they received orders to move to the left bank of the Somme, between Roncy-le-Grand and Pargny, which was done under heavy fire. William's death is recorded as 'Killed in action', and he is buried in Ham British Cemetery, Muille-Villette. But as the cemetery was used by the 61st Casualty Clearing Station, it is more probable that he died of wounds received some time earlier.

W. WETHERALL

William Weatherall (the spelling of the surname varies in the records) was born at Sandhurst in 1895. He was the youngest of five children, two of whom died young. His mother died when he was just four years old, and although his father later lived with a widow, he never married her. Like his father, William worked as a farm labourer after leaving school, before joining the 2nd Battalion, Hampshire Regiment towards the end of 1913, attesting at Guildford. The battalion were in India when war broke out, and returned to England just before Christmas. Three months later, they sailed via Malta and Egypt to Gallipoli, where they arrived on 25th April 1915. They remained there until the following January when all units were evacuated, and returned to Egypt. On 25th February, orders were received for a move to France. They sailed for Marseilles, and moved to an area east of Pont Remy, southeast of Abbeville, in the second half of March. The battalion fought in the Battle of the Somme later the same year, in the Arras Offensive and the Battles of Langemarck and Cambrai in 1917. In May 1918, the battalion were between Saint Omer and Hazebrouck. On the 25th, they moved into the front and support lines on the edge of Bois de Rual. 'N' Company carried out a raid to capture German prisoners, but returned empty-handed, having not found any of the enemy. Apart from some intermittent shelling on the 26th, the next few days were 'quiet.' However, there were casualties on each day, amounting to six killed and fifteen wounded by the time they were relieved. William was one of the latter, and died in a nearby Casualty Clearing Station on the 29th; he is buried in Ebblinghem Military Cemetery.

G. WHITE

George Arthur White was born at Eversley in 1896, one of five brothers. His father, a carpenter and builder, died when George was only eight years old. Although his mother and brothers are listed in the 1911 census, George is missing; this may mean he was working locally as a farm labourer, and both households assumed the other would record him. George was conscripted into the Royal Garrison Artillery, attesting at Camberley, and was mobilised in January 1916, part of the first group to do so. By 1918, he was part of VIII Corps, Heavy Trench Mortar Battery. Until the middle of 1915, Trench Mortars were improvised weapons, inaccurate in their firing, with ammunition prone to explode prematurely, being of more danger to their operators than the enemy. The invention of the 3-inch Stokes mortar at the beginning of the year, was to change all this, and became standard issue in the Army for several decades. Trench mortars were used in a variety of defensive and offensive roles, from the suppression of an enemy machine gun, sniper post, or other local feature, to the co-ordinated firing of barrages. Larger mortars were sometimes used for cutting barbed wire, especially where Field Artillery could not be used. The 9.45 inch Heavy Mortars became available towards the end of 1916, and were known as 'Flying Pigs'. But even as late as July 1918, there were problems with 'prematures', with the War Diary recording "an examination of the bombs was ordered, and firing suspended pending result of enquiry." Towards the end of March when the Germans launched their offensive, and for the first week of April, all the men of George's unit were engaged in the construction of Heavy Trench Mortar gun positions in the battle zone. It was during this period when more British prisoners of war were taken by the enemy than at any other, and it is probable George was one of those captured. The death of Private White, G. is recorded on 7th July 1918, and he is buried in Niederzwehren Cemetery, one of four cemeteries in Germany where the Commonwealth War Graves have been concentrated.

H. WITHAM

Herbert Witham, known as Bertie, was born, along with his twin sister Beatrice, at Aldershot in 1888. His father had served in the army for eighteen years, including a spell in India, and reached the rank of Sergeant, with two of Bertie's five siblings born in Ireland. By 1901, his father was employed in the Officers' Mess at the Royal Military Academy at Sandhurst, and the family had moved to Yorktown Road. Bertie's mother died in 1903, and his father remarried the following year. Bertie joined the Army, attesting at Aldershot, and in 1911 was stationed at Tempe, near Bloemfontein in South Africa, home to various military bases and units. He served with the Veterinary Section of the Army Service Corps. As Bertie's Service Record no longer exits, it is not possible to follow him through the war. By May 1918, he was an acting Staff Sergeant with the 42nd Division Train. Each Division of the army had a certain amount of transport under its own command, known as the Divisional Train. It was the 'workhorse' of the Division in terms of carrying stores and supplies, providing the main supply line to the transport of the brigades of infantry and artillery and other attached units. The unit was at Pas en Artois, a few miles east of Doullens, from the 6th. Entries in the War Diary are mainly concerned with the movement of supplies and men. On the 11th Driver Lomas, who had been sentenced to two years imprisonment with hard labour, was handed over to the Assistant Provost Marshall, who was responsible for the Division's Military Police. Although no details of his offence are recorded, the length of the sentence indicates something serious, such as desertion. Three days later, one of the American Infantry Brigades joined the Division, and another two days after that, fresh vegetables were purchased locally. Between these last two entries was another. "15th May. At midnight, bombs dropped by enemy aeroplane on No. 4 Company Camp – Saddle Sergeant Witham, B. killed, A/Cpl Huish, E.J. wounded." Bertie was buried in Couin New British Cemetery.

A. WOODAGE

Arthur Woodage was born at Arborfield in 1891, one of six children. His father had served in the Royal Berkshire Regiment for six years, with postings to Ireland, Barbados, Bermuda and Nova Scotia, before being discharged on medical grounds, having contracted hepatitis. The Medical Officer described him as "a very weakly man, prematurely aged in appearance." This may explain why he moved between various labouring jobs within Berkshire, as Arthur's siblings were born at Bucklebury, Ufton Nervet and Finchampstead before the family moved to Little Sandhurst. Arthur's mother, a Canadian, died in 1902, and his father two years later. Arthur joined the 1st Battalion, Yorkshire Regiment as a bandsman in 1907, attesting at Aldershot, and appears in the 1911 census at Khartoum in the Sudan. The 1st Battalion were in India when war broke out, but remained there during the entire period of the conflict. But Arthur was transferred to the 2nd Battalion at some point, and although not in the first draft that landed at Zeebrugge in early October 1914, he had joined the fighting by the middle of the following month. In March 1915, the battalion fought in the Battle of Neuve Chapelle where Arthur won the Distinguished Conduct Medal, the second highest award for bravery after the Victoria Cross. The citation, published on 3rd June 1915 reads, "For conspicuous gallantry and devotion to duty at Neuve Chapelle on 13th March 1915, in voluntarily leaving his trench (his battalion not being engaged at the time) under very heavy fire, and attending on the wounded, regardless of danger. The gallantry of this bandsman was very noticeable." He was also awarded the Order of St George, 3rd Class, an award given by the Russian Emperor. Meanwhile, on 9th May, the battalion took part in the Battle of Aubers, a combined attack with the French, aimed at piercing the German line, and capturing high ground from which the Germans had a view of the entire Allied positions. More than 11,000 British casualties were sustained, the vast majority within yards of their own front-line trench, although the Yorkshires escaped lightly. Mile for mile, this was one of the highest rates of loss during the entire war. A week later, the second phase, known as the Battle of Festubert, began. Learning lessons from the earlier failure, a longer, more intense bombardment preceded the attack, but shrapnel was used, which was less effective than high explosive, which was not available. Observers reported a high proportion of dud shells failed to explode. The Yorkshires were not involved on the first day, but were under heavy artillery fire for the whole period, with 'C' Company sustaining "a good many casualties," including seven deaths. The following day, 'A' and 'D' Companies were sent forward to support the Scots Fusiliers, where they remained until late on the 17th; meanwhile, the rest of the battalion marched to a position on the right of the British attacking line later in the afternoon. Arthur, now a Lance Corporal, was killed in the fighting; his body was never recovered, and his name is listed on the Le Touret Memorial.

W. WYETH

William Henry Wyeth was born at Hurst in 1895, where he was baptised on 30th June. He was one of six children. Within a couple of years, the family had moved to the Sandhurst area, where his father, who had worked as a labourer, got a job as coachman at the Royal Military College. After leaving school, William worked as an errand boy, making deliveries for a greengrocer. He was conscripted into the Royal Garrison Artillery, attesting at Camberley, and was mobilised in January 1916, part of the first group to do so. William served with the 14th Trench Mortar battery, part of the 19th Division, and was involved in several phases of the Battle of the Somme in 1916, including the Battle of Albert at the start of July. By the end of November, William's battery was just to the southwest of Arras. The War Diary for the period is not very informative about locations, actions, or casualties, but the batteries spent three days cutting the enemy wire for an infantry raid, scheduled for the beginning of December. William was killed on the last day of November, and another gunner from the same gun three days later; both men were just in the wrong place at the wrong time, and are buried in Faubourg d'Amiens Cemetery, Arras.

OTHER GRAVES

There is one grave in the churchyard of a war casualty who is not on the list of names inside the church.

The late Sergt. ARTHUR M. HODGE,
Royal Garrison Artillery, Deepnall
House, Sandhurst. Died of pneumonia.

ARTHUR HODGE/MUGGERIDGE

The Commonwealth War Grave in Sandhurst churchyard lists Sergeant A. Hodge of the Royal Garrison Artillery, with the additional information that he served under the name of A. Muggeridge. He was born at Ockley, near Dorking, Surrey, in 1888, and registered as Arthur Muggeridge Penfold, his parents marrying soon after. A sister was born the following year. Soon afterwards, his parents separated, his father moving to Sussex, where he worked as a domestic coachman. His mother, Alice Muggeridge, assumed the name Eliza, and married Walter Hodge in 1891, who was employed driving a horse and cart for a miller in Ockley, and would have two more children. By the age of thirteen, Arthur had left school, and was working as an errand boy in Hastings, Sussex, before becoming a labourer. He joined the Royal Garrison Artillery on 19th February 1908, attesting at Horsham, Sussex, when he was described as just over 5'7" tall, weighing 9½ stone, with grey eyes, dark brown hair, and a fresh complexion; he also had a mole above the right nipple, a brown birth mark on the right side of his breast bone, a small scar on his left wrist, and a pulse rate of 90. After completing three months of training, he was posted to No. 46 Company, manning one of the coastal forts of the south-eastern defences. In September, Arthur was transferred to No. 88 Company, and spent just over three years in Hong Kong, before returning to England, and serving with No. 2 Company, occupied with Eastern Coast Defences, based at Sheerness, Kent. Whilst abroad, he passed a course in signalling, and took refresher courses every twelve months up to the outbreak of war. Also while in Hong Kong, he had a mild attack of bronchitis, and a bout of fever, which was possibly thought to be malaria, which recurred after his return. He suffered another bout of bronchitis just before Christmas in 1914, while at Coalhouse Fort, Tilbury, Essex, which put him in hospital for a week, and was confined again with another bout on 28th January the following year, and died on 8th February. By now, his mother and stepfather were living in Sandhurst, where they ran a laundry, which is why he is buried in the town.

Wokingham St Sebastian's

St Sebastian's Church

Part of the parish of Wokingham St Sebastian's falls inside the boundary of Bracknell Forest Borough. Only those men who were born or lived in this part of the parish have been included.

Sidney Bedford
James Sydney Bedford – see Crowthorne

Charles Alfred Chamberlain
Charles Alfred Chamberlain – see Crowthorne

Joseph Giles
Joseph Giles – see Crowthorne

William Charles Greenman
William Charles Greenman -– see Crowthorne

Frank Langley
Frank Langley – see Crowthorne

Henry Lovick
Henry Lovick – see Crowthorne

Frederick John Pither
Frederick John Pither – see Crowthorne

William Arthur Sharp
William Arthur Sharp - see Crowthorne

Frank Sutton
Frank Sutton - see Crowthorne

The late Pte. W. WERRELL, Pinewood Avenue, Ellis Road, Crowthorne.—Died of wounds.

WILLIAM WERRELL

William Werrell was born at Ramsdell, near Basingstoke, in 1880. He was the youngest of four children, but was only twelve months old when his father, who worked as a domestic coachman, died. His mother moved back to her native Wiltshire, remarried in 1886, and had a further five children, one of whom died in infancy. William's step-father ran a local hotel and also worked as a carpenter, but he too died, in 1898. The family moved again, to Owlsmoor, where William's mother worked as a laundress, possibly at the Royal Military College, where one of her sons worked as a kitchen lad. William by now had left school, and was working as a bricklayer's labourer. He had joined the 1/4th Battalion, Royal Berkshire Regiment, a Territorial Battalion, attesting at Wokingham, but did not go to France until 1916, presumably because he was supporting his widowed mother and younger step-siblings. He was probably mobilised in March, and may have taken part in some phases of the Battle of the Somme later that year, as the War Diary records two drafts of men joining in May, plus another four men in June. His first winter abroad was bitterly cold, but the battalion were in billets after Christmas, training with bombs and Lewis Guns. In February 1917, they moved back into the trenches, but with overnight temperatures registering twenty degrees of frost, digging was impossible, and water froze in the buckets as it was being carried forward to the trenches. Mild spells were invariably accompanied by fogs and mists, masking the German withdrawal to the Hindenburg Line, all buildings and infrastructure being destroyed as they went. The Third Battle of Ypres started on the last day of July in a great storm, and this was followed by a month of heavy rain. On 16th August, the battalion played a small part in an attack near Langemarck, but still suffered casualties to around one third of their fighting strength. At the end of September, the Berkshires moved up to Sombrin, and went into the front line the following day. The War Diary for the 2nd and 3rd October records "enemy artillery activity normal", and they were relived on the 4th. Next day, three Officers were hospitalised, suffering the effects of gas. Although there are no other reports of casualties, William died of wounds on the 8th, possibly also from the effects of gas, and is buried in Dozinghem Military Cemetery.

The late Pte. J. W. WHITAKER, 3rd Batt., Maisonette, Ellis Road, Crowthorne.—Died.

JOSEPH WHITTAKER

Joseph William Whittaker was born in 1882 at Eton, one of five children. His father worked as a steam engine fitter, but by 1901, his parents had separated, and Joseph's father was living in Kent with a common-law wife and another young son. Joseph's mother died later that year, and he went to live with an elder married brother, initially in London, and then in Ellis Road, Crowthorne. By now he had left school, and was working as a carman, driving a horse and cart and making deliveries. He joined the army under the Derby Scheme, attesting at Wokingham, and joined the 8th Battalion, Royal Berkshire Regiment. He was mobilised in March 1916, and was probably one of the draft of 164 men who joined the battalion in mid July. The first couple of weeks were spent at Baisieux Wood, before moving into reserve trenches on 13th August, and the front line on the 18th. Earlier in the day, 1st Battalion, The Black Watch had failed in an attack on a German line, and the Berkshires would make another attempt. Unfortunately, during the preliminary bombardment, one of the British guns was firing 'short', dropped shells in the British trench, burying many men, and badly damaging it, making movement along it impossible. They were barely in position when the attack started, and with smoke blowing across the line, and the German barrage and machine gun fire so heavy, they tried to dig in short of the objective, but were forced back to the start position with over 160 casualties. On 3rd September, the Berkshires were in support of another attack on German lines, and were called upon to help, but again, the attack was unsuccessful, and no ground was taken, and the battalion suffered another hundred casualties. After this, the fighting settled down to the usual monotony of trench warfare, and the weather was atrocious, leaving the mud waist deep in places. They celebrated Christmas a day early with a dinner, beer, oranges, nuts and cigars, and spent a miserable day in the front line on the 25th. At the beginning of February the following year, the battalion moved to the area south of Peronne. The War Diary contains few entries during this period, but the men went into the front line on the 22nd, and were relieved four days later. Joseph was killed on the 25th, one of five men during the month. After the war, his grave could not be found, and his name is listed on the Thiepval Memorial.

OTHER GRAVES

There is one grave in the churchyard of a war casualty who is not listed
on the Roll of Honour inside the church.

SIDNEY G. HARVEY

Sidney George Harvey was born in 1883 at 11 Summerhouse Road, Stoke Newington, London, the second of four children (a fifth died in infancy). At the time, his father was employed as a coachman, but by 1901, he was working as a grocer in Tottenham. Sidney, by this time, had left school, and was sharing a house in Westbourne Grove Terrace, Paddington with eight other draper's assistants. He married Jenny Green in 1906, and after the birth of their first son a few months later, moved to Bracknell, living on the London Road. Sidney worked as a postman from 1909, and five more children were born in the following years. He volunteered early in the conflict, attesting at Dalston, not far from where he grew up, and joined the 2nd Battalion, Oxfordshire and Buckinghamshire Light Infantry, where he was soon made a Corporal. Landing in France two days after Christmas 1914, the battalion was not involved in any major action until the Battle of Aubers on 9th May 1915, but it is not known whether Sidney took part. The Regimental History also records that many casualties occurred on the 17th, when the enemy shelled the trenches all day with great accuracy, causing great destruction of the breastworks, and wounding 270 men. The previous night, the battalion had assisted the 2nd Battalion, Inniskilling Fusiliers in an attack on two German trenches which had met with a lot of opposition. Sidney was probably wounded on one of these two dates, brought back to England, and died in Chatham Casualty Hospital, Kent, on 23rd June 1915. He is buried in Wokingham (St Sebastian) Churchyard, behind the church in a private grave, erected by the family, the headstone of which has fallen over (at the time of writing). He is not among the official War Graves in the churchyard; these are all men who died in the nearby Pinewood Hospital. His parents had moved to Crowthorne by 1911 (their address is given as Forest Road, just east of the High Street), and probably attended St Sebastian's Church on Nine Mile Ride. Sidney is listed on the Roll of Honour inside Holy Trinity Church, Bracknell.

POSTSCRIPT

The Armistice, when it came, was a surprise to many soldiers on the ground. While it was a relief and a cause for celebration, it left many at a loss. They had survived, but what of the future? When could they go home, and what would they find? Their whole life, for up to four years, had been one of fighting in the mud and trenches, and they could not conceive of a different one. Younger men had gone straight from school to military training and then the trenches – 'normal' working life was something they had never experienced. Others had unfinished apprenticeships or degree courses, now useless and forgotten. An entry in an autograph book kept by a nurse at one of the many hospitals in France treating the wounded, sums up the attitude of the time: "We held them on the Marne, we beat them on the Aisne, we gave them equal at Neuve Chapelle, and here we go again." Many questioned what they had been fighting for, and what had been achieved. There were hopes a more equal society; had not all classes fought together, suffering the same hardships and privations? Did the humble farm labourer not deserve the same future as the monied landowner? The street sweeper and the solicitor? But the world was a different place, and the country to which they returned had changed. Women had replaced absent men in the workplace (and there were almost two million more women than men), the country was almost bankrupt (Britain incurred debts during the war equivalent to 136% of its gross national product), and the swathes of unskilled, many with physical or mental scars, returning from the front, found no jobs, no money, and sometimes no waiting families. Rationing had been imposed in early 1918, limited to meat, sugar, and butter, but not bread. Inflation doubled between 1914 and 1920; income tax rose from 6% before the war, to 60% for the richest. The value of the pound sterling fell by more than 60%.

The end of the fighting was not followed by an immediate return home by every man overseas. Surrendering Germans had to be guarded and escorted, their captured and abandoned equipment and ammunition destroyed, dismantled or otherwise dealt with. British equipment also had to be returned to home shores in an orderly and organised fashion. The land and infrastructure had to be returned to returning civilian populations, and the inevitable looting and 'souvenir hunters' discouraged or imprisoned. After four long years of chaos, order was not something that could be reinstated overnight. The territories of German and her allies needed occupying forces until such time as the politics had been sorted out. The Naval Blockade on Germany would be maintained for several months until the Peace Treaty was signed at Versailles at the end of June 1919.

Illness was still prevalent, and soon a flu pandemic, originating in America, but known as the Spanish Flu, would sweep the world, striking down many who had survived the fighting. However ordered the return, many felt they were being treated unfairly. Young conscripts, still being trained at home, were the first to be discharged. Why were those who had sacrificed years serving their country not the first? Next to return were those in jobs considered 'essential' to the recovering country. Were miners more necessary than shopkeepers; were farm workers or clerks more important? Should those with injuries gain preferential treatment? But within twelve months, the British army of 3.8 million men had been reduced to less than one million, and by 1922, only 230,000 remained in the country's fighting force.

Lloyd George, who had been Prime Minister since 1916 in a coalition government, won the General Election of 1919 with the promise of "a country fit for heroes to live in." For the soldiers who came back from the trenches, there was the thanks of a grateful country, a suit of civilian clothes, a pair of medals, and a small cash payment. A private was given the equivalent of a few weeks' wages, an officer got rather more, and Sir Douglas Haig, who commanded the British Expeditionary Force from 1915, was given an earldom and £100,000, and eventually was the subject of the last equestrian statue in London. Most returning men were successfully re-integrated into the British economy, although their War Bonus was spent on new clothes, the army diet having caused them to grow and put on weight. But the ambitious wartime program of 'reconstruction' was abandoned during the economic slump of 1921, and many men found themselves with no job, reduced to selling matches, cards and war mementoes on street corners, and visiting soup kitchens and food distribution centres. The economic impacts of the war were huge as industry had been completely focussed on providing materials and resources for the armed forces, producing everything from ships to uniforms. Britain's pre-war economy had been built on exports and the four core industries of coal, ship-building, textiles and iron. During the war, Britain's previous markets had developed their own industries, and, after an initial post-war boom, a balance of payments crisis ensued. By 1922, one and half million men were unemployed. Despite an ambitious post-war building program, housing facilities were woefully short, none having been built during the war years. The seriously wounded were often denied their pensions as medical tribunals discharged their rights. Local newspapers of the time reported cases of domestic abuse or abandonment as men struggled to adapt, many having married in haste before going off to fight. Some returned to find their wives living with other men.

The British Legion was set up to help those who fought, and many Comrades of the Great War Clubs were formed, with men keen to consolidate and foster the comradeship of the trenches (Bracknell's Comrades had their own clubhouse in Park Road). It very quickly began to dawn on large numbers of demobilised soldiers, whatever their wartime rank, the dream of coming home to the secure job, which they believed was their right, was not going to come true. A letter from an ex-Officer was published in The Times in February 1920: "During the War, all those who put on the King's uniform had a great access of friends. We were heroes in those days. Our relations, too, even our rich relatives, took a new interest in us. On leave from the Front we were welcome and honoured guests - especially as we gained promotion: 'My Cousin the Major' ... when at last we came home, were demobilised and doffed our uniforms, we realised how much our welcome had depended on the glamour of our clothes, with all that they implied. In mufti, we were no longer heroes, we were simply 'unemployed', an unpleasant problem. Many businessmen think they did their part in the war at home, just as much as those on active service, and that no obligation rests on them to help ex-officers. I know that many of them worked long hours, even overworked in their country's cause, but they got a reward in experience, in an increase of income, and in good positions. And although the strain of long hours is great, their offices did not admit poison gas, mud, and shells, with the ever present threat of sudden death. There is a large balance outstanding to the credit of the ex-officer. Are you going to withhold payment until it is too late?" There were thinkers among the rank and files too, among them a

Private from the Machine Gun Corps: "One universal question which I have never seen answered: two or three million pounds a day for the 1914-18 war, yet no monies were forthcoming to put industry on its feet on our return from that war. Many's the time I've gone to bed, after a day of 'tramp, tramp' looking for work, on a cup of cocoa and a pennyworth of chips between us; I would lay puzzling why, why, after all we had gone through in the service of our country, we have to suffer such poverty, willing to work at anything but no work to be had. I only had two Christmases at work between 1919 and 1939." Another ex-soldier, who fell on hard times, recounts a couple of experiences from 1923. "I had a walk round and eventually sat on a seat on the Embankment. I must have dozed off because it was dark as I woke up, so I decided to stay put till morning. I woke as the dawn was breaking and what a sight it was. All the seats were full of old soldiers in all sorts of dress - mostly khaki - and a lot more were lying on the steps, some wrapped up in old newspapers. Men who had fought in the trenches, now unwanted and left to starve were all huddled together …. Later I met a man crying in a doorway. He had on an army greatcoat and a turban and a tray round his neck with lucky charms on it. Another, unwanted, after three years in the trenches. He and his wife were penniless when some crook offered a chance to earn easy money for five shillings He pawned his wife's wedding ring to get it, and in return he got a tray, a turban and a dozen-or-so lucky charms to sell at 6d each. Now, after a day without anything to eat or drink, he was broken-hearted at the thought of going home to his wife without a penny. He was an ex-CSM *(Company Sergeant Major)*." In later life, Jim Hooley, who grew up in a poor area in Stockport in the years after the war, remembered the frequent sight of people, unable to pay their rent, being evicted by bailiffs: "The furniture would be taken out of the house and left on the pavement. The father would stay to watch it, while neighbours looked after his wife and children. One case always stood out in my memory. On my way to school I had to pass an old disused public house. A family had taken up residence in this building. I knew the boy who lived there: his mother and father were quite respectable. However, one morning on my way to school I saw a crowd of people round the old building. Making my way to the front of the crowd I could see the old familiar scene - another eviction. Next morning, on my way to school, I again saw a crowd round the old pub. On looking at the scene, I saw three First World War medals placed on an old sideboard which the bailiffs had taken out of the house the day before. A lady in the crowd told me that the father had got back into the building during the night and hanged himself." The writer and broadcaster J. B. Priestly wrote an account of a reunion of his old battalion in 1934: "Several of us had arranged with the secretary to see that original members of the battalion, to whom the price of the dinner was prohibitive, were provided with free tickets. But this, he told me, had not worked very well; and my old platoon comrades confirmed this, too, when I asked about one or two men. They were so poor, these fellows, that they said they could not attend the dinner, even if provided with free tickets, because they felt that their clothes were not good enough."

Despite the economic problems, the post-war administration established a genuine mass-democracy in Britain. The Representation of the People Act of 1918 enfranchised all males over the age of 21, and all women over the age of 30, and abolished the pre-war property qualifications. The 1920s, and perhaps the following decade, was one of the brief interludes when a three-party democracy existed in British politics. However, the post-war period wrought one important change: the Labour Party replaced the Liberals as the principle opposition to the Conservatives. In conjunction with coming to terms with mass-democracy, Britain also experienced fraught industrial relations. From 1914 to 1918, trade union membership had doubled, to a little over eight million. Work stoppages and strikes became frequent in 1917–1918 as the unions expressed grievances regarding prices, alcohol control, pay disputes, fatigue from overtime and working on Sundays, and inadequate housing. A notable clash took place in Glasgow in 1919, where protestors battled with the police, and eventually the army, over shorter working hours. The most potent symbol of the industrial malcontent fostered after the First World War was the general strike of 1926. In a similar fashion to democracy, the welfare provision began to develop. The school leaving age was increased to fourteen, and the Unemployment Insurance Act of 1920, extending National Insurance provision to eleven million more workers.

The aftermath years were a time of paradox; the men who returned from the horrors of the trenches wanted to forget, and where those who had stayed behind, and had lost husbands and brothers, and sons and fathers were equally determined never to forget. It was a world where questioning whether the war had been right was attacked as a slur on the memory of the dead. The last living link with the war was broken when Harry Patch, the last veteran who served in the trenches, died on 25th July 2009, aged 111. The Head Teacher at Crowthorne Church of England School summed up the mood of the time at the unveiling of their Roll of Honour: "We hope in all the years to come, the families and scholars of every generation will never fail to give honour to the memory of these 'old boys' who made the supreme sacrifice for England. They are very dear to us of today, and we ask all who succeed to us that their names and records shall not be forgotten. We transmit this as a precious heritage."

Many returned with scars, both physical, and more damagingly, mental, from which they would never recover. The ones who survived are often the forgotten ones; those who died are remembered annually. As one veteran, who had obviously given some thought to what would happen when the War finally ended, summed up to a younger companion in the days after the Armistice, "Peace is going to bring one glorious mess, an unequal fight against a public who will soon forget our sacrifices, and new generations who will know nothing of the war and what it meant to those who served."

It is hoped this book will go some way to redressing some of the mess.

Acknowledgements

I would like to thank the following people and organisations for their help in compiling the three volumes of Bracknell's Great War Fallen.

CROWTHORNE
Crowthorne Church of England School for allowing me access to see the Roll of Honour
Daphne Harris for information on some of the men from the village found during her research

SANDHURST
Sandhurst (St Michael and All Angels) Church for allowing me access to see the Roll of Honour
Maurice Clark and Teresea Birchnell-Wood from Sandhurst Historical Society for sharing their research with me

WOKINGHAM
Wokingham St Sebastian's Church for giving me a copy of the Roll of Honour

Staff at The National Archives, Kew, Berkshire Record Office, Reading, and Reading Central Library for their help during my visits for research

The staff at Bracknell and Harmanswater Libraries for obtaining books through inter-library loans to assist my research

John Chapman for assistance with men in the Royal Berkshire Regiment

Andrew French, Assistant Honorary Curator at the Berkshire Yeomanry Museum, Windsor, for information on the men from that regiment

The relatives of men who supplied information for inclusion in these biographies

All those organisations and individuals who made a contribution to the costs of publishing these volumes

Cath Murray for turning my ideas for the book covers into reality

The staff at Grosvenor Publishing for dealing with my queries over the publication of these volumes

BIBLIOGRAPHY

History of the Royal Regiment of Artillery: Western Front 1914-1918
General Sir Martin Farndale

The Royal Berkshire Regiment 1914-1918
F. Loraine Petre

The 2nd Battalion Royal Berkshire Regiment in World War One
Ian Cull

Coldstream Guards 1914-1918
Ross of Bladensburg

Devonshire Regiment 1914-1918
C. T. Atkinson

Faithful; The Story of The Durham Light Infantry
S. G. P. Ward

A Contemptible Little Flying Corps
I. McInnes and J. V. Webb

Gloucestershire Regiment in the War 1914-1918
Everard Wyrall

The Grenadier Guards in The Great War 1914-1918
Sir Frederick Ponsonby

Regimental History, The Royal Hampshire Regiment
C. T. Atkinson

From Trench and Turret, Royal Marine's Letters and Diaries 1914-18
S. M. Holloway

Annals of The King's Royal Rifle Corps: Vol 5: "The Great War"
Major-Gen. Sir Steuart Hare

Die-Hards in The Great War (Middlesex Regiment)
Everard Wyrall

History of The Rifle Brigade in the War of 1914-1918
Capt. Reginald Berkley and Brig. Gen. William W. Seymour

Britain's Sea Soldiers: A Record of the Royal Marines during the War 1914-1919
General Sir H. E. Blumberg

History of the Somerset Light Infantry 1914-1918
Everard Wyrall

The Queen's Own Royal West Regiment
C. T. Atkinson

Worcestershire Regiment in The Great War
Capt. M. Fitzm. Stacke

King's Own Yorkshire Light Infantry in The Great War 1914-1918
R. C. Bond

The Goodchilds of Grundisburgh: Four Brothers in the First World War
Henry Finch

Old Soldiers Never Die
Frank Richards

Indian Corps in France
Merewether Merewether and Sir Frederick Smith

The Pride of Pirton
Tony French, Chris Ryan and Jonty French

Bloody Red Tabs: General Officer Casualties of the Great War, 1914 1920
Frank Davies and Graham Maddocks

Boy Soldiers of the Great War
Richard van Emden

First Day on the Somme
Martin Middlebrook

APPENDIX I

BATTLES

MAJOR BATTLES ON THE WESTERN FRONT

1914

Battle of Mons	23rd to 24th August
Battle of Cateau	26th August to 1st September
Battle of the Marne	7th to 10th September
Battle of the Aisne	12th to 15th September
Defence of Antwerp	4th to 10th October
Battle of La Bassee	10th October to 2nd November
Battle of Messines	12th October to 2nd November
Battle of Armentieres	13th October to 2nd November
First Battle of Ypres	19th October to 22nd November

1915

Battle of Neuve Chapelle	10th March to 22nd April
Second Battle of Ypres	22nd April to 25th May
Battle of Aubers	9th to 10th May
Battle of Festubert	15th to 25th May
Battle of Loos	25th September to 18th October

1916

Battle of the Somme	1st July to 18th November
Battle of Albert	1st to 13th July
Battle of Bazentin	14th to 17th July
Battle of Delville Wood	15th July to 3rd September
Attack at Fromelles	19th July
Attacks on High Wood	20th to 25th July
Battle of Pozieres	23rd July to 3rd September
Battle of Guillemont	3rd to 6th September
Battle of Ginchy	9th September
Battle of Flers-Courcelette	15th to 22nd September
Battle of Morval	25th to 28th September
Battle of Thiepval	26th to 28th September

Battle of Le Transloy	1st to 18th October
Battle of Ancre Heights	1st October to 11th November
Battle of Ancre	13th to 18th November

1917

Operations on the Ancre	11th January to 13th March
German Retreat to the Hindenburg Line	14th March to 5th April
Arras Offensive	9th April to 16th June
Battle of Vimy	9th to 14th April
First Battle of the Scarpe	9th to 14th April
Second Battle of the Scarpe	23rd to 24th April
Battle of Arleux	28th to 29th April
Third Battle of the Scarpe	3rd to 4th May
Battle of Messines	7th June to 14th June
Battle of Langemarck	16th to 18th August
Third Battle of Ypres	31st July to 10th November
Battle of Pilkem	31st July to 2nd August
Battle of Langemarck	16th to 18th August
Battle of the Menin Road	20th to 25th September
Battle of Polygon Wood	26th September to 3rd October
Battle of Broodseinde	4th October
Battle of Poelcapelle	9th October
First Battle of Passchendaele	12th October
Second Battle of Passchendaele	26th October to 10th November
Cambrai Operations	20th November to 30th December

1918

First Battles of the Somme 1918 (the German Spring Offensive)	
	21st March to 4th July
Battle of St Quentin	21st March to 23rd March
First Battle of Bapaume	24th to 25th March
Battle of Rosieres	26th to 27th March
First Battle of Arras	28th March
Battle of Avre	4th April
Battle of the Ancre	5th April
Battles of the Lys	9th to 29th April
Battle of Estaires	9th to 11th April
Battle of Messines	10th to 11th April
Battle of Hazebrouck	12th to 15th April
Battle of Bailleul	13th to 15th April
First Battle of Kemmel	17th to 19th April
Battle of Bethune	18th April
Second Battle of Kemmel	25th to 26th April
Battle of Scherpenberg	29th April
Battle of the Aisne	27th May to 6th June
Battles of the Marne	20th July to 2nd August
Battle of Amiens	8th to 11th August

Second Battles of the Somme 1918	21st August to 3rd September
Battle of Albert	21st to 23rd August
Second Battle of Bapaume	31st August to 3rd September
Advance in Flanders	18th August to 6th September
Second Battles of Arras	26th August to 3rd September
Battles of the Hindenberg Line	12th September to 12th October
Battle of Havrincourt	12th September
Battle of Epehy	18th September
Battle of the Canal du Nord	27th September to 1st October
Battle of the St Quentin Canal	29th September to 2nd October
Battle of Beaurevoir	3rd to 5th October
Battle of Cambrai	8th to 9th October
Final Advance in Flanders	28th September to 11th November
Battle of Ypres	28th September to 2nd October
Battle of Coutrai	14th to 19th October
Final Advance in Artois	2nd October to 11th November
Final Advance in Picardy	17th October to 11th November
Battle of the Selle	17th to 25th October
Battle of Valenciennes	1st to 2nd November
Battle of the Sambre	4th November
Germany signs Armistice	11th November

THE MESOPOTAMIA CAMPAIGN

1914

Capture of Basra	5th to 21st November
Capture of Qurna	3rd to 19th December

1915

Capture of Nasiriyeh	27th June to 24th July
First Advance on Baghdad (including capture of Kut-al-Amara)	
	12th September to 7th October
Battle of Clesiphon	22nd to 24th November
Retreat to Kut-al-Amara	25th November to 3rd December

1916

Siege of Kut-al-Amara	7th December 1915 to 29th April 1916
Efforts to relieve Kut-al-Amara	
Battle of Sheik Sa'ad	7th January
Battle of the Wadi	13th January
Battle of the Hanna	21st January
Attack on the Dujaila Redoubt	7th to 9th March
Battles of the Hanna and Fallahiyeh	5th to 8th April
Battles of Bait Alsa and Sannaiyat	7th to 22nd April
Surrender of the Kut-al-Amara Garrison	29th April

1917

Battle of Mohammed Abdul Hussan	9th January
Battles of the Hal Salient, Dahra Bend, and the Shumran Peninsula	
	11th January to 24th February
Capture of Baghdad	11th March
Battle of Istanbulat	21st April
Battle of 'The Boot' at Band-i-Adhaim	30th April
Battle of Tikrit	5th November

1918

Action of Khan Badghdadi	26th March
Turkey signs Armistice	1st October

THE GALLIPOLI CAMPAIGN

1915

Naval bombardment of the Straights Forts	9th February to 16th March
Naval attempt to force the Straights	18th March
Landings at Cape Helles and Anzac Cove	25th April
First Battle of Krithia	28th April
Second Battle of Krithia	6th May
The Third Battle of Krithia	4th June
Battle of Gully Ravine	28th June
Landings at Suvla Bay and the ANZAC attack on Chunuk Bair	
	6th to 9th August
Battle of Scimitar Hill and attack on Hill 60	21st August
Evacuation of ANZAC bridgehead and Suvla Bay	
	10th to 19th December
Evacuation of Cape Helles bridgehead	10th December to 9th January 1916

THE CAMPAIGN IN EGYPT AND PALESTINE

1915

Defence of the Suez Canal	26th January to 12th August
Operations in the Sinai Peninsula	15th November to 9th January 1917
Operations against the Senussi in the Western Desert	
	23rd November to 8th February 1917

1916

Operations against the Sultan of Darfur	1st March to 31st December
Arab revolt in the Hejuz	6th June to 22nd September
Battle of Romani	4th to 5th August

1917

First Battle of Gaza	26th to 27th March
Second Battle of Gaza	17th to 19th April

Third Battle of Gaza   27th October to 7th November
Affair of Huj, Action of El Mughar, and Capture of Junction Station
                                              8th to 14th November
Battle of Nabi Samweil   20th to 24th November
Capture of Jerusalem   7th to 9th December
Battle of Jaffa   21st to 22nd December

1918
Operations in the Jordan Valley   19th February to 4th May
Battles of Megiddo, Sharon and Nablus   19th to 25th September
Final Offensive beyond the Jordan   to 26th October
Armistice   31st October 1918

THE CAMPAIGN IN SALONIKA

1915
Landing at Salonika   21st October

1916
Occupation of Mazirko   2nd October
Capture of Karajakois   30th September to 2nd October
Capture of Yenikoi   3rd to 4th October
Battle of Tumbitza Farm   17th November to 7th December

1917
First Battle of Doiran   22nd April to 8th May
Capture of Ferdie and Essex Trenches   15th May
Capture of Bairakli and Kumli   16th May
Capture of Homonodos   14th October

1918
Capture of the Roche Noir Salient   1st to 2nd September
Second Battle of Doiran   18th to 19th September
Passage of the Vardar and the Pursuit to the Strumica Valley
                                           20th to 30th September
Armistice   30th September

THE CAMPAIGN IN ITALY

1917
First troops arrive   5th November

1918
Battle of the Piave River   15th to 23rd June
Battle of Vittorio Veneto   24th October to 3rd November
Armistice   3rd November

NAVAL BATTLES

1914
Battle of Heligoland Bight   28th August
Battle of Coronel   1st November
Battle of the Falkland Islands   8th December
Raid on Scarborough and Hartlepool   16th December

1915
Battle of Dogger Bank   24th January

1916
Battle of Jutland   31st May to 1st June

1917
Battle of Otranto Straights   14th to 15th May

1918
Zeebrugge Raid   23rd April

APPENDIX II

CEMETERIES AND MEMORIALS

The following list of cemeteries and memorials contain at least one man
from Bracknell Forest Borough.

ABBEVILLE COMMUNAL CEMETERY EXTENSION

The town of Abbeville is on the main road from Paris to Boulogne (N1), about 80 kms
south of Boulogne.

For much of the First World War, Abbeville was headquarters of the Commonwealth lines
of communication and various hospitals were stationed there from October 1914 to January
1920. The communal cemetery was used for burials from November 1914 to September 1916,
the earliest being made among the French military graves. The extension was begun in September
1916.

A.I.F. BURIAL GROUND, FLERS

A.I.F. BURIAL GROUND is 2 kms north of the village of Flers, in the Department of the Somme.

Flers was captured on 15 September 1916, in the Battle of Flers-Courcelette, when it was
entered by the New Zealand and 41st Divisions behind tanks, the innovative new weapons that
were used here for the first time. The village was lost during the German advance of March 1918
and retaken at the end of the following August.

The cemetery was begun by Australian medical units, posted in the neighbouring caves, in
November 1916 to February 1917. It was very greatly enlarged after the Armistice when almost
4,000 Commonwealth and French graves were brought in from the battlefields of the Somme,
and later from a wider area.

AIRE COMMUNAL CEMETERY

Aire is a town about 14 kms south-south-east of St. Omer.

From March 1915 to February 1918, Aire was a busy but peaceful centre used by Commonwealth
Forces as Corps Headquarters. The Highland Casualty Clearing Station was based there as was the
39th Stationary Hospital (from May 1917). It was used again when the 54th Casualty Clearing
Station came to Aire and the town was, for a while, within 13 kms of the German lines.

AIX-NOULETTE COMMUNAL CEMETERY EXTENSION

Aix-Noulette is a village in the Department of the Pas-de-Calais, about 13 kms south of Bethune.

The Cemetery Extension was begun by French troops early in 1915, and the two French plots
are next to the Communal Cemetery. It was taken over by the 1st and 2nd Divisions in February,

1916, and used by fighting units and Field Ambulances until October, 1918. It was increased after the Armistice by the concentration of graves from the battlefields to the east.

ALBERT COMMUNAL CEMETERY EXTENSION

Albert is a town 28 kms north-east of Amiens.

It was held by French forces against the German advance on the Somme in September 1914. It passed into British hands in the summer of 1915; and the first fighting in July 1916, is known as the Battle of Albert, 1916. It was captured by the Germans on 26th April 1918, and before its recapture on the following 22nd August (in the Battle of Albert, 1918), it had been completely destroyed by artillery fire.

The Extension was used by fighting units and Field Ambulances from August 1915 to November 1916, and more particularly in and after September 1916, when Field Ambulances were concentrated at Albert. From November 1916, the 5th Casualty Clearing Station used it for two months. From March 1917, it was not used (except for four burials in March 1918) until the end of August 1918, when Plot II was made by the 18th Division.

ALLONVILLE COMMUNITY CEMETERY

Allonville is a village in the Department of the Somme, 8 kms north-east of Amiens.

The communal cemetery was used from August 1916 to February 1917 by the 39th Casualty Clearing Station then posted at Allonville, and from April to July 1918, by Australian fighting units.

AMARA WAR CEMETERY

Amara is a town on the left bank of the Tigris some 520 kms from the sea.

Amara was occupied by the Mesopotamian Expeditionary Force on 3rd June 1915 and it immediately became a hospital centre. The accommodation for medical units on both banks of the Tigris was greatly increased during 1916 and in April 1917, seven general hospitals and some smaller units were stationed there.

NOTE: Whilst the current climate of political instability persists it is not possible for the Commission to manage or maintain its cemeteries and memorials located within Iraq. Alternative arrangements for commemoration have therefore been implemented and a two volume Roll of Honour listing all casualties buried and commemorated in Iraq has been produced. These volumes are on display at the Commission's Head Office in Maidenhead and are available for the public to view.

ANCRE BRITISH CEMETERY, BEAUMONT-HAMEL

ANCRE BRITISH CEMETERY is about 2 kms south of the village of Beaumont-Hamel.

The village of Beaumont-Hamel was attacked on 1st July 1916 but without success. On 3rd September a further attack was delivered between Hamel and Beaumont-Hamel and on 13th and 14th November, the Allies finally succeeded in capturing it. Following the German withdrawal to the Hindenburg Line in the spring of 1917, V Corps cleared this battlefield and created a number of cemeteries, of which ANCRE BRITISH CEMETERY (then called Ancre River No.1 British Cemetery) was one. There were originally 517 burials almost all of the 63rd (Naval) and 36th Divisions, but after the Armistice the cemetery was greatly enlarged when many more graves from the same battlefields and smaller burial grounds.

ARNEKE BRITISH CEMETERY
The village of Arneke is approximately 50 kms south-east of Calais and about 8 kms north-west of the town of Cassel.

The cemetery was begun by the 13th Casualty Clearing Station which moved to Arneke from the Proven area in October 1917. It was joined by two further Clearing Stations in April 1918. The cemetery was used by these hospitals until the end of May, and again from July to September 1918. In November it was used for a short time by the 4th and 10th Stationary Hospitals. A few French soldiers were buried from clearing stations in April 1918 and French units buried at the north-west end of the cemetery, mainly in May and June 1918.

ARRAS MEMORIAL AND ARRAS FLYING SERVICES MEMORIAL
The two memorials will be found in the FAUBOURG-D'AMIENS CEMETERY, which is in the Boulevard du General de Gaulle in the western part of the town of Arras.

The ARRAS MEMORIAL commemorates almost 35,000 servicemen from the United Kingdom, South Africa and New Zealand who died in the Arras sector between the spring of 1916 and 7 August 1918, the eve of the Advance to Victory, and have no known grave.

The ARRAS FLYING SERVICES MEMORIAL commemorates almost 1,000 airmen of the Royal Naval Air Service, the Royal Flying Corps, and the Royal Air Force, either by attachment from other arms of the forces of the Commonwealth or by original enlistment, who were killed on the whole Western Front and who have no known grave.

ASCOT (ALL SAINTS) CHURCHYARD EXTENSION
This cemetery is located off Priory Road, Chavey Down, and contains seven WWI burials.

ATH COMMUNAL CEMETERY
The town of Ath is located east of the town of Tournai on the N7.

The 38 Commonwealth burials of the First World War in ATH COMMUNAL CEMETERY date from November 1918 to March 1919, and are mainly those of men who died at No. 2 Australian Casualty Clearing Station.

AUBERCHICOURT BRITISH CEMETERY
Auberchicourt is a village 11.5 kms east of Douai on the road to Valenciennes.

The village was occupied by Commonwealth troops in October 1918. The cemetery was begun at the end of that month and used until February 1919 while three Canadian Casualty Clearing Stations were in the neighbourhood. These original graves are in Plot I, but the cemetery was enlarged after the Armistice when graves (mainly of 1918-19, but also of August 1914) were brought in from the surrounding battlefields and from the following smaller burial grounds.

AUCHONVILLERS MILITARY CEMETERY
Auchonvillers is approximately 20 kms south of Arras.

From the outbreak of the war to the summer of 1915, this part of the front was held by French troops, who began the military cemetery in June 1915. It continued to be used by Commonwealth field ambulances and fighting units, but burials practically ceased with the German withdrawal in February 1917.

AWOINGT BRITISH CEMETERY

Awoingt is a village some 3 kms east-south-east of Cambrai.

AWOINGT BRITISH CEMETERY was begun in the latter half of October 1918 and used until the middle of December; the village had been captured on 9/10th October. By 28th October, three Casualty Clearing Stations were posted in the neighbourhood, and the great majority of the burials were made from those hospitals.

BAILLEUL COMMUNAL CEMETERY EXTENSION (NORD)

Bailleul is a large town in France, near the Belgian border, 14.5 kms south-west of Ieper.

Bailleul was occupied on 14th October 1914 and became an important railhead, air depot and hospital centre, with several Casualty Clearing Stations quartered in it for considerable periods. It was a Corps headquarters until July 1917, when it was severely bombed and shelled, and after the Battle of Bailleul (13-15th April 1918), it fell into German hands and was not retaken until 30th August 1918.

The earliest Commonwealth burials at Bailleul were made at the east end of the communal cemetery and in April 1915, when the space available had been filled, the extension was opened on the east side of the cemetery. The extension was used until April 1918, and again in September, and after the Armistice graves were brought in from the neighbouring battlefields and other burial grounds.

BAILLEUL ROAD EAST CEMETERY, ST LAURENT-BLANGY

St. Laurent-Blangy is a village adjoining the north-east side of Arras.

A greater part of the village was included in the front taken over by British troops in March, 1916, and the remainder fell into British hands on the first day of the Battles of Arras, the 9th April, 1917.

BAILLEUL ROAD EAST CEMETERY was begun in April, 1917, and carried on by fighting units until the following November. After the Armistice isolated graves from a very wide area north, east and south of Arras were brought in.

BARD COTTAGE CEMETERY

The Cemetery is located near Ieper, on the Diksmuidseweg road (N369) in the direction of Boezinge (BARD COTTAGE CEMETERY is the first cemetery on the left, the second being TALANA FARM CEMETERY).

For much of the First World War, the village of Boesinghe (now Boezinge) directly faced the German line across the Yser canal. Bard Cottage was a house a little set back from the line, close to a bridge called Bard's Causeway, and the cemetery was made nearby in a sheltered position under a high bank. Burials were made between June 1915 and October 1918; after the Armistice, 46 graves were brought in from the immediate area.

BARLIN COMMUNAL CEMETERY EXTENSION

Barlin is a village about 11 kms south-west of Bethune on the D188.

The extension was begun by French troops in October 1914 and when they moved south in March 1916 to be replaced by Commonwealth Forces, it was used for burials by the

6th Casualty Clearing Station. In November 1917, Barlin began to be shelled and the hospital was moved back to Ruitz, but the extension was used again in March and April 1918 during the German advance on this front.

BASRA MEMORIAL

Until 1997, the Basra Memorial was located on the main quay of the naval dockyard at Maqil, on the west bank of the Shatt-al-Arab, about 8 kms north of Basra. Because of the sensitivity of the site, the Memorial was moved by presidential decree. The move, carried out by the authorities in Iraq, involved a considerable amount of manpower, transport costs and sheer engineering on their part, and the Memorial has been re-erected in its entirety. The Basra Memorial is now located 32 kms along the road to Nasiriyah, in the middle of what was a major battleground during the first Gulf War. The Basra Memorial commemorates more than 40,500 members of the Commonwealth forces who died in the operations in Mesopotamia from the autumn of 1914 to the end of August 1921 and whose graves are not known.

NOTE: Whilst the current climate of political instability persists it is not possible for the Commission to manage or maintain its cemeteries and memorials located within Iraq. Alternative arrangements for commemoration have therefore been implemented and a two volume Roll of Honour listing all casualties buried and commemorated in Iraq has been produced. These volumes are on display at the Commission's Head Office in Maidenhead and are available for the public to view.

BASRA WAR CEMETERY

Basra is a town on the west bank of the Shatt-al-Arab, 90 kms from its mouth in the Persian Gulf. The cemetery now contains 2,551 burials of the First World War, 74 of them unidentified. The headstones marking these graves were removed in 1935 when it was discovered that salts in the soil were causing them to deteriorate. The names of those buried in the graves affected are now recorded on a screen wall.

The cemetery also contains the BASRA (TANOOMA CHINESE) MEMORIAL, commemorating 227 unidentified casualties of the Chinese Labour Corps who were attached to the Inland Water Transport during the First World War. A panel in their memory was added to the screen wall when it became evident that their graves in TANOOMA CHINESE CEMETERY could no longer be maintained.

NOTE: Whilst the current climate of political instability persists it is not possible for the Commission to manage or maintain its cemeteries and memorials located within Iraq. Alternative arrangements for commemoration have therefore been implemented and a two volume Roll of Honour listing all casualties buried and commemorated in Iraq has been produced. These volumes are on display at the Commission's Head Office in Maidenhead and are available for the public to view.

BAVINCOURT COMMUNAL CEMETERY

Bavincourt is a village and commune in the Department of the Pas-de-Calais, a little north of the main road from Doullens to Arras. Five soldiers from the United Kingdom, who fell in May 1916, and March 1917, are buried in two groups in the Communal Cemetery, near the entrance.

BAZENTIN-LE-PETIT COMMUNAL CEMETERY AND BAZENTIN-LE-PETIT COMMUNAL CEMETERY EXTENSION

Bazentin is a village in the Department of the Somme, to the north-east of Albert, containing the villages of Bazentin-le-Grand and Bazentin-le-Petit.

Bazentin was in German hands until 14th July 1916, when the 3rd and 7th Divisions captured the two villages (and the communal cemetery) and held them against counter-attacks. The ground was lost in April 1918 during the great German advance but recaptured on the following 25th August.

The COMMUNAL CEMETERY contains two Commonwealth burials dating from August 1916. The COMMUNAL CEMETERY EXTENSION was begun immediately after the capture of the village and used until December 1916 as a front-line cemetery. It was enlarged after the Armistice when 50 graves were brought in from the battlefields of Bazentin and Contalmaison.

BEAURAIN BRITISH CEMETERY

Beaurain (not to be confused with Beaurains near Arras) is a village in the Department of the Nord 19 kms south of Valenciennes and 4 kms from Solesmes railway station.

It was captured on 23rd October, 1918; the British Cemetery was made in the fortnight after the capture of the village.

BEAURAINS ROAD CEMETERY, BEAURAINS

Beaurains is a village on the southern outskirts of Arras.

The cemetery was begun a few days before Beaurains was captured by Commonwealth forces on 18th March 1917. It was a month before the Battle of Arras began, and the Germans were still in nearby Tilloy-les-Mofflaines. The cemetery was used (sometimes under the name of Ronville Forward Cemetery) until the beginning of June, and later for a short time in August and September 1918, in the Second Battle of Arras. It contained, at the date of the Armistice, the graves of 129 British soldiers, 15 French soldiers and four German prisoners. It was enlarged after the armistice when graves were brought in from the surrounding battlefields and cemeteries.

BEERSHEBA WAR CEMETERY

Beersheba is a southern town on the edge of the Negev Desert, 75 kms south-west of Jerusalem.

The cemetery was made immediately on the fall of the town, remaining in use until July 1918, by which time 139 burials had been made It was greatly increased after the Armistice when burials were brought in from a number of scattered sites and small burial grounds.

BERLIN SOUTH-WESTERN CEMETERY

The cemetery is located in the village of Stahnsdorf, lying approx 22 kms south west of Berlin and approx 14 kms to the east of Potsdam.

In 1922-23 it was decided that the graves of Commonwealth servicemen who had died all over Germany should be brought together into four permanent cemeteries. Berlin South-Western was one of those chosen and in 1924-25, graves were brought into the cemetery from 146 burial grounds in eastern Germany.

BERNAFAY WOOD BRITISH CEMETERY, MONTAUBAN
BERNAFAY WOOD BRITISH CEMETERY is 10 kms east of Albert and 2 kms south of Longueval.

The Bois De Bernafay is a pear-shaped wood close to the east end of Montauban village. It was taken on 3rd and 4th July 1916, lost on 25th March 1918, in the retreat to the Ancre, but finally regained 27th August.

The cemetery was begun by a dressing station in August 1916 and used as a front-line cemetery until the following April. It contained at the Armistice 284 burials but was then increased when graves were brought in from Bernafay Wood North Cemetery and from the battlefields immediately east of the wood.

BEAUMONT-HAMEL BRITISH CEMETERY
Beaumont-Hamel is a village 10 kms north of Albert. It was attacked and reached on 1st July 1916, but it could not be held. It was attacked again, and this time taken, on 13th November 1916, and the British cemetery (originally titled as 'V Corps Cemetery No. 23') was made by units taking part in that and subsequent operations until February 1917. It was increased after the Armistice when graves were brought in from the surrounding battlefields.

BEAURAIN BRITISH CEMETERY
Beaurain (not to be confused with Beaurains near Arras) is a village in the Department of the Nord 19 kms south of Valenciennes and 4 kms from Solesmes railway station. It was captured by the 5th Division on 23rd October, 1918; the British Cemetery was made in the fortnight after the capture of the village.

BETHUNE TOWN CEMETERY
Bethune is a town 29 kms north of Arras.

For much of the First World War, Bethune was comparatively free from bombardment and remained an important railway and hospital centre, as well as a corps and divisional headquarters. The 33rd Casualty Clearing Station was in the town until December 1917. Early in 1918, Bethune began to suffer from constant shell fire and in April 1918, German forces reached Locon, five kms to the north. The bombardment of 21st May did great damage to the town and it was not till October that pressure from the Germans was relaxed.

BINFIELD CEMETERY
The cemetery is situated in Church Lane, to the east of All Saints Church. There are two WWI graves in the cemetery.

BLEUET FARM CEMETERY
The cemetery is located to the northwest of the town of Ieper near a village called Elverdinge. Bleuet Farm was used as a dressing station during the 1917 Allied offensive on this front. The cemetery was begun in a corner of the farm and was in use from June to December 1917, though a few of the burials are of later date. Two graves were brought into the cemetery after the Armistice from isolated positions close by.

BOULOGNE EASTERN CEMETERY

Boulogne Eastern Cemetery, one of the town cemeteries, lies in the district of St Martin Boulogne, just beyond the eastern (Chateau) corner of the Citadel (Haute-Ville).

Boulogne was one of the three base ports most extensively used by the Commonwealth armies on the Western Front throughout the First World War. It was closed and cleared on 27th August 1914 when the Allies were forced to fall back ahead of the German advance, but was opened again in October, and from that month to the end of the war, Boulogne and Wimereux formed one of the chief hospital areas. Until June 1918, the dead from the hospitals at Boulogne itself were buried in the CIMETIERE DE L'EST, one of the town cemeteries, the Commonwealth graves forming a long, narrow strip along the right hand edge of the cemetery. In the spring of 1918, it was found that space was running short in the Eastern Cemetery in spite of repeated extensions to the south, and the site of the new cemetery at Terlincthun was chosen.

BOUZINCOURT RIDGE CEMETERY, ALBERT

Bouzincourt is a village 3 kms north-west of Albert on the D938 road to Doullens.

The village remained partly in German hands after the battles of March 1918. It was attacked at the end of June 1918, and cleared in the latter half of August. In the first week of September, nearby the battlefields were cleared and after the Armistice, 500 further graves were brought in from the immediate neighbourhood.

BOVES EAST COMMUNAL CEMETERY

Boves is a village in the Department of the Somme, 9.7 kms from Villers-Bretonneux.

Boves has two communal cemeteries, on either side of the river. The 49th Casualty Clearing Station was at Boves from 23rd April to the end of August 1918 and the 1st Canadian and 4th Canadian during August 1918. The burials in the two communal cemeteries and the extension to the West cemetery are mainly those of soldiers who died in the three hospitals.
BOVES EAST COMMUNAL CEMETERY contains 15 Commonwealth burials of the First World War.
BOVES WEST COMMUNAL CEMETERY contains 51 Commonwealth burials of the First World War and 12 French graves.
BOVES WEST COMMUNAL CEMETERY EXTENSION was made in August 1918 and after the Armistice, 32 graves were brought into it from Boves Military Cemetery.

BRACKNELL (LARGES LANE) CEMETERY

Larges Lane runs behind the Bracknell and Wokingham College and is accessed from the westbound carriageway of London Road, just east of the Met Office roundabout. The cemetery lies to the left on the bend just past Bracknell Football Club.

BRANDHOEK NEW MILITARY CEMETERY

Brandhoek New Military Cemetery is located 6.5 km west of Ieper town centre, on the Zevekotestraat.

During the First World War, Brandhoek was within the area comparatively safe from shell fire, which extended beyond Vlamertinghe Church. Field ambulances were posted there continuously.

Until July 1917 burials had been made in the Military Cemetery, but the arrival of three Casualty Clearing Stations in preparation for the new Allied offensive launched that month made it necessary to open the New Military Cemetery, followed in August by the New Military Cemetery No 3.

BRAY MILITARY CEMETERY

Bray-sur-Somme is a village about 9 kms south-east of Albert.

The cemetery was begun in April 1916 by fighting units and field ambulances. In September 1916, the front line having been pushed further east, it was used by the XIV Corps Main Dressing Station and in 1917, three Casualty Clearing Stations came forward and used it. In March 1918, the village and the cemetery fell into German hands, but were retaken by the 40th Australian Battalion on 24th August, and during the next few days the cemetery was used again. After the Armistice graves were brought in from the battlefields immediately north and south of the village and in 1924, further isolated graves were brought in.

BROOKWOOD MILITARY CEMETERY

The main entrance to BROOKWOOD MILITARY CEMETERY is on the A324 from the village of Pirbright, Surrey.

BROOKWOOD MILITARY CEMETERY is owned by the Commission and is the largest Commonwealth war cemetery in the United Kingdom, covering approximately 37 acres.

In 1917, an area of land in Brookwood Cemetery (The London Necropolis) was set aside for the burial of men and women of the forces of the Commonwealth and Americans, who had died, many of battle wounds, in the London district.

BUCQUOY ROAD CEMETERY, FICHEUX

BUCQUOY ROAD CEMETERY is situated on the D919 heading south from Arras to Ayette.

In November 1916, the village of Ficheux was behind the German front line, but by April 1917, the German withdrawal had taken the line considerably east of the village and in April and May, the VII Corps Main Dressing Station was posted near for the Battles of Arras. It was followed by the 20th and 43rd Casualty Clearing Stations, which remained at Boisleux-au-Mont until March 1918, and continued to use the BUCQUOY ROAD CEMETERY begun by the field ambulances. From early April to early August 1918 the cemetery was not used but in September and October, the 22nd, 30th, and 33rd Casualty Clearing Stations came to Boisleux-au-Mont and extended it. By the date of the Armistice, it contained 1,166 burials but was greatly increased when graves were brought in from the surrounding battlefields and from small cemeteries in the neighbourhood.

BUSIGNY COMMUNAL CEMETERY EXTENSION

Busigny is a village about 10 kms south-west of Le Cateau and 24 kms north-east of St. Quentin. It was captured by the 30th American Division and British cavalry on 9th October 1918, in the Battle of Cambrai, and in the course of the next two months three Casualty Clearing Stations came successively to the village. The majority of the burials were made from these three hospitals. The cemetery extension was begun in October 1918, and used until February 1919.

After the Armistice it was enlarged when graves were brought in from a wide area between Cambrai and Guise.

BUZANCY MILITARY CEMETERY

Buzancy is a village in the Department of the Aisne, 7 kms south of Soissons and 50 kms west of Reims, Northern France.

Buzancy was reached (though not held) by the 1st American Division on 21st July, 1918, after an advance begun on the 18th. It was attacked on the 23rd July, and taken on the 28th.

The Military Cemetery was made beside a French Military Cemetery from which the graves have been removed to Ambleny; and the original graves contain 96 burials. After the Armistice, graves were brought in from the surrounding battlefields.

CABARET-ROUGE BRITISH CEMETERY, SOUCHEZ

Souchez is a village 3.5 kms north of Arras on the main road to Bethune.

Caberet Rouge was a small, red-bricked, red-tiled café that stood close to this site in the early days of the First World War. The café was destroyed by shellfire in March 1915, but it gave its unusual name to this sector and to a communication trench that led troops up the front-line. Commonwealth soldiers began burying their fallen comrades here in March 1916. It was greatly enlarged in the years after the war when as many as 7,000 graves were concentrated here from over one hundred other cemeteries in the area. For much of the twentieth century, Cabaret Rouge served as one of a small number of 'open cemeteries' at which the remains of fallen servicemen newly discovered in the region were buried. Today the cemetery contains over 7,650 burials of the First World War, over half of which remain unidentified.

CAIX BRITISH CEMETERY

The village of Caix is situated about 28 kms south-east of Amiens.

Caix was occupied by Commonwealth troops in March 1917, lost during the German advance in March 1918, and recaptured on 8th August 1918 by the Canadian Corps.

CAIX BRITISH CEMETERY (called at first Caix New British Cemetery) was made after the Armistice when graves (mainly of March and August 1918) were brought in from the battlefields and from other smaller cemeteries.

CAMBRAI EAST MILITARY CEMETERY

Cambrai is a town about 32 kms south-east of Arras on the main straight road to Le Cateau. It was occupied by German forces on 26th August 1914, and it remained in German hands until 9th October 1918. The Battle of Cambrai in 1917 left the Allied line still five miles from the city on the southwest side, and the German offensive of March 1918, drove it far to the west, but the Battle of Cambrai in 1918, the last of the Battles of the Hindenburg Line, delivered the very badly hit city into the hands of Commonwealth forces. Two Casualty Clearing Stations were later posted to the town. CAMBRAI EAST MILITARY CEMETERY was made by the Germans during their occupation and laid out with the greatest care, with monuments erected in it to the French, Commonwealth and German dead. On 11th August 1918, as an inscription in the cemetery records, the Bavarian Commandant handed over to the city the care and maintenance of the cemetery.

The graves have now been regrouped, including those brought from the battlefields east and south of the city, as well as graves of Commonwealth prisoners.

CAMBRAI MEMORIAL, LOUVERVAL

The small village of Louverval is on the north side of the D930, Bapaume to Cambrai road.

The Memorial stands on a terrace in LOUVERVAL MILITARY CEMETERY, and commemorates more than 7,000 servicemen of the United Kingdom and South Africa who died in the Battle of Cambrai in November and December 1917 and whose graves are not known.

CAMBRIN CHURCHYARD EXTENSION

Cambrin is a village about 24 kms north of Arras and about 8 kms east of Bethune, on the road to La Bassee.

At one time, the village of Cambrin housed Brigade Headquarters, but until the end of the First World War, it was only about 800 metres from the front line trenches. The village contains two cemeteries used for Commonwealth burials; the churchyard extension, taken over from French troops in May 1915, and the Military Cemetery "behind the Mayor's House."

The churchyard extension was used for front line burials until February 1917 when it was closed, but there are three graves of 1918 in the back rows. The extension is remarkable for the very large numbers of graves grouped by battalion, all dating from 25th September 1915, the first day of the Battle of Loos.

CANADIAN CEMETERY NO 2, NEUVILLE-ST, VAAST

Neuville-St. Vaast is a village about 6 kms north of Arras and 1 kilometre east of the main road from Arras to Bethune.

The cemetery was established by the Canadian Corps after the successful storming of Vimy Ridge on 9th April, 1917, and some of those buried in the cemetery fell in that battle or died of wounds received there, though the majority of the graves were made later for the burial of the dead recovered from surrounding battlefields and from isolated graves which were transferred into the cemetery over a period of years after the Armistice.

CHATBY MEMORIAL

Chatby is a district on the eastern side of the city of Alexandria. The CHATBY MEMORIAL is situated within CHATBY WAR MEMORIAL CEMETERY which is located centrally within the main Alexandria cemetery complex.

In March 1915, the base of the Mediterranean Expeditionary Force was transferred to Alexandria from Mudros, and the city became a camp and hospital centre for Commonwealth and French troops. After the Gallipoli campaign of 1915, Alexandria remained an important hospital centre during later operations in Egypt and Palestine, and the port was much used by hospital ships and troop transports bringing reinforcements and carrying the sick and wounded out of the theatres of war.

The CHATBY MEMORIAL stands at the eastern end of the ALEXANDRIA (CHATBY) WAR MEMORIAL CEMETERY and commemorates almost 1,000 Commonwealth servicemen who died during the First World War and have no other grave but the sea. Many of them were lost when hospital ships or transports were sunk in the Mediterranean, sailing to or from Alexandria. Others died of wounds or sickness while aboard such vessels and were buried at sea.

More than 700 of those commemorated on the memorial died when their vessels were topedoed or mined. Officers and men of the merchant services lost in these incidents are commemorated on appropriate memorials elsewhere.

CHATHAM NAVAL MEMORIAL

The Memorial overlooks the town of Chatham and is approached by a steep path from the Town Hall Gardens.

After the First World War, an appropriate way had to be found of commemorating those members of the Royal Navy who had no known grave, the majority of deaths having occurred at sea where no permanent memorial could be provided.

An Admiralty committee recommended that the three manning ports in Great Britain - Chatham, Plymouth and Portsmouth - should each have an identical memorial of unmistakable naval form, an obelisk, which would serve as a leading mark for shipping. The Chatham Naval Memorial was unveiled by the Prince of Wales (the future King Edward VIII) on 26th April 1924.

CHAUNY COMMUNAL CEMETERY BRITISH EXTENSION

Chauny is a commune 35 kms west of Laon. The Cemetery Extension was made after the Armistice for the burial of remains brought in from the battlefields of the Aisne and from the smaller cemeteries in the surrounding countryside; the majority of them having died in 1918 and most of the rest in September 1914.

CHESTER FARM CEMETERY

Chester Farm Cemetery is located 5 kms south of Ieper town centre, on the Vaartstraat.

Chester Farm was the name given to a farm about 1 km south of Blauwepoort Farm, on the road from Zillebeke to Voormezeele. The cemetery was begun in March 1915 and was used by front line troops until November 1917.

CHOCQUES MILITARY CEMETERY

Chocques is 4 kms north-west of Bethune on the road to Lillers.

Chocques was occupied by Commonwealth forces from the late autumn of 1914 to the end of the war. The village was at one time the headquarters of I Corps and from January 1915 to April 1918, No.1 Casualty Clearing Station was posted there. Most of the burials from this period are of casualties who died at the clearing station from wounds received at the Bethune front. From April to September 1918, during the German advance on this front, the burials were carried out by field ambulances, divisions and fighting units.

After the Armistice it was found necessary to concentrate into this Cemetery a large number of isolated graves plus some small graveyards from the country between Chocques and Bethune.

COJEUL BRITISH CEMETERY, ST MARTIN-SUR-COJEUL

St. Martin-sur-Cojeul is a village about 8 kms south-south-east of Arras on the D33.

The village of St. Martin-sur-Cojeul was taken by the 30th Division on 9th April 1917, lost in March 1918, and retaken in the following August.

COJEUL BRITISH CEMETERY was begun in April 1917, and used by fighting units until the following October. It was very severely damaged in later fighting.

COLCHESTER CEMETERY

Colchester Cemetery was opened in 1856 and now belongs to the Corporation. There are 266 Commonwealth burials of the 1914-1918 war. After the war a Cross of Sacrifice was erected on a site overlooking both the plot and the group of war graves, in honour of all the servicemen buried here.

COLOGNE SOUTHERN CEMETERY

The city of Cologne lies in the west of Germany, approx 30kms to the north of Bonn.

More than 1,000 Allied prisoners and dozens of German servicemen were buried in COLOGNE SOUTHERN CEMETERY during the First World War. Commonwealth forces entered Cologne on 6th December 1918, less than a month after the Armistice, and the city was occupied under the terms of the Treaty of Versailles until January 1926. During this period the cemetery was used by the occupying garrison. In 1922, it was decided that the graves of Commonwealth servicemen who had died all over Germany should be brought together into four permanent cemeteries at Kassel, Berlin, Hamburg and Cologne. Over the course of the following year, graves were transferred to Cologne Southern Cemetery from over 180 different burial grounds in Hanover, Hessen, the Rhine and Westphalia.

COMBLES COMMUNITY CEMETERY EXTENSION

The large village of Combles is 16 kms east of Albert and 13 kms south of Bapaume.

It was entered on 26th August 1916, and remained in Allied occupation until the 24th March 1918, when the place was captured by the Germans. It was retaken on the 29th August 1918. The cemetery was begun in October 1916, by French troops, but the 94 French graves made in 1916 have been removed to another cemetery. The first British burials took place in December, 1916. From March 1917, to the end of May 1918, the Extension was not used. During the next three months, 194 German soldiers were buried but these graves, too, have been removed; and in August and September further burials were made by the 18th Division. After the Armistice almost one thousand graves from the battlefields in the neighbourhood were brought in.

CORBIE COMMUNAL CEMETERY EXTENSION

Corbie is a small town 15 kms east of Amiens.

Corbie was about 20 kms behind the front when Commonwealth forces took over the line from Berles-au-Bois southward to the Somme in July 1915. The town immediately became a medical centre, with Nos 5 and 21 Casualty Clearing Stations based at La Neuville until October 1916 and April 1917 respectively. In November 1916, the front moved east, but the German advance in the Spring of 1918 came within 10 kms of the town, and brought with it field ambulances of the 47th Division and the 12th Australian Field Ambulance.

The communal cemetery was used for burials until May 1916, when the plot set aside was filled and the extension opened. The majority of the graves in the extension are of officers and men who died of wounds in the 1916 Battle of the Somme. The remainder relate to the fighting of 1918.

COUIN NEW BRITISH CEMETERY

Couin is a village 15 kms east of Doullens.

Couin Chateau was used as a divisional headquarters from 1915 to 1918. The BRITISH CEMETERY was begun in May 1916 by the field ambulances of the 48th (South Midland) Division, and was used by units and field ambulances during the Battle of the Somme in 1916. It was closed at the end of January 1917 because further extension was not possible.

The NEW BRITISH CEMETERY was opened across the road and was used by field ambulances from January 1917 (with a long interval in 1917-18) to the end of the war.

COURCELETTE BRITISH CEMETERY

Courcelette is a village some 10 kms north-east of the town of Albert, just off the D929 road to Bapaume.

The commune and the village of Courcelette were the scene of very heavy fighting and taken on 15th September 1916. It was destroyed by German artillery after its capture and remained very close to the front line until the German retreat in the following spring.

The cemetery was begun in November 1916 (as Mouquet Road or Sunken Road Cemetery), and used until March 1917. The original 74 burials are now parts of Plot I, Rows A to F. On 25th March 1918, Courcelette passed into German hands, but was retaken on 24th August. The cemetery was greatly enlarged after the Armistice when almost 2,000 graves were brought in, mostly those of men who died around Courcelette and Pozieres in 1916.

COXYDE MILITARY CEMETERY

Coxyde Military Cemetery is located approximately 500 metres beyond the village of Koksijde.

In June 1917, Commonwealth forces relieved French forces on 6 kms of front line from the sea to a point south of Nieuport (now Nieuwpoort), and held this sector for six months. Coxyde (now Koksijde) was about 10 kms behind the front line. The village was used for rest billets and was occasionally shelled, but the cemetery, which had been started by French troops, was found to be reasonably safe. It became the most important of the Commonwealth cemeteries on the Belgian coast and was used at night for the burial of the dead brought back from the front line.

The French returned to the sector in December 1917 and continued to use the cemetery, and during 1918, Commonwealth naval casualties from bases in Dunkirk (now Dunkerque) were buried there. After the Armistice, the remains of 44 British soldiers were brought into the cemetery. Ten of them had been buried in isolated graves.

CRANBOURNE (ST PETER) CHURCHYARD

The churchyard surrounds the church in Hatchet Lane. There are five WWI graves.

CROISILLES BRITISH CEMETERY

Croisilles is a village about 13 kms south-east of Arras.

Croisilles was taken on 2nd April 1917, lost on 21st March 1918 and recaptured on the following 28th August, after heavy fighting.

Plots I and II of the cemetery, were made between April 1917 and March 1918, and the rest was formed after the Armistice when graves were brought in from the neighbouring battlefields and from some smaller burial grounds.

CROUY-VAUXROT FRENCH NATIONAL CEMETERY, CROUY

Crouy is a village in the Department of the Aisne, 4 kms north-east of Soissons on the road to Laon.

There are now fifty WWI war casualties commemorated in this site. Of these, nearly half are unidentified, and special memorials are erected to ten soldiers who are believed to be among them. All were brought in after the Armistice and fell in September and October, 1914.

CROWTHORNE (ST JOHN THE BAPTIST) CHURCHYARD

The churchyard surrounds the church which is situated in Church Road, Crowthorne.

DANTZIG ALLEY BRITISH CEMETERY, MAMETZ

Mametz is a village about 8 kms east of the town of Albert.

It was carried by the 7th Division on 1st July 1916, the first day of the Battle of the Somme, after very hard fighting at Dantzig Alley (a German trench) and other points. The cemetery was begun later in the same month and was used by field ambulances and fighting units until the following November. The ground was lost during the great German advance in March 1918, but regained in August, and a few graves were added to the cemetery in August and September 1918. At the Armistice, the cemetery consisted of 183 graves, but it was then very greatly increased by graves (almost all of 1916) brought in from the battlefields north and east of Mametz and from other smaller burial grounds,

DELHI WAR CEMETERY AND DELHI 1914-18 MEMORIAL

DELHI WAR CEMETERY was created in 1951 when graves from many cemeteries in northern India were moved into the site to ensure their permanent maintenance. Among them are graves from cantonment cemeteries in Allahabad, Cawnpore, Dehra Dun and Lucknow. It also contains the DELHI 1914-18 MEMORIAL, commemorating 153 casualties buried in Meerut Cantonment Cemetery, where their graves could no longer be maintained.

DELSAUX FARM CEMETERY, BEUGNY

This cemetery is near the village of Beugny, 19 kms south-west of Cambrai on the Bapaume-Cambrai road (RN30).

Delsaux Farm was a point on the German defensive system known as the Beugny-Ytres line, which was reached by Commonwealth troops on 18th March 1917, and passed on the following day. The farm was lost on 23rd March 1918, but it was retaken on 2nd September 1918, and on the next day the same division occupied Beugny village.

After their advance in March 1918, the Germans made a cemetery (Beugny Military Cemetery No.18) at the cross-roads, and in it buried 103 Commonwealth and 82 German dead. The site was extended in October - November 1918 by two Casualty Clearing Stations, which came to Delsaux Farm and made the present cemetery. A little later, the German graves of March 1918 were removed and the 103 Commonwealth dead reburied. The rest of the cemetery was made when graves were later brought in from the battlefield.

DELVILLE WOOD CEMETERY, LONGUEVAL

The cemetery is on the east side of Longueval, a village 11 kms east of Albert.

Delville Wood was a tract of woodland, nearly 1 kilometre square, the western edge of which touched the village. On 14th July 1916, the greater part of Longueval was taken, and most of

Delville Wood on the following day. The wood now formed a salient in the line, with Waterlot Farm and Mons Wood on the south flank still in German hands, and, owing to the height of the trees, no close artillery support was possible for defence. Battles for control ebbed and flowed until the beginning of August, but it was then held until the end of April 1918 when it was lost during the German advance, but retaken on the following 28th August. DELVILLE WOOD CEMETERY was made after the Armistice, when graves were brought in from a few small cemeteries and isolated sites, and from the battlefields. Almost all of the burials date from July, August and September 1916.

DERNANCOURT COMMUNAL CEMETERY EXTENSION

Dernancourt is a village 3 kms south of Albert.

Field ambulances used the Communal Cemetery for Commonwealth burials from September 1915 to August 1916, and again during the German advance of March 1918. It contains 127 Commonwealth burials of the First World War. The XV Corps Main Dressing Station was formed at Dernancourt in August 1916, when the adjoining EXTENSION was opened. Five further Casualty Clearing Stations came over the next two years, but on 26th March 1918, Dernancourt was evacuated ahead of the German advance, and the extension remained in their hands until the village was recaptured on 9th August 1918. In September it was again used by Casualty Clearing Stations under the name of "Edgehill", due to the rising ground on the north-west.

At the Armistice, the Extension contained more than 1,700 burials; it was then enlarged when graves were brought in from isolated positions in the immediate neighbourhood and other small cemeteries.

DICKEBUSCH NEW MILITARY CEMETERY EXTENSION

From Ieper town centre the Dikkebusseweg (N375), is reached via Elverdingsestraat.

The New Military Cemetery was begun in February 1915, and was used until May 1917 by fighting units and field ambulances, with a few further burials taking place in March and April 1918. The Extension was used from May 1917 to January 1918.

DOIRAN MILITARY CEMETERY AND DOIRAN MEMORIAL

THE DOIRAN MEMORIAL stands near DOIRAN MILITARY CEMETERY, which is situated in the north of Greece close to the Yugoslav frontier and near the south-east shore of Lake Doiran.

The DOIRAN MEMORIAL stands roughly in the centre of the line occupied for two years by the Allies in Macedonia, but close to the western end, which was held by Commonwealth forces. It marks the scene of the fierce fighting of 1917-1918, which caused the majority of the Commonwealth battle casualties.

From October 1915 to the end of November 1918, the British Salonika Force suffered some 2,800 deaths in action, 1,400 from wounds and 4,200 from sickness. The campaign afforded few successes for the Allies, and none of any importance until the last two months. The action of the Commonwealth force was hampered throughout by widespread and unavoidable sickness, and by continual diplomatic and personal differences with neutrals or Allies. On one front there was a wide malarial river valley and on the other, difficult mountain ranges, and many of the roads and railways it required had to be specially constructed.

The memorial serves the dual purpose of Battle Memorial of the British Salonika Force (for which a large sum of money was subscribed by the officers and men of that force), and place of commemoration for more than 2,000 Commonwealth servicemen who died in Macedonia and whose graves are not known.

The memorial stands near DOIRAN MILITARY CEMETERY. The cemetery (originally known as Colonial Hill Cemetery No.2) was formed at the end of 1916 as a cemetery for the Doiran front. The graves largely reflect the fighting of April and May 1917 (the attacks on the Petit-Couronne), and 18-19th September 1918 (the attacks on Pip Ridge and the Grand-Couronne). In October and November 1918, after the final advance, a few burials were added by the 25th Casualty Clearing Station.

After the Armistice, graves were brought into the cemetery from the battlefields and from some small burial grounds nearby.

DON COMMUNAL CEMETERY, ANNOEULLIN
Don is a town and commune in the Department of the Nord, 12 kms south-west of Lille.

Annoeullin was held by the Germans from an early date in the War until shortly before the Armistice. No.15 Casualty Clearing Station came to Don on the 25th October 1918, and remained until the 19th January 1919, and No. 32 came at the end of November and left at the end of December. From these two hospitals, soldiers were buried in Don Communal Cemetery, and later a number of bodies were brought in from the neighbouring fields.

DOVER (ST. JAMES'S) CEMETERY
During the First World War, Dover was a port of embarkation for troops bound for the Western Front and between August 1914 and August 1919, some 1,300,000 Commonwealth sick and wounded were landed there. The port was bombed in 1915 and again in August 1916.

There are 373 identified burials of the 1914-1918 war here. In addition there are 19 unidentified burials, 9 of whom can be named as victims of the Zeebrugge Raid, and these 9 are inscribed on a Special Memorial on the Cross of Sacrifice in the Zeebrugge Plot.

DOULLENS COMMUNAL CEMETERY EXTENSION NO 1
Doullens is a town in the Department of the Somme, approximately 30 kms north of Amiens on the N25 road to Arras.

Doullens was Marshal Foch's headquarters early in the First World War, and the scene of the conference in March 1918, after which he assumed command of the Allied armies on the Western Front. From the summer of 1915 to March 1916, the town was a junction between the French Tenth Army on the Arras front and the Commonwealth Third Army on the Somme. The citadel, overlooking the town from the south, was a French military hospital, and the railhead was used by both armies. In March 1916, Commonwealth forces succeeded the French on the Arras front, and five Casualty Clearing Stations came to Doullens at various times during the remainder of the War. From February 1916 to April 1918, these medical units continued to bury in the French extension (No 1) of the communal cemetery. In March and April 1918, the German advance and the desperate fighting on this front threw a severe strain on the Canadian Stationary Hospital in the town. The extension was filled, and a second extension begun on the opposite side of the communal cemetery.

DOZINGHEM MILITARY CEMETERY

The cemetery is located to the north-west of Poperinge near Krombeke.

Westvleteren was outside the front held by Commonwealth forces in Belgium during the First World War, but in July 1917, in readiness for the forthcoming offensive, groups of casualty clearing stations were placed at three positions, called by the troops Mendinghem, Dozinghem and Bandaghem.

Three Casualty Clearing Stations were posted at Dozinghem and the military cemetery was used by them until early in 1918.

DUD CORNER CEMETERY, LOOS

Loos-en-Gohelle is a village 5 kms north-west of Lens.

The name "Dud Corner" is believed to be due to the large number of unexploded enemy shells found in the neighbourhood after the Armistice. Only burials were made here during hostilities, the remainder of the graves were brought in later from isolated positions near Loos and to the North, and other small cemeteries.

DUHALLOW A.D.S. CEMETERY

The Cemetery is located on the Diksmuidseweg, N369 road, in the direction of Boezinge. Duhallow Advanced Dressing Station, believed to have been named after a southern Irish hunt, was a medical post 1.6 kms north of Ypres (now Ieper). The cemetery was begun in July 1917 and in October and November 1918, it was used by the 11th, 36th, and 44th Casualty Clearing Stations.

The cemetery contains many graves of the artillery and engineers and 41 men of the 13th Company Labour Corps, killed when a German aircraft dropped a bomb on an ammunition truck in January 1918. After the Armistice, the cemetery was enlarged when graves were brought into this cemetery from isolated sites and a number of small cemeteries on the battlefields around Ypres. Special memorials commemorate a number of casualties known to have been buried in two of these cemeteries, whose graves were destroyed by shellfire.

DUISANS BRITISH CEMETARY, ETRUN

Duisans and Etrun are villages in the Department of the Pas-de-Calais, about 9 kms west of Arras.

The area around Duisans was occupied by Commonwealth forces from March 1916, but it was not until February 1917 that the site of this cemetery was selected for the 8th Casualty Clearing Station. The first burials took place in March and from the beginning of April the cemetery grew very quickly. Most of the graves relate to the Battles of Arras in 1917, and the trench warfare that followed. From May to August 1918, the cemetery was used by divisions and smaller fighting units for burials from the front line. In the autumn of 1918, three Clearing Stations remained at Duisans for two months, while a fourth was there from November 1918 to November 1920.

DURY CRUCIFIX CEMETERY

Dury is a village about 17 kms east-south-east of Arras. The cemetery was begun by Canadian units immediately after the capture of the village, and contained 72 graves at the Armistice.

It was then enlarged by the concentration of graves from the battlefields of April and May 1917, and March, August and September 1918, north and west of Dury.

EASTHAMPSTEAD (SS MICHAEL AND MARY MAGDALENE) CHURCHYARD

The churchyard surrounds the church which is located on the north side of Crowthorne Road, opposite Church Hill House. Most of the War graves are on the north side of the church, with the exception of one to the west.

EAST MUDROS MILITARY CEMETERY

The Cemetery is on the Greek island of Limnos (Lemnos) in the northeast Aegean Sea.

Because of its position, the island of Lemnos played an important part in the campaigns against Turkey during the First World War. It was occupied by a force of marines on 23rd February 1915 in preparation for the military attack on Gallipoli, and Mudros became a considerable Allied camp. The 1st and 3rd Canadian Stationary Hospitals, the 3rd Australian General Hospital, and other medical units were stationed on both sides of Mudros Bay, and a considerable Egyptian Labour Corps detachment was employed. After the evacuation of Gallipoli, a garrison remained on the island and the 1st Royal Naval Brigade was on Lemnos, Imbros and Tenedos for the first few months of 1916. On 30th October 1918, the Armistice between the Entente Powers and Turkey was signed at Mudros.

EAST MUDROS MILITARY CEMETERY was begun in April 1915 and used until September 1919.

EBBLINGHEM MILITARY CEMETERY

Ebblinghem is a village halfway between St. Omer and Hazebrouck.

The cemetery was begun by the 2nd and 15th Casualty Clearing Stations, who came to Ebblinghem in April 1918 at the beginning of the German offensive, and used the cemetery until July. Further graves were added after the war from nearby cemeteries.

EPEHY WOOD FARM CEMETERY, EPEHY

Epehy is a village between Cambrai and Peronne about 18 kms north-east of Peronne.

The village was captured at the beginning of April 1917. It was lost on 22nd March 1918 and retaken (in the Battle of Epehy) on 18th September 1918.

The cemetery takes its name from the Ferme du Bois, a little to the east. Graves mainly date from the capture of the village in September 1918 and also after the Armistice when graves were brought in from the battlefields surrounding Epehy and smaller nearby cemeteries.

ERQUELINNES COMMUNAL CEMETERY

Erquelinnes is located 21 kms south east of Mons.

ERQUELINNES COMMUNAL CEMETERY contains 67 Commonwealth burials of the First World War, all of which were made by the Germans in October and November 1918.

ESQUELBECQ MILITARY CEMETERY

Esquelbecq is a village near the Belgian frontier, 24 kms north of Hazebrouck, and the same distance south of Dunkirk.

The cemetery was opened in April 1918 during the early stages of the German offensive in Flanders, when the 2nd Canadian and 3rd Australian Casualty Clearing Stations came to Esquelbecq. It was closed in September 1918.

ESSEX FARM CEMETERY

Boezinge is a village in the province of West Flanders, north of Ieper on the Diksmuidseweg road (N369).

The land south of Essex Farm was used as a dressing station cemetery from April 1915 to August 1917. The burials were made without definite plan, and some of the divisions which occupied this sector may be traced in almost every part of the cemetery.

ETAPLES MILITARY CEMETERY

Etaples is a town about 27 kms south of Boulogne.

During the First World War, the area around Etaples was the scene of immense concentrations of Commonwealth reinforcement camps and hospitals. It was remote from attack, except from aircraft, and accessible by railway from both the northern and the southern battlefields. In 1917, 100,000 troops were camped among the sand dunes and the hospitals, which included eleven general, one stationary, four Red Cross hospitals, and a convalescent depot, could deal with 22,000 wounded or sick. In September 1919, ten months after the Armistice, three hospitals and the Q.M.A.A.C. convalescent depot remained.

The cemetery is the largest in France under the Commission.

EUSTON ROAD CEMETERY, COLINCAMPS

Colincamps is a village 11 kms north of Albert. Colincamps and "Euston", a road junction a little east of the village, were within the Allied lines before the Somme offensive of July 1916. The cemetery was started as a front line burial ground during and after the unsuccessful attack on Serre on 1st July, but after the German withdrawal to the Hindenburg Line in March 1917, it was scarcely used. It was briefly in German hands towards the end of March 1918, when it marked the limit of the German advance, but the line was held and pushed forward by the New Zealand Division allowing the cemetery to be used again for burials in April and May 1918. The cemetery is particularly associated with three dates and engagements; the attack on Serre on 1st July 1916; the capture of Beaumont-Hamel on 13th November 1916; and the German attack on the 3rd New Zealand (Rifle) Brigade trenches before Colincamps on 5th April 1918. After the Armistice, more than 750 graves were brought in from small cemeteries in the neighbouring communes and the battlefields.

FAUBOURG D'AMIENS CEMETERY, ARRAS

Faubourg-d'Amiens Cemetery is in the western part of the town of Arras in the Boulevard du General de Gaulle, near the Citadel.

The French handed over Arras to Commonwealth forces in the spring of 1916, and the system of tunnels upon which the town is built were used and developed in preparation for the major offensive planned for April 1917. The Commonwealth section of the FAUBOURG D'AMIENS CEMETERY was begun in March 1916, behind the French military cemetery established earlier. It continued to be used by field ambulances and fighting units until November

1918. The cemetery was enlarged after the Armistice when graves were brought in from the battlefields and from two smaller cemeteries in the vicinity.

FAUQUISSART MILITARY CEMETERY, LAVENTIE

Fauquissart and Fleurbaix are hamlets of Laventie, a town near Armentieres in the Pas de Calais.

FAUQUISSART MILITARY CEMETERY was begun in November 1914 by the 2nd Royal Berks and the 2nd Rifle Brigade, and used until June 1915.

FERME BUTERNE MILITARY CEMETERY, HOUPLINES

Ferme Buterne Military Cemetery will be found 1 kilometre south-east of the village of Houplines.

Houplines was in Allied hands (but near the front line) from 17th October 1914, when it was taken by the 4th Division. It fell into German hands in April 1918 during their great advance, but was recovered in September. The village contained four Commonwealth cemeteries in addition to plots in the communal cemetery, but the graves were regrouped after the war and only two cemeteries remain.

FIFTEEN RAVINE BRITISH CEMETERY, VILLERS-PLOUICH

Villers-Plouich is a village about 13 kms south-west of Cambrai.

"Fifteen Ravine" was the name given by the Army to the shallow ravine, once bordered by fifteen trees, which ran at right angles to the railway about 800 metres south of the village of Villers-Plouich, but the cemetery is in fact in "Farm Ravine," on the east side of the railway line, nearer to the village.

The cemetery, sometimes called FARM RAVINE CEMETERY, was begun in April 1917, a few days after the capture of the ravine. It continued in use during the Battle of Cambrai (November 1917) and until March 1918, when the ravine formed the boundary between the Third and Fifth Armies. On 22nd March, the second day of the great German offensive, the ground passed into their hands after severe fighting, and it was not regained until the end of the following September.

In March 1918, the cemetery contained 107 graves, but it was greatly enlarged after the Armistice when graves were brought in from the battlefields south-west of Cambrai and other cemeteries.

FINS NEW BRITISH CEMETERY, SOREL-LE-GRAND

Fins is a village on the road between Cambrai and Peronne.

Fins and Sorel were occupied at the beginning of April 1917, in the German Retreat to the Hindenburg Line. They were lost on the 23rd March 1918, and regained in the following September.

The first British burials at Fins were carried out in the CHURCHYARD and the CHURCHYARD EXTENSION, and the NEW BRITISH CEMETERY was not begun until July 1917. It was used until March 1918, when it comprised about 590 graves; it was then used by the Germans, who added 255 burials, including 26 British. In September and October 1918, about 73 British soldiers were buried and the cemetery completed, by the concentration of 591 graves after Armistice from the surrounding battlefields and from other smaller cemeteries.

FLATIRON COPSE CEMETERY, MAMETZ

The cemetery is on the right hand side of D929, Amiens-Albert-Bapaume, 10 kms east of Albert. Flatiron Copse was the name given by the army to a small plantation a little to the east of Mametz Wood. The ground was taken on 14th July 1916, and an advanced dressing station was established at the copse. The cemetery was begun later that month, and it remained in use until April 1917. Two further burials were made in August 1918, and after the Armistice, more than 1,100 graves were brought in from the neighbouring battlefields and smaller cemeteries

FORT WILLIAM (ST. ANDREW) EPISCOPALIAN CHURCHYARD

This site is on the end of a pedestrian-only High Street.

The two WWI graves are west of the church.

FRETOY COMMUNAL CEMETERY

FRETOY COMMUNAL CEMETERY contains three Commonwealth burials from the First World War.

GAZA WAR CEMETERY

Gaza is 3 kms inland from the Mediterranean coast, 65 kms southwest of Tel Aviv.

Gaza was bombarded by French warships in April 1915. At the end of March 1917, it was attacked and surrounded by the Egyptian Expeditionary Force in the First Battle of Gaza, but the attack was broken off when Turkish reinforcements appeared. The Second Battle of Gaza, 17-19th April, left the Turks in possession, and the Third Battle of Gaza, begun on 27th October, ended with the capture of the ruined and deserted city on 7th November 1917. Casualty Clearing Stations arrived later that month, and General and Stationary hospitals in 1918.

Some of the earliest burials were made by the troops that captured the city. About two-thirds of the total were brought into the cemetery from the battlefields after the Armistice. The remainder were made by medical units after the Third Battle of Gaza, or, in some cases, represent reburials from the battlefields by the troops who captured the city.

GEZAINCOURT COMMUNAL CEMETERY EXTENSION

Gezaincourt is a village a little south-west of the town of Doullens.

The COMMUNAL CEMETERY at Gezaincourt contains nine Commonwealth burials of the First World War, made between October 1915 and March 1916

The adjoining EXTENSION was opened in March 1916 and used until March 1917, and again from March to October 1918. In most cases, the burials were carried out from casualty clearing stations and, in June to August 1918, from the 3rd Canadian Stationary Hospital.

GIAVERA BRITISH CEMETERY, ARCADE

Giavera is 12 kms east of Montebelluna and 20 kms west of Conegliano on the S248, the road that joins the two towns.

The Italians entered the war on the Allied side, declaring war on Austria, in May 1915. Commonwealth forces were at the Italian front between November 1917 and November 1918. On 4th December 1917, the XIth and XIVth British Corps relieved the Italians on the Montello sector of the Piave front. The Commonwealth troops on the sector were not involved in any large operations, but they carried out continuous patrol work across the River Piave, as well as much successful counter-battery work. In January 1918, an additional sector of the defence on the right was taken over by the Commonwealth troops. Between December and March, the Royal Flying Corps carried out a large number of successful raids on enemy aerodromes, railway junctions, and other objectives. Sixty-four hostile aeroplanes and nine balloons were destroyed during this period against British losses of twelve machines and three balloons. In March 1918, the Commonwealth troops on the Montello sector were relieved. On 4th November, the Armistice came into effect, and active hostilities ceased.

Men who died in defending the Piave from December 1917 to March 1918, and those who fell on the west of the river during the Passage of the Piave, are buried in this cemetery.

GLYMPTON CHURCHYARD, GLYMPTON, OXFORDSHIRE
Although one of the men listed on the Binfield War Memorial is buried in GLYMPTON CHURCHYARD, he did not die until 1923 and is therefore not classed as a War Grave.

GOMIECOURT SOUTH CEMETERY
Gomiecourt is a village in the Department of the Pas-de-Calais, 16 kms south of Arras and 6 kms north-west of Bapaume. It was captured on 23rd August 1918, and the cemetery made at the end of August 1918. Gomiecourt South Cemetery contains around two hundred Commonwealth burials of the First World War; 27 German burials form a separate plot on the south-west side.

GOMMECOURT BRITISH CEMETERY NO 2, HEBUTERNE
Gommecourt is a village 19 kms south-west of Arras.

Hebuterne village remained in Allied hands from March 1915 to the Armistice, although during the German advances of the summer of 1918, it was practically on the front line. Gommecourt and Gommecourt Wood were attacked on 1st July 1916, with only temporary success, but the village was occupied on the night of 27-28th February 1917, remaining in Allied hands until the Armistice. Gommecourt was later "adopted" by the County Borough of Wolverhampton.

GOMMECOURT BRITISH CEMETERIES NO. 1, NO. 2, NO. 3 and NO. 4 were made in 1917 when the battlefields were cleared.

GONNEHEM BRITISH CEMETERY
Gonnehem is a village about 7 kms north-west of Bethune and 7 kms east of Lillers.

The cemetery was begun in the middle of April 1918, when the German front line came within 3.2 kms of the village. It was used until September. After the Armistice graves were brought in from the battlefields east of Gonnehem.

GOUZEAUCOURT NEW BRITISH CEMETERY
Gouzeaucourt is a large village 15 kms southwest of Cambrai and 15 kms northeast of Peronne.

The village was captured on the night of 12-13th April 1917. It was lost on 30th November 1917 in the German counterattack at the end of the Battle of Cambrai, and recaptured the same day. It was lost again on 22nd March 1918, and finally retaken by the 21st Division on 8th October.

The cemetery was begun in November 1917, taken over by the Germans in 1918, and used again by Commonwealth forces in September and October 1918, but the original burials are only 55 in number. It was enlarged after the Armistice when graves were brought in from other cemeteries and from the battlefield of Cambrai.

GRANGEGORMAN MILITARY CEMETERY, DUBLIN

The cemetery is situated on Blackhorse Avenue, off Navan Rd, facing the wall of the Phoenix Park, and just up the road from McKee Barracks.

The cemetery was opened in 1876, and was used for the burial of British service personnel and their near relatives. It contains war graves from both World Wars. Some of the graves were re-located to this site at a later date. A Screen Wall Memorial of a simple design standing nearly two metres high and fifteen metres long has been built of Irish limestone to commemorate the names of those war casualties whose graves lie elsewhere in Ireland and can no longer be maintained. Arranged before this memorial are the headstones of the war dead, buried in Cork Military Cemetery, but now commemorated here.

GREEN HILL CEMETERY

Heading North from Anzac, you will encounter the cemetery after 17.6 kms on the right, adjacent to the track.

The eight month campaign in Gallipoli was fought by Commonwealth and French forces in an attempt to force Turkey out of the war, to relieve the deadlock of the Western Front in France and Belgium, and to open a supply route to Russia through the Dardanelles and the Black Sea.

The Allies landed on the peninsula on 25-26th April 1915; the 29th Division at Cape Helles in the south, and the Australian and New Zealand Corps north of Gaba Tepe on the west coast, an area soon known as Anzac. On 6th August, further troops were put ashore at Suvla, just north of Anzac, and the climax of the campaign came in early August when simultaneous assaults were launched on all three fronts. Green Hill and Chocolate Hill (which form together Yilghin Burnu), rise from the eastern shore of the salt lake. They were captured on 7th August 1915, but once taken, no further advance was then made. GREEN HILL CEMETERY was made after the Armistice when isolated graves were brought in from the battlefields of August 1915, and from small burial grounds in the surrounding area.

GREVILLERS BRITISH CEMETERY

Grevillers is a village in the Department of the Pas de Calais, 3 kms west of Bapaume.

The village was occupied by Commonwealth troops on 14th March 1917, and in April and May, three Casualty Clearing Stations were posted nearby. They began the cemetery and continued to use it until March 1918, when Grevillers was lost to the Germans during their great advance. On the following 24th August, the New Zealand Division recaptured Grevillers, and in September, another three Casualty Clearing Stations came to the village and used the cemetery again. After the Armistice, two hundred graves were brought in from the battlefields to the south of the village.

GROVE TOWN CEMETERY, MEAULTE

Meaulte is a village just south of Albert.

In September 1916, the 34th and 2/2nd London Casualty Clearing Stations were established at this point, known to the troops as Grove Town, to deal with casualties from the Somme battlefields. They were moved in April 1917 and, except for a few burials in August and September 1918, the cemetery was closed.

GUARDS CEMETERY, WINDY CORNER, CUINCHY

Cuinchy is a village about 7 kms east of the town of Bethune and north of the N41 which runs between Bethune and La Bassee.

A little west of the crossroads known to the army as 'Windy Corner', was a house used as a battalion headquarters and dressing station. The cemetery grew up beside this house. The original cemetery was begun in January 1915, and used extensively in and after February. It was closed at the end of May 1916, when it contained 681 graves. After the Armistice it was increased when more than 2,700 graves were brought in from the neighbouring battlefields - in particular the battlefields of Neuve-Chapelle, the Aubers Ridge and Festubert - and from certain smaller cemeteries.

HAIDAR PASHA CEMETERY AND HAIDAR PASHA MEMORIAL

Haidar Pasha is a suburb of Istanbul between Scutari (Uskudar) and Kadikoy on the Asiatic side of the Bosphorous.

The HAIDAR PASHA MEMORIAL stands within the war graves plot of HAIDAR PASHA CEMETERY, and commemorates more than thirty Commonwealth servicemen of the First World War who died fighting in South Russia, Georgia and Azerbaijan, and in post-Armistice operations in Russia and Transcaucasia, whose graves are not known. An Addenda panel was later added to commemorate over 170 Commonwealth casualties who are buried in cemeteries in South Russia and Transcaucasia whose graves can longer be maintained.

The war graves plot also contains the HAIDAR PASHA CREMATION MEMORIAL, which commemorates 122 soldiers of the Indian Army who died in 1919 and 1920, who were originally commemorated at Mashiak and Osmanieh Cemeteries. In 1961, when these cemeteries could no longer be maintained, the ashes of the Hindus, whose remains were cremated in accordance with their faith, were scattered near this memorial, while the remains of their comrades of the Muslim faith were brought here and re-interred.

HAIDAR PASHA CEMETERY was first established for Crimean war burials and was used during the First World War by the Turks for the burial of Commonwealth prisoners of war. After the Armistice, when Istanbul was occupied, further burials were made mainly from No. 82 General Hospital, and graves were brought in from other civil cemeteries in the area.

HAM BRITISH CEMETERY, MUILLE-VILLETTE

Ham is a small town about 20 kms south west of St. Quentin.

In January, February, and March 1918, the 61st (South Midland) Casualty Clearing Station was posted at Ham, but on 23rd March the Germans, in their advance towards Amiens, crossed the Somme at Ham, and the town remained in German hands until the French First Army re-entered it on the following 6th September.

Ham British Cemetery was begun in January-March 1918 as an extension of MUILLE-VILLETTE GERMAN CEMETERY, made by the Casualty Clearing Station. In 1919, these graves were regrouped and others were added from the German cemetery and from other cemetreies.

HASLAR ROYAL NAVAL CEMETERY

During both wars, Gosport was a significant sea port and Naval depot, with many government factories and installations based there, as well as the Haslar Naval Hospital.

HASLAR ROYAL NAVAL CEMETERY, which was attached to the Naval Hospital of 2,000 beds, contains 763 First World War graves, two of which are unidentified, scattered throughout the cemetery.

HAWTHORN RIDGE CEMETERY NO. 2, AUCHONVILLERS

Auchonvillers is approximately 20 kms south of Arras.

HAWTHORN RIDGE CEMETERY NO.1 was made by the V Corps, who cleared the Ancre battlefields in the spring of 1917; HAWTHORN RIDGE CEMETERY NO. 2 is 460 metres south of NO. 1. It was made in the spring of 1917, and seven isolated graves were brought in after the Armistice.

HAZEBROUCK COMMUNAL CEMETERY

Hazebrouck is a town lying about 56 kms south-east of Calais.

From October 1914 to September 1917, casualty clearing stations were posted at Hazebrouck. The Germans shelled and bombed the town between September 1917 and September 1918, making it unsafe for hospitals, but in September and October 1918, No. 9 British Red Cross Hospital was stationed there.

Commonwealth burials began in the communal cemetery in October 1914 and continued until July 1918. At first, they were made among the civilian graves, but after the Armistice these earlier burials were moved into the main Commonwealth enclosure.

HEBUTERNE MILITARY CEMETERY

Hebuterne is a village 15 kms north of Albert (Somme) and 20 kms south-west of Arras.

HEBUTERNE MILITARY CEMETERY was begun in August 1915, and used by fighting units and Field Ambulances until the spring of 1917; it was reopened in 1918.

HEDAUVILLE COMMUNAL CEMETERY EXTENSION

Hedauville is approximately 5 kms northwest of Albert, on the road to Doullens.

The extension was begun at the end of March 1918, when the front line was consolidated a short distance east of the village following the German offensive. It was used by field ambulances and fighting units until the following August. The extension contained 95 graves at the Armistice, but was later increased when graves were brought in from the surrounding battlefields of March-August 1918.

HEILLY STATION CEMETERY, MERICOURT-L'ABBE

Mericourt-l'Abbe is a village approximately 19 kms northeast of Amiens and 10 kms southwest of Albert.

The 36th Casualty Clearing Station was at Heilly from April 1916. It was joined in May by the 38th, and in July by the 2/2nd London, but these hospitals had all moved on by early June 1917. The cemetery was begun in May 1916, and was used by the three medical units until April 1917. From March to May 1918, it was used by Australian units, and in the early autumn for further hospital burials, when the 20th Casualty Clearing Station was there briefly in August and September 1918. The last burial was made in May 1919.

HELLES MEMORIAL

The Anzac and Suvla cemeteries are first signposted from the left hand junction of the Eceabat-Bigali Road. The HELLES MEMORIAL stands on the tip of the Gallipoli Peninsula. It takes the form of an obelisk over 30 metres high that can be seen by ships passing through the Dardanelles.

The eight month campaign in Gallipoli was fought by Commonwealth and French forces in an attempt to force Turkey out of the war, to relieve the deadlock of the Western Front in France and Belgium, and to open a supply route to Russia through the Dardanelles and the Black Sea. The Allies landed on the peninsula on 25-26th April 1915; the 29th Division at Cape Helles in the south, and the Australian and New Zealand Corps north of Gaba Tepe on the west coast, an area soon known as Anzac. On 6th August, further landings were made at Suvla, just north of Anzac, and the climax of the campaign came in early August when simultaneous assaults were launched on all three fronts. However, the difficult terrain and stiff Turkish resistance soon led to the stalemate of trench warfare. From the end of August, no further serious action was fought and the lines remained unchanged. The peninsula was successfully evacuated in December and early January 1916. The HELLES MEMORIAL serves the dual function of Commonwealth battle memorial for the whole Gallipoli campaign, and place of commemoration for many of those Commonwealth servicemen who died there and have no known grave. The United Kingdom and Indian forces named on the memorial died in operations throughout the peninsula, the Australians at Helles. There are also panels for those who died or were buried at sea in Gallipoli waters. The memorial bears more than 21,000 names.

HENINEL COMMUNAL CEMETERY EXTENSION

Heninel is a village some 10 kms south-east of Arras on the D33.

Heninel village was captured in a snowstorm on 12th April 1917. The extension was begun in April 1917 and was used by fighting units until the following November.

HENINEL-CROISILLES ROAD CEMETERY

Heninel and Croisilles are villages approximately 5 kms and 8 kms southeast of Arras.

Heninel was captured on 12th April 1917, the attack continuing eastwards on the two following days. In April 1918, this ground was lost, and the eleven German graves were made when the cemetery was in German hands. After the Armistice, graves were brought in from a wide area round Heninel.

HOLLYBROOK MEMORIAL, SOUTHAMPTON

The Hollybrook Memorial is situated in SOUTHAMPTON (HOLLYBROOK) Cemetery behind the plot of First World War graves near the main entrance.

The Hollybrook Memorial commemorates by name almost 1,900 servicemen and women of the Commonwealth land and air forces whose graves are not known, many of whom were lost in transports or other vessels torpedoed or mined in home waters. The memorial also bears the names of those who were lost or buried at sea, or who died at home but whose bodies could not be recovered for burial.

HONNECHY BRITISH CEMETERY

Honnechy is a village in the Department of the Nord, 8 kms south-west of Le Cateau.

The village was part of the battlefield of Le Cateau in August 1914, and from that time it remained in German hands until the 9th October 1918. It had been a German Hospital centre, and from its capture until the end of October, it was a British Field Ambulance centre. The village was inhabited by civilians during the whole of the War.

The cemetery stands on the site of a German Cemetery, begun in the Battle of Cambrai 1917, and used by German troops and then by British until the 24th October 1918. The 300 German graves were removed to another burial ground, leaving 44 British graves; and the cemetery was re-made in 1922 and 1923 by the concentration of British graves, almost entirely from German Cemeteries.

HOOGE CRATER CEMETERY

HOOGE CRATER CEMETERY is 4 kms east of Ieper town centre on the Meenseweg (N8), connecting Ieper to Menen.

Hooge Chateau and its stables were the scene of very fierce fighting throughout the First World War. On 31st October 1914, the staff of the 1st and 2nd Divisions were wiped out when the chateau was shelled; from 24th May to 3rd June 1915, the chateau was defended against German attacks, and in July 1915, the crater was made by a mine sprung by the 3rd Division. It changed hands several times in the course of the conflict, and was retaken for the final time on 28th September 1918. The cemetery was begun early in October 1917. It contained originally 76 graves, but was greatly increased after the Armistice when graves were brought in from the battlefields of Zillebeke, Zantvoorde and Gheluvelt and the other smaller cemeteries.

ISLINGTON CEMETERY AND CREMATORIUM

The cemetery is located on High Road, East Finchley, London.

ISLINGTON CEMETERY contains almost 350 First World War graves, scattered throughout the cemetery. A screen wall in the western part bears the names of those whose graves could not be marked individually.

JERUSALEM WAR CEMETERY AND JERUSALEM MEMORIAL

The JERUSALEM MEMORIAL stands in JERUSALEM WAR CEMETERY, 4.5 kms north of the walled city, and is situated on the neck of land at the north end of the Mount of Olives, to the west of Mount Scopus.

At the outbreak of the First World War, Palestine (now Israel) was part of the Turkish Empire, and it was not entered by Allied forces until December 1916. The advance to Jerusalem took a further year, but from 1914 to December 1917, about 250 Commonwealth prisoners of war were buried in the German and Anglo-German cemeteriesof the city. By 21st November 1917, the Egyptian Expeditionary Force had gained a line about five kms west of Jerusalem, but the city was deliberately spared bombardment and direct attack. Very severe fighting followed, lasting until the evening of 8th December, when all the city's prepared defences were captured. Turkish forces left Jerusalem throughout that night and in the morning of 9th December, the Mayor came to the Allied lines with the Turkish Governor's letter of surrender. Jerusalem was occupied that day and on 11th December, General Allenby formally entered the city, followed by representatives of France and Italy. JERUSALEM WAR CEMETERY was begun after the occupation of the city, with 270 burials. It was later enlarged to take graves from the battlefields and smaller cemeteries in the neighbourhood.

KANTARA WAR MEMORIAL CEMETERY

Kantara War Memorial Cemetery is situated at Kantara East on the eastern side of the Suez Canal, 160 kms northeast of Cairo and 50 kms south of Port Said.

In the early part of the First World War, Kantara was an important point in the defence of Suez against Turkish attacks, and marked the starting point of the new railway east towards Sinai and Palestine, begun in January 1916. Kantara developed into a major base and hospital centre, and the cemetery was begun in February 1916 for burials from the various hospitals, continuing in use until late 1920. After the Armistice, the cemetery was more than doubled in size when graves were brought in from other cemeteries and desert battlefields, notably those at Rumani, Qatia, El Arish and Rafa.

Near the entrance to the cemetery is the KANTARA MEMORIAL, bearing the names of 16 New Zealand servicemen of the First World War who died in actions at Rumani and Rafa, and who have no known grave.

KARASOULI MILITARY CEMETERY

Karasouli Military Cemetery is on the edge of the town of Polikastro (formerly Karasouli) which lies some 56 kms from Thessaloniki.

The cemetery was begun in September 1916 for the use of casualty clearing stations on the Doiran front. At the Armistice, it contained about 500 burials, but was greatly increased when graves were brought in from other cemeteries.

KIRECHKOI-HORTAKOI MILITARY CEMETERY

The cemetery is some 15 kms north east of Thessaloniki, on the outskirts of the village of Exochi (formerly Kirechkoi).

XVI Corps Headquarters were at Kirechkoi from January 1916, soon after the opening of the Salonika campaign, until the advance to the Struma in September 1916. The cemetery was begun in March 1916, but it remained a very small one until September 1917, when three General Hospitals came to the neighbourhood. In June, July and September 1918, other hospitals were brought to the high and healthy country beside the Salonika-Hortakoi road, and in September 1918, the influenza epidemic began, which raged for three months and filled three-quarters of the cemetery. The last burial took place in January 1919, but in 1937, twelve graves were brought into the cemetery from Salonika Protestant Cemetery, where their permanent maintenance could not be assured.

KLEIN-VIERSTRAAT BRITISH CEMETERY

KLEIN-VIERSTRAAT BRITISH CEMETERY is located 6 kms south-west of Ieper town centre, on the Molenstraat.

The village of Kemmel and the adjoining hill, Mont Kemmel, were the scene of fierce fighting in the latter half of April 1918, in which both Commonwealth and French forces were engaged. The cemetery was begun in January 1917 by field ambulances and fighting units before the middle of January 1918. After the Armistice, graves were brought in from two smaller cemeteries and from the battlefields of Dikkebus, Loker and Kemmel.

KORTRIJK (ST JAN) COMMUNAL CEMETERY

Kortrijk Communal Cemetery is located 28 kms east of Ieper town centre on the N8 Meenseweg.

Courtrai (now Kortrijk) was in German hands for most of the First World War. In April 1915, its railway junction was severely damaged by Allied airmen, and on 16th October 1918, the town was entered by the 12th Royal Irish Rifles.

St. Jean (now St. Jan) Cemetery was largely used and extended by the Germans, who erected a screen wall bearing the names of the dead by nationalities (the German Extension is in the commune of Heule). In November 1918, No. 44 Casualty Clearing Station was posted at Kortrijk for a week, and it was followed for a period of eight months by No. 62. These two units made a new plot in the southwest part of the cemetery, in which Commonwealth soldiers were buried. This plot was enlarged after the Armistice when graves were brought in from the German plots, the German extension and LA MADELEINE CEMETERY.

LA FERT-SOUS-JOUARRE MEMORIAL

La Ferte-sous-Jouarre is a small town 66 kms to the east of Paris, located on the main road (N3).

The LA FERTÉ-SOUS-JOUARRE MEMORIAL commemorates 3,740 officers and men of the British Expeditionary Force who fell at the battles of Mons, Le Cateau, the Marne, and the Aisne between the end of August and early October 1914 and have no known graves.

LA TARGETTE BRITISH CEMETERY, NEUVILLE-ST. VAAST

Neuville-St. Vaast is a village 6.5 kms north of Arras.

LA TARGETTE BRITISH CEMETERY, formerly known as Aux-Rietz Military Cemetery, was begun at the end of April 1917 and used by field ambulances and fighting units until September 1918. Nearly a third of the graves have an artillery connection. Sixteen graves were brought into the cemetery from the immediate neighbourhood after the Armistice.

LAPUGNOY MILITARY CEMETERY

Lapugnoy is a village 6 kms west of Bethune.

The first burials were made in September 1915, but it was most heavily used during the Battle of Arras, which began in April 1917. The dead were brought to the cemetery from casualty clearing stations, chiefly at Lapugnoy and Lozinghem, but between May and August 1918, the cemetery was used by fighting units.

LARCH WOOD (RAILWAY CUTTING) CEMETERY

Larch Wood Cemetery is located 4 kms south-east of Ieper town centre, on the Komenseweg.

The cemetery was begun in April 1915 at the north end of a small plantation of larches. It was used by troops holding this sector until April 1918. It was enlarged after the Armistice when graves were brought in from the battlefields of Ypres and from other smaller cemeteries.

LE TOUQET RAILWAY CROSSING CEMETERY

Le Touquet Railway Crossing Cemetery is located 15 km south of Ieper town centre, on a road leading from the Rijselseweg N365.

The cemetery was used from October 1914 to June 1918, and contains the graves of 28 men of the 1st Rifle Brigade killed in October and November 1914 during fierce German attacks on the 11th Infantry Brigade.

LE TOURET MEMORIAL AND LE TOURET MILITARY CEMETERY

LE TOURET MEMORIAL is located at the east end of LE TOURET MILITARY CEMETERY, on the south side of the Bethune-Armentieres main road. It commemorates over 13,400 British soldiers who were killed in this sector of the Western Front from the beginning of October 1914, to the eve of the Battle of Loos in late September 1915, and who have no known grave. Almost all of the men commemorated on the Memorial served with regular or territorial regiments from across the United Kingdom, and were killed in actions that took place along a section of the front line that stretched from Estaires in the north to Grenay in the south. This part of the Western Front was the scene of some of the heaviest fighting of the first year of the war. Soldiers serving with Indian and Canadian units who were killed in this sector in 1914 and 1915, whose remains were never identified, are commemorated on the NEUVE CHAPELLE and VIMY MEMORIALS, while those who fell during the northern pincer attack at the Battle of Aubers Ridge, are commemorated on the PLOEGSTEERT MEMORIAL.

The Cemetery was begun by the Indian Corps in November 1914, and it was used continuously by Field Ambulances and fighting units until March 1918. It passed into German hands in April 1918, and after its recapture, a few further burials were made in September and October.

LE TREPORT MILITARY CEMETERY

Le Treport is a coastal town approximately 30 kms northeast of Dieppe. During the First World War, it was an important hospital centre. In 1917, a divisional rest camp and a tank training depot were also established in the neighbourhood. The hospitals had been closed by March 1919.

LE VERTANNOY BRITISH CEMETERY, HINGES

Le Vertannoy is a hamlet nearly 1 km west of the village of Hinges, which is a small village 2 kms northwest of the town of Bethune in the Department of the Pas-de-Calais.

The cemetery was begun in April 1918, during the Battles of the Lys, and was used by field ambulances, burial officers and fighting units until the following September.

LEBUCQUIERE COMMUNAL CEMETERY EXTENSION

Lebucquiere is a village 8 kms east of Bapaume.

Lebucquiere village was occupied by Commonwealth forces on 19th March 1917, following the German withdrawal to the Hindenburg Line. It was recaptured by the Germans on 23rd March 1918, and finally reoccupied on 3rd September 1918.

The communal cemetery extension was begun on 24th March 1917 and was used by the 1st Australian Division and other units for almost a year. After the reoccupation of the village in September 1918, it was used again for a fortnight. At the Armistice, the cemetery contained 150 burials, but it was then greatly enlarged when graves were brought in from the surrounding battlefields.

LEEDS (LAWNS WOOD CEMETERY)

During the First World War, the major hospitals in Leeds were the 2nd Northern General with 1,800 beds, and the East Leeds War Hospital with 1,900. The cemetery is located in Otley Road, Leeds.

LEEDS (LAWNS WOOD) CEMETERY contains 138 burial of the First World War, 88 of them forming a war graves plot in Section W. As these graves could not be marked individually, the names of the dead are recorded on a screen wall. The rest of the First World War burials scattered throughout the cemetery. A further screen wall bears the names of 105 casualties of both wars buried in LEEDS GENERAL CEMETERY, where their graves could no longer be maintained.

LIEVIN COMMUNAL CEMETERY EXTENSION
Lievin is a small town in the Department of the Pas-de-Calais, 3.5 kms west of Lens. It was captured by the Canadian Corps on 14th April 1917, and remained in British hands until the end of the War. The Extension was made after the Armistice by the concentration of graves from the battlefields north and south of Lens and from other smaller cemeteries.

LIGNY-ST. FLOCHEL BRITISH CEMETERY, AVERDOINGT
Ligny-St.Flochel is a village about 6.5 kms east of St.Pol. The cemetery was started at the beginning of April 1918 when the 7th Casualty Clearing Station came back from Tincques ahead of the German advance. Two more Casualty Clearing Stations followed in the next four months, but all three had left by November 1918.

LIJSSENTHOEK MILITARY CEMETERY
LIJSSENTHOEK MILITARY CEMETERY is located 12 kms west of Ieper town centre.

During the First World War, the village of Lijssenthoek was situated on the main communication line between the Allied military bases in the rear and the Ypres battlefields. Close to the Front, but out of the extreme range of most German field artillery, it became a natural place to establish casualty clearing stations. The cemetery was first used by the French, and in June 1915, it began to be used by casualty clearing stations of the Commonwealth forces.

From April to August 1918, the casualty clearing stations fell back before the German advance and field ambulances (including a French ambulance) took their places.

LILLERS COMMUNAL CEMETERY AND LILLERS COMMUNAL CEMETERY EXTENSION
Lillers is a small town about 15 kms west-north-west of Bethune.

It was used for billets and headquarter offices from the autumn of 1914 to April 1918. At that time, it was a hospital centre with six Casualty Clearing Stations in the town at one time or another. These units buried their dead on the right of the central path of the communal cemetery. In April 1918, the Germans advanced as far as Robecq; Lillers came under shell-fire, and the units holding this front continued to bury beyond the cemetery boundary, in the extension.

LONDON CEMETERY AND EXTENSION, LONGUEVAL
Longueval is a village 40 kms northeast of Amiens and 12 kms east-north-east of Albert. High Wood was fiercely fought over during the Battle of the Somme until cleared on 15th September 1916. It was lost during the German advance of April 1918, but retaken the following August. The original LONDON CEMETERY at High Wood was begun when 47 men of the 47th Division were buried in a large shell hole on 18th and 21st September 1916. Other

burials were added later, mainly of officers and men of the 47th Division who died on 15th September 1916, and at the Armistice the cemetery contained just over a hundred graves. The cemetery was then greatly enlarged when remains were brought in from the surrounding battlefields, but the original battlefield cemetery is preserved intact within the larger cemetery, now known as the LONDON CEMETERY AND EXTENSION.

LONDON CEMETERY, NEUVILLE-VITASSE

Neuville-Vitasse is a village in the department of the Pas-de-Calais, 5 kms southeast of Arras.

Neuville-Vitasse was captured by the same Division on 9th April, almost entirely lost at the end of March 1918, but regained at the end of the following August. It was later "adopted" by the Metropolitan Borough of Paddington.

THE LONDON CEMETERY was made in April 1917, and greatly extended after the Armistice when graves were brought in from other burial grounds and from the battlefields between Arras, Vis-en-Artois and Croisilles.

LONE PINE CEMETERY, ANZAC

LONE PINE CEMETERY, ANZAC is signposted from the road between Eceabat and Bigali in Turkey.

The eight month campaign in Gallipoli was fought by Commonwealth and French forces in an attempt to force Turkey out of the war, to relieve the deadlock of the Western Front in France and Belgium, and to open a supply route to Russia through the Dardanelles and the Black Sea. Lone Pine was a strategically important plateau in the southern part of Anzac which was briefly in the hands of Australian forces, retaken by the Turks and became a strong point, before the Australians recaptured it. The original battle cemetery of around fifty graves was enlarged after the Armistice when scattered graves were brought in from the neighbourhood, and nearby cemeteries.

LONGUEAU BRITISH CEMETERY

The town of Longueau is situated on the southeastern outskirts of Amiens.

LONGUEAU BRITISH CEMETERY was begun in April 1918, when the Allied line was re-established before Amiens; it was used by fighting units and field ambulances until the following August. After the Armistice graves were also brought in from the surrounding battlefields and smaller cemeteries

LONGUENESSE (ST. OMER) SOUVENIR CEMETERY

St. Omer is a large town 45 kms southeast of Calais. Longuenesse is a commune on the southern outskirts of St. Omer.

St. Omer was the General Headquarters of the British Expeditionary Force from October 1914 to March 1916. St. Omer suffered air raids in November 1917 and May 1918, with serious loss of life.

The cemetery takes its names from the triangular cemetery of the St. Omer garrison, properly called the Souvenir Cemetery (Cimetiere du Souvenir Francais) which is located next to the War Cemetery.

LOOS BRITISH CEMETERY
Loos (Loos-en-Gohelle) is a village to the north of the road from Lens to Bethune.

The cemetery was begun by the Canadian Corps in July 1917. Further burials were performed after the Armistice by the concentration of graves from the battlefields and smaller cemeteries over a wide area north and east of the village.

LOOS MEMORIAL
The LOOS MEMORIAL forms the sides and back of DUD CORNER CEMETERY. Loos-en-Gohelle is a village 5 kms northwest of Lens, and DUD CORNER CEMETERY is located about 1 kilometre west of the village. It stands almost on the site of a German strong point, the Lens Road Redoubt, captured by the 15th (Scottish) Division on the first day of the battle. The name "Dud Corner" is believed to be due to the large number of unexploded enemy shells found in the neighbourhood after the Armistice. The LOOS MEMORIAL commemorates over 20,000 officers and men who have no known grave, who fell in the area from the River Lys to the old southern boundary of the First Army, east and west of Grenay.

LUTTERWORTH (ST MARY) CHURCHYARD
The market town of Lutterworth is located in Leicestershire, just to the west of the M1, about ten miles south of Leicester.

MADRAS 1914-1918 WAR MEMORIAL, CHENNAI
MADRAS WAR CEMETERY is about 5 kms from the airport and 14 kms from the central railway station. The MADRAS 1914-1918 MEMORIAL is situated at the rear of the cemetery. It bears the names of more than 1,000 servicemen who died during the First World War, who lie in many civil and cantonment cemeteries in various parts of India where it is not possible to maintain their graves in perpetuity.

MARFAUX BRITISH CEMETERY
Marfaux is a commune 18.5 kms from Reims and 16 kms from Epernay.

It was captured by the Germans in May 1918, and retaken, after severe fighting, on 23rd July, by the 51st (Highland) and 62nd (West Riding) Divisions, and the New Zealand Cyclist Battalion.

The cemetery was begun after the Armistice by the concentration of graves from the battlefields and from other Military Cemeteries in the Marne.

MAROEUIL BRITISH CEMETERY
Maroeuil is a village in the Department of the Pas-de-Calais, 6 kms northwest of Arras. The cemetery was begun by the 51st (Highland) Division when Commonwealth forces took over the Arras front in March 1916, and it retained its association with that division until the summer of 1918. Almost half of the graves are those of Highland territorials, and many of those remaining are of London territorials who were at Maroeuil from July to December 1916. The cemetery also contains the graves of 25 officers and men of tunnelling companies of the Royal Engineers who died in mine explosions. The cemetery was protected from observation by

the crest of the hill behind it and whenever possible, bodies were brought back to it from the front line by tramway.

MAROILLES COMMUNAL CEMETERY

Maroilles is a village in the Department of the Nord, some 30 kms southeast of Valenciennes,

Maroilles was the scene of fighting on 25th August 1914, but then remained in German hands until it was captured on 5th November 1918. The cemetery contains just twenty War Graves.

MARTEVILLE COMMUNAL CEMETERY, ATTILLY

Marteville is situated 8 kms west of St Quentin; the British Plot is on the northern side of the Communal Cemetery. The village of Attilly was occupied in April 1917, and British burials were made in the Communal Cemetery by fighting units in April and May 1917, and January, March, September and October 1918, and by the enemy in March 1918.

MEAULTE MILITARY CEMETERY

Meaulte is a village in the Department of the Somme, immediately south of Albert.

It was held by Commonwealth forces (and inhabited by three-quarters of its civilian population) from 1915 to 26th March 1918, when it was evacuated after a rearguard fight by the 9th (Scottish) Division. It was recaptured on 22nd August 1918.

The military cemetery was begun in December 1915, and used until February 1917. A few further burials were made after the recapture of the village and after the Armistice, graves (mainly of 1918) being brought in from the neighbouring battlefields and other burial grounds.

MENIN ROAD NORTH MILITARY CEMETERY AND MENIN ROAD SOUTH MILITARY CEMETERY

Menin Road South Military Cemetery is located 2 kms east of Ieper town centre.

The Menin Road ran east and a little south from Ypres (now Ieper) to a front line which varied only a few kilometres during the greater part of the war. The position of this cemetery was always within the Allied lines. It was first used in January 1916, and continued to be used by units and Field Ambulances until the summer of 1918. The cemetery was increased after the Armistice when graves were brought in from isolated positions on the battlefields to the east and other cemeteries.

MENIN ROAD NORTH MILITARY CEMETERY was on the north side of the road at almost the same point. It was used by the units and Field Ambulances of another Corps from May 1915, until August 1916, and again to a small extent in 1917 and 1918.

MERVILLE COMMUNAL CEMETERY

Merville is a town 15 kms north of Bethune and about 20 kms southwest of Armentieres.

Merville was the scene of fighting between the Germans and French and British cavalry early in October 1914, but from the 9th of that month until 11th April 1918, it remained in Allied hands. In October 1914, and in the autumn of 1915, the town was the headquarters of the Indian Corps. It was a railhead until May 1915, and a billeting and hospital centre from 1915-1918; several Casualty Clearing Stations also were there.

On the evening of 11th April 1918, in the Battles of the Lys, the Germans forced their way into Merville, and the town was not retaken until 19th August. The cemeteries were not used again until the concentration of battlefield burials into the Extension began, after the Armistice.

MERVILLE COMMUNAL CEMETERY was used by French troops (chiefly cavalry) in October 1914, and for Commonwealth burials from that date until August 1916 (in the case of officers, to March 1918).

MERVILLE COMMUNAL CEMETERY EXTENSION was opened in August 1916, and used by Commonwealth and Portuguese hospitals until April 1918. It was enlarged after the Armistice when graves were brought in from the battlefields immediately north and east of Merville.

METZ-EN-COUTURE COMMUNAL CEMETERY BRITISH EXTENSION

Metz-en-Couture is a village situated in the extreme southeastern corner of the Department of the Pas-de-Calais.

The village was captured on the 4th and 5th April 1917, evacuated on 23rd March 1918, and retaken the following 6th September. It was noted for its extensive system of underground cellars. It was later "adopted" by the County Borough of Halifax.

The Communal Cemetery was used by the enemy for the burial of German soldiers and also of three R.F.C. Officers, whose graves have now been removed to the British Extension. On the east side of it, a German Extension was made containing the graves of 252 German soldiers, and one man of the Chinese Labour Corps; the German graves have now been removed to other cemeteries and the Chinese grave to the British Extension.

The British Extension was begun in April 1917, and used until March 1918, and two graves were added in the following September. Further burials from METZ-EN-COUTURE BRITISH CEMETERY No. 2, were moved after the Armistice.

MIKRA BRITISH CEMETERY, KALAMARIA

Mikra British Cemetery is situated approximately 8 kms south of Thessaloniki, in the municipality of Kalamaria (behind the army camp of Ntalipi).

At the invitation of the Greek Prime Minister, M. Venizelos, Salonika (now Thessalonika) was occupied by three French Divisions and the 10th (Irish) Division from Gallipoli in October 1915. Other French and Commonwealth forces landed during the year, and in the summer of 1916, they were joined by Russian and Italian troops. In August 1916, a Greek revolution broke out at Salonika, with the result that the Greek national army came into the war on the Allied side.

The town was the base of the British Salonika Force and it contained, from time to time, eighteen general and stationary hospitals. Three of these hospitals were Canadian, although there were no other Canadian units in the force.

The earliest Commonwealth burials took place in the local Protestant and Roman Catholic cemeteries, and the Anglo-French (now Lembet Road) Military Cemetery was used from November 1915 to October 1918. The British cemetery at Mikra was opened in April 1917, remaining in use until 1920. The cemetery was greatly enlarged after the Armistice when graves were brought in from a number of burial grounds in the area.

MOEUVRES COMMUNAL CEMETERY EXTENSION

Moeuvres is a village 10 kms west of Cambrai. It remained in German hands during the Battle of Cambrai, 1917, in spite of three days of desperate attack. It was partly taken by on 11th September 1918, and cleared on the 19th. The communal cemetery was extended to the west by the Germans between November 1917 and March 1918. The British Extension was made between September and October 1918, and was enlarged after the Armistice when graves were brought in from the battlefields on the Cambrai-Bapaume road.

MONT HUON MILITARY CEMETERY, LE TREPORT

Le Treport is a small seaport 25 kms northeast of Dieppe.

During the war, Le Treport was an important hospital centre and by July 1916, the town contained three general hospitals, a Convalescent Depot and Lady Murray's British Red Cross Society Hospital. Canadian and USA General Hospitals arrived later, but all of the hospitals had closed by March 1919.

MONTECCHIO PRECALCINO COMMUNAL CEMETERY EXTENSION

Montecchio Precalcino is a town in the Province of Vicenza, 4 kms north of Dueville and 17 kms north of the town of Vicenza.

The Italians entered the war on the Allied side, declaring war on Austria in May 1915. Commonwealth forces were at the Italian front between November 1917 and November 1918, and rest camps and medical units were established at various locations in northern Italy behind the front, some of them remaining until 1919.

Between April 1918 and February 1919, those who died from wounds or disease in three Clearing Stations were buried either here or at Dueville. Certain graves were brought in after the Armistice from other burial grounds in the area.

MOREUIL COMMUNAL CEMETERY ALLIED EXTENSION

Moreuil is a village in the Department of the Somme, 18 kms southeast of Amiens.

The village and Moreuil Wood were the scene of desperate fighting in March and April 1918, in which Commonwealth and French infantry, and the Canadian Cavalry Brigade, took part. The village was lost to the Germans, but was retaken on 8th August. The extension was made after the Armistice when graves were brought in from the neighbouring battlefields

NETLEY MILITARY CEMETERY

The cemetery lies within a park maintained by Hampshire County Council on the site of the former hospital.

NETLEY MILITARY CEMETERY is a permanent military cemetery, the property of the Ministry of Defence. The cemetery was at the back of the Royal Victoria Military Hospital and was used during both wars for burials from the hospital.

NETTLETON (ST MARY) CHURCHYARD

The village of Nettleton is in Wiltshire. The graveyard contains just one War Grave.

NEUVE-CHAPELLE BRITISH CEMETERY AND NEUVE-CHAPELLE MEMORIAL

The village of Neuve Chapelle is some 5 kms north of La Bassee and 20 kms west-south-west of Lille.

NEUVE-CHAPELLE BRITISH CEMETERY was begun during the Battle of Neuve-Chapelle, which began on 10th March, 1915, and used until the following November. The Cemetery was known at one time as Moggs Hole Cemetery.

The Indian Memorial at Neuve Chapelle commemorates over 4,700 Indian soldiers and labourers who lost their lives on the Western Front during the First World War and have no known graves. The location of the memorial was specially chosen as it was at Neuve Chapelle in March 1915 that the Indian Corps fought its first major action as a single unit.

NEW MUNICH TRENCH BRITISH CEMETERY, BEAUMONT-HAMEL

Beaumont-Hamel is a village about 24 kms southwest of Arras.

It was attacked and taken on the 13th November 1916. Munich Trench was occupied by the 51st (Highland) Division on the 15th November 1916; New Munich Trench being dug on the previous night by the 2/2nd Highland Field Company and a company of the 8th Royal Scots, and lengthened by the 8th Devons in December.

The cemetery was made in the spring of 1917, when units cleared the battlefield.

NIEDERZWEHREN CEMETERY

The city of Kassel lies in the centre of Germany, approx 165 kms south of Hannover.

The cemetery was begun by the Germans in 1915 for the burial of prisoners of war who died at the local camp. During the war, almost 3,000 Allied soldiers and civilians, including French, Russian and Commonwealth, were buried there. In 1922-23, it was decided that the graves of Commonwealth servicemen who had died all over Germany should be brought together into four permanent cemeteries. Niederzwehren was one of those chosen and in the following four years, more than 1,500 graves were brought into the cemetery from 190 burial grounds in Baden, Bavaria, Hanover, Hesse and Saxony.

NORFOLK CEMETERY, BECORDEL-BECOURT

Becordel-Becourt is a village just east of Albert. The cemetery was begun in August 1915 and used until August 1916. After the Armistice it was nearly doubled in size when graves were brought in from the battlefields nearby.

NOYON NEW BRITISH CEMETERY AND NOYON OLD BRITISH CEMETERY

Noyon is a town 32 kms northwest of Soissons, on the road to Roye (D6/D934)

Noyon was the British G.H.Q. on 26th to 28th August 1914. It was entered by the Germans on 1st September 1914, by the French on 18th March 1917, and by the Germans again in March 1918. The French finally retook it on 29th and 30th August 1918. It was twice bombarded by the enemy, and in 1918 practically destroyed.

NOYON OLD BRITISH CEMETERY was made by the 46th Casualty Clearing Station and the 44th Field Ambulance in March 1918, in a woodyard near the railway station. It contained the graves of 144 soldiers from the United Kingdom, one American medical officer, two Italian and three French soldiers. All these graves except the French were removed after the Armistice, to the New British Cemetery.

Noyon French National and New British Cemeteries are side by side, on the hill north of the town. The former was made in 1919, and contains the graves of 1,721 French soldiers, of whom 693 are unidentified.

NOYON NEW BRITISH CEMETERY was made after the Armistice by the concentration of graves from other burial grounds and from the battlefields.

OOSTTAVERNE WOOD CEMETERY

Oosttaverne Wood Cemetery is located 6 kms south of Ieper town centre on the Rijselseweg N336.

The "Oosttaverne Line" was a German work running northward from the river Lys to the Comines Canal, passing just east of Oosttaverne. It was captured on 7th June 1917, the first day of the Battle of Messines. There were two cemeteries, No. 1 and No. 2, used until September 1917. The present cemetery was completed after the Armistice when graves were brought in from the surrounding battlefields (including many from Hill 60) and from smaller cemeteries.

OVILLERS MILITARY CEMETERY

Ovillers is a village about 5 kms northeast of the town of Albert.

On 1st July 1916, the first day of the Battle of the Somme, the two villages of Ovillers and La Boiselle were attacked, but not captured until 17th July. They were lost during the German advance in March 1918, but they were retaken on the following 24th August.

OVILLERS MILITARY CEMETERY was begun before the capture of Ovillers, as a battle cemetery behind a dressing station. It was used until March 1917, by which time it contained 143 graves. The cemetery was increased after the Armistice when Commonwealth and French graves where brought in, mainly from the battlefields of Pozieres, Ovillers, La Boiselle and Contalmaison.

OXFORD ROAD CEMETERY

The cemetery is located to the northeast of the town of Ieper. Oxford Road was the name given to a road running behind the support trenches, from a point west of the village of Wieltje, southeastwards to the Potijze-Zonnebeke road. The original OXFORD ROAD CEMETERY was used by the units fighting on this front from August 1917 to April 1918. In October 1917, another cemetery, known as OXFORD ROAD CEMETERY NO. 2, was started close by, and now forms part of the cemetery as it appears today. After the Armistice, scattered graves from the battlefields east and southeast of Ypres (now Ieper) were brought into the cemetery.

PEAKE WOOD CEMETERY, FRICOURT

Fricourt is a village about 5 kms east of Albert.

Peake Wood was the name given by the army to a copse on the southeast side of the road to Contalmaison. The wood fell into Allied hands on 5th July 1916, but the cemetery was not begun until later in the month. It was used as a front line cemetery until February 1917, but was in German hands from the end of March 1918, until nearly the end of the following August.

PERNES BRITISH CEMETERY

Pernes-en-Artois is a small town on the main road from Lillers to St. Pol.

The cemetery was not begun until April 1918, when the 1st and 4th Canadian Casualty Clearing Stations came to Pernes, driven back by the German advance. In May, two further Clearing Stations arrived, and in August, they were joined by another. Almost all the burials were made by these units, but a few of the graves were brought into the cemetery after the Armistice.

PICQUIGNY BRITISH CEMETERY

Picquigny is a small town in the Department of the Somme, about 13 kms northwest of Amiens.

During the first four years of the First World War, Picquigny was on the lines of communication for French and Commonwealth forces, and there are ten burials from these years in the communal cemetery, opposite the church.

At the end of March 1918, two Clearing Stations were brought to Picquigny to deal with casualties of the German advance on Amiens, and the British Cemetery was opened a little west of the town.

PIETA MILITARY CEMETERY

The Cemetery is located in Triq id-Duluri (Our Lady of Sorrows Street), 2 kms southwest of Valletta on the road to Sliema.

From the spring of 1915, the hospitals and convalescent depots established on the islands of Malta and Gozo dealt with over 135,000 sick and wounded, chiefly from the campaigns in Gallipoli and Salonika, although increased submarine activity in the Mediterranean meant that fewer hospital ships were sent to the island from May 1917.

PLOEGSTEERT MEMORIAL

The PLOEGSTEERT MEMORIAL stands in BERKS CEMETERY EXTENSION, which is located 12.5 kms south of Ieper town centre. It commemorates more than 11,000 servicemen of the United Kingdom and South African forces who died in this sector during the First World War and have no known grave. The memorial serves the area from the line Caestre-Dranoutre-Warneton to the north, to Haverskerque-Estaires-Fournes to the south, including the towns of Hazebrouck, Merville, Bailleul and Armentieres, the Forest of Nieppe, and Ploegsteert Wood. The original intention had been to erect the memorial in Lille. Most of those commemorated by the memorial did not die in major offensives, but were killed in the course of the day-to-day trench warfare which characterised this part of the line, or in small scale set engagements, usually carried out in support of the major attacks taking place elsewhere. It does not include the names of officers and men of Canadian or Indian regiments (they are found on the Memorials at VIMY and NEUVE-CHAPELLE), nor those lost at the Battle of Aubers Ridge on 9th May 1915, who are commemorated on the LE TOURET MEMORIAL.

BERKS CEMETERY EXTENSION, in which the memorial stands, was begun in June 1916, and used continuously until September 1917. In 1930, graves were brought in from

ROSENBERG CHATEAU MILITARY CEMETERY AND EXTENSION, about 1 km to the northwest, when it was established that these sites could not be acquired in perpetuity. This had been used by fighting units from November 1914 to August 1916. The extension was begun in May 1916 and used until March 1918. Together, the ROSENBERG CHATEAU CEMETERY AND EXTENSION were sometimes referred to as 'Red Lodge'.

HYDE PARK CORNER (ROYAL BERKS) CEMETERY is separated from BERKS CEMETERY EXTENSION by a road. It was begun in April 1915, and used at intervals until November 1917. Hyde Park Corner was a road junction to the north of Ploegsteert Wood. Hill 63 was to the northwest, and nearby were the 'Catacombs', deep shelters capable of holding two battalions, which were used from November 1916 onwards.

POELCAPELLE BRITISH CEMETERY

POELCAPELLE BRITISH CEMETERY is located 10 kms north-east of Ieper town centre on the Brugseweg (N313).

Poelcapelle (now Poelkapelle) was taken by the Germans from the French on 20th October 1914, entered by the 11th Division on 4th October 1917, evacuated by Commonwealth forces in April 1918, and retaken by the Belgians on 28th September 1918.

POELCAPELLE BRITISH CEMETERY was made after the Armistice when graves were brought in from the surrounding battlefields and smaller cemeteries.

POPERINGHE OLD MILITARY CEMETERY AND POPERINGHE NEW MILITARY CEMETERY

POPERINGHE OLD MILITARY CEMETERY is located some 10 kms west of Ieper town centre, in the town of Poperinge itself.

The town of Poperinghe (now Poperinge) was of great importance during the First World War because, although occasionally bombed or bombarded at long range, it was the nearest place to Ypres which was both considerable in size and reasonably safe. It was at first a centre for Casualty Clearing Stations, but by 1916 it became necessary to move these units further back, and field ambulances took their places.

The earliest Commonwealth graves in the town are in the communal cemetery, which was used from October 1914 to March 1915. The Old Military Cemetery was made in the course of the First Battle of Ypres and was closed, so far as Commonwealth burials are concerned, at the beginning of May 1915. The New Military Cemetery was established in June 1915.

PORTSDOWN (CHRIST CHURCH) MILITARY CEMETERY

The cemetery is to the rear of the church in Portsdown, Hampshire

PORTSMOUTH NAVAL MEMORIAL

The Memorial is situated on Southsea Common overlooking the promenade.

After the First World War, an appropriate way had to be found of commemorating those members of the Royal Navy who had no known grave, the majority of deaths having occurred at sea where no permanent memorial could be provided.

An Admiralty committee recommended that the three manning ports in Great Britain - Chatham, Plymouth and Portsmouth - should each have an identical memorial of unmistakable naval form, an obelisk, which would serve as a leading mark for shipping. The Portsmouth Naval Memorial was unveiled by the Duke of York (the future George VI) on 15th October 1924.

POTIJZE CHATEAU WOOD CEMETERY

The cemetery is located to the northeast of Ypres.

The old chateau grounds contain three Commonwealth War Graves Commission cemeteries, all formed in the spring of 1915, and used for the burial of Commonwealth soldiers until 1918.

POZIERES BRITISH CEMETERY, OVILLERS-LA-BOISSELLE AND POZIERES MEMORIAL

Pozieres is a village 6 kms northeast of the town of Albert.

The POZIERES MEMORIAL relates to the period of crisis in March and April 1918, when the Allied Fifth Army was driven back by overwhelming numbers across the former Somme battlefields, and the months that followed before the Advance to Victory, which began on 8th August 1918.

The Memorial commemorates over 14,000 casualties of the United Kingdom, and 300 of the South African Forces, who have no known grave, and who died on the Somme from 21st March to 7th August 1918. The memorial encloses POZIERES BRITISH CEMETERY, the original burials of 1916, 1917 and 1918, carried out by fighting units and field ambulances. The remaining plots were made after the Armistice, when graves were brought in from the battlefields immediately surrounding the cemetery, the majority of them of soldiers who died in the autumn of 1916 during the latter stages of the Battle of the Somme, but a few represent the fighting in August 1918.

PROSPECT HILL CEMETERY, GOUY

Gouy is a village to the east of the road between Cambrai and St. Quentin.

On 3rd October 1918, the 1st King's Own Yorkshire Light Infantry captured Prospect Hill. The cemetery was made by the 50th Division and the 18th Field Ambulance immediately after. After the Armistice graves were brought in, mainly from the battlefields north of Gouy, and almost exclusively of men who died in October 1918.

PROWSE POINT MILITARY CEMETERY

Prowse Point Military Cemetery is located 11.5 kms south of Ieper town centre.

This cemetery is unique on the Salient for being named after an individual. It is the site of a stand which featured the heroism of a Major Charles Prowse - later as Brigadier-General C.B. Prowse, D.S.O. (Somerset Light Infantry); he would be killed on the first day of the Battle of the Somme, and is buried in Louvencourt Military Cemetery.

The cemetery was used from November 1914 to April 1918.

PUCHEVILLERS BRITISH CEMETERY

Puchevillers is a village on the D11 about 19 kms northeast of Amiens.

In June 1916, just before the opening of the Battles of the Somme, the 3rd and 44th Casualty Clearing Stations came to Puchevillers; later, the South Midland Casualty Clearing Station also used the cemetery. There are also graves of men who died in the German advance in 1918, many of whom were buried by the 49th Clearing Station in March 1918, or by the 48th Labour Group in August.

QUEANT ROAD CEMETERY, BUISSY

Buissy is a village about 2 kms south of the main Arras to Cambrai road (D939) and about 25 kms from Arras.

The village was reached by the Third Army on 2nd September 1918, after the storming of the Drocourt-Queant line, and it was evacuated by the Germans on the following day.

Queant Cemetery was made by the 2nd and 57th Casualty Clearing Stations in October and November 1918. It then consisted of 71 graves, but was greatly enlarged after the Armistice when 2,200 graves were brought in from the battlefields of 1917-1918 between Arras and Bapaume, and from other smaller burial grounds in the area

RAILLENCOURT COMMUNAL CEMETERY EXTENSION

Raillencourt is a village in the Department of the Nord, about 5 kms west of Cambrai on the main road to Arras.

The village was captured by the Canadian Corps on 28th September 1918, in the Battle of the Canal du Nord. The extension to the communal cemetery was made by the Canadian Corps after the capture of the village. It was enlarged in 1923 when graves were brought in from NORTH CEMETERY, RAILLENCOURT.

REDOUBT CEMETERY, HELLES

From Helles, continue on the road to Alciptepe, and the cemetery will be found on your left.

The eight month campaign in Gallipoli was fought by Commonwealth and French forces in an attempt to force Turkey out of the war, to relieve the deadlock of the Western Front in France and Belgium, and to open a supply route to Russia through the Dardanelles and the Black Sea.

The Allies landed on the peninsula on 25-26th April 1915; the 29th Division at Cape Helles in the south, and the Australian and New Zealand Corps north of Gaba Tepe on the west coast, an area soon known as Anzac. REDOUBT CEMETERY takes its name from the chain of forts made by the Turks across the southern end of the peninsula in the fighting for Krithia and the Redoubt Line on which the advance halted in May.

The cemetery was begun by the 2nd Australian Infantry Brigade in May 1915, and continued in use until the evacuation. It was greatly increased after the Armistice when the battlefields were cleared and graves were brought in from other smaller cemeteries.

RED CROSS CORNER CEMETERY, BEUGNY

Beugny is a village 5 kms northeast of Bapaume.

The cemetery was started between April 1917 and March 1918 by field ambulances and fighting units. When the cemetery fell into German hands in March 1918, they added the 25 Commonwealth burials (all from 21st March 1918), and began another cemetery alongside (BEUGNY MILITARY CEMETERY NO. 3). Commonwealth forces retook the cemetery in September 1918. The German graves were removed after the Armistice, and the Commonwealth burials among them were transferred, partly to DELSAUX FARM CEMETERY, and partly to FAVREUIL BRITISH CEMETERY.

ROCLINCOURT MILITARY CEMETERY

Roclincourt is a village a little to the east of the road from Arras to Lens.

The French troops, who held this front before March 1916, made a military cemetery (now removed), on the southwest side of which the present Commonwealth cemetery was made. It was begun in April 1917, and contains many graves of 9th April, the first day of the Battles of Arras. It continued in use, as a front-line cemetery, until October 1918, and after the Armistice graves, mostly from the battlefield north of Roclincourt, were brought in.

ROCQUIGNY-EQUANCOURT ROAD BRITISH CEMETERY, MANANCOURT

Rocquigny and Equancourt are two villages in the Department of the Somme, some 13 kms north of Peronne and 12 kms southeast of Bapaume.

Etricourt was occupied by Commonwealth troops at the beginning of April 1917 during the German withdrawal to the Hindenburg Line. It was lost on the 23rd March 1918 when the Germans advanced, but regained at the beginning of September.

The cemetery was begun in 1917 and used until March 1918, mainly by the 21st and 48th Casualty Clearing Stations posted at Ytres, and to a small extent by the Germans, who knew it as "Etricourt Old English Cemetery". Burials were resumed by Commonwealth troops in September 1918, and the 3rd Canadian and 18th Casualty Clearing Stations buried in it in October and November 1918.

ROISEL COMMUNAL CEMETERY EXTENSION

Roisel is a small town 11 kms east of Peronne.

The town was occupied by British troops in April 1917, and evacuated after a strong defence by the 66th (East Lancashire) Division in the evening of 22nd March 1918. It was retaken in the following September.

ROISEL COMMUNAL CEMETERY EXTENSION was begun by German troops, who buried immediately to the north of the Communal Cemetery. It was developed in October and November 1918, by four Casualty Clearing Stations, and it was completed after the Armistice by the concentration of British and German graves from the country north, east and south of Roisel.

ROMERIES COMMUNAL CEMETERY EXTENSION

Romeries is a village approximately 16 kms south of Valenciennes and 4 kms northeast of Solesmes.

Part of the II Corps retired through this area during the Retreat from Mons in August 1914, and in October 1918, Commonwealth forces returned during the Advance to Victory. Briastre was captured on 10th October 1918, Belle Vue Farm on 20th October, Romeries itself and Beaudignies on 23rd October, and Englefontaine on 26th October. The Battle of the Sambre, the last great action of the war, carried the front forward into Belgium and ended with the Armistice. ROMERIES COMMUNAL CEMETERY EXTENSION is one of the burial grounds of those who died between these dates. After the Armistice, graves were brought in from isolated positions on the battlefield and other small cemeteries.

ROYAL IRISH RIFLES GRAVEYARD, LAVENTIE

Laventie is a village and commune, in the Department of the Pas-de-Calais, about 11 kms southwest of Armentieres.

The Rue-du-Bacquerot runs southeast of Laventie, towards Fleurbaix; and the position of the road behind the British front line, during the greater part of the war, made it the natural line of a number of small British cemeteries. One of these was begun in November 1914, and used, at first, particularly by the 1st Royal Irish Rifles.

The ROYAL IRISH RIFLES GRAVEYARD was carried on by fighting units until July 1916. It was increased after the Armistice by the concentration of graves (chiefly of 1914-15 and 1918), from the battlefields east of Estaires and Bethune, and from other smaller cemeteries.

RUE-PETILLON MILITARY CEMETERY, FLEURBAIX

Fleurbaix is a village 5 kms southwest of Armentieres on the D22.

British soldiers began burying their fallen comrades at Rue Pétillon in December 1914, and the cemetery was used by fighting units until it fell into German hands during the Spring Offensive of 1918. The Allies recaptured this sector of the front in September 1918, and when the war ended in November, the cemetery was the site of twelve Battalion burial grounds. Many of those laid to rest here had died of wounds in a dressing station that was located in the buildings adjoining the cemetery, which were known as 'Eaton Hall' during the war. The cemetery was enlarged in the years after the Armistice when graves were concentrated here from the battlefields around Fleurbaix and a number of smaller burial grounds.

STE. MARIE CEMETERY, LE HAVRE

STE. MARIE CEMETERY is one of the town cemeteries, but it is actually situated in the commune of Graville-St. Honorine, overlooking Le Havre from the north. During the First World War, Le Havre was one of the ports at which the British Expeditionary Force disembarked in August 1914. Except for a short interval during the German advance in 1914, it remained No. 1 Base throughout the war, and by the end of May 1917 it contained three general and two stationary hospitals, and four convalescent depots. The first Commonwealth burials took place in mid August 1914. A memorial marks the graves of 24 casualties from the hospital ship 'Salta' and her patrol boat, sunk by a mine on 10th April 1917. The memorial also commemorates by name the soldiers, nurses and merchant seamen lost from the 'Salta' whose bodies were not recovered, and those lost in the sinking of the hospital ship 'Galeka' (mined on 28th October 1916), and the transport ship 'Normandy' (torpedoed on 25th January 1918), whose graves are not known.

ST PATRICK'S CEMETERY, LOOS

The cemetery is near Loos-en-Gohelle, Pas de Calais.

St. Patrick's Cemetery was begun during the Battle of Loos by French and British troops, and used in 1916. It was closed in June 1918, but a small number of graves were brought into it after the Armistice from the battlefields between Loos and Hulluch.

ST SEVER CEMETERY EXTENSION, ROUEN

ST SEVER CEMETERY and ST. SEVER CEMETERY EXTENSION are located within a large communal cemetery, situated on the eastern edge of the southern Rouen suburbs of Le Grand Quevilly and Le Petit Quevilly. During the First World War, Commonwealth camps and hospitals were stationed on the southern outskirts of the city. Almost all of the hospitals at Rouen remained there for practically the whole of the war. They included eight general, five stationary, one British Red Cross and one labour hospital, and No. 2 Convalescent Depot. A number of the dead from these hospitals were buried in other cemeteries, but the great majority were taken to the city cemetery of St. Sever. In September 1916, it was found necessary to begin an extension, where the last burial took place in April 1920.

SAILLY-SAILLISEL BRITISH CEMETERY

Sailly-Saillisel British Cemetery is 16 kms east of Albert and 10 kms south of Bapaume.

Sailly-Saillisel, standing at the north end of a ridge, was the objective of French attacks in September and October 1916, and was captured on 18th October. The village remained in Allied hands until 24th March 1918 when it was lost during the German advance, but was recaptured on 1st September 1918. The cemetery was made after the Armistice when graves were brought in from isolated positions, chiefly south and east of the village, and from small burial grounds.

SALONIKA (LEMBET ROAD) MILITARY CEMETERY

The Cemetery is on the northern outskirts of Thessalonika.

At the invitation of the Greek Prime Minister, M. Venizelos, Salonika (now Thessalonika) was occupied by three French Divisions and the 10th (Irish) Division from Gallipoli in October 1915. Other French and Commonwealth forces landed during the year and in the summer of 1916, they were joined by Russian and Italian troops. In August 1916, a Greek revolution broke out at Salonika, with the result that the Greek national army came into the war on the Allied side. The town was the base of the British Salonika Force and it contained, from time to time, eighteen general and stationary hospitals. Three of these hospitals were Canadian, although there were no other Canadian units in the force. The earliest Commonwealth burials took place in the local Protestant and Roman Catholic cemeteries. SALONIKA (LEMBET ROAD) MILITARY CEMETERY (formerly known as the Anglo-French Military Cemetery) was begun in November 1915, and Commonwealth, French, Serbian, Italian and Russian sections were formed. The Commonwealth section remained in use until October 1918, although from the beginning of 1917, burials were also made in MIKRA BRITISH CEMETERY. After the Armistice, some graves were brought in from other cemeteries in Macedonia, Albania and from Scala Cemetery, near Cassivita, on the island of Thasos.

SANCTUARY WOOD CEMETERY

Sanctuary Wood Cemetery is located 5 kms east of Ieper town centre.

Sanctuary Wood is one of the larger woods in the commune of Zillebeke. It was named in November 1914, when it was used to screen troops behind the front line. There were three Commonwealth cemeteries at Sanctuary Wood before June 1916, all made in May-August 1915. The first two were on the western end of the wood, the third in a clearing further east. All were practically obliterated in the Battle of Mount Sorrel, but traces of the second were found and it became the nucleus of the present Sanctuary Wood Cemetery.

At the Armistice, the cemetery contained 137 graves. From 1927 to 1932, the cemetery was extended as far as 'Maple Avenue', when graves were brought in from the surrounding battlefields. They came mainly from the communes immediately surrounding Ypres, but a few were taken from Nieuport (on the coast) and other smaller cemeteries.

SANDHURST (ST MICHAEL) CHURCHYARD
There are two WWI graves in the graveyard surrounding the church, located in Lower Church Road.

SAVY BRITISH CEMETERY
Savy is a village 6.5 kms west of St Quentin. After hard fighting, it was taken on the 1st April 1917, with Savy Wood captured the following day. On 21st March 1918, Savy and Roupy were successfully defended, but the line was withdrawn after nightfall. The village and the wood were retaken on 17th September 1918. SAVY BRITISH CEMETERY was made in 1919, and the graves from the battlefields and from small cemeteries in the neighbourhood were brought in.

SERRE ROAD CEMETERY NO. 1
The village of Serre is 11 kms north-north-east of Albert.

In June 1916, the road out of Mailly-Maillet to Serre and Puisieux entered No Man's Land about 1,300 metres south-west of Serre. On 1st July 1916, attacks north and south of this road were made, and although parties reached Serre, the attack failed; a further attack on 13th November also failed. Early in 1917, the Germans fell back to the Hindenburg Line, and on 25th February, Serre was occupied. The village changed hands once more in March 1918, and remained under German occupation until they withdrew in August.

In the spring of 1917, the battlefields of the Somme and Ancre were cleared, and a number of new cemeteries were made, three of which are now named from the Serre Road. SERRE ROAD CEMETERY NO. 1 was begun in May 1917. The rest of the cemetery was added after the Armistice, when graves were brought in from the nearby battlefields and from nearby smaller cemeteries.

SERY-LES-MEZIERES COMMUNAL CEMETERY
Sery-les-Mezieres is a commune 38 kms west of Laon.

There are 4 First World War Commonwealth burials in the Military Section of the southeast part of the cemetery.

SHINFIELD (ST MARY) CHURCH CEMETERY
The cemetery is to the south of the church, hidden in a housing estate. It is best reached by taking the small path to the right of the house opposite the church.

SHREWSBURY GENERAL CEMETERY
Burials from the Military Hospitals in Shrewsbury were made in this cemetery. It is located off Roman Road, to the southwest of the city centre.

SKOPJE BRITISH CEMETERY

The war cemetery is northeast of the town, one kilometre north of the railway station in Bulevar Jugoslavija.

Skopje was captured by the Bugarians in October 1915, and re-entered by French cavalry at the end of September 1918. SKOPJE BRITISH CEMETERY was created after the Armistice when burials were gathered together from Kumanovo British Cemetery, Prilep French Military Cemetery, Veles British and French Military Cemteries and other burial grounds. The great majority of those who died were men of the Royal Amy Service Corps who died of influenza after the Armistice with Bulgaria.

SOISSONS MEMORIAL

The town of Soissons stands on the left bank of the River Aisne, approximately 100 kms northeast of Paris.

The original British Expeditionary Force crossed the Aisne in August 1914, a few kilometres west of Soissons, and re-crossed it in September a few kilometres east. For the next three and a half years, this part of the front was held by French forces and the city remained within the range of German artillery. At the end of April 1918, five divisions of Commonwealth forces (IX Corps) were posted to the French 6th Army in this sector to rest and refit following the German offensives on the Somme and Lys. Here, at the end of May, they found themselves facing the overwhelming German attack which, despite fierce opposition, pushed the Allies back across the Aisne to the Marne. Having suffered 15,000 fatal casualties, IX Corps was withdrawn from this front in early July, but was replaced by XXII Corps, who took part in the Allied counter attack that had driven back the Germans by early August and recovered the lost ground.

THE SOISSONS MEMORIAL commemorates almost 4,000 officers and men of the United Kingdom forces who died during the Battles of the Aisne and the Marne in 1918, and who have no known grave.

SOFIA WAR CEMETRY

SOFIA WAR CEMETERY is part of the Sofia Protestant Cemetery, a section of the main town cemetery. It contains the graves of Commonwealth servicemen who died as prisoners of war, or with the occupying forces, following the Bulgarian capitulation in September 1918.

STAGLIENO CEMETERY, GENOA

The Italians entered the war on the Allied side, declaring war on Austria, in May 1915. Commonwealth forces were at the Italian front between November 1917 and November 1918, and rest camps and medical units were established at various locations in northern Italy behind the front, some of them remaining until 1919.

From November 1917 to the end of the war, Genoa was a base for Commonwealth forces, and the three Stationary Hospitals were posted in the city.

TALANA FARM CEMETERY

From Ieper, the Cemetery is located on the Diksmuidseweg road (N369) in the direction of Boezinge. The commune of Boesinghe (now Boezinge) lies on both sides of the Yser Canal. The village itself is on the west side of the canal, and was, during the greater part of the War, directly faced by the German front line on the east side; but to the south of it the German line sloped away from the canal, and Talana Farm was just one kilometre from the edge of the Salient. Dragoon Camp was across the canal, due east of the village, and within the German lines until 31st July, 1917. Talana Farm was one of a group of farm houses named by the army from episodes of the South African war. The cemetery was begun by French troops in April 1915, taken over by the British in June 1915, and was used by fighting units until March 1918.

TEHRAN WAR CEMETERY and TEHRAN MEMORIAL

TEHRAN WAR CEMETERY is situated within the British Embassy residential compound at Gulhek, which is approximately 13 kms from Tehran. Within the cemetery is the TEHRAN MEMORIAL commemorating casualties from both World Wars.

The War Cemetery was built in 1962. There are now 412 Commonwealth burials of the 1914-1918 war, thirteen of which are unidentified, commemorated in this site.

TERLINCTHUN BRITISH CEMETERY, WIMILLE

TERLINCTHUN BRITISH CEMETERY is situated on the northern outskirts of Boulogne.

The first rest camps for Commonwealth forces were established near Terlincthun in August 1914, and during the whole of the First World War, Boulogne and Wimereux housed numerous hospitals and other medical establishments. The cemetery at Terlincthun was begun in June 1918 when the space available for service burials in the civil cemeteries of Boulogne and Wimereux was exhausted. It was used chiefly for burials from the base hospitals, but also contains the graves of 46 RAF personnel killed at Marquise in September 1918 in a bombing raid by German aircraft. In July 1920, the cemetery contained more than 3,300 burials, but for many years, Terlincthun remained an 'open' cemetery and graves continued to be brought into it from isolated sites and other burials grounds throughout France, where their maintenance could not be assured.

THIEPVAL MEMORIAL

The Thiepval Memorial will be found on the D73, next to the village of Thiepval, off the main Bapaume to Albert road (D929).

On 1st July 1916, supported by a French attack to the south, thirteen divisions of Commonwealth forces launched an offensive on a line from north of Gommecourt to Maricourt. Despite a preliminary bombardment lasting seven days, the German defences were barely touched, and the attack met unexpectedly fierce resistance. Losses were catastrophic and with only minimal advances on the southern flank, the initial attack was a failure. In the following weeks, huge resources of manpower and equipment were deployed in an attempt to exploit the modest successes of the first day. However, the German Army resisted tenaciously, and repeated attacks and counter-attacks meant a major battle for every village, copse and farmhouse gained. At the end of September, Thiepval was finally captured. The village had been an original objective of 1st July. Attacks north and east continued throughout October and into November in increasingly difficult weather conditions. The Battle of the Somme finally ended on 18th November with the onset of winter.

In the spring of 1917, the German forces fell back to their newly prepared defences, the Hindenburg Line, and there were no further significant engagements in the Somme sector until the Germans mounted their major offensive in March 1918.

The THIEPVAL MEMORIAL, the Memorial to the Missing of the Somme, bears the names of more than 72,000 officers and men of the United Kingdom and South African forces who died in the Somme sector before 20th March 1918, and who have no known grave. Over 90% of those commemorated died between July and November 1916. The memorial also serves as an Anglo-French Battle Memorial in recognition of the joint nature of the 1916 offensive, and a small cemetery containing equal numbers of Commonwealth and French graves lies at the foot of the memorial.

TILLOY BRITISH CEMETERY, TILLOY-LES-MOFFLAINES
Tilloy-les-Mofflaines is a village 3 kms southeast of Arras, on the south side of the main road to Cambrai. It was taken by Commonwealth troops on 9th April 1917, but it was partly in German hands again from March to August 1918.

The cemetery was begun in April 1917 by fighting units and burial officers, and includes casualties from later fighting in 1917 and the first three months of 1918, and the clearing of the village in August 1918. These 390 original burials were increased after the Armistice when graves were brought in from a wide area east of Arras and from smaller burial grounds.

TINCOURT NEW BRITISH CEMETERY
Tincourt is a village about 7 kms east of Peronne and Tincourt.

The villages of Tincourt and Boucly were occupied by British troops in March 1917, during the German Retreat to the Hindenburg Line. From the following May until March 1918, Tincourt became a centre for Casualty Clearing Stations. On 23rd March 1918, the villages were evacuated, and they were recovered, in a ruined condition, about 6th September. From that month until December 1918, Casualty Clearing Stations were again posted to Tincourt.

The cemetery was begun in June 1917, and used until September 1919. After the Armistice it was used for the reburial of soldiers found on the battlefield, or buried in small French or German cemeteries.

TORQUAY CEMETERY AND EXTENSION
The cemetery is located on the outskirts of the town.

TROIS ARBRES CEMETERY, STEENWERCK
Steenwerck is a village on the D77, about 6 kms southeast of Bailleul, and to the east of the road from Bailleul to Estaires. It remained untouched for much of the First World War, but on 10th April 1918, it was captured by the Germans and remained in their possession until the beginning of October. The site for TROIS ARBRES CEMETERY was chosen for the 2nd Australian Casualty Clearing Station in July 1916, and used by that hospital until April 1918. A few further burials were made in the cemetery after the German withdrawal at the end of 1918, and after the Armistice, over 700 graves were brought into it from the battlefields of Steenwerck, Nieppe, Bailleul and Neuve-Eglise.

TYNE COT CEMETERY AND TYNE COT MEMORIAL
TYNE COT CEMETERY is located 9 kms northeast of Ieper town centre, on the Tynecotstraat, a road leading from the Zonnebekeseweg (N332).

'Tyne Cot' or 'Tyne Cottage' was the name given by the Northumberland Fusiliers to a barn which stood near the level crossing on the Passchendaele-Broodseinde road. The barn, which had become the centre of five or six German blockhouses, or pill-boxes, was captured by the 3rd Australian Division on 4th October 1917, in the advance on Passchendaele. One of these pill-boxes was unusually large, and was used as an advanced dressing station after its capture. From 6th October to the end of March 1918, 343 graves were made, on two sides of it. The cemetery was in German hands again from 13th April to 28th September, when it was finally recaptured, with Passchendaele, by the Belgian Army. TYNE COT CEMETERY was greatly enlarged after the Armistice when remains were brought in from the battlefields of Passchendaele and Langemarck, and from a few small burial grounds. It is now the largest Commonwealth war cemetery in the world in terms of burials. At the suggestion of King George V, who visited the cemetery in 1922, the Cross of Sacrifice was placed on the original large pill-box. There are three other pill-boxes in the cemetery.

The TYNE COT MEMORIAL forms the north-eastern boundary of TYNE COT CEMETERY and commemorates nearly 35,000 servicemen from the United Kingdom and New Zealand who died in the Ypres Salient after 16th August 1917, and whose graves are not known. The memorial stands close to the farthest point in Belgium reached by Commonwealth forces in the First World War until the final advance to victory.

VAILLY BRITISH CEMETERY
Vailly-sur-Aisne is a small town within the Department of the Aisne, on the north bank of the Aisne River. It is 13 kms east of Soissons and 18 kms south of Laon.

The village was the point at which the 3rd Division crossed the river Aisne on 13th and 14th September 1914 during the Allied advance from the Marne. It fell to the German forces in 1915, was retaken by the French during the Chemin des Dames Offensive in April 1917, lost again to the Germans in June 1918, and finally captured by the French on 15th September 1918. VAILLY BRITISH CEMETERY was established after the Armistice when the remains of Commonwealth soldiers were brought here from other burial grounds and battlefields throughout the region. Most of those buried here were killed during the Battle of the Aisne in September 1914, but the cemetery is also the final resting place of over sixty Commonwealth soldiers who were killed or mortally wounded in the summer of 1918.

VALENCIENNES (ST ROCH) COMMUNAL CEMETERY
VALENCIENNES (ST ROCH) COMMUNAL CEMETERY is situated on the northeast side of Valenciennes, about 1.5 kms from the centre.

Valenciennes remained in German hands from the early days of the First World War until the beginning of November 1918, when it was entered and cleared by the Canadian Corps; 5,000 civilians were found in the town. In November and December 1918, four Casualty Clearing Stations were posted at Valenciennes, and the last of them did not leave until October 1919.

The Communal Cemetery of St. Roch was initially used by the Germans in August and September 1914, but Commonwealth plots were made adjoining the German, containing the graves of October 1918 to December 1919; and bodies brought from other cemeteries or from the battlefields.

VALLEY CEMETERY, VIS-EN-ARTOIS
Valley Cemetery lies south of Vis-en-Artois, some 12 kms southeast of Arras.

The cemetery was begun on 31st August 1918 with the burial of 31 officers and men of the 3rd Canadian Infantry Battalion, who had died the previous day in the capture of Orix Trench; ten further burials were made during the early part of September. In 1924-25, remains were brought in from the battlefields and from Thilloy German Cemetery. This was just to the north of the voillage of Ligny-Thilloy, and was a Dressing Station cemetery containing the graves of four Australian soldiers, three from the United Kingdom, and about three hundred Germans.

VERMAND COMMUNAL CEMETERY

Vermand is a village 12 kms east of St Quentin, in the Department of the Aisne.

Vermand was later "adopted" by the Borough of Cambridge. The Communal Cemetery was used in April and May 1917, and March and September 1918, for British burials.

VERMELLES BRITISH CEMETERY

Vermelles is a village 10 kms northwest of Lens.

Vermelles was in German hands from the middle of October 1914 to the beginning of December 1914, when it was recaptured by the French. The cemetery was begun in August 1915 (though a few graves are slightly earlier), and during the Battle of Loos, when the Chateau was used as a dressing station, From April 1917 to the Armistice, the cemetery was closed; but after the Armistice some graves were re-grouped and others were brought in rom the battlefields to the East.

VIEILLE-CHAPELLE OLD MILITARY CEMETERY AND VIEILLE-CHAPELLE NEW MILITARY CEMETERY, LACOUTURE

Vieille-Chapelle is a village northeast of Bethune.

The Old Military Cemetery (now removed) was closed in November 1915, as being too near the school; and the New Military Cemetery was begun in that month and used by fighting units and Field Ambulances until March 1918. The village and the cemetery fell into German hands in the following month during the Battles of the Lys; but in September 1918, on the German retirement, some further burials took place. The remainder of the cemetery was made after the Armistice, by the concentration of British, Indian and Portuguese graves from the neighbouring battlefields and from other cemeteries, but the Portuguese graves were removed to RICHEBOURG-L'AVOUE PORTUGUESE NATIONAL CEMETERY in 1925; three German prisoners' graves have also been removed.

VILLERS-PLOUICH COMMUNAL CEMETERY

Villers-Plouich is a village in the Department of the Nord, 24 kms north of Gouzeaucourt.

Villers-Plouich was captured in April 1917, lost in March 1918; and regained at the end of the following September, when the 1st East Surreys were the first troops to enter the village. It was later "adopted" by the Borough of Wandsworth.

VIMY MEMORIAL

The Vimy Memorial overlooks the Douai Plain from the highest point of Vimy Ridge, about eight kms northeast of Arras on the N17 towards Lens.

On the opening day of the Battle of Arras, 9 April 1917, the four divisions of the Canadian Corps, fighting side by side for the first time, scored a huge tactical victory in the capture of the 60 metre high Vimy Ridge. After the war, the highest point of the ridge was chosen as the site of the great memorial to all Canadians who served their country in battle during the First World War, and particularly to the 60,000 who gave their lives in France. It also bears the names of 11,000 Canadian servicemen who died in France - many of them in the fight for Vimy Ridge - who have no known grave.

VIS-EN-ARTOIS MEMORIAL

Vis-en-Artois and Haucourt are villages on the straight main road from Arras to Cambrai about 10 kms southeast of Arras. This Memorial bears the names of over 9,000 men who fell in the period from 8th August 1918 to the date of the Armistice in the Advance to Victory in Picardy and Artois, between the Somme and Loos, and who have no known grave. They belonged to the forces of Great Britain and Ireland and South Africa; the Canadian, Australian and New Zealand forces being commemorated on other memorials to the missing.

VLAMERTINGHE MILITARY CEMETERY AND VLAMERTINGHE NEW MILITARY CEMETERY

VLAMERTINGHE is located 5 kms west of Ieper town centre (Vlamertinge is the modern spelling of Vlamertinghe).

For much of the First World War, Vlamertinghe was just outside the normal range of German shell fire, and the village was used both by artillery units and field ambulances. VLAMERTINGHE MILITARY CEMETERY was started by French troops in 1914, and was taken over by Commonwealth forces in April 1915. It was used by fighting units and field ambulances until June 1917, when the land adjoining the cemetery was claimed for a military railway, preventing further extension.

From June 1917, the VLAMERTINGHE NEW MILITARY CEMETERY was begun in anticipation of the Allied offensive launched on this part of the front in July. Although the cemetery continued in use until October 1918, most of the burials are from July to December 1917.

VOORMEMZEELE ENCLOSURES NOS 1, 2 AND 3

The VOORMEZEELE ENCLOSURES are located 4 kms southwest of Ieper town centre, on the Voormezeele Dorp.

Origianlly four, but now reduced to three, the Voormizeele Enclosures were originally regimental groups of graves, begun very early in the First World War, and gradually increased until the village and the cemeteries were captured by the Germans after very heavy fighting on 29th April 1918. No.1 and No.2 are now treated as a single cemetery.

WANQUETIN COMMUNAL CEMETERY EXTENSION

Wanquetin is a village approximately 12 kms west of Arras and approximately 6 kms north of Beaumetz. A few burials were made in the communal cemetery from March to November 1916, but in October 1916, the 41st Casualty Clearing Station came to the village, and by the end of November it had become necessary to begin the extension. The last graves made in the cemetery were 23 men of the 3rd Canadian Machine Gun Battalion, killed on 24th September 1918 in a German daylight air raid over Warlus.

WARFIELD (ST MICHAEL THE ARCHANGEL) CHURCHYARD EXTENSION

The Churchyard Extension is on the opposite side of Church Lane from the church. It contains two graves from WWI.

WARLENCOURT BRITISH CEMETERY

Warlencourt British Cemetery lies on the east side of the D929, to the southeast of Warlencourt village and 5 kms southwest of Bapaume.

Warlencourt, the Butte de Warlencourt, and Eaucourt-L'Abbaye, were the scene of very fierce fighting in 1916. Eaucourt was taken early in October, but the Butte (a Roman mound of excavated chalk, about seventeen metres high, once covered with pines) was attacked by that and other divisions, but not relinquished by the Germans until the following 26th February, when they withdrew to the Hindenburg Line. The cemetery was made late in 1919, when graves were brought in from small cemeteries and the battlefields of Warlencourt and Le Sars.

WARLOY-BAILLON COMMUNAL CEMETERY EXTENSION

Warloy-Baillon is a village about 21 kms northeast of Amiens along the D919 to Arras.

The first Commonwealth burial took place in the communal cemetery in October 1915, and the last on 1st July 1916. By that date, field ambulances had come to the village in readiness for the attack on the German front line eight kilometres away, and the extension was begun on the eastern side of the cemetery. The fighting from July to November 1916, on the northern part of the Somme front, accounts for the majority of the burials in the extension, but some are from the German attack in the spring of 1918.

WASSIGNY COMMUNAL CEMETERY

Wassigny is a commune 32 kms northeast of St Quentin and 11 kms south of Le Cateau, just off the D27.

Wassigny was captured on 18th-19th October, 1918. The French and German War Graves have been removed from the Communal Cemetery.

WAVANS BRITISH CEMETERY

Wavans is a village 14 kms northwest of Doullens and 32 kms northeast of Abbeville.

Wavans British Cemetery was made by the 21st Casualty Clearing Station bewteen May and September 1918.

WESTOUTRE BRITISH CEMETERY

WESTOUTRE BRITISH CEMETERY is located 11.5 kms southwest of Ieper town centre on a road leading from the N375 Dikkebusseweg.

The village of Westoutre (now Westouter) remained in Allied hands from the early months of the First World War to the Armistice, but in the summer of 1918, after the Battles of the Lys, it was less than two and a half kilometres from the front line.

WESTOUTRE BRITISH CEMETERY was begun in October 1917. It was used until the following April, and again in August-October 1918. A further fifty graves were brought into it from the battlefields of the Ypres salient, from BIXSCHOTE GERMAN CEMETERY and KEMMEL FRENCH CEMETERY after the Armistice. French units used the cemetery in April-August 1918, but these graves were later removed.

WIMEREUX COMMUNAL CEMETERY
Wimereux is a small town situated approximately 5 kms north of Boulogne.

It was the headquarters of the Queen Mary's Army Auxilliary Corps during the First World War, and in 1919 became the General Headquarters of the British Army. From October 1914 onwards, Boulogne and Wimereux formed an important hospital centre, and until June 1918, the medical units at Wimereux used the communal cemetery for burials, the southeastern half having been set aside for Commonwealth graves, although a few burials were also made among the civilian graves. By June 1918, this half of the cemetery was filled, and subsequent burials from the hospitals at Wimereux were made in the new military cemetery at Terlincthun.

WOKINGHAM (ALL SAINTS) CHURCHYARD
Travelling from Bracknell, All Saints Church is on the right side of the London Road, just before the one-way system is reached. There are seven graves from WWI in the churchyard.

WOKINGHAM (ST SEBASTIAN) CHURCHYARD
The graveyard is situated around the church on Nine Mile Road, just west of the traffic lights outside Ravenswood Village. Most of the graves, from patients who died at nearby Pinewood Hospital, are to the west of the church, but one is on the north side.

WORTHING (BROADWATER) CEMETERY
Located on South Farm Road, Worthing, north of the railway station.

The entrance to the cemetery is just south of Broadwater Green.

YPRES (MENIN GATE) MEMORIAL
Ypres (now Ieper) is a town in the Province of West Flanders. The Memorial is situated at the eastern side of the town on the road to Menin (Menen) and Courtrai (Kortrijk). Each night at 8pm, the traffic is stopped at the MENIN GATE while members of the local Fire Brigade sound the 'Last Post' in the roadway under the Memorial's arches.

The MENIN GATE is one of four memorials to the missing in Belgian Flanders, which covers the area known as the Ypres Salient. Broadly speaking, the Salient stretched from Langemarck in the north to the northern edge in Ploegsteert Wood in the south, but it varied in area and shape throughout the war. The Salient was formed during the First Battle of Ypres in October and November 1914, when a small British Expeditionary Force succeeded in securing the town before the onset of winter, pushing the German forces back to the Passchendaele Ridge. The Second Battle of Ypres began in April 1915, when the Germans released poison gas into the Allied lines north of Ypres. This was the first time gas had been used by either side, and the violence of the attack forced an Allied withdrawal and a shortening of the line of defence.

There was little more significant activity on this front until 1917, when in the Third Battle of Ypres, an offensive was mounted by Commonwealth forces, to divert German attention from a weakened French front further south. The initial attempt in June to dislodge the Germans from the Messines Ridge was a complete success, but the main assault northeastward, which began at the end of July, quickly became a dogged struggle against determined opposition and the rapidly deteriorating weather. The campaign finally came to a close in November with the capture of Passchendaele. The German offensive of March 1918 met with some initial success, but was eventually checked and repulsed in a combined effort by the Allies in September. The battles of the Ypres Salient claimed many lives on both sides, and it quickly became clear that the commemoration of members of the Commonwealth forces with no known grave would have to be divided between several different sites.

The site of the MENIN GATE was chosen because of the hundreds of thousands of men who passed through it on their way to the battlefields. It commemorates casualties from the forces of Australia, Canada, India, South Africa, and the United Kingdom, who died in the Salient. In the case of United Kingdom casualties, only those prior to 16th August 1917, with a few exceptions, are listed. United Kingdom and New Zealand servicemen who died after that date are named on the memorial at TYNE COT, a site which marks the furthest point reached by Commonwealth forces in Belgium until nearly the end of the war. New Zealand casualties that died prior to 16th August 1917 are commemorated on memorials at BUTTES NEW BRITISH CEMETERY and MESSINES RIDGE BRITISH CEMETERY.

ZANTVOORDE BRITISH CEMETERY

ZANDVOORDE BRITISH Cemetery is located 8 kms southeast of Ieper town centre, on the Kruisekestraat a road leading from the Meenseweg (N8), connecting Ieper to Menen.

On 30th October 1914, the village of Zantvoorde (now Zandvoorde) was held by the 1st and 2nd Life Guards, numbering between three and four hundred men. It was bombarded for over an hour with heavy guns and then taken by the 39th German Division and three attached battalions. The whole front of the 3rd Cavalry Division was driven back to the Klein-Zillebeke ridge. The village could not be retaken, and remained in German hands until 28th September 1918. The Household Cavalry Memorial, unveiled by Lord Haig in May 1924, stands on the south side of the village at the place where part of the Brigade was annihilated in 1914.

ZANTVOORDE BRITISH CEMETERY was made after the Armistice, when remains were brought in from the battlefields and nearby German cemeteries. Many were those of soldiers who died in the desperate fighting round Zantvoorde, Zillebeke and Gheluvelt in the latter part of October 1914.

For further information on all cemeteries and memorials, see the Commonwealth War Graves Commission website www.cwgc.org

Appendix III

Other Natives

According to SDGW, the following men were born or grew up in what is now the borough of Bracknell Forest, but their name does not appear on any of the local war memorials. In some cases, they had moved away, in some cases there was no family to put their name forward, but there may be other reasons why their name was not included

CROWTHORNE

Leonard Albert Day
Regiment   2nd Battalion, Royal Berkshire Regiment
Date of death   5th March 1917
Cemetery   Thiepval Memorial
Birth registration and census returns suggest this man may have been born in Addlestone, Surrey

George Henry Field
Regiment   11th Battalion, Royal Sussex Regiment
Date of death   24th September 1917
Cemetery   Zantvoode British Cemetery

Henry Reginald Hazard
Regiment   573rd Company, Army Service Corps
Date of death   28th June 1918
Cemetery   Salonika (Lembet Road) Military Cemetery

Reginald Arthur James
Regiment   7th Battalion, Royal Fusiliers
Date of death   12th February 1917
Cemetery   Ancre British Cemetery, Beaumont-Hamel

Arthur Wynne
Regiment   2nd Battalion, Royal West Surrey Regiment
Date of death   25th September 1915
Cemetery   Loos Memorial
Census returns suggest this man may have been born in Sandhurst

SANDHURST

Percy Alderman
Regiment   1/4th Battalion, Hampshire Regiment
Date of death   21st January 1916
Cemetery   Basra Memorial

Harry Beaven
Regiment   4th Battalion, Rifle Brigade
Date of death   11th June 1915
Cemetery   Torquay Cemetery and Extension, Devon

Alfred Frederick Bedbrook
Regiment   2/4th Battalion, Royal West Surrey Regiment
Date of death   8th October 1915
Cemetery   Pieta Military Cemetery

George Albert Day
Regiment   9th Battalion, Rifle Brigade
Date of death   29th August 1916
Cemetery   Thiepval Memorial

Edward Fullbrook
Regiment   7th Battalion, Somerset Light Infantry
Date of death   17th August 1917
Cemetery   Oosttaverne Wood Cemetery
Birth registration and census entries suggest this man may have been born at Sunninghill

George Sidney Gough
Regiment   1st Battalion, Grenadier Guards
Date of death   15th May 1915
Cemetery   Le Touret Memorial

John David Gough
Regiment   1st Battalion, Rifle Brigade
Date of death   2nd November 1914
Cemetery   Le Touret Railway Crossing Cemetery

George Ernest Hennes
Regiment   19th Battalion, Durham Light Infantry
Date of death   23rd April 1918
Cemetery   Pozieres Memorial

James Iles
Regiment   2nd Dragoon Guards
Date of death   22nd March 1918
Cemetery   Pozieres Memorial

Alexander Beauclerk James
> Regiment   17 Battalion, Royal Welsh Fusiliers
> Date of death   31 July 1917
> Cemetery   Poelcapelle British Cemetery

Birth registration and census returns suggest this man may have been born in Reading, and resident in Sandhurst, Kent

Joseph James Johnson
> Regiment   1st Battalion, North Staffordshire Regiment
> Date of death   20th March 1915
> Cemetery   Ferme Buterne Military Cemetery, Houplines

Frank Kercher
> Regiment   1st Garrison Regiment, Bedfordshire Regiment
> Date of death   20th October 1918
> Cemetery   Delhi War Cemetery

Arthur Patrick Malone
> Regiment   Woking Pay Office, Army Pay Corps
> Date of death   4th November 1918
> Cemetery   Brookwood Military Cemetery

John Mileham
> Regiment   'C' Battery, 63rd Brigade, Royal Field Artillery
> Date of death   2nd August 1916
> Cemetery   Doullens Communal Cemetery Extension No 1

Arthur John L Owen
> Regiment   6th Labour Company, Lincolnshire Regiment
> Date of death   5th April 1917
> Cemetery   Etaples Military Cemetery

Reginald James Paice
> Regiment   Oxfordshire Hussars
> Date of death   28th April 1915
> Cemetery   Bailleul Communal Cemetery Extension Nord

Arthur Richard Squires
> Regiment   9th Battalion, Royal Fusiliers
> Date of death   18th February 1916
> Cemetery   Vermelles British Cemetery

Charles Thomas Stubbs
> Regiment   1st Battalion, Bedfordshire Regiment
> Date of death   16th April 1918
> Cemetery   Aire Communal Cemetery

John Willmott
    Regiment   2nd Battalion, Worcestershire Regiment
    Date of death   20th September 1914
    Cemetery   La Ferte-sous-Jouarre Memorial

David Wood
    Ship   Royal Navy, H.M.S. 'Heliotrope'
    Date of death   8th August 1919
    Cemetery   Haidar Pasha Cemetery

APPENDIX IV

OTHER RESIDENTS

The following men listed their place of residence as one of the parishes with the borough
of Bracknell Forest when they attested, or had next of kin living in the parish
when they lost their lives.

CROWTHORNE

Arthur Howard Addey-Jibb
Regiment	94th Field Ambulance, Royal Army Medical Corps
Date of death	12th April 1918
Cemetery	Hondeghem Churchyard

William Adnams
Regiment	6th Battalion, Royal Berkshire Regiment
Date of death	24th February 1917
Cemetery	Dernacourt Communal Cemetery Extension

*Records may indicate a surviving relative living in Crowthorne; there is no evidence the deceased
man ever did*

Arthur Frederick Annetts
Regiment	8th Battalion, Royal Berkshire Regiment
Date of death	17th November 1915
Cemetery	Wokingham (St Sebastian) Churchyard

Wilfred Bingham
Regiment	Royal Engineers Training Centre (Newark)
Date of death	27th July 1916
Cemetery	Wokingham (St Sebastian) Churchyard

Iden Claud Murdoch Bishop
Regiment	12th Battalion, Royal Sussex Regiment
Date of death	30th June 1916
Cemetery	Loos Memorial

Claude Milberne Blandy

Regiment	110th Brigade, Ammunition Column, Royal Field Artillery
Date of death	8th April 1916
Cemetery	St Sever Cemetery, Rouen

Charles Joshua Brant

Regiment	2nd Battalion, Royal Berkshire Regiment
Date of death	1st July 1916
Cemetery	Ovillers Military Cemetery

Frederick Arthur Brant

Regiment	20th Battalion, Middlesex Regiment
Date of death	28th September 1918
Cemetery	Tyne Cot Memorial

Records may indicate a surviving relative living in Crowthorne; there is no evidence the deceased man ever did

Alfred Butler

Regiment	2nd Battalion, Royal Berkshire Regiment
Date of death	16th August 1917
Cemetery	Tyne Cot Memorial

Harold Chapman

Regiment	7th Battalion, Canadian Infantry
Date of death	15th August 1917
Cemetery	Vimy Memorial

William Clark

Regiment	2nd Battalion, Royal Berkshire Regiment
Date of death	16th October 1915
Cemetery	Sailly-sur-la-Lys Canadian Cemetery

Albert William Edwards

Regiment	13th Battery, 8th Brigade, Royal Field Artillery
Date of death	20th July 1920
Cemetery	Birmingham (Witton) Cemetery

Florence Mary Faithfull

Regiment	65th British General Hospital, Voluntary Aid Detachment
Date of death	15th January 1918
Cemetery	Basra War Cemetery
	Nurse, accidentally drowned

Records may indicate a surviving relative living in Crowthorne; there is no evidence the deceased woman ever did

Geoffrey Mitchell Hodgson

Regiment	Eastern Ontario Regiment, Canadian Light Infantry
Date of death	14th October 1915
Cemetery	Vimy Memorial

Records may indicate a surviving relative living in Crowthorne; there is no evidence the deceased man ever did

Alexander Irving

Regiment	1st Battalion, Seaforth Highlanders
Date of death	15th February 1919
Cemetery	Brookwood Cemetery

William Keefe

Regiment	2nd Battalion, Royal Berkshire Regiment
Date of death	16th August 1917
Cemetery	Tyne Cot Memorial

Edward Harry Macnaghten

Regiment	12th Battalion, Royal Irish Fusiliers (attached)
Date of death	1st July 1916
Cemetery	Thiepval Memorial
	His batman won the Victoria Cross, bringing in seven wounded soldiers in an attempt to rescue his man

Records may indicate a surviving relative living in Crowthorne; there is no evidence the deceased man ever did

Percy Selby Redgrave Maynard

Regiment	2nd Battalion, Hampshire Regiment
Date of death	28th April 1915
Cemetery	Helles Memorial

William Lucius Palmer

Regiment	3rd Battalion, Monmouthshire Regiment
Date of death	8th May 1915
Cemetery	Ypres (Menin Gate) Memorial

Records may indicate a surviving relative living in Crowthorne; there is no evidence the deceased man ever did

Alfred Charles Parker

Regiment	3rd Battalion, Royal Berkshire Regiment
Date of death	11th May 1916
Cemetery	Wokingham (St Sebastians) Churchyard

Percival Perry

Ship	Royal Navy, H.M.S. 'Bulwark'
Date of death	26th November 1914
Cemetery	Portsmouth Naval Memorial

George Edwin Pollard
Regiment	10th Battalion, West Yorkshire Regiment
Date of death	21st March 1918
Cemetery	Arras Memorial

William Povey
Regiment	65th Battery, Royal Field Artillery
Date of death	19th April 1915
Cemetery	Wimereux Communal Cemetery

Records may indicate a surviving relative living in Crowthorne; there is no evidence the deceased man ever did

Robert Frederick Rogers
Regiment	6th Dragoons (Inniskilling)
Date of death	4th August 1917
Cemetery	Tincourt New British Cemetery

Charles Rose
Regiment	1st Battalion, Hampshire Regiment
Date of death	15th September 1914
Cemetery	Crouy-Vauxrot French National Cemetery, Crouy

William James Tanner
Ship	Royal Navy, submarine 'K5'
Date of death	20th January 1921
Cemetery	Portsmouth Naval Memorial
	Accidentally sank off the Isles of Scilly

Albert Wardell
Regiment	1st Battalion, Royal Berkshire Regiment
Date of death	15th May 1915
Cemetery	Le Touret Memorial

Records may indicate a surviving relative living in Crowthorne; there is no evidence the deceased man ever did

SANDHURST

Frederick Alexander
Regiment	1/21st Battalion, London Regiment
Date of death	9th December 1917
Cemetery	Arras Memorial

Records may indicate a surviving relative living in Sandhurst; there is no evidence the deceased man ever did

Jeremiah Patrick Baldwin
Regiment	3/10th Battalion, Middlesex Regiment

Date of death   4th October 1917
Cemetery   Tyne Cot Memorial

Albert Ernest Barefoot
Regiment   2nd Battalion, Royal Berkshire Regiment
Date of death   20th June 1915
Cemetery   Royal Irish Rifles Graveyard, Laventie

Joseph James J Bracey
Regiment   11th Battalion, Hampshire Regiment
Date of death   16th October 1918
Cemetery   Erquelinnes Communal Cemetery

Arthur Clifford Evans
Regiment   3rd Battalion, London Regiment
Date of death   13th May 1917
Cemetery   Duisans British Cemetery, Etrun
Records may indicate a surviving relative living in Sandhurst; there is no evidence the deceased man ever did

William Jesse Hawkins
Regiment   2nd Battalion, Royal Berkshire Regiment
Date of death   18th August 1917
Cemetery   Brandhoek New Military Cemetery No. 3

George Aubrey Kennedy Lawrence
Regiment   Royal Flying Corps
Date of death   28th January 1917
Cemetery   Brookwood Cemetery

James Pengelly
Ship   Royal Navy, HMS 'India'
Date of death   8th August 1915
Cemetery   Portsmouth Naval Memorial

Charles Thomas Anderdon Pollock
Regiment   1st/4th Battalion, East Yorkshire Regiment (attached)
Date of death   31st March 1918
Cemetery   Moreuil Communal Cemetery Allied Extension
Records may indicate a surviving relative living in Sandhurst; there is no evidence the deceased man ever did

Charlie Frederick Roach
Regiment   Training Depot (Guildford), Royal Engineers
Date of death   22nd February 1919
Cemetery   Brookwood Cemetery
                                Discharged from the Army 18th December 1917, cause "General paralysis of insane"

Records may indicate a surviving relative living in Sandhurst; there is no evidence the deceased man ever did

Herbert Alonzo M Rowe
Regiment	1st Battalion, North Staffordshire Regiment
Date of death	24th June 1916
Cemetery	Ypres (Menin Gate) Memorial

Records may indicate a surviving relative living in Sandhurst; there is no evidence the deceased man ever did

John Charles Spratley
Regiment	11th Battalion, Australian Infantry
Date of death	29th March 1915
Cemetery	Cairo War Memorial Cemetery

Charles Richard Chenevix Trench
Regiment	2nd/5th Battalion, Sherwood Foresters
Date of death	21st March 1918
Cemetery	Arras Memorial

Frederick John Winfield
Regiment	17th Battalion, London Regiment
Date of death	23rd March 1918
Cemetery	Sailly-Saillisel British Cemetery

Records may indicate a surviving relative living in Sandhurst; there is no evidence the deceased man ever did

Lightning Source UK Ltd.
Milton Keynes UK
UKOW06n0902180614

233611UK00001B/2/P